VOTE FOR US

VOTE FOR *US*

How to TAKE BACK OUR ELECTIONS and CHANGE THE FUTURE of Voting

JOSHUA A. DOUGLAS

59 John Glenn Drive
Amherst, New York 14228

Published 2019 by Prometheus Books

Inquiries should be addressed to
Prometheus Books
59 John Glenn Drive
Amherst, New York 14228
VOICE: 716–691–0133 • FAX: 716–691–0137
WWW.PROMETHEUSBOOKS.COM

23 22 21 20 19   5 4 3 2 1

Library of Congress Cataloging-in-Publication Data

Names: Douglas, Joshua A., author.
Title: Vote for US : how to take back our elections and change the future of voting / by Joshua A. Douglas.
Description: Amherst, NY : Prometheus Books, 2019. | Includes bibliographical references and index.
Identifiers: LCCN 2018042342 (print) | LCCN 2018056617 (ebook) | ISBN 9781633885110 (ebook) | ISBN 9781633885103 (pbk.)
Subjects: LCSH: Elections—United States. | Voting—United States. | Politics, Practical—United States.
Classification: LCC JK1976 (ebook) | LCC JK1976 .D67 2019 (print) | DDC 324.6/30973—dc23
LC record available at https://lccn.loc.gov/2018042342

Printed in the United States of America

To Caitlyn and Harrison—
I hope you can be proud of the democracy you will inherit.
I'd vote for you any day.

CONTENTS

A life is not important except in the impact it has on other lives.
—Jackie Robinson[1]

Elections aren't just about who votes, but also who doesn't vote.
—Michelle Obama[2]

PROLOGUE

West Powell had a story to tell. In doing so, he changed our democracy for the better.

The forty-five-year-old African American with a big smile and a soft voice did not set out to have such a large impact. He just wanted to feel whole again, feel like part of society, feel like his small voice would at least be heard. He was finishing up a physical therapy degree and feared that he wouldn't be able to find a job. Maybe, just maybe, if he told his story, someone would listen. Sure, it seemed futile. But even long shots have a chance, right?

If only Powell lived in a different state, not Kentucky, then perhaps things would be easier. But he had a family and a home. In any event, he wanted to feel like he was part of his community, not outside of it.

The problem was that over twenty-five years earlier, Powell had made a dumb mistake. He had just graduated from Holmes High School in Covington, Kentucky, which is just south of Cincinnati, when he and his brother broke into an auto salvage yard and stole a car radio. He was caught and convicted of a felony. He served his time, met a woman, and started a family. He opened his own computer repair shop. But he strived for more.

Adding insult to injury, he also lost his right to vote—for life. States have varying rules on felon disenfranchisement. Two states—Maine and Vermont—actually allow prisoners to vote while in jail, and many at least reinstate the right to vote after a person finishes his or her prison sentence and parole. But in deep red Kentucky, felons are disenfranchised forever. The only recourse is to ask the governor to restore someone's civil rights, and you can imagine how often that works.

So Powell decided to speak up. He wasn't even thinking about voting rights as much as his application for a physical therapy license. He had earned a 4.0 GPA in school but feared that the state would not let him finish his licensure exam. He needed to have his record expunged.

For several years the Kentucky legislature had considered a bill to allow certain low-level felons[3] to regain their rights, but it had always failed to pass. Why would this year, 2015, be any different? What would convince the legislators—especially conservative Republicans who tended to support felon disenfranchisement—to change their minds this time?

The answer was West Powell. His voice shook as he began telling his story to the Kentucky Senate Judiciary Committee, which was considering a bill to allow some felons to seek an expungement of their record. "My name is West Powell," he said softly. "I'm a forty-five-year-old father of five. I have four girls, one boy. I was trying to have a boy, but the four girls came first, so, that's that."[4] The lawmakers chuckled.

Then he told the committee about the mistake he had made back in 1989, when he was still a teenager. "Me and my brother—he's sitting back there—came up with a stupid idea to steal a car stereo from an auto parts place, and we got caught doing it." He went on to explain how he spent eleven months in jail because he violated his probation curfew of 10:00 p.m., but only because his job made him work until 11:00. Once out of prison he cleaned up his life, but he had a hard time finding a new job given that he had to "check the box" on any job application to indicate that he was a felon. He went to school to learn about computers and then opened a computer repair shop. "Since I can't get a job, I'll just make my job—so if any of you guys need laptops repaired . . . iPad screens replaced, I do a lot of those, I do cell phones as well," he quipped. He then talked about his physical therapy degree, noting that his clinical exams were coming up. Part of that process included a background check, and "I'm sweating bullets" about what would come back. "All of that work I've done may be going down the tubes," he lamented. "I've beared [*sic*] this cross for a long time," he testified. "I know I made a mistake. I think I've paid for that mistake—four times over. . . . I'm not a criminal. I was a stupid kid and made a stupid mistake."[5]

Four minutes later, Powell was done. His short statement would reverberate across the state, impacting thousands of Kentucky felons.

Republican senator Whitney Westerfield was in the hearing room that day. He listened intently as Powell gave his testimony. Westerfield is a pro-law enforcement conservative who ran unsuccessfully for Kentucky attorney general in 2015. He was initially opposed to allowing felons to seek an expungement of their records, and he thought that nothing would change his mind. Why should someone who had violated the social contract and committed a crime be given any leniency?

Yet, as Senator Westerfield listened to Powell's story, something stirred inside of him. Something clicked. He changed his mind on the spot. He texted a fellow Republican: "If I'm still here in January [after the next election], then we are going to make this happen!"[6] Westerfield became an unlikely advocate for Powell's cause. As Westerfield explained to the media, "This guy has done what we ask everybody in the justice system to do: correct the behavior and don't do it again. We ought to be able to help that guy." He continued, "This isn't about [Powell]. It's about the nearly 100,000 others like him across Kentucky that can benefit [from] this hope-giving, redemption-providing bill."[7] The bill passed in 2016, and Powell and thousands like him are now eligible to have their records expunged and regain their right to vote. Kentucky officials must follow through by making the administrative process quick and seamless for eligible individuals.

Reflecting on this effort a few years later, Powell remembers being mostly worried about his physical therapy exams at the time, but he now recognizes the impact he had on the most important right in our democracy: the right to vote. In particular, he considered how our elected leaders don't necessarily reflect the full electorate because so many people are cut out of the system. "If you have only one section of the population voting," he told me, "then politicians only hear their voice."[8] This can lead to skewed representation and skewed policies.

West Powell secured an expungement of his record and finished his physical therapy degree. He has voted in every election since. "It gives me a voice," he told me. "I'm not just a silent person anymore who can't participate in the voting process. They can't ignore me anymore. Somebody has to speak to me now to get my vote. I'm a voter—so show me what you have to offer!"[9]

West Powell after receiving his felony expungement papers.
[Photo courtesy of West Powell III and Kentucky Office of
Governor Matt Bevin.]

It's time to take back our democracy, one voter and one inspiring story at a time.

"Oh no!" you might be saying to yourself. Not another book that clamors for us to "rise up" or "resist," using broad platitudes with few practical solutions. Do we really need someone else arguing for seemingly impossible changes to our democracy without providing real-life guidance on how to make it happen?

This is not that book.

It instead offers a different path, explaining how to reform our democracy from the ground up through the stories of individuals who are already seeing success. Positive voting rights enhancements at the state and local levels can fundamentally change American elections.

These new election rules expand voter eligibility, improve the voter registration process, and make voting more convenient and more reflective of the public's will. Some states have eased their rules on felon disenfranchisement. A few localities have expanded the voter rolls, allowing high school students to vote in local elections and creating a new genera-tion of engaged citizens. Election Day itself is becoming more convenient. Voters with disabilities face fewer hurdles. Activists are putting voter IDs into voters' hands. Reform advocates are taking politics out of redistricting and promoting campaign finance reform.

This is the untold story of voting rights in America. Although the media and the general public emphasize the ways in which entrenched politicians rig the rules to keep themselves in power, there is also much to celebrate in how individuals on the ground are helping to enhance our democracy. We must not bury these positive stories among the common refrain of voter suppression. This is the necessary counterattack to the doom-and-gloom that dominates our discourse. Pro-voter enhancements can provide all of us with hope for a brighter democratic future.

Everyday Americans are the main drivers of this early success. Call it the Democracy Movement, and its advocates today's Democracy Cham-pions. People like Rob Richie, Molly McGrath, Katie Fahey, and Jen Hitchcock—inspiring individuals you will meet in this book—have become Democracy Champions in their communities. This is the antidote to politi-cians who craft rules for our democracy that primarily benefit themselves. It is the way to fight back against big corporations and moneyed interests that impact the rules of the game. Citizens who care about our democracy can take a stand, organize, and push for meaningful reforms to state and local election processes. We *can* fix our election system. However, it won't happen solely by legislative protests and filing lawsuits, by merely playing defense against voter suppression. Instead, we—all of us—must dedicate ourselves to expanding and enhancing the right to vote. The power of grassroots movements to improve our electoral system will change the reality of voting rights in America.

The pages that follow tell the stories of the seemingly ordinary indi-viduals who are at the forefront of these extraordinary efforts. The book follows people like Scott Doyle of Larimer County, Colorado, who devel-oped a more convenient and secure way to vote through countywide Vote Centers instead of home-based precincts, which increased turnout signifi-cantly. You'll hear from energetic youth like Joshua Cardenas, who began a movement to lower the voting age to sixteen for local elections in San Francisco. You'll see how someone like Alison Smith, a stay-at-home mom in Maine, became a public champion for campaign finance reform, which led to the first statewide adoption of public financing in the United States.

Speaking with these individuals, while writing this book, has been immensely inspiring. Their stories provide me with hope for a better democracy. May they inspire you as well. Once you feel that call to action, flip to the back of the book, where the appendix lists organizations working on these initiatives in all fifty states. Give one of them a call and see how you can help.

Imagine: voter turnout at record levels. Young people, armed with better civics education, engaged with politics in a positive way. Individuals with disabilities having the same, easy access to the voting booth as everyone else. District lines and election processes that create fair elections, where ideas—not election rules—dictate the outcomes.

The new voter expansion is happening in our communities through the hard work of these dedicated Americans—today's Democracy Champions. The challenge for all of us is to expand upon their successes.

CHAPTER 1

THE TALE OF A SIXTEEN-YEAR-OLD VOTER

I n the fall of 2013, Ben Miller, a sixteen-year-old junior in high school, did something no other person his age had ever done in America: he registered to vote and cast his ballot.[1]

Miller was taking advantage of a new law in Takoma Park, Maryland, a suburb of Washington, DC, that allows sixteen- and seventeen-year-olds to vote in local elections.[2] This reform has immense potential. By lowering the voting age to sixteen, at least for local elections, and coupling it with improved civics education, we can usher in a whole new generation of engaged voters. Fostering democratic participation among young people and revamping their civics education—as we will discuss in chapter 10—will provide benefits for years to come.

CITIES IN MARYLAND PLANT THE SEED

Sometimes it just takes an innovative city council member to propose an idea that might seem radical at first, but on further examination makes a lot of sense. In this case, that council member was Tim Male, a scientist and environmental advocate who served on Takoma Park's City Council from 2011 to 2017.

Male watched with interest in early 2013 as Scotland debated whether to lower the voting age to sixteen for its 2014 Independence Referendum. He thought the idea made sense for Takoma Park's local elections as well.[3] The reform was part of a broader effort, backed by both Male and fellow council member Seth Grimes, to enact a Right to Vote resolution for the city to affirm the importance of voting rights. In addition to lowering the voting age, the proposal would also allow voter registration on Election Day (a major reform we will learn more about in chapter 3) and require landlords to provide election and registration information to new tenants.[4]

Male and Grimes found an ally in Rob Richie, a Takoma Park resident and the executive director of FairVote, a nonprofit advocacy organization that promotes voting rights.[5] FairVote once housed the National Youth Rights Association, which supports lowering the voting age to sixteen as a major policy goal. Richie had spoken with Bill Bystricky, the head of the National Youth Rights Association at the time, who in turn approached Male at a fund-raising dinner to offer his assistance for the legislative effort.[6] Male and Richie both had read studies from Austria and Denmark showing that younger voting-eligible teenagers are more likely to vote than their slightly older peers.[7] Male and the others, along with young residents, crafted a strategy to build support for the idea. Teenagers—including Richie's two children—spoke to the city council about the value they placed in civic engagement and their involvement in the community.

The council passed the Right to Vote resolution to highlight voting as a fundamental right.[8] But Male and Grimes wanted concrete action, not just nice-sounding platitudes. So they also pushed the council to amend its charter to lower the voting age to sixteen for city elections.[9] The key to enacting this local law was to have young residents make the case through a compelling narrative about how they would benefit from this positive electoral reform, demonstrating that they were civically engaged and could become lifelong voters. Individual advocacy from everyday teenagers convinced council members to support the measure.

Relatively speaking, turnout was high among sixteen- and seventeen-year-olds in November 2013, the first election when they could vote. Though there were few young voters in terms of raw numbers—because Takoma Park itself is small—over 40 percent of the newly enfranchised and registered sixteen- and seventeen-year-olds voted, as compared to an overall turnout rate of 11 percent.[10] Most impressively, these young people came out to vote even though the ballot included no contested elections that year! Turnout among sixteen- and seventeen-year-olds has grown in subsequent elections.[11] Sixteen- and seventeen-year-olds are now participating at a higher rate than older voters, showing how they have embraced their new voting power. Male is proud of the fact that young people in the city "have become more engaged—hosting candidate forums and debates, asking candidates to make commitments, showing up at city council meetings or to meet council members."[12] Lowering the voting age has changed the culture of the local community.

In 2015, the neighboring city of Hyattsville, Maryland, also lowered the voting age to sixteen for its elections.[13] Hyattsville council member Patrick Paschall read about the success in Takoma Park and decided to introduce a similar measure in his own city. The effort passed the city council only after teenagers attended the crucial council meeting on the topic, where, according to Bystricky of the National Youth Rights Association, "one by one they flipped the opposing city council members."[14] This was particularly significant because, as Bystricky put it, "Hyattsville is a working-class town whose leadership was known for sticking to the tried and true."[15] As in Takoma Park, once the city lowered its voting age, many young people embraced their new voting power and went to the polls.

Greenbelt, Maryland, then came on board.[16] In 2017, the city council voted unanimously to direct its staff to research the voting age issue, with an eye toward making the change for upcoming elections. To demonstrate that young voters would actually show up to vote, the city's Youth Advisory Committee—a group of young people that advises the city council on issues that affect younger residents—conducted a survey of 159 local high school students: 92.45 percent said that if given the opportunity, they would vote in local elections.[17] This contrasts with a 2015 questionnaire of Greenbelt residents, which indicated that about 77 percent would oppose a measure to lower the voting age.[18] Yet as advocates in other cities have found, people often have a knee-jerk reaction against the idea but frequently change their minds after they learn about the merits of the reform. After a youth-led campaign, 53 percent of Greenbelt voters endorsed a nonbinding referendum in November 2017 to support lowering the voting age for the city's elections. The city council then gave its approval.[19] Young advocates were instrumental in achieving this success. As Ema Smith, the chair of the Youth Advisory Committee, explained, "there's this misconception [that] teenagers are apathetic and don't care what goes on in government, but I feel my peers, at least some of them, do care and want to have a voice in their local government."[20]

THE MOVEMENT GROWS IN CALIFORNIA

If small towns like Takoma Park, Hyattsville, and Greenbelt see this kind of positive impact on democracy by lowering the voting age, imagine what would happen if larger cities were to adopt this reform. In 2016, young advocates in Berkeley, California, convinced voters that sixteen- and seventeen-year-olds should be allowed to vote for their school board representatives.[21] Once again, the voters who would benefit from this change—youths themselves—were vital to the campaign.[22]

In September 2015, a group of about a dozen students at Berkeley High School began meeting to discuss issues such as racism and sexual assault in their school. Those discussions led to a realization that they could have a say in school policies and become more engaged in the local community if they could vote for school board members.[23] Around the same time, Josh Daniels, himself a Berkeley school board member, sat down with local organizer Kad Smith to plan their next initiative, having just convinced the city council to pass a soda tax. Over coffee, they discussed ways to improve the city and honed in on local youth engagement. Daniels and Smith decided to meet with a handful of local high school students to hear their ideas. The students mentioned sexual harassment, bullying . . . and voting. That set off a series of meetings over the next year where these young people convinced various stakeholders that they should be allowed to vote for school board members. Daniels gives all of the credit to those energetic teens. "We supported them, but we would not have done this if they had not done all of the hard work."[24]

After these young people made their case to the local government, the Berkeley City Council unanimously voted to put the reform on the ballot. The president of the PTA and the school board president both endorsed the idea. The students essentially ran the campaign in their communities. They canvassed at BART stations (the local public transit), grocery stores, and farmers markets. They knocked on doors and spoke with neighbors. The measure to lower the voting age for school board elections passed in 2016 with over 70 percent of the vote.[25]

Across the bay that same year, San Francisco came quite close to lowering the voting age to sixteen for all city elections, suggesting that the reform effort is likely to succeed there in the near future.

Teenager Joshua Cardenas was one of the first advocates of youth voting in San Francisco.[26] He turned eighteen two weeks after the November 2014 election, which included several local measures that concerned him. He turned his disappointment at not being allowed to vote that year into a new cause: advocating to lower the voting age for local elections. At the time, Cardenas was a member of San Francisco's Youth Commission, a group that advises the city on issues affecting young residents. His role with the Youth Commission helped to bring this issue to the forefront.[27]

After months of research, Cardenas authored a resolution urging the city's leaders to lower the voting age to sixteen, which passed the Youth Commission by a fourteen to one vote. Young residents were already engaged in San Francisco's civic life through various advocacy organizations; why not give them a more direct say through voting?

Cardenas then convinced two members of San Francisco's governing body, the board of supervisors, to endorse the plan. Supervisor John Avalos helped Cardenas along the way. Avalos was always interested in youth advocacy, particularly after he met a young woman in 2008 who was inspired by the Barack Obama campaign and who had talked to Avalos about engaging young people in democracy.[28] When Cardenas came to Supervisor Avalos with a proposal to lower the voting age for city elections, the supervisor immediately jumped on board. He recognized that voting is habit-forming and that young voters could be important actors in San Francisco's civic life. He agreed to support a measure before the board of supervisors that would certify a ballot proposition for the city's voters to consider. Passing it through the board, however, would require a heavy lift.

Young people were key advocates for the reform, holding a press conference on the steps of city hall and directly approaching stakeholders to make the case for their own suffrage. The San Francisco Board of Education unanimously endorsed the measure after about one hundred students showed up at a board meeting to demonstrate their civic involvement. Importantly, the board of education agreed to enhance civics education in the city's high schools to work in tandem with lowering the voting age. Education and outreach, particularly from youths themselves, made all the difference.[29]

Initially, only four of the eleven city supervisors supported lowering the voting age. Most of the others thought the idea was crazy. However, five of them were convinced after hearing directly from young people about their desire to participate in local democracy. Teenagers packed the hearing room to show their enthusiasm and dedication. The measure passed nine to two, allowing the issue to go to the voters in a ballot proposition.[30]

Joshua Cardenas displays a campaign sign to lower the voting age to sixteen in San Francisco. [Photo courtesy of Joshua E. Cardenas.]

Cardenas went off to college and other young activists took the lead. Oliver York was fifteen years old on Election Day in 2014, and he lamented his inability to participate in elections for another three years. As he told the website *Vox*, "more than half of all the San Francisco ballot measures directly affected young people like me. But we had no say."[31] So he began to organize and campaign.

As York explained, youth advocates drove the campaign, often convincing people who were initially skeptical to change their minds. He told *Vox*, "We've [had] students meeting with legislators. We've had students going out and knocking on doors. And we have students leading conversations at their high schools about why voting really matters."[32]

Hundreds of young people went out almost every night of the week and on weekends to obtain endorsements from organizations and to go door-to-door to speak with voters. Adele Carpenter, the director of the San Francisco Youth Commission, noted that their dedication to the campaign "counters the story that young people are not interested in voting or democracy."[33]

When advocates conducted polling in early 2016, the measure to lower the voting age had the support of only about 36 percent of the electorate.[34] But young people pounded the pavement and knocked on doors throughout the summer and fall. The measure ultimately failed by about 52 percent to 48 percent—but garnering 48 percent of the vote was a significant increase over the initial polling, demonstrating the power of education and advocacy on this issue.[35] While the proponents obviously wanted to win, the close outcome gave them hope. The organizers plan to put the measure on the ballot again in the near future and believe it has a strong chance of success, especially as they continue to educate more people about its merits.

As Joshua Cardenas looked back on his experience in San Francisco, he expressed pride that the effort brought young people into the political process.[36] Grassroots movements like these often have a lifelong impact, meaning that in some ways the advocates have already won. It might take several tries to pass, but that does not mean we should give up on the ideal of voter expansions, even at the local level.

A STATEWIDE PUSH IN NEW YORK

Although most efforts to lower the voting age so far have focused on local elections, the idea may also spread to states—especially once people see how well it works in the places that have done it. This is important in part because some states (such as New York) have not given their localities permission to pass their own election rules. In those states, where localities lack what's known as "home rule" authority,[37] a statewide reform is the only way to expand the electorate to include younger people.

Young activists in New York want to lower the voting age for statewide elections. In the fall of 2016, Eli Frankel, then a high school sophomore in Brooklyn, started an organization with some friends called the Youth Progressive Policy Group.[38] The organization identified lowering the voting age as its first main project. The theory: if we want to engage younger individuals in civic life, then we should start with voting. Until beginning his research, Frankel didn't even know that similar reform efforts were underway in other parts of the country. He simply recognized that many high school students are interested in politics, especially once they realize that policy decisions will affect them for years to come.[39]

Frankel emailed his state assembly member, Robert Carroll, about the idea. He didn't hear back. Undeterred, he and his friends attended an event that Carroll was sponsoring in the community. They approached Carroll after the event and presented their idea to lower the voting age for state elections. Carroll was intrigued. After further discussion, Carroll agreed to draft legislative language and sponsor the bill. He recommended lowering the voting age to seventeen, not sixteen, as an incremental way to improve the chance it would pass. He also added mandates in the bill that high schools provide a set number of days of civics education and that schools give students who turn seventeen an opportunity to register to vote. That registration aspect is unique: high schools would have to provide students with one of two forms, a registration form or an opt-out form, meaning that individuals would have to make an affirmative choice whether or not to register to vote.[40]

Frankel then organized a lobbying effort for the bill. In May 2017, he led about forty other high school students to Albany (the state capital) to promote the idea to the state's General Assembly. He also held conversations with the governor's office to seek the governor's support. Frankel even wrote an op-ed for the *New York Daily News* to educate the public.[41] He and his group continue to fight for this reform.

As of this writing, the voting age bill is still pending before the state legislature. But Frankel is undeterred. He realizes that persistence is important and that a reform like this may take years to pass. To eventually achieve success and fundamentally alter our democratic system, we need to start somewhere. We need someone like Frankel to light the spark. Frankel was not even seventeen himself when he embarked on this effort. Yet he was still able to begin the grassroots work needed to expand the electorate across the state. All it takes is dedicated people like Eli Frankel—as well as other voters and policy makers—who are willing to work to improve our democracy.

THE LEGAL LANDSCAPE

Changing the voting age is not without precedent.

The US Constitution sets a baseline for the voting age, forbidding a state or locality from denying the right to vote to anyone aged eighteen or older. But that hasn't always been the case. When the United States was founded, the minimum voting age was twenty-one. This was the original British rule, so states likely copied it when they created their own voter eligibility requirements. Common lore has it that the British practice stemmed from medieval times, when men who reached the age of twenty-one were thought to be strong enough to wear a suit of heavy armor and were thus eligible for knighthood. Setting the voting age at twenty-one for American elections was therefore a historical accident, held over from the prior British practice.[42]

That all changed with state reforms and then the ratification of the Twenty-Sixth Amendment to the US Constitution in 1971, which lowered the voting age to eighteen for all federal, state, and local elections. The impetus for this change? The Vietnam War and the fact that young adults were asked to fight for their country but could not vote for the very leaders who had sent them overseas. "Old enough to fight, old enough to vote" became the rallying cry for this effort.[43] Crucial to the ultimate success of this voter expansion were states like Georgia and Kentucky, which lowered the voting age for state elections well before the ratification of the Twenty-Sixth Amendment. Youth protests also helped to bring the issue to the forefront in the public's mind. Youth advocacy groups championed the cause.

Even though the US Constitution sets the minimum voting age at eighteen, such that a state or locality cannot raise it, no legal doctrine prevents a state from lowering the minimum voting age for federal, state, or local elections. That's because the Constitution gives states the authority to dictate voting rules for federal elections so long as they do not conflict with the Constitution's mandates,[44] and the Constitution says nothing about going lower than eighteen. States also have full authority to decide voter eligibility rules for state elections and can be more expansive than what the US Constitution requires. Cities and towns can make this reform for their own local elections if state law gives them that authority.[45] Essentially, there are no legal obstacles to states lowering the voting age to sixteen for federal or state elections, and cities can do so for their own elections if state law permits it.

WHY LOWERING THE VOTING AGE TO SIXTEEN MAKES SENSE

Lowering the voting age may seem like a radical idea, but adopting this kind of bold, positive reform could dramatically improve our elections. This change to our voting laws is not as far-fetched as you might think. Several countries allow sixteen-year-olds to vote, including Argentina, Austria, Brazil, Scotland, and others.[46] Enfranchising sixteen- and seventeen-year-olds will bring new people into the democratic process, increase turnout, improve civic knowledge, and create a stronger culture of democratic participation.[47]

Our elections are in dire need of all these improvements. Turnout in the United States is abysmal. In 2016—a presidential election year, when turnout is usually the highest—40 percent of the population stayed on the sidelines.[48] That is "normal" and seemingly acceptable for US elections, a symptom of pervasive voter apathy. Many other countries would consider that level of voter engagement an immense failure. The French presidential election of 2017, for example, saw turnout at 75 percent, which was the *lowest* in decades.[49]

Younger voters in particular have the lowest turnout rates. Turnout for eighteen- to twenty-nine-year-olds during the 2016 presidential election was less than 50 percent.[50] The youngest voters in that age group are the least likely to vote. That is, turnout for eighteen- and nineteen-year-olds was likely *much* lower than 50 percent. One estimate for the 2012 presidential election put turnout among eighteen- to twenty-four-year-olds at 38 percent, compared to about 70 percent for voters aged sixty-five and older.[51] In the 2014 midterm election, turnout among eighteen- to twenty-nine-year-olds was under 20 percent![52] If we think that 20 percent or lower turnout among the youngest voters in a midterm election is unconscionable—and we should—then we need to devise strategies to fix the problem. The shameful reality of low youth engagement in our elections calls into question the very strength of our democracy. Simply put, we can do better. And we must.

Voting is habit-forming. Studies show that people who skip the first election after they become eligible are less likely to turn out for future elections, while individuals who begin voting early in their lives are more likely to sustain that habit for years to come.[53] Young people do not vote in part because they never voted previously; nonvoting is a habit too. If we begin the habit of voting earlier in life for local elections, then overall turnout a few years later is likely to increase. Adopting this reform for local elections will have an outsized effect once these individuals turn eighteen and can vote in state and national races. Sixteen-year-olds are more likely to vote when they first become eligible because they are immersed in their communities and can benefit from education and encouragement from parents, teachers, their high school environment, and community organizations. Eighteen-year-olds, by contrast, are in a period of transition, moving out of the house and going off to college or entering the workforce. They are less likely to jump through the hoops of registering, requesting an absentee ballot, filling it out, and sending it back—all for the first time ever—while simultaneously experiencing so many other changes in their lives. No wonder so few of them vote.

As to whether sixteen-year-olds are mature enough to vote, nothing magical happens at age eighteen, but studies of cognitive brain development show that something magical does happen to the brain by at least age sixteen when it comes to the kind of thinking necessary for voting.[54] Psychologically speaking, by age sixteen the brain is fully developed for "cold" cognition, which requires measured deliberation and thought before acting—the very description of voting. This contrasts with "hot" cognition, which involves impulse control and reacting to peer pressure in the moment. Brains are not fully developed for appropriate hot cognition until at least age twenty-one. If sixteen-year-olds are as cognitively capable of voting as eighteen-year-olds or twenty-eight-year-olds, then why don't we let them cast a ballot?

Turning sixteen also comes with a variety of new legal obligations. Sixteen-year-olds can obtain a driver's license in many states and must comply with driving laws. They can work but must pay taxes on their wages. Most states set the age of sexual consent at age sixteen or seventeen and allow individuals to drop out of high school at that time as well.[55] Yet these young Americans have no say on critical issues of public policy that affect them—like how their local tax dollars are spent—at the ballot box. They are treated like adults in many ways but cannot vote on the very laws they must follow, even though they are cognitively capable of doing so. They also can't influence school board choices, which most directly affect them. That dichotomy is fundamentally unfair. Just think of the students from Parkland, Florida, after the 2018 shooting at their high school: they drove a national discussion on gun control and school safety, yet they could not actually influence policy at the ballot box. Individuals like Emma González and David Hogg continually reminded legislators that they would be voters in a few short years, but how much more powerful could they have been in that moment of national discussion if they and their peers were *already* voters?

The last common objection to lowering the voting age is that doing so will effectively give parents a second vote. This conventional wisdom does not play out in practice. Almost anyone with a teenager in the house will agree that telling that person how he or she must vote will backfire. Sure, some young voters might follow their parents, but that outcome is not inevitable. Younger individuals are independent thinkers. One study of American youths showed that over half of them "either misperceive or reject their parents' political party affiliations."[56] A 2014 survey found that about half of millennials self-identified as political independents.[57] Young voters are not "in the bag" for either side. Here's my own example: in his first election after he turned eighteen, my nephew—a dyed-in-the-wool liberal—chose Republican Charlie Baker over Democrat Martha Coakley for Massachusetts governor because, after reading the policy positions and ideas of each candidate, he found Baker to be much more credible.

The experience in Scotland tells the same story. In the Scottish Independence Referendum of 2014, about 40 percent of youths aged sixteen and seventeen said they would vote differently from their parents.[58]

IT WORKED IN SCOTLAND

The United States is missing a huge opportunity to create a culture of democratic participation early in the lives of young people. Look at what happened in Scotland: the country lowered the voting age to sixteen for the 2014 Independence Referendum while also encouraging high school teachers to include instruction about politics in the classroom.[59] By all measures—even among those who initially opposed it—lowering the voting age has been a brilliant success.

Seventy-five percent of sixteen- and seventeen-year-olds voted in that 2014 Referendum, a higher rate than the turnout among eighteen- to twenty-four-year-olds.[60] The move was so successful that in 2015 the Scottish Parliament unanimously agreed to lower the voting age for all elections. Conservatives, who initially opposed the reform, wrote about how the experience of engaging young people during the Referendum campaign changed their minds and caused them to support a lower voting age for all Scottish elections.[61] The young Scottish voters proved themselves to be immensely engaged, passionate, and knowledgeable. Scotland had previously suffered from decreasing turnout in its parliamentary elections. After lowering the voting age, turnout in the 2016 parliament election improved significantly. According to one report, lowering the voting age to sixteen caused about half of the increase.[62]

Part of the reason for the success was that civics teachers engaged these newly enfranchised young voters in their classrooms. As we'll see in chapter 10, the Scottish experience offers useful lessons for how we should teach our American teenagers about politics and elections. For now, the important point is that we should learn from Scotland on the merits of lowering the voting age. I spent two weeks in Scotland learning about the reform, and quite literally everyone I spoke with—from policy experts to the random guys at the pub—thought it made perfect sense. Although some were skeptical at first, they all seemed pleased with the results: a lower voting age engaged young people, and, indeed, the entire community.

Scotland shows us that if we give young people a chance—as well as a stronger foundation of civics education in schools—then they will be thoughtful and independent. They have unique policy preferences that our leaders usually ignore because they are not a reliable voting constituency, but they are the citizens who will have to deal with the consequences of policy choices for years to come. Indeed, far from any clear partisan effect, lowering the voting age will just require politicians to consider more carefully the needs of young people, which ultimately will benefit everyone. Scottish politicians of all political parties have found the youth engagement invigorating.

A common storyline weaves its way through the efforts in Takoma Park, Hyattsville, Greenbelt, Berkeley, San Francisco, and New York: enterprising individuals, many of whom are teenagers, are engaged in a grassroots movement to expand the electorate in their communities. Of course, young people cannot do it entirely on their own. They benefit greatly from pro-democracy organizations such as Generation Citizen and its subsidiary Vote16USA. The aim of Generation Citizen is to engage young people in civic life, and Vote16USA assists by promoting a voting age of sixteen and helping with advocacy, providing funding and strategic planning.[63] Vote16USA's Youth Advisory Board, comprised of young people, generates energy for the movement.[64] This demonstrates how individuals can use good government organizations to channel their pro-democracy efforts into concrete action.

Lowering the voting age is a bold idea, to be sure, but it's one that could have long-term effects on voter turnout and democratic representation. Why not engage young people as soon as they are cognitively capable of making electoral choices? Why don't we use our schools to better educate our young citizens about the importance of voting and the various public policy issues they must decide as voters? The ideas are working already in some communities both in the United States and abroad. Even more cities, like Washington, DC, Boulder, Colorado, and Northampton, Massachusetts, are considering the reform, though in 2018 voters in Golden, Colorado, rejected a ballot measure to lower the voting age in that city.[65] The problem was that advocates had little time for a robust campaign given that the measure was approved for the ballot only a few months before Election Day. Sustained advocacy and education are key. That's why proponents have spent so much time explaining the merits to those who are willing to listen, such as lawmakers in DC. As of fall 2018, a majority of DC council members had endorsed a proposal to lower the voting age for all elections in the nation's capital—including the presidential election.[66] Although the measure stalled toward the end of 2018, its prospects for eventual passage look strong because young people have continued to press the issue. The time has come to expand the conversation and make this change on a widespread basis. The positive effects on democracy will last for decades.

Passing bold reforms in some places, especially for local elections first, will normalize them and give activists in other jurisdictions success stories to cite as they campaign for positive changes in their own communities. Down the road, the same measures to expand the right to vote more broadly may not seem that far-fetched. City by city, state by state, we can expand the eligible electorate and build a more inclusive, engaged culture of democratic participation.

In addition to promoting voting rights for young people, what other reforms can we make today to expand the electorate? What's working right now? Let's hear from a guy named Denver from Tennessee who once robbed a bank. He'll show us how to change hearts and minds.

SECOND CHANCES

Denver Schimming of Tennessee had found his calling. But that's only after he saw the depths of despair.

In 1991, Schimming robbed a bank after, he notes, "a week of severe alcohol abuse, deep depression, and deep desperation."[1] He completed a prison sentence of forty-six months. He then reentered society with a one-way bus ticket to Nashville, a few dollars from his prison job, and the clothes on his back. Yet he slowly cleaned up his life to the point where he started to wonder whether he was allowed to vote. After a little research he came to one conclusion: Tennessee's law was extremely convoluted.

Under Tennessee law, felons could not vote while they served their time, but if their convictions had occurred between 1986 and 1996, then most of them automatically regained their right to vote upon finishing their sentence. It turned out that Schimming had actually regained his voting rights without even realizing it. But other felons who had completed their sentences, but had convictions from other time periods, had to hire an attorney and petition a court to seek a restoration of their right to vote in an adversarial proceeding. Schimming thought this was both confusing and fundamentally unfair. He eventually became the face of the effort in 2005 to change the law and lessen the burden on future ex-felons, allowing them to regain their rights by filling out a simple form.

Schimming's initial interest in helping stemmed from a meeting he attended where a local lawyer spoke about the rights of former offenders. "A light went off," he told me. "I realized that I had a personal responsibility to try and help the cause."[2] He then contacted Tennessee representative Larry Turner, who every year had introduced a bill in the state legislature to make it easier for those convicted of felonies who had served their time to regain their voting rights without having to hire an attorney or petition a judge. Even though Turner's proposal had failed in the past, Schimming told Turner that he wanted to join the effort. Schimming's advocacy just may have made the difference this time around.

Schimming took off work every Wednesday during the legislative session to petition legislators, meet with voters, and lobby for a new law. He spoke on college campuses. He appeared on television and radio programs. He went to the state capitol building to knock on legislators' doors and visited their districts to speak with their constituents. He began each of these meetings by telling his personal story: he made a mistake many years ago, paid for it dearly, and yet remained a valuable member of his community. The conversations changed minds, particularly among the Republican-controlled Senate leadership. As he put it, "many of these legislators had never personally spoken with a former offender. They were able to put a human face to the issue."[3]

A bill that streamlined the process for re-enfranchisement, requiring a simple form that one can download online, passed in July 2006. To be clear, Tennessee's current law is not a perfect model to emulate across the country, as it still places unnecessary hurdles on ex-felons who have otherwise paid their debt to society.[4] But at the very least, it's better than the prior version thanks to the advocacy of people like Schimming. As he explained, "when you're afforded the opportunity to vote, you think, 'Yes, I am fully vested in my city, state, [and] country. I'm just as much a citizen as anyone else.' I think it shows rehabilitation; I think it shows a mindset that you're looking forward, not backward. No one should ever lose that right because of a felony conviction."[5] Reflecting on his efforts a decade later, which have helped thousands of Tennessee voters regain their rights, he said with pride, "It was a year I'll never forget."[6]

A GROWING TREND

This is a nationwide movement. Individuals and legislators on the ground in various communities are finding ways to reduce the harsh effects of strict felon disenfranchisement laws. State laws vary widely: while Iowa and Kentucky disenfranchise virtually all felons for life, felons in Maine and Vermont can vote from jail using an absentee ballot and never lose their right to vote.[7] Pro-democracy advocates are lobbying governors, legislators, and local politicians in places with the harshest laws. Many states have eased their rules and given former offenders a second chance, providing a positive way to expand democratic participation. We already saw in the prologue how one person, West Powell of Kentucky, changed minds in his state, making Kentucky's worst-in-the-country felon disenfranchisement law a little bit better by opening the door for some offenders to regain their right to vote through an expungement of their records. All it took was Powell speaking up and an influential legislator, Republican Whitney Westerfield, being willing to listen. Others are doing the same work in their own communities.

The stakes could not be higher. According to the Sentencing Project, a nonprofit organization that works to improve the US criminal justice system, as of the 2016 election, state laws had disenfranchised nearly 6.1 million Americans because of a felony conviction. That amounts to about 2.5 percent of the total US voting age population, or one out of every forty adults. For comparison, in 1976 America had "only" about 1.17 million disenfranchised felons. Felon disenfranchisement disproportionately harms African Americans: these laws take away the right to vote from one in thirteen blacks of voting age, amounting to over 7.4 percent of all African American adults. In some states, such as Kentucky, where it has been historically tough to regain one's rights, the law disenfranchises almost a quarter of the adult black population. Systemically removing the right to vote from minority communities perpetuates discrimination because they then have reduced electoral power to create meaningful change.[8] Nationwide, half of today's disenfranchised individuals have fully finished their sentences and are living as regular citizens in our communities; another quarter are out of prison and are on probation or parole. That leaves only 25 percent of the disenfranchised population currently in jail.[9]

Yet there is continuing progress to reduce these numbers. In Wyoming, a bipartisan group of lawmakers enacted a law that automatically gives voting rights back to nonviolent felons once they serve their time.[10] Nevada also recently passed a law to restore voting rights to some former felons.[11] Lawmakers in Minnesota and Mississippi have considered proposals to ease their felon disenfranchisement rules.[12] Nebraska's legislature passed a bill in 2017 to repeal the state's two-year waiting period to regain the right to vote after a felon completes his or her sentence, but the governor vetoed the proposal and the legislature failed to override the veto.[13] Also in 2017, Alabama's Republican governor signed a bill, passed by the Republican-controlled legislature, to give voting rights back to thousands of people by redefining what it means to commit a "crime of moral turpitude."[14] In an ironic twist of fate, Republican Roy Moore, while running unsuccessfully for Alabama's US Senate seat during a 2017 special election, complained (erroneously) that Democrats were illegally registering new voters—the very ex-felons that the Republican legislature had lawfully re-enfranchised—all while allegations about Moore's sexual misconduct toward teenagers engulfed his campaign.[15]

THE POWER OF INDIVIDUAL STORIES

There are countless people just like Denver Schimming who are working to re-enfranchise felons. Andres Idarraga of Rhode Island was convicted of a felony when he was twenty years old and served six-and-a-half years in prison.[16] While incarcerated, he dedicated his time to educating himself about economics, history, and politics. He read two books that changed his worldview: biographies of Supreme Court Justice Thurgood Marshall and South African revolutionary and President Nelson Mandela. As Idarraga recounted, he learned from Marshall's biography the power of becoming involved in one's community to effect change. He gained from Mandela's story the power of direct political action. Through these books, he acquired a new framework for thinking about education and the possibilities of political change by harnessing the grassroots efforts of everyday people.[17]

Once out of prison, Idarraga joined an organization called the Family Life Center (now known as Open Doors), which seeks to assist formerly incarcerated individuals.[18] He also began reading about felon disenfranchisement and the unfair costs it imposes. Denying the franchise creates both a tangible and a symbolic harm, because voting is how we engage the population in our democracy. It is, as Idarraga noted, the most direct way an individual can become involved in society. Taking that right away impugns a person's dignity and standing in the community. Idarraga also learned about the history of felon disenfranchisement and how it had served as a potent method after the Civil War to strip power away from minority populations, with southern states in the late 1800s and early 1900s specifically targeting "black" crimes as the basis for disenfranchisement.[19] The racist origins of felon disenfranchisement have detrimental modern-day effects. The Rhode Island law disproportionately harmed African American and Hispanic voters: one in five black men and one in eleven Hispanic men in Rhode Island had lost their voting rights due to a felony conviction.[20]

As a volunteer for the Family Life Center, Idarraga advocated for the state to ease its felon disenfranchisement rule. He targeted specific organizations and individuals. Along with fellow volunteers, he walked the streets and knocked on doors. His aim was to educate his fellow citizens. He believed that once people understood the effects of felon disenfranchisement, they would support a ballot referendum to change the law. Importantly, community organizers and political experts—the usual suspects who push for reform—were not the main drivers of this effort. Instead, people who had never been involved in politics before saw that they could strengthen their communities by walking the streets and speaking with their neighbors. Their advocacy also had the laudable effect of encouraging more people to vote.

Andres Idarraga, who fought for felon re-enfranchisement in Rhode Island. [Photo by John Abromowski.]

In 2006, Rhode Island voters passed a ballot referendum to allow felons to vote once they are released from prison, instead of having to wait until they complete their probation and parole. Idarraga registered to vote shortly thereafter. He was one of 15,500 residents of the state who regained their fundamental right to vote.[21] The experience of advocating for this change, Idarraga recounted, was "life altering."[22] It gave him a new understanding of the responsibility and importance of civic participation. "I'm learning . . . how to give back to society and that starts with participating in the democratic process and encouraging others to vote."[23] Voting, he said, is "the only way to exert power, have one's voice heard, and show accountability for our democratic system."[24]

Idarraga eventually enrolled at Brown University, studying comparative literature and economics while also working full time. He then went on to Yale Law School and is now a successful lawyer. Rhode Island's prior law would have barred him from voting until he was fifty-eight years old, a thirty-one-year wait. Instead, he is now a regular voter and has never missed an election since he regained his rights.

Muhamad As-saddique Abdul-Rahman of Virginia voted for the first time in 2016 after Virginia eased its felon disenfranchisement rule. He was fifty-three years old and had completed his prison sentence years earlier. He explained to the media what voting meant to him personally: "I was not whole when I came out of prison, both politically and emotionally. But having my right to vote back has made me feel whole as a human being."[25] He elaborated, "as an ex-felon, myself, I couldn't vote and I didn't feel—as a citizen I didn't feel whole. I was paying taxes. I had to follow laws, and I had no say in what these laws were."[26]

Abdul-Rahman spent months canvassing in Richmond, Virginia, to encourage people—especially the newly enfranchised—to vote in the 2016 election. He actively sought out former felons to educate them about re-enfranchisement and to help them register to vote. People like Katrina Miller were the beneficiaries. She did not realize that she had regained her voting rights until Abdul-Rahman looked up her status.[27] Another new voter called her mother immediately after receiving the certificate saying that she had regained her right to vote. Others had their certificates framed. In total, Abdul-Rahman helped to register over 1,400 individuals in 2016, about 800 of them former felons who could now vote for the first time.[28]

Maryland offers another example of positive progress at the state and local levels. In 2016, the Maryland legislature restored voting rights to over 40,000 released felons, allowing them to vote even while they are on probation or parole.[29] This followed the action in Takoma Park, Maryland (the innovator in lowering the voting age to sixteen), which restored voting rights to felons for local elections.[30] Maryland's reform came about thanks to people like Etta Myers. Myers was wrongfully convicted of murder based on faulty eyewitness testimony and was sentenced to life imprisonment. After thirty-six years in jail, a Maryland appeals court threw out her conviction because the jury instructions at her trial were improper. Once she was finally released, she worked to change Maryland law. As she wrote in a column for the *USA Today*, "After so long in prison, I want to start living like the rest of society. I long to take part in our democracy and make my voice heard. Voting is a right that gives me the ear of people in power and through that, I have the power to change what I know to be wrong: our country's enormous problem with mass incarceration, which disproportionately impacts black and brown people."[31] Her story, along with lobbying from various advocacy organizations, convinced a majority of the legislature to make this change.

This is the tale of today's voter enhancements, achieved one person, one community, and one state at a time. Stories from people like Denver Schimming and Andres Idarraga represent the power of change, the power of forward thinking, and the power of local advocacy. These individuals offered themselves up to their neighbors, other members of their communities, and local political leaders. Their neighbors talked to their own friends, legislators spoke with their colleagues, and the conversations spread. State and local politicians are relatively easy to reach and will meet with their constituents. They are usually willing to listen. All it takes is some courage.

Of course, in many states the authority to actually change the law is in the hands of elected officials themselves. That means that we, as a community, must demonstrate political support for their positive actions on this issue. Individuals need to tell their stories and then politicians need to act. We must reward our elected leaders when they support an inclusive view of our political community—and hold them accountable at the ballot box if they don't. Let's flip the burden and make them explain why we should *not* re-enfranchise felons who have done their time and paid their debt to society. And let's applaud those, like Virginia's governor Terry McAuliffe, who do the right thing.

VIRGINIA IS FOR LOVERS—AND VOTERS

Terry McAuliffe's hand must have been tired.

In April 2016, McAuliffe, the Democratic governor of Virginia, issued an executive order to re-enfranchise more than 200,000 felons who had completed their sentences.[32] Virginia has one of the harshest felon disenfranchisement rules in the country; the law essentially bans felons from voting for life unless they obtain clemency from the governor,[33] previously a rare occurrence. As with most felon disenfranchisement measures, the Virginia law disproportionately harmed minority voters given the reality of our criminal justice system, which tends to capture more racial minorities within its domain. Indeed, almost 25 percent of Virginia's African American population was disenfranchised because of felony convictions. McAuliffe's decision to lift the lifetime ban for felons who had served their time therefore reduced a significant barrier to voting for thousands of people, especially racial minorities.

McAuliffe's move was controversial, to say the least. But it was the right thing to do. Individuals who have served their time still suffer the consequences of their poor decisions years later. They are essentially told that they are forever outside of our political community. Without a vote, they have little voice, even though they now may be model, law-abiding citizens. McAuliffe took to his pen to undo that injustice.

Initially, McAuliffe issued a single order that re-enfranchised thousands of felons in one fell swoop. Virginia's Republican lawmakers immediately sued. They argued that the governor's order violated the Virginia Constitution—and they won. In a four to three decision, the Supreme Court of Virginia ruled that the governor could not unilaterally re-enfranchise thousands of felons in a single order.[34] Instead, the governor had the power to restore voting rights only on a case-by-case basis.

Fine, McAuliffe responded. I'll just sign thousands of individual orders. "My faith remains strong in all of our citizens to choose their leaders, and

I am prepared to back up that faith with my executive pen," he said. "The struggle for civil rights has always been a long and difficult one, but the fight goes on."[35] He then signed 13,000 individual orders restoring the right to vote to citizens who had previously regained their rights through his prior order before the Supreme Court of Virginia struck that down. His administration reviewed each individual's record to ensure they had completed their sentence and period of supervised release. He promised to continue signing individual orders to re-enfranchise thousands more people. (His office used an autopen, a machine that copies his signature, so his hand was spared.) During his term as governor, McAuliffe restored voting rights to over 150,000 felons, calling it his proudest achievement while in office.[36] These new voters were able to participate in the 2017 gubernatorial election. The winner, Democratic governor Ralph Northam, has continued this voting rights restoration program.[37]

A COMMUNITY EFFORT

Former felons aren't the only ones engaged in these lobbying efforts to reform laws that prohibit felons from voting for life. Community groups can make a big difference as well. In Minnesota, for instance, an organization called Restore the Vote is a coalition of various stakeholders who promote felon re-enfranchisement. The coalition includes over seventy-five groups with varying interests but a singular purpose: improve our democracy by expanding the electorate.[38] Many other states have similar organizations.

There are also scores of lawmakers, on both sides of the aisle, who are willing to consider the issue, just as Kentucky's Republican senator Whitney Westerfield did when he heard West Powell's tale. Understanding how felon disenfranchisement harms the dignity of those who have cleaned up their lives can make all the difference.

Yet there is still a stigma attached to felon voting rights that our society must overcome. Joshua Lewis Berg wrote of his experience registering voters in California when a man declined his assistance.[39] Berg quickly surmised that the individual was a former felon who had served his time and thought he could not vote, even though California law re-enfranchises felons after their release from parole. The man had just assumed that he had lost his rights permanently. Better education regarding the scope of voting rights would have helped. We need more individuals and community groups on the ground to educate our fellow citizens about their rights.

Florida's recent success exemplifies how a grassroots movement can have a big impact on this issue.[40] Florida—along with Kentucky, Iowa, and Virginia (until its governor issued the executive order)—had one of the strictest felon disenfranchisement laws in the country, taking away felons' voting rights for life. Florida disenfranchised about 1.7 million individuals, including a whopping 20 percent of the state's African American population. To put this 1.7 million number in perspective, Donald Trump beat Hillary Clinton in Florida in 2016 by just under 113,000 votes.[41] Under Florida law, felons could regain their right to vote only through a governor's order, but Florida's Republican governor Rick Scott was particularly stingy in using this power.

So activists, using the name Second Chances, secured over 70,000 signatures as the first step toward a state constitutional amendment to undo Florida's strict felon disenfranchisement rule. The constitutional amendment would automatically re-enfranchise everyone—other than those convicted of murder or sexual assault—once they have served their time and completed their parole or probation.

Desmond Meade was at the forefront of this movement. Formerly homeless, a drug addict, and a felon, Meade eventually cleaned up his life and earned a law degree even though he knew that Florida would prohibit him from taking the bar exam because of his conviction. He turned his attention toward reforming Florida's felon disenfranchisement rule, joining thousands of volunteers to convince the state's citizens to vote for the measure.[42] I heard Meade speak in February 2018 at a conference in New Orleans called the Unrig the System Summit, which was a gathering of people interested in improving our democracy. He broke down crying while he told his story of despair—he had almost committed suicide—and eventual redemption. He lamented, however, that although he was now a well-known community leader, he still could not vote.

In November 2018, the state's voters passed the constitutional amendment by a wide margin, with almost two-thirds of voters approving the measure.[43] The state's voters recognized the importance of giving Meade and others like him another chance to be full members of our democracy.

Although the new Republican governor, Ron DeSantis, tried to slow-walk the implementation of the amendment, the state must put the law into effect immediately and allow these individuals to vote. The stakes could not be higher: as Florida is perennially a battleground state, these new voters could quite literally help decide the next presidential election.

Dedicated people on the ground are the key to this re-enfranchisement movement. Although not always glamorous work, these efforts are essential to secure the fundamental right to vote for more people. Felon disenfranchisement might seem reasonable in the abstract. These people committed a crime against our society, after all, so why should we let them vote? But once lawmakers and citizens hear the actual stories of real people who suffer the harms—once the public sees these individuals as neighbors, brothers, and friends—and once people understand the significant impact felon disenfranchisement has on racial minorities, then the moral argument becomes much clearer. Felon disenfranchisement for life is morally wrong. We must change hearts and minds. We must create a groundswell of support. To so do, we need to share these stories with one another and with those who can make a difference.

A POSITIVE IMPACT ON OUR DEMOCRACY

Re-enfranchising felons, at least after they have completed their sentences, is not only good for civic engagement and the overall strength of our democratic institutions. It also helps people who have served their time reintegrate into society. There is a personal benefit for each individual who regains the right to vote and a personal toll for every citizen who remains disenfranchised. Civic engagement will help ex-felons rehabilitate themselves, likely leading to fewer future crimes. Although establishing a direct causal link is difficult, one study showed that recidivism rates, which measure how often a convict commits another crime, are lower in states that re-enfranchise felons as opposed to those that bar them from voting for life.[44] As newly enfranchised voter Jonathan Quarles put it, "if you deny a person the right to vote, they will never be equal in a society."[45]

This is why flipping the narrative on ex-felon voting rights is so important. Most commentary about felon disenfranchisement in America highlights the massive impact of these prohibitions, particularly on racial minorities. That focus is accurate, at least on a broad, social level, and the truth of felon disenfranchisement tells a troubling story about our democracy. But that story is incomplete. A full discussion of felon disenfranchisement must recognize the progress occurring on the ground in states and cities throughout the country.

On the personal, local level, things are improving, with more and more states easing their felon disenfranchisement rules. Individuals on the ground are coming forward with their stories and taking the fight to state legislatures, state courts, and the public at large. Public opinion polls generally show that Americans favor re-enfranchisement for felons who have completed their prison sentences.[46] Although much more can be done, state-level reforms have helped to ease felon disenfranchisement laws and restore the constitutional right to vote for thousands of people. Every felon who regains the right to vote is another citizen who can participate in our democracy. This movement will only grow stronger as more and more people critically examine our felon disenfranchisement laws. It's a matter of fundamental fairness. The stories of people working on this movement have planted the seeds for wider growth. We must continue to expand upon these early successes.

Increasing the electorate can also impact who wins an election. We already saw how the Virginia governor's race in 2017 included former felons who had regained their rights, possibly tipping the scales toward Democrat Ralph Northam. Also consider the Virginia House race in 2017 that initially looked like a one-vote victory for the Democratic challenger but then ended up in a tie, which the Republican incumbent won in a coin flip—keeping the state legislature under Republican control. One vote made the difference. Might that vote have come from an ex-felon who now could vote?[47] Yet this isn't just a ploy to help Democrats. Any candidate or political party can campaign toward a newly enfranchised group to advocate for support, which is perhaps one reason why felon re-enfranchisement has gained bipartisan support in most places.

Indeed, these efforts are occurring in so-called blue states *and* so-called red states. Felon re-enfranchisement doesn't have to be a partisan issue, even if many still consider it only through a political lens. When Virginia governor Terry McAuliffe re-enfranchised thousands of voters in 2016, critics claimed that as a Hillary Clinton supporter, he was simply trying to add Democratic voters to the rolls in that battleground state. Although there is some evidence that ex-felons support Democratic candidates more than Republican candidates, any disparity simply may be due to demographics. Former felons are disproportionately racial minorities and have lower socioeconomic backgrounds, which are factors that correlate with voting for Democrats.[48] Of course, it is impossible to know for sure which candidate a former felon will support. Plenty of ex-felons voted for Hillary Clinton, Donald Trump, or someone else in the 2016 election. Regardless of the politics, whether we should let ex-felons vote after they have served their time is about doing what is right for our democracy, nothing more. Politicians should expand voter eligibility wherever possible and win on ideas, not election rules that limit who may participate. Denying voting rights to otherwise-eligible people because of how they may vote is antithetical to the very essence of democracy and good governance. Making a mistake (even an admittedly big one) years or even decades earlier shouldn't mean that someone can never be a full citizen once again. Should we really couple a criminal conviction with eliminating the fundamental right to vote, often for life? How can felons, once they have served their sentences, hope to become a full part of our society and community if they cannot participate in our elections? This is the human and moral reality with which we must all grapple.

Lawsuits to challenge felon disenfranchisement generally have not succeeded in reducing the impact of these laws. Attorneys have argued that the practice violates the constitutional right to vote and discriminates against racial minorities. But most courts have upheld the laws even when presented with evidence of their discriminatory effect, ruling that neither the US Constitution nor the federal Voting Rights Act prohibits the practice.[49] These results, though perhaps wrong, show that we cannot rely solely on judicial challenges as the primary strategy to counter the adverse effects of felon disenfranchisement laws. Voting rights advocates must ensure that they put sufficient resources into expanding the electorate through a grassroots movement that focuses on the stories of individuals who are denied the right to vote. Little by little, community by community, we will return the franchise to thousands of people who have cleaned up their lives, showing them that they are once again valued members of our society. As West Powell, the former felon who convinced Kentucky to change its law, explained, "I'm part of society again. So I want to make sure I'm voting to have people in office who represent most of the things I want to get done."[50]

Re-enfranchising ex-felons will add to the voter rolls and bring more people into the political process. This could improve overall turnout. Of course, adding more eligible voters increases the denominator in the turnout ratio (the number of people who vote divided by the eligible electorate), so the challenge is both to allow these individuals to vote and also ensure they actually go to the polls. That is, felon re-enfranchisement could perversely reduce the overall turnout percentage if these individuals do not also go out and vote.

Therefore, grassroots efforts to expand the voter rolls are a good place to start, but they cannot be the end of our advocacy. We must also find ways to increase overall participation and turnout by breaking down barriers to registration and voting for *all* voters.

How do we help to improve overall turnout? Steve Trout of Oregon has some ideas about that.

CHAPTER 3

WHAT DO TACO TRUCKS HAVE TO DO WITH VOTER REGISTRATION?

I t had never really made sense to Kate Brown. Why do voters have to jump through so many hoops? Why must they take affirmative steps and opt in to a voter registration system before the state will allow them to vote? Why can't the state just register all eligible voters automatically?

Brown was a state senator in Oregon who recognized that voting should be as easy as possible so long as it also remained free from fraud. As her deputy chief of staff recounted, Brown believed that reforming the state's voter registration process was vital to a flourishing democracy. Online voter registration, which the state adopted in 2010, had helped, but it did not solve the problem that voters were still required to take an affirmative step just to exercise their fundamental right to vote. Brown would rise to become Oregon's secretary of state and then governor, and her goal of easing voter registration remained a top priority.[1]

In fact, one of the first bills Brown signed as Oregon governor was an automatic voter registration (AVR) law she had championed as secretary of state.[2] This law drastically enhanced convenience for voters—with compelling results: a significant improvement in voter turnout. AVR's success is now sweeping the nation, with a dozen states adopting their own versions and more on the way. This is the kind of pro-voter, bipartisan measure that can truly advance our democracy. Individual champions have led the way.

The stories of this reform—as well as other improvements to voter registration—demonstrate the power of local advocacy, innovative thinking, and dedicated public servants.

A PRACTICAL PROBLEM WITH A SIMPLE SOLUTION

Most people have probably never heard of Steve Trout. But those who follow elections know what he helped to achieve. Along with Kate Brown, Oregon's secretary-of-state-turned-governor, Trout was a central figure behind the idea of automatic voter registration. To be sure, others had floated the concept as well.[3] But under Trout's guidance, Oregon was the first state to implement AVR. This reform can have a significant impact on our elections nationwide, increasing voter turnout just like it did in Oregon.

Trout was the elections director of Oregon, working for Secretary of State Brown after she won election to that office. Early during his service, the state faced turmoil over its registration system—a common problem in many states. Activists on the left were threatening lawsuits, claiming that the state was not fully complying with its obligations under the federal National Voter Registration Act to make registration easy at DMV offices. Activists on the right were making noise about the state's outdated voter rolls, saying that ineligible people were still registered, but these complaints often came just before the election when there wasn't sufficient time to respond. Trout worried about the time and expense of dealing with these allegations while also trying to keep the voter registration lists as accurate as possible as Election Day neared.[4]

Around this time, Oregon was considering whether to join ERIC, the Electronic Registration Information Center.[5] ERIC is a nonprofit organization made up of member states that is dedicated to helping states clean up their voter rolls in a cost-effective and efficient manner, providing a valuable resource for states to compare their voter lists. Started with just seven states, the membership as of early 2019 was up to twenty-five states and Washington, DC.[6] Oregon joined ERIC in 2014, and one of its obligations as a member was to send a postcard to anyone it could identify as eligible to vote but who was not yet registered. The state would have to compare its DMV lists to the voter registration rolls to determine who was not registered and should receive a postcard, with the hope that the postcard would spur these individuals to then register. According to Trout, other states saw a response rate of about 1 to 3 percent from these postcards.[7] That is, only about 1 to 3 percent of the mailed postcards resulted in new voter registrations—better than nothing, but still not great. To Trout, that didn't seem like a good use of taxpayer funds if other options were available. The state was already spending money to defend its outdated voter rolls and it would now have to use funds to send out postcards to non-registered voters, with only a minimal improvement to its registration and turnout rates. There had to be a better way.

Trout went home one night and thought it over. As he told me, he tried to flip the problem around in his mind. What if the state just registered everyone who was eligible and left it to individuals who objected to ask *not* to be on the voter list? What if Oregon adopted an opt-out mechanism instead of its current system of requiring voters to opt-in?

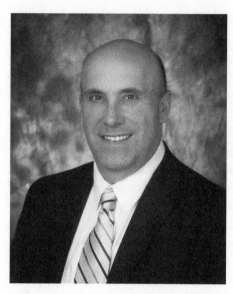

Steve Trout, Oregon elections director. [Photo by Cecil Photography.]

A new, opt-out voter registration process could use information that the state already possessed. Anytime someone visits the DMV in Oregon to obtain or renew a driver's license, the person already provides the DMV with all of the relevant information for voter registration—name, address, age, proof of citizenship, and a signature. Although they are supposed to be given the opportunity to register to vote at that time, for whatever reason a large number of these people fail to take the additional steps that would put them on the voter rolls. To close the gap, the state simply matched the DMV database with the voter registration database. If an eligible voter was listed in the DMV database, but not on the voter registration rolls, the state would add the person to the voter registration list and mail out a notification letter that provided an opportunity to opt-out.

Logistically, the idea worked because the DMV's electronic database could "talk" to the online voter registration database by the push of a button. In addition, moving to automatic voter registration would cut off the lawsuits about outdated voter rolls because the state would update the registration list dynamically by comparing the DMV list with the voter registration list, thereby helping to minimize the potential of fraud. Oregon could make it easier to vote while also ensuring the integrity of its voter list. It seemed like a win-win.

It wasn't that easy, explained Gina Zejdlik, Kate Brown's deputy chief of staff who had worked for Brown since Brown's days in the state Senate. Zejdlik was one of the key players who helped to push the idea of automatic voter registration. The reform, she told me, seemed extremely radical to many people at the time. It was completely different from how every other state registered voters. Even the state's own lawyers were wary of the idea because of its novelty.[8]

Opponents lined up to derail the plan. Their main argument was that voting is a privilege, not a right, and that individuals should have to take affirmative steps to exercise this privilege. Of course, most of us think of voting as the most fundamental *right* in our democracy, not merely a privilege. Voting is not the same as, say, driving. We have the privilege to drive so long as we comply with the state's requirements and obtain a driver's license. We have the right, as members of a democracy, to participate in governance equally with everyone else. Our entire democracy rests on the notion that our leaders have legitimacy because we *all* had the opportunity to select them in a free and fair election. As Zejdlik remembered, advocates promoted the idea of voting as a fundamental right, such that the state should make it easy to participate, while also highlighting that AVR would clean up the voter rolls.[9]

Indeed, as Trout explained, there was something for everyone in the proposal. For progressives, who often worry about voter access, it provided a path to expand the registration rolls to make it easier to participate. For conservatives, who usually seem more concerned about the potential of fraud, it enhanced election integrity because it ensured that voters provided proof of their eligibility.[10]

Once Secretary of State Brown, Elections Director Trout, and other proponents introduced the concept, the campaign to pass automatic voter registration was on. That's when individuals on the ground stepped up their advocacy. They were, in fact, vital to the success of this movement. Brown's office received assistance from nongovernmental organizations and other partners to lobby lawmakers, educate the public, and rally support for the idea. For instance, the Oregon Bus Project, a volunteer-based pro-democracy group, promoted the reform, explaining to the public how AVR would help to increase political participation among young voters.[11] The work of individuals and groups such as the Bus Project validated the effort and demonstrated that the change was not that radical.

The Oregon legislature initially rejected the idea in 2013. Advocates had not adequately told the story of why the state needed to reform the registration process, and county clerks were concerned about bearing the increased costs of compliance. Zejdlik, Kate Brown's aide, recalled that proponents faced hurdles at almost every step of the way.[12] The law eventually passed in 2015—with additional state funding for county clerks in response to their concerns—but only after advocates promoted a compelling, positive narrative and stayed persistent in their message of improving the voting process for all.[13]

For instance, one vital aspect of the effort was to tell a story to the state's citizens about why automatic voter registration would improve Oregon's election system. Many voters erroneously assumed that Oregon was already putting them on the voter rolls and that they did not need to do anything to register to vote. That was a big problem. Paradoxically, voters thought the state already had automatic voter registration when it did not, leaving them off of the voter rolls as a result.[14] To clear up this confusion, advocates dubbed the bill the New Motor Voter law, rather than "automatic voter registration." Motor Voter was already a well-known concept, based on a 1993 federal law that requires states to offer voter registration when someone obtains a driver's license.[15] The New Motor Voter law would simply switch who was the primary actor to register the voter, putting the responsibility on the state instead of the individual.

The data on improved turnout due to AVR are impressive. Oregon added at least 225,000 citizens to its voter registration list and cleaned up outdated records. Almost 100,000 of these new registrants voted in the

2016 election.[16] One study showed that "[m]ore than 116,000 people registered who were unlikely to have done so otherwise, and more than 40,000 of these previously disengaged people voted in the November [2016] election."[17] Another study found that AVR increased the racial, age, and income diversity of Oregon's electorate and that AVR alone contributed to a turnout increase of 2 to 3 percent.[18] That's a lot better than the 1 to 3 percent increase in voter registrations—not turnout—the state could expect using the postcard method from ERIC.

One consequence of AVR, however, is the rise of "unaffiliated" voters who are not listed as members of a political party, which could impact the primary process.[19] That's in part because Oregon uses a "closed" primary system, where only party members may vote to choose a party's nominee. This means that voters must affirmatively select a political party before they can participate in a primary. Under AVR, the state sends a postcard to people who are newly registered explaining that they can return the card or log onto the state's elections website to affiliate with a political party if they wish.[20] Yet those who do not eventually affiliate with a party cannot vote in a party primary. The state should find other ways to reach these voters or consider switching to an open primary system where the political parties can allow unaffiliated voters to participate in their primaries.

Given its initial success, the state is now looking at other ways to improve AVR. For example, Trout is studying whether it is possible to compare the electronic voter registration database with public university records or tax statements to capture potential voters who don't have a driver's license. The key will be to figure out how to ensure that these other databases require voters to show proof of eligibility and provide a signature. The focus must be on making the experience as easy and convenient as possible for each voter while also ensuring the integrity of the system.

As we will see in the next chapter, in addition to AVR, Oregon also runs its elections entirely through the mail. The state mails out a ballot to every registered voter, which the voter can mail back or drop off at designated sites.[21] With increased participation through automatic voter registration, this combined AVR/vote-by-mail system truly makes voting easy and convenient.

Oregon proved that AVR works. It improves turnout. By spreading the story of its adoption and understanding its positive effects, innovative reforms such as these—which may have once seemed radical—can become normalized and mainstream.

THE IDEA SPREADS TO "RED" STATES

Conservative states like West Virginia have followed Oregon's lead. Automatic voter registration came about there through a political compromise. That effort shows how voting rights advocates can succeed by going on the offense instead of merely opposing laws that make it harder to vote.

In 2016, Republicans in West Virginia were pushing a strict voter ID requirement. The bill passed the state House and was under consideration in the Senate. As it went through the Senate Judiciary Committee, Democratic senator Corey Palumbo added an amendment to include AVR. The voter ID law, along with the automatic voter registration amendment, eventually passed both houses with bipartisan support, and Democratic governor Earl Ray Tomblin signed it into law.[22]

To implement automatic voter registration successfully, then secretary of state Natalie Tennant formed a working group of government agencies, election officials, and advocacy organizations. The advocacy groups were integral to the early success of the new policy, selling the idea to their constituents. As Julie Archer of the West Virginia Citizen Action Group explained, her organization was eager to help election officials create a system that would modernize voter registration.[23] Importantly, the implementation effort was bipartisan. AVR is a cheaper, easier, and more secure way of running the state's registration system. It also makes elections a lot more convenient for thousands of voters.[24]

Automatic voter registration, once seen as an innovative or even radical reform, is now spreading throughout the country, with over a dozen states approving its implementation. People of all political persuasions support it because it improves elections for everyone. After Oregon and West Virginia, early adopters included California, Georgia, Vermont, and Washington, DC.[25] Alaska voters approved it in 2016.[26] In 2017, Illinois Republican governor Bruce Rauner signed AVR into law.[27] Rhode Island also came on board in 2017, and Colorado adopted it through an administrative process that same year.[28] Massachusetts, New Jersey, and Washington State followed suit with legislation in 2018.[29] Also in 2018, voters in Michigan and Nevada approved the reform through ballot measures.[30] As legislators and voters have recognized, automatic voter registration will go a long way toward positively impacting thousands of citizens, easing their path to participating in our democracy.

USING THE INTERNET TO MAKE VOTER REGISTRATION EASIER

The story of automatic voter registration echoes the path of another similar reform, online registration, where individuals can register to vote and update their registration with the click of a mouse. It took one innovative state, in this case Arizona, to be the first mover on this issue. Now over thirty-seven states have online voter registration, positively helping voters in every election.[31]

Craig Stender, a soft-spoken IT expert for the Arizona Department of Motor Vehicles, was one of the driving forces behind Arizona's adoption and implementation of online voter registration. Although Stender demurred when I spoke with him, saying that it was actually the Arizona secretary of state's chief information officer, Mike Totherow, who came up with the idea for online voter registration, Stender's IT expertise made all the difference. Stender had moved from the state's Department of Transportation to the Arizona secretary of state's office to help implement the Help America Vote Act of 2002, a federal law that required states to update their voting technology.[32] In addition, one major task was to transition the state's voter database from a paper to an electronic format. While doing so, Stender recognized that the Motor Vehicle's online database and the state's election office could "talk" to each other over the internet.[33]

The state was already using an online motor vehicle registration system, which included a digitized image of each person and his or her signature. The Motor Vehicle Division could simply share that information with the state's voter database, fostering easy verification. The preexisting digital files made online voter registration both more convenient and more secure. Paper registrations have three main problems: forms can be lost in the mail, groups conducting registration drives may not turn in the forms on time, and data entry mistakes can occur when election officials copy the information from paper registrations to a computer database. Stender's work on Arizona's system, called EZ Voter, showed how an online voter registration process could solve all three problems while also improving security.

Stender possessed the technological knowledge and creativity to implement the reform, but many election officials call Tammy Patrick the "matriarch" of online voter registration.[34] That's because Patrick has been instrumental in voter registration's growth across the country. Patrick, who now works for the Democracy Fund, a bipartisan foundation that promotes democracy reform, was at the time the elections administrator for Maricopa County, Arizona (the state's largest county, which includes Phoenix). She joined the office in 2003 and was an early champion of online voter registration. In particular, she has shown many states how it can help voters, reduce costs, and make the registration lists more accurate and secure. Patrick also served on the bipartisan Presidential Commission on Election Administration, created after the 2012 election, which recommended online voter registration as a key component of election reform.[35]

Although Arizona was first, other states quickly took notice. Election officials such as Tammy Patrick had to educate their fellow election workers and the general public, making the case for online voter registration to both legislators and voters. Advocacy and support from everyday Americans matter even for the adoption of seemingly complex technological changes to our election system. Without public support, legislators would have little incentive to actively pursue reforms to election administration.

Consider the example of Florida, one of the most contentious battleground states in recent presidential elections. Based on the adoption of online voter registration in other states, Florida's State Association of Supervisors of Elections—a nonprofit organization composed of the state's county clerks—began looking into the issue. The Association plays an active role in shaping Florida's election rules. It found that the substance of the idea had merit but that the politics might be difficult to overcome. The group learned that many people, particularly Republicans, assumed that online voter registration was simply a guise for Democrats to increase the voter rolls in their favor. Yet the reality is that both Republican- and Democratic-controlled states have adopted online voter registration without any obvious political effects.[36] The Association sought to dispel the myth of a partisan motivation and instead explain how online voter registration was truly a nonpartisan concept. Indeed, the bipartisan Association was unanimous in its recommendation that Florida adopt this reform. Brian Corley, the Republican supervisor of elections for Pasco County who was instrumental in this advocacy effort, summed up the Association's views on this issue in a way that should make any election administrator— or anyone who cares about fair elections—swell with pride: "We should make the rules easy. Candidates and parties should win on ideas, not on election rules."[37] That mentality, shared among election officials of both political parties and promoted to legislators and the general public, drove the debate around online voter registration in Florida.[38]

The key was to explain the effects the policy would have on real voters, highlighting the convenience and cost-reducing benefits. These on-the-ground advocacy and educational efforts ultimately led the Florida legislature to pass, with bipartisan support, an online voter registration bill. The state implemented its new system on October 1, 2017.[39] Shortly thereafter, Brian Corley proudly visited a high school to help sixteen- and seventeen-year-olds preregister to vote using the online portal so that they were officially on the voter rolls by their eighteenth birthdays.[40]

States have also found ways to work with advocates who run voter registration drives. Under a paper registration model, advocacy organizations send out people with clipboards or set up information tables at events to register voters. One benefit is that these organizations have a paper record of who they had registered, meaning that the groups can follow up on Election Day to encourage these individuals to vote. Online voter registration inherently makes that follow-up harder because organizations do not know who they had successfully registered. So Washington—which in 2008 was the second state to adopt online voter registration—began offering specialized URLs for organizations to use during their in-person voter registration drives. A group can create a specific URL and then bring a laptop to a farmers market or county fair to register voters using the online portal.[41] It can also engage in internet-based voter registration drives, embedding the state's online form within the organization's website. The system provides the organization with publicly available information on any voters that the group registered through the specialized URL, allowing the group to engage in the same Election Day get-out-the-vote efforts as before.[42]

Online voter registration enhances the voter experience drastically. Instead of having to go to the post office or county clerk's office, or printing and mailing a registration form, voters can access the state's online voter registration system twenty-four hours a day from wherever they are. (States still accept paper registrations for those who want to use them.) The system improves accuracy because there are fewer mistakes when a voter, as opposed to a county clerk staffer, inputs the data. For instance, a voter will probably notice immediately if his or her name or birthday contains a typo. Online registration reduces the costs associated with printing registration documents and processing thousands of forms as the registration deadline nears. One study found that it cost Arizona eighty-three cents to process a paper registration but only three cents, at most, to process an online submission.[43] Election officials need not work through thousands of paper registration forms and instead can focus on other pressing matters as an election nears. Technology experts say there are few security concerns, though of course we must be ever vigilant given Russia's hacking of some state databases before the 2016 election.[44] The system is wildly popular among all demographics for one simple reason: it makes registering more convenient. In particular, younger voters—who have the lowest turnout rates—are more likely to register using online voter registration, and those who register online are more likely to turn out to vote.[45] This all may sound technical and dull, yet online registration is vitally important to improve turnout and democratic representation.

We must embrace new technologies to modernize the way we run our elections. But it takes on-the-ground advocacy to turn nice ideas into electoral reality. It requires creativity, thoughtfulness, and buy-in from election officials, legislators, and everyday voters. This is a win-win all around. That's probably why over thirty-seven states have adopted online voter registration.[46] The remaining states should follow suit.

ALLOWING VOTERS TO REGISTER ON ELECTION DAY ITSELF

Same day registration, also known as Election Day Registration (EDR), is another useful tool that can improve access to the polls. In EDR states, voters may show up to the polls on Election Day (or, in some states that allow it, to the county clerk's office during the early voting period) and both register and vote at the same time.[47] (Some states require same-day registrants to visit the county clerk's office instead of their polling place and complete a provisional ballot on Election Day, which will count so long as the voters' information checks out.) These voters must show proof of residency and identity before they can vote. Voter turnout in EDR states is much higher than in states without EDR, which makes perfect sense: many voters do not start paying attention to the election until the weekend or day before Election Day, but if they live in a state with a pre–Election Day registration deadline (such as thirty days before Election Day, which is common), they are essentially cut out of the process if they haven't registered ahead of time.[48] We shouldn't assume that they are ill-informed— they can easily educate themselves on the candidates and issues—and they shouldn't suffer disenfranchisement just because they did not jump through the right administrative hoops well before Election Day.

Maine was first state to adopt same-day registration back in 1973. Minnesota (1974), Wisconsin (1976), Oregon (1976), and Ohio (1977) quickly followed suit, although Ohio and Oregon eventually repealed their EDR laws due to opposition from entrenched politicians in Ohio and political controversy over a local election with many new registrants in Oregon.[49] The motivations for same-day registration were both political and practical. Researchers from the organization Dēmos explain that "the specific motivations for EDR's enactment in Maine, Wisconsin, and Minnesota have variously been attributed to a national Democratic campaign to boost turnout among the party's base voters or, alternatively, to homegrown desires for consistent, statewide voter registration rules and procedures."[50] But regardless of partisanship, any effort to make voting easier—so long as there are appropriate safeguards—is good for democracy.

As of this writing, Election Day Registration exists in fifteen states plus DC, which include both red and blue states from across the country.[51] In 2018, voters approved ballot measures to adopt same-day registration in both Maryland and Michigan.[52] As Dēmos explains, EDR has multiple benefits: it increases voter turnout (especially for younger people, racial minorities, and low-income voters), eliminates an arbitrary pre–Election Day voter registration deadline, and helps citizens and the state update the voter rolls dynamically.[53] There's simply no reason—in today's technology-dependent world—that states still need thirty days before Election Day to prepare their voter lists. The system is secure, especially given that voters must show both proof of residency and some form of identification when registering and voting. Most states take additional fail-safe measures such as mailing a verification form to a voter's address after the election to check the accuracy of the registration information and imposing stiff penalties for fraud. Academic research has confirmed that EDR does not increase voter fraud.[54]

Election Day Registration helps actual voters, as seen through its proven results. According to a report titled *America Goes to the Polls* by the group Nonprofit VOTE, in the 2016 election the top six states for voter turnout—Minnesota (74.8%), Maine (72.8%), New Hampshire (72.5%), Colorado (72.1%), Wisconsin (70.5%), and Iowa (69.0%)—all have EDR.[55] The bottom five states for voter turnout—Hawaii (43%), West Virginia (50.8%), Texas (51.6%), Tennessee (52.0%) and Arkansas (53.1%)—all had a voter registration deadline that is three to four weeks before Election Day.[56] As Dēmos's researchers note, "there is little doubt that restrictive pre–election registration deadlines are a deterrent to participation for many voters, and that EDR is a reform that boosts voter turnout."[57] More states should consider this reform. Individuals can contact their representatives to demand better accessibility for the voting process and advocate for measures like EDR.

ENSURING YOUTH ARE ALREADY ON THE VOTER ROLLS BY THEIR EIGHTEENTH BIRTHDAY

Turning eighteen is an exciting time in someone's life, when society deems that person to be a legal adult in virtually all respects. Beyond a few jurisdictions that have lowered the voting age for local elections (see chapter 1), it is the moment when young people can begin participating in our democracy through voting. Yet too many young Americans are not even on the voter rolls when they turn eighteen, and pre–Election Day registration requirements already add an immediate obstacle to voting at the moment they become eligible. Plus, with all of the changes going on in someone's life—graduating from high school, moving out of their childhood home, and entering the workforce or going to college—it is no wonder that registering to vote may be low on the priority list. What if we found a way to ensure that voter registration was part of everyone's eighteenth birthday present?

As of 2018, twelve states and DC allow individuals to preregister to vote when they turn sixteen so they are on the voter rolls automatically on their eighteenth birthday. Another four states open up preregistration when a person turns seventeen. That's sixteen states plus DC that permit individuals to register at least a year before their eighteenth birthday. Five other states allow for registration slightly later, but before someone turns eighteen.[58] California uses a dual system, combining the opportunity to preregister for sixteen- and seventeen-year-olds with automatic voter registration, showing how these reforms can supplement each other. But in other states, individuals must wait until their eighteenth birthday before they can register to vote.

Preregistration is a positive step for democracy that all states should adopt. The reform may seem small, but it can have a big impact on improving democratic participation. One study showed that preregistration may increase voter turnout, particularly when there is direct outreach to youth, especially at school.[59] Voting is habit-forming, so capturing young people early is important for increasing overall turnout. What can you do? Contact your state legislators to demand they adopt preregistration in your state if it does not already exist. Voters also must speak out when a state repeals its preregistration mechanism, as North Carolina did in 2016.[60] There is no good reason—beyond partisan overreach and a blatant desire to shape the electorate for political gain—to eliminate a program that is proven to bring more young people into the democratic process. We must demand that our legislators refrain from partisan tactics to rig election outcomes and vote them out if they refuse to heed our calls.

ENGAGING THE COMMUNITY TO REGISTER VOTERS

Last, but certainly not least, are the efforts of individuals on the ground to register new voters. Voting rights groups are actively engaged in expanding the voter rolls. The key is to reach out to voters individually to explain the importance of voting. Take the example of Mi Familia Vota, a nonprofit, nonpartisan organization dedicated to promoting civic engagement among Latino communities. Its voter registration drive in Texas partners with high schools, community colleges, and universities to register voters, educate them about the issues, and encourage them to vote on Election Day. Mi Familia Vota's strategy is to go school-by-school, classroom-by-classroom to reach young Latinos. In the lead-up to the 2016 election, for instance, volunteers and staffers gave a forty-five-minute presentation in college and high school classrooms in Texas where they distributed voter registration forms and explained the importance of a strong turnout among the Latino community. The presentation explained to students that Latinos make up roughly 40 percent of Houston's population, but that hardly any of the area's elected officials are Latino.[61] Most students were not aware of this disparity and did not recognize that their political participation could change that number. Direct communication, with salient facts, helped convince many young voters to register and vote. Many of these students then joined the advocacy effort, participating in phone banks or going door-to-door to speak with their own neighbors about the importance of voting.[62] Similarly, the Texas secretary of state engaged high school principals, naming them deputy voter registrars, which is an official designation that allows these individuals to register people to vote.[63]

Reaching voters where they are can ensure success in expanding who participates on Election Day. Here is one of my favorite examples, which was the inspiration for the title of this chapter: in 2016, Mi Familia Vota distributed thousands of voter registration forms to taco trucks in Latino communities throughout Harris County, Texas (which includes Houston). At 10:00 p.m. on the day of the registration deadline, several taco truck owners called Carlos Duarte, Mi Familia Vota's Texas director, to say they had run out of forms and needed more. As Duarte explained to me, the ultimate goal is to create an environment in which "discussion about voting is all over the place in the Latino community."[64]

The efforts seemed to work, though progress, of course, has been slow. Turnout among Latino voters in Harris County rose in 2016,[65] while the overall turnout rate for Latinos in the state has slowly crept up.[66] Consistent exposure to information about voting can increase the likelihood that new voters will participate. We need to expand upon this kind of grassroots effort.

A taco truck in Texas that also registers voters. [Photo by Miao Zhang.]

Individuals can help by promoting voter registration in their own communities. It takes no special training or education. Kathy Jones, a parent in Alabama, knows this well. She created a volunteer group called Tennessee Valley Votes to promote voter registration in her local high school months before an upcoming election. The goal was to ensure that every senior in the high school was registered to vote. "We felt like there was a real need to get the students engaged as early as possible, and to catch them before they graduate and go off to college is really a great opportunity," she said.[67]

Local laws also can make a difference. Registration, after all, happens on the ground in our communities. That's one reason why Seattle passed a local ordinance that requires landlords to provide voter registration information to any new tenant when they move in.[68] Through this simple change, Seattle found a way to reach many new voters as soon as they join the community.

The takeaway from all of these stories is that there are many useful reforms to the voter registration system—automatic voter registration, Election Day Registration, preregistration for those younger than eighteen, and even local reforms to the registration process—that can spread throughout the country. The antiquated requirement that new voters register a month before Election Day can leave some people out of our democracy with no corresponding benefit to the state. Not paying attention that early doesn't mean that people will vote without educating themselves and it shouldn't result in someone's effective disenfranchisement. We can find ways to expand the electorate by breaking down these barriers. These efforts should go hand-in-hand with fighting back against voter restrictions such as aggressive purges of the voter rolls.

We seem to view all voting rules through a partisan lens, which makes it more difficult to adopt common sense reforms such as automatic or online voter registration. That's what happened in both Oregon and Florida: partisan bickering almost derailed the movements. The reforms passed only after individuals made the case through compelling stories of how the systems would help voters, reduce costs, and improve election integrity. Once these new policies worked in one place, other states took notice. Slowly, but surely, these changes—initiated by innovative election thinkers and supported by everyday people and advocacy organizations—can positively transform our elections, ultimately bringing more people into our democracy.

Improving registration, of course, is just an initial step. We also need to make Election Day itself more convenient for all voters. We must make it easy to go to the polls so that people don't face unnecessary hurdles to political participation. Scott Doyle, a baseball-loving Republican from Larimer County, Colorado, has some ideas on that topic. We'll meet him next.

CHAPTER 4

HOW VOTING CAN BE
AS EASY AS FOOD SHOPPING

It was the highly contested presidential election of 2000, and Scott Doyle, the deputy county clerk in Larimer County, Colorado, witnessed something that infuriated him: eligible voters had shown up at the county courthouse to vote, yet the police were blocking the courthouse doors because it was past the poll closing time. It was a problem that anyone could have faced. These individuals couldn't vote because they had initially gone to the wrong precinct and then could not make it to their correct polling place in time. They tried the courthouse as a last resort but were turned away. As a result, they weren't able to vote in that highly consequential election, which wasn't finally decided until the Supreme Court issued its opinion in *Bush v. Gore* over a month after Election Day. "There's got to be a better way," Doyle thought.[1]

Doyle—who had no prior election experience—had joined the Larimer County Clerk and Recorder's office a few months earlier to help revamp the office's business operations. That office administers elections in Larimer County, which is in the northern part of Colorado, bordering Wyoming. Its biggest city is Fort Collins, about an hour north of Denver. Doyle had an entirely different career before he joined the county clerk's office, working as an environmental engineer for twenty-five years. He took the job as deputy county clerk to use his business and engineering expertise in the name of public service.

That 2000 election experience upset him to no end. Why did voting seem so much harder than so many other simpler things, like picking up his groceries at whichever store was closest? "I always scratched my head wondering why I had to rush home to vote or go super early in the morning before heading off to work, when I could go to any Walmart anywhere and buy what I needed," he told me in his warm, pleasant way.[2] "Then I saw people who were turned away from voting because of this very problem" of simply not going to the right place.[3]

Doyle sat down with a pencil and paper and began to sketch out different models of voting. Looking at the number of precincts in the county, along with the population, he realized that a Vote Center model could work. In a system using Vote Centers, voters may visit any Vote Center in the county to vote, as opposed to having to go to the precinct closest to their home. Doyle brought the idea to the county clerk and recorder at the time, but for whatever reason she was not interested in pursuing it. She was term limited from the position, however, so she encouraged Doyle to run for the office and promote the idea. He won.

Fast-forward to 2003, when Doyle faced another problem. As the county's head election official, he was charged with ensuring that the county's voting system complied with the new requirements of the federal Help America Vote Act of 2002, or HAVA, which was Congress's response to the presidential election debacle of 2000.[4] HAVA required, among other things, the replacement of outdated voting equipment throughout the country. Although Congress provided some money for states and counties to purchase new machines, it would not cover new machines for all 143 polling sites in Larimer County.

So Doyle and his colleagues put on their creative hats. Might his pencil sketches of a Vote Center model help them comply with HAVA, save money, and make the voting process smoother for voters, all at the same time? They held brainstorming sessions. They bandied about various ideas on how to comply with the new federal requirements. They consulted IT experts. The result was the creation and implementation of Vote Centers, a new and innovative way to vote. As a commentary on Colorado election reforms explained, "In a culture where workplace, residence, and recreational locations may be distributed across a metropolitan area and extensive commuting is the norm, it seemed reasonable to the new clerk and his staff to do what smart retailers had done for decades and provide multiple voting locations where the modern and mobile American could drop in at his or her convenience."[5]

THE POWER OF VOTE CENTER CONVENIENCE

The idea is actually quite simple: instead of having to visit a precinct based on one's home address, why not allow someone to vote anywhere in the county? A voter might find it more convenient to vote closer to work or school. Voters could go out during their lunch break, or leave work a little early, and not have to worry about traveling back home to vote at a home precinct. The ballot will reflect the races for one's home district, but there essentially would be no "wrong" place to vote within the county. A voter who recently moved to a new home within the county also would not have to worry about which precinct is "correct." Election officials would not deal with confused voters who are not sure if they are in the right place. Provisional ballots—which a voter must use if his or her name is not on the voter rolls for that precinct—would be minimized. Voters would not be sent away, or told to drive to a different precinct, in the hubbub of Election Day. So long as the technology exists, why must modern Election Day be tied so closely to where you live?

The technology, in fact, does exist. Doyle found that by simply tying electronic poll books to one another through an encrypted network, the county can update, in real time, who has voted in each Vote Center. Once a voter casts a ballot at one polling site, the other polling sites receive an immediate update to their electronic poll books, preventing the person from voting again. Working with the County's Information Technology department, Doyle's office learned that this real-time update helped to improve the election system's security while also facilitating voter convenience. It also made the check-in process faster as compared to using a paper poll book.[6]

As with any new voting change, especially one using technology, the potential for election fraud is always present. But local experiences with Vote Centers in a handful of states show that they are safe, especially because the electronic poll books are on a secure, encrypted network. Moreover, Vote Centers may actually deter fraud: by allowing for real-time updates to the electronic poll books, the innovation ensures that someone cannot vote more than once, at least within the county itself. Hacking is always a concern in this day and age, so election officials are keenly attuned to the security of the network. There have been no noted problems. Plus, there's always the option to let voters cast provisional ballots on paper if issues arise.

Vote Centers also greatly reduce costs. Elections are run through local-level government agencies, not the federal or even state governments. Your city or county's tax dollars fund our election infrastructure. Anything to lower costs, while improving the election process, is a win-win. That's precisely the case for Vote Centers. A study in Indiana showed that the adoption of Vote Centers can decrease costs in both the short and long term, especially given that they reduce the number of poll workers and the number of voting machines that need constant updating.[7]

Although the technology requires an initial outlay of money, the long-term savings—especially in using fewer polling sites throughout the county—are significant. Extra precincts require more facilities, machines, and poll workers. Fewer Vote Centers, which can process a higher number of voters more efficiently, cut down on these expenses. In addition, county officials can change the number of poll workers at each Vote Center based on demand, giving election officials more flexibility and saving them money.

By implementing Vote Centers, in conjunction with the use of early voting days, Doyle and his colleagues were able to reduce the number of precincts that the county needed—from 143 home-based precincts to 24 Vote Centers—while still processing more voters.[8] The results were impressive. During the 2004 election, the county's website explains, "[e]ven when lines were long, the average voter reported casting his/her ballot within 20 minutes of arriving at a Vote Center."[9] Doyle put it another way: "We try and move people through like a checkout line at Albertsons," the supermarket chain.[10]

Vote Centers also can increase turnout, especially among infrequent voters. That was the finding of Robert Stein and Greg Vonnahme, political scientists at Rice University.[11] Stein noted that "[o]f all the election reforms that have been adopted, this is the only one anybody's been able to find that has an effect on turnout and cost."[12] (As we'll see below, universal vote-by-mail may now rival Vote Centers in this regard.) Colorado's counties experienced these positive effects firsthand. Though perhaps caused by several factors in addition to Vote Centers, turnout in Fort Collins in 2004 soared after the county adopted the Vote Center model.[13] Doyle takes pride in the significant increase in voter turnout in every place that has used Vote Centers. As he put it, "The minute we put the Vote Centers into place, turnout skyrocketed—especially for municipal elections!"[14]

That's likely one reason that Larimer County voters overwhelmingly support the use of Vote Centers. They are more convenient. They save time. They are secure. They save money. What's not to like?

A BIPARTISAN APPROACH

Views on the merits of Vote Centers do not fall along partisan lines. This is one of those reforms in which everyone benefits. Doyle himself is a Republican. Yet his number one goal, as the head of elections for Larimer County, was to find a way to make the voting process as strong, tamper free, and easy as possible. He said that he received some Republican pushback initially, especially when he located a Vote Center on a college campus near many Democratic voters, but his mentality was that the system was good for voters overall. "I wanted to make voting easier for everyone," he explained.[15] "If some Republicans didn't like it, they should have run against me in the next primary."[16] In reality, there is no evidence that Vote Centers help one party's voters over the others'. *Everyone* benefits. This is the ultimate feel-good story in local voting innovation.

Doyle retired in 2013, and as the local newspaper proudly explained, his legacy as the head of elections was in enhancing "the ease of voting in this county. . . . In doing so, he also had a hand in ensuring some of the highest-turnout elections in the history of the county."[17] Now he spends his time relaxing and watching baseball. He's still eager, however, to speak with anyone about the benefits of Vote Centers. Indeed, although in full retirement mode—in summer 2018 he spent time away from his email because he was fishing for walleye along the US–Canadian border—he was very excited when I contacted him for this book.

Not surprisingly, the initial success of Vote Centers prompted other jurisdictions to start using them, showing the power of local innovation that spreads across the country. Places in both red and blue states jumped on board. Indiana's Republican secretary of state sent a bipartisan delegation of Indiana legislators and local election officials to Colorado to learn about the mechanism, and five counties in Indiana participated in a pilot program to use Vote Centers from 2007–2010.[18] Given how well the pilot program went, Indiana's Republican-led legislature then passed a law to approve the use of Vote Centers for any county in the state.[19] Over fifteen counties in Indiana now offer Vote Centers; that number is growing every election cycle. In 2005, the Indiana secretary of state named Scott Doyle an "Honorary Secretary of State" because of the success of the program.[20]

Scott Doyle of Larimer County, CO, the creator of the Vote Center Model. [Photo courtesy of Scott Doyle.]

Yet overall, the adoption of Vote Centers is not widespread. They are limited to a handful of counties in a few states.[21] Places such as Doña Ana County, New Mexico, and Teton County, Wyoming, now regularly use Vote Centers for their elections.[22] But chances are that most voters have never even heard of them.

If Vote Centers are so useful—if they save money, improve convenience, remain secure, increase turnout, and are popular among voters— then why haven't more places adopted them? Why, fifteen years after Scott

Doyle came up with the idea in Larimer County, Colorado, are only a few places making voting as convenient as possible by employing the Vote Center model?

There are a few reasons. For one, some people hold on to the traditional notion of voting with their neighbors at the local school, community center, or church. We have idealized Election Day as a community, neighborly activity, and Vote Centers seem to cut against that romantic vision. Yet we must recognize that the nature of our society, and of our election processes, must change with the times. Should we revert to a bygone era that fails to recognize that many people may be far from their home precincts on Election Day—resulting in fewer people voting? Or do we want to be forward thinking in our elections so that we include as many eligible voters as possible?

In addition, state legislatures have to approve the use of Vote Centers in their states, and then county clerks and other local election officials must adopt them. Achieving this change takes political willpower. That hurdle, in turn, requires all of us to vote for election officials—secretaries of state and county clerks, among others—who will make voting convenience a top priority. Election officials like Scott Doyle want to serve the public. Their goals are to foster smooth, secure, well-run elections. But if their constituents seem uninterested in innovative voting reforms, they won't have the proper incentives to try out these methods. A reluctant public—one that is resistant to change—only makes their jobs harder. A public, however, that understands the importance of positive voting enhancements will arm these local election officials with the political willpower to approach their state legislatures, city councils, and county election boards to fight for these changes. There are thousands of Scott Doyles around the country who serve the public's interest and who seek innovative solutions to election problems, regardless of ideology or partisan effect. We must give them the tools and resources to succeed.

"VOTE AT HOME—AND SAVE OUR COUNTRY"[23]

Phil Keisling has another idea to make voting more convenient. The Oregonian is traversing the country to promote what he calls vote-at-home, which has worked extremely well in his state. Many of our activities take place at home: we shop, bank, and connect with people without ever leaving our couches. Why not vote at home as well? Once again, this innovation—more commonly referred to as vote-by-mail—is a win-win: it improves turnout, reduces costs, and enhances election integrity, all thanks to the power of grassroots advocacy at the local level.

In three states—Colorado, Oregon, and Washington—every voter automatically receives a ballot by mail.[24] In several other states, such as California, North Dakota, and Utah, numerous counties also use vote-by-mail, though it's not yet implemented statewide. Colorado, which pioneered the Vote Center model, still uses Vote Centers in addition to a vote-by-mail system, offering the utmost in electoral convenience: voters can choose to return the ballot by mail or drop box or, if they prefer, visit a Vote Center on Election Day. The key to vote-by-mail is that every eligible and registered voter in the relevant jurisdiction *automatically* receives a ballot mailed to his or her home address. This is unlike absentee balloting, in which a voter must affirmatively request the ballot. Instead, whether or not you even know that there is an election about to take place, you receive a ballot within a few weeks of Election Day. You can then mail in your completed ballot or drop it off at one of the many official ballot drop sites located throughout the county. Predictably, turnout has soared in vote-by-mail jurisdictions, while costs have plummeted. Indeed, states with universal vote-by-mail routinely have higher turnout than even battleground states without vote-by-mail.[25] Young voters in particular have higher turnout rates in vote-by-mail states. As discussed below, the system is just as secure as any other voting method.

This innovation, like many of the others discussed in this book, began not with a statewide push, but at the local level. San Diego first pioneered vote-by-mail in 1981 for a referendum about whether to use public funds for the construction of a convention center.[26] The genesis in Oregon, which saw the first statewide adoption of vote-by-mail, was a local election in Linn County, Oregon, on a school bond measure in the early 1980s with a laughable turnout: two voters! The measure passed 2–0, and given that whether someone showed up at the polls is a public record, the unanimous result sacrificed the secrecy of the ballot—everyone knew how those two people had voted. The county clerk, Del Riley, expressed concern about this poor turnout: would he have to keep holding elections where hardly anyone showed up? Riley approached the Republican secretary of state at the time, Norma Paulus, who in turn sent a delegation to San Diego to learn about that city's mail-in balloting process and whether it might increase turnout. Those efforts led the Oregon legislature to pass a law allowing localities to adopt vote-by-mail for local elections, so long as the county also had at least one open polling place on Election Day.[27]

Counties steadily began to use the process. The state then expanded vote-by-mail in a few elections, culminating in the voters passing, by a two to one margin, a statewide initiative in 1998 to adopt vote-by-mail for all elections.[28]

Phil Keisling was front and center of that effort.[29] Keisling was a freshman state representative in 1989 when he voted against a bill to expand vote-by-mail from local and special elections to party primary contests. He was "swayed by the 'crunch of autumn leaves' argument—that vision of walking to my local school on a crisp, fall afternoon, exchanging neighborly hellos, and pulling the voting booth curtain under the watchful gaze of octogenarian poll workers."[30]

Keisling then became Oregon's secretary of state in 1991, and he faced a familiar complaint: counties in the state had to run elections on a limited budget and turnout was often low. The arguments from local election officials changed his mind on the merits of vote-by-mail. As he wrote, "once I grasped the dramatic cost savings from no longer having to operate and staff thousands of traditional polling stations, and realized how much voter turnout had soared in local and special elections—by a factor of three or even five—I saw that I'd been confusing a particular ritual of democracy with its essence, which is participation."[31] That last statement is worth repeating: the essence of our democracy is participation, so any secure voting reform that improves participation is worthy of consideration.

Oregon first used vote-by-mail in lower-stakes and low-participation local elections, employing it statewide for the first time in a 1993 referendum that one publication called "a complicated and boring measure put on the ballot by the Legislature involving voter approval of repayment of urban renewal district bonds."[32] Yet turnout in that boring referendum was 39 percent, exceeding expectations.[33] Then, in a 1994 congressional race, a Republican challenger came close to winning in part because the

Republican Party had sent absentee ballot request forms to all of its registered voters, boosting participation among Republicans.[34] These results led Republicans to generally support vote-by-mail. Democrats, like Phil Keisling, continued to push forward—once he changed his own mind and understood the merits of the system.

When Senator Bob Packwood resigned his US Senate seat in 1995, Keisling, as the secretary of state, was responsible for choosing the method of voting for the statewide special election to replace him—and he chose vote-by-mail. This was the first Senate election to use an entirely mailed ballot. Turnout in that election, which Democrat Ron Wyden won, was almost 66 percent—a record for an Oregon special election—and the process saved the state around $1 million.[35] By 1998, the state's voters were ready to adopt vote-by-mail for all Oregon elections.

One major reason for vote-by-mail's success was that county clerks— and the voters themselves—bought into the idea and pushed it forward. This was really out of necessity. Once some counties offered vote-by-mail for a few local elections, voters wanted it for other elections as well. Given Oregon's lax requirements for absentee balloting, voters began to request absentee ballots in droves for elections that were not using universal vote-by-mail. In some places, over half of the votes cast in an election were through absentee ballots. Wasco County, for example, reported that in one election, 86 percent of the ballots were cast absentee by mail.[36] But the clerks still had to open the same number of polling places to accommodate in-person voters. The clerks were essentially running dual election systems for every election. Something had to give. The dual system cost more money and created immense voter confusion. Voters would wonder, was this election a vote-by-mail one or not? Would they receive a ballot automatically, or did they need to request an absentee ballot or show up at the polls? People "voted with their feet," as Wasco County election officer Karen LeBreton Brown explained. "They had said we want Vote by Mail."[37]

Voters seem to love the process, as their views and actions well demonstrate. A 2003 poll found that 81 percent of Oregonians preferred vote-by-mail to visiting a polling place in person.[38] One researcher notes that vote-by-mail may improve turnout by up to 10 percent and can boost participation among prior voters, increasing the likelihood that they will turn out again in low-profile elections.[39] Other researchers, considering the impact of Colorado's first implementation of universal vote-by-mail in 2014, found that turnout in that election was about 3.3 percent higher than if the state had not used vote-by-mail.[40] The increase was largest among young voters, who traditionally vote at lower rates.[41] Voters who were less likely to vote based on historical models turned out at a much higher level: "[r]egistered voters assigned a 10 percent chance of voting, for instance, turned out at a 31 percent rate."[42] Perhaps most profoundly, vote-by-mail improved turnout among Republican voters slightly more than Democratic voters, while those unaffiliated with a political party saw the largest increase.[43] These results show that vote-by-mail is not a partisan initiative.

Keisling—whose wide smile belies his scholarly demeanor—emphasizes that "vote-by-mail" is somewhat of a misnomer. Most people do not mail in their ballots. They instead receive the ballot by mail, fill it out at home, and then drop it off at a secure drop box or county clerk's office. It is also not "absentee balloting on steroids," because with absentee balloting a voter must affirmatively request the ballot, and in many states they must offer a valid reason for needing to vote absentee. That requires foresight and voter action well before Election Day.

With Oregon's system, however, some voters may receive their ballots without even realizing that an election is about to take place. The mailed ballot will include national and statewide races as well as any elections for their specific district. They can then educate themselves, from the comfort of their own home, before returning their ballot either via mail or in person. This produces a more informed electorate. It also alerts voters—with enough time to study the candidates and issues—to local races that they previously may have ignored. Keisling himself admitted that he had not realized there was a local election in his community in 2017 until he received his ballot in the mail about two weeks before Election Day. He lives and breathes elections, yet he did not know about the election until the county mailed him a ballot. So he sat down and learned about the candidates and issues before casting his vote.[44]

"Universal Ballot Delivery to Your Home by Mail" does not sound as sexy, but that is technically how Oregon's elections work. And the people love it.

In 2017, Keisling, now the Director of the Center for Public Service at Portland State University, created the National Vote at Home Institute.[45]

The goal of this organization is to increase voter engagement by promoting vote-at-home policies. Keisling uses the term "vote-at-home" instead of vote-by-mail because, he notes, voters receive the ballot at home, where they can fill it out at their convenience after taking the time to educate themselves. This can lead to more informed choices. The National Vote at Home Institute's goal is to have over 100 million voters use vote-at-home by the 2022 midterm elections and to implement vote-at-home policies in at least a dozen states.[46]

Sure, that might seem like a long shot, but Keisling is not deterred. Instead, he sees a lot of opportunity for other jurisdictions to come on board. In forty-seven states, voters are responsible for connecting themselves to their ballot. They must either request an absentee ballot or physically go to their polling place. But in Oregon, Washington, and Colorado (as well as numerous counties in other states), Keisling explains, "The vote-at-home system reverses the polarity in that equation. If the government knows you are a properly registered voter, it is the government's obligation to send you your ballot."[47] It *should* be the government's obligation to make the voting process as easy as possible. The outcome of elections should depend on the best ideas winning with everyone participating, not on who has the easiest time wading through the state's procedures.

Washington State takes the concept of universal vote-by-mail even further by paying for return postage, making it that much easier for voters to participate by mail without having to find a drop box. King County—which includes Seattle—ran a pilot program in two small jurisdictions for a special election in early 2017 in which the county prepaid for the postage on every ballot. Election officials expected turnout of about 30 percent but saw 37 percent turnout in one jurisdiction and 40 percent in the other. The county's elections director was thrilled with this increase, commenting, "when I was elected, one of my commitments was to remove barriers to voting. As we increase access with pre-paid postage and ballot drop boxes, we're beginning to see a real impact."[48] Washington expanded the program and paid for postage for all mail-in ballots in 2018.[49]

The upshot of this political history is that vote-by-mail can be successful when implemented first at the local level. It will then spread to other places as voters themselves demand greater convenience for the voting process. Neither political side will necessarily benefit more than the other from its adoption. It's a nonpartisan solution to our current poor turnout and voter apathy. Vote-by-mail is a key success story, pushed by people like Phil Keisling who simply want to make our democracy stronger.

Yet it takes political will to so do. Voters are the key. As Keisling says, it is up to voters, as "consumers of democracy," to advocate for the government to connect them with their ballot. The voters can choose how to deliver it. If a voter wants to feel the "crunch of leaves in the fall," interacting with their neighbors while voting, they can bring their completed ballot to the closest drop box, county courthouse, or elections office with others in their community. Voters who want more convenience, however, can simply put it in the mail. Everyone wins. Shouldn't we reach forward, not step backward, in our voting processes by finding ways to include as many people as possible in our most important democratic ritual?

Vote-by-mail is now the reality for all elections in Oregon, Washington, and Colorado.[50] California is in the process of rolling out vote-by-mail for the entire state. In Utah, almost all of the twenty-nine counties used vote-by-mail in the 2018 election. So did the majority of counties in North Dakota.[51] A few other states allow vote-by-mail for certain elections, or at least permit no-excuse absentee balloting. Seven states and DC provide for "permanent absentee balloting" for anyone, where a voter is put on a list of those who will receive an absentee ballot automatically in future elections.[52] Yet in other places, absentee balloting is not the same as a true vote-by-mail system, as the voter must take the affirmative step of requesting their absentee ballot for every election ahead of Election Day.[53] Importantly, universal vote-by-mail states have higher turnout than states that still use primarily in-person voting.[54] Voters want this reform. It's a voting practice that improves turnout, enhances convenience, and costs less. So, as Keisling says, why not "vote at home [and] save your country?"[55]

OVERCOMING BARRIERS TO ELECTORAL IMPROVEMENTS LIKE VOTE-BY-MAIL

Given all of these benefits, why hasn't vote-by-mail spread to more places?[56] There are a few possible reasons, but all are surmountable with the right advocacy.

First, some voters may feel reluctant to move away from the idealized notion of going to a polling place alongside one's neighbors. There is
something nostalgic about visiting your local precinct each Election Day to
take part, as a community, in your civic duty. In fact, I personally know the
poll workers at my own precinct only because I see them each time I vote.

But that idealized notion must give way to the realities of today's world.
We may remember fondly the weekly trip to the supermarket, yet online
grocery shopping is the wave of the future. We may long for the days of
visiting the movie rental shop to find the latest new releases (something I
surely enjoyed on Saturday nights as a teenager), but streaming services
have replaced that weekend night ritual. So too with voting. The need to
innovate, so long as we do so securely, is more important than hanging on
to an outdated method of casting one's ballot. If we want to engage more
voters, we need to find them where they are and create processes that make
it easy for them to participate.

Second, there are misconceptions about vote-by-mail, such as that it is
the same as absentee balloting or that it will open the door to election fraud.
True, there are documented instances of absentee balloting fraud.[57] Yet
there has been virtually zero evidence of voter fraud in universal vote-by-
mail systems.[58] The process may be harder to exploit if everyone is using it,
especially since all voters receive the same mailed ballot. A voter will know
if his or her ballot did not arrive at home. In addition, election officials in
vote-by-mail states are trained to look diligently for signature matches—
comparing the signature from when the person registered to the signature
on the ballot—to ensure a vote is valid. Drop boxes are bolted down and
often near security cameras. Oregon Secretary of State (and eventual Governor) Kate Brown noted that between 2000 and 2010, voters in Oregon
submitted over 15 million votes by mail. The state investigated thousands
of allegations of voter fraud. The result? Only nine prosecutions.[59] Similarly, Keisling highlights that since 2000, there have been over 100 million
votes cast through vote-by-mail yet only about a dozen isolated instances
of credible voter fraud. That's (approximately) .00001 percent of all votes
cast![60] That paltry number is not for a lack of vigilance. Brown notes that
Oregon trains its county clerks, using forensic experts, to conduct a rig-
orous signature match for every ballot.[61] In addition, the penalties for voter
fraud are harsh, providing a strong deterrent.

Academics who study election procedures have generally confirmed Brown's statements: Oregon's vote-by-mail system has produced hardly any election fraud. As Reed College political scientist Paul Gronke explained, the state's "signature verification process, the tracking system for each ballot, and postal services cooperation in preventing ballots from being delivered to names not recognized as receiving mail at an address reduce the risk of large scale attempts to cast fraudulent ballots."[62] Or as Keisling puts it, "there's a reason why fraudsters don't try to counterfeit pennies and go for the $20s and $100s instead."[63]

In fact, vote-by-mail may be superior to electronic voting machines that lack a paper trail. As of 2018, five states (Delaware, Georgia, Louisiana, New Jersey, and South Carolina) conducted all of their elections using electronic machines without any paper trail, and several other states have these machines in at least part of the state.[64] By contrast, vote-by-mail necessarily has a paper trail that is useful both for recounts and ballot security.

Third, some express concern that a vote-by-mail system may not preserve the secret ballot.[65] With vote-by-mail, the argument goes, an employer or family member could strong-arm someone to vote contrary to how he or she really wants. Yet that's a potential issue with any method of voting by mail, including absentee balloting, but few people advocate for doing away with that system. Plus, there is simply no evidence that coercion has affected votes to any measurable degree in vote-by-mail states.

Not everyone agrees that vote-by-mail is necessarily positive. MIT Professor Charles Stewart has pointed to problems with absentee balloting and the concern about "lost votes" due to mail-in voting.[66] But absentee balloting, by definition, occurs in a "dual" system, where counties must offer absentee balloting *and* manage in-person precincts. The dynamics are different when the entire election is via mail, with the state automatically sending each voter a ballot and using a more robust ballot identification and signature verification system. Stewart's reticence certainly suggests caution and deliberation. States would be wise to implement a vote-by-mail system first for lower profile or local elections to ensure the process runs smoothly, particularly to account for ballot delivery and security concerns. But the potential integrity hurdles do not mean that states should abandon the effort altogether.

Once again, voters are the key. Election officials need public support to adopt pro-voter measures such as vote-by-mail. It's not only up to election officials. Anyone concerned about the political process can advocate for measures that can improve turnout and fix our system.

IS ONLINE VOTING NEXT?

Given that I advocate for a more convenient voting process, people often ask me, "why not internet voting?" "I do my banking online," the argument goes, "so why can't I vote online as well?" The rise of vote-at-home procedures also has tech-savvy people clamoring for online voting. But even though voting via the internet may sound like a good idea, experts have shown that our security infrastructure just isn't ready yet.

In 2000, no states allowed online voting. In 2016, by contrast, thirty-two states permitted some form of electronic transmission of ballots.[67] People serving in the military overseas, for example, can submit their ballots online or via fax in some states. Alaska used to allow any absentee voter to send in their ballot via the web and still permits ballot transmission by fax. Utah let Republican Party members vote online for the 2016 caucuses—though many voters experienced significant problems in casting their ballots.[68] Overall, internet voting has not yet become mainstream.

The reason? Online voting is still too open to hacking. Just think about Russia, which infiltrated at least one state's voter registration database prior to the 2016 election.[69] One official at the Department of Homeland Security explained that "online voting, especially online voting in large scale, introduces great risk into the election system by threatening voters' expectations of confidentiality, accountability and security of their votes and provides an avenue for malicious actors to manipulate the voting results."[70] Scholars, too, have remained skeptical. As Professor Ron Rivest, an internet security expert at MIT, told the *Washington Post*, "The Chinese are very good at getting into everybody's systems. They've attacked most of the Fortune 500 companies successfully."[71] When the District of Columbia developed a pilot program for online voting in 2010 and invited the public to try to hack it, it took a team from the University of Michigan only forty-eight hours to infiltrate the system. To notify the DC election officials that the team was (virtually) inside, the team uploaded the University of Michigan fight song, "The Victors," to start playing on the final voting confirmation screen.[72] The researchers explained that they "successfully changed every vote and revealed almost every secret ballot" and that the election officials did not detect the intrusion for almost two business days—until the Michigan fight song began to play![73] This experience shows that we are not quite ready for online voting on a wide scale. Or as election law Professor Rick Hasen puts it, "when it comes to voting, the Internet is simply not ready for prime time."[74]

That does not mean, of course, that we should abandon the effort—although having a paper trail is particularly useful for a recount. Anything that is more convenient and increases turnout among all groups of voters is a positive step so long as the system also remains secure. New technology such as blockchain, where data are securely linked, could produce stronger, tamper-free online voting solutions. Indeed, in 2018, West Virginia piloted a program for overseas military voters in two counties to vote through a blockchain-based app.[75] But until states run several trials and refine the technology, widespread internet voting is still a ways off. The experience with online voting so far shows that we need to move forward deliberately and carefully.

VOTING CONVENIENCE SHOULD BE THE DEFAULT

Vote Centers work well in places as politically diverse as Colorado and Wyoming, New Mexico and Utah. Vote-by-mail has transformed elections in Oregon and Washington. Colorado essentially uses both, with Vote Centers available on Election Day for those who don't mail in or drop off their ballots ahead of time. Both reforms make voting more convenient and improve turnout. Perhaps the politics are such that a particular jurisdiction may want to adopt one model over the other. What we can't do, however, is remain stagnant in our voting processes, failing to innovate in a positive way to improve our elections.

Any opposition to voting enhancements that improve turnout should come with actual evidence that the new system is somehow less secure or is otherwise inferior. Internet voting is not feasible just yet given the evidence of its vulnerabilities. By contrast, Vote Centers and vote-by-mail/

vote-at-home have proven to work. The key is to start small, learn best practices, and then innovate as the process spreads. Individual voters can play a significant role by advocating for these reforms for their local and state elections.

Incremental changes to our voting processes are possible. Some Kentucky precincts have transitioned to electronic poll books and iPads for voter check-in to speed up the process on Election Day.[76] Indiana, in addition to using Vote Centers in some places and allowing voters to cast a ballot before Election Day at the county election office, has considered a bill to allow no-excuse absentee balloting, meaning that anyone could take advantage of vote-by-mail.[77] Under current law, a voter must select one of eleven possible reasons for needing to mail in an absentee ballot. Yet the state has admitted that it never actually checks a person's excuse to verify its validity.[78] Michigan voters approved a ballot measure in 2018 that, among other things, adopts no-excuse absentee balloting.[79] As Republican state senator Wayne Schmidt noted, "we are talking about a small change to encourage people, not to have to lie, whether or not they'll be in town. I think it just encourages people to get out there."[80] Indeed, *encouraging people to vote is the baseline* for all pro-democracy legislators, regardless of party. Moving to no-excuse absentee balloting is but a step toward more universal vote-by-mail, which Oregon and other states have already proven can work well. These incremental actions can lay the groundwork for even bolder changes.

Polling place locations also matter. Boost Mobile, the cell phone company, recognized this fact and determined that it could help the minority communities where it has most of its stores while also garnering some goodwill in the process. Working with the creative agency 180LA, Boost Mobile sought to have counties use its stores as polling places, even offering to have its employees trained as poll workers. This would increase the number of polling places in minority communities. For the 2016 election, only a few counties took the company up on its offer, so just four of its stores in California and two in Chicago became polling sites. The company asserts that turnout in these precincts was higher than it had been when they were located elsewhere. Imagine the possibilities if this idea spread. The campaign won the *Ad Age* Creativity Award for "Campaign of the Year."[81]

Even little things to improve the voting process can help. One precinct in Texas has a tradition of applauding after any first-time voter casts his or her ballot. Ashley Daniels, a student who received the applause in 2016, championed the idea as a way to improve turnout among her peers: "I feel like the more newcomers they applaud, the more people will go. If we go out and say 'Oh yeah we went and they made us feel really good,' I feel like my other classmates in school will go, as well."[82] This is an easy—and fun!—reform that all in-person voting precincts could adopt. Sure, it's hokey, but it can create a spirit of community and positive feeling about participating in our democracy. Small advances are possible. We have to start somewhere; that means we have to start.

It should be easy to participate in our elections. The voting process should adapt with the times. No one should be denied the ability to vote because of unnecessary hurdles. We must think creatively about ways to improve our election processes—which includes both enhancing access and promoting integrity—with the ultimate goal of increasing turnout.

Those are universal, fundamental ideals that can reshape our democracy. The underlying premise is inclusivity. Let's ensure that everyone can participate, easily and without hassle, and then let the best candidates and the best ideas win the day. That, after all, is what democracy is supposed to be about.

Yet some voters have an especially harder time participating in our elections given their circumstances. Individuals with disabilities face unique hurdles on Election Day. What can we do specifically to help them—and all voters in the process? We turn to that vexing issue next, where we will meet two blind voters in New Hampshire who can show us the way.

CHAPTER 5

ALL FOR ONE AND ONE FOR ALL: VOTING MACHINE EDITION

C hris Stewart, a blind law student, did something he found both remarkable and somewhat routine: he registered to vote using his iPhone.

In 2016, Kentucky secretary of state Alison Lundergan Grimes successfully brought her state into the twenty-first century by implementing online voter registration, joining over thirty other states in making it possible to register online.[1] When creating the online registration system, Grimes was particularly attuned to the need to ensure accessibility for voters with disabilities. Just a few days after GoVoteKy.com went live, Grimes gave the keynote speech at an election law conference put on by the *Kentucky Law Journal* at the University of Kentucky College of Law. On the way to her speech, Stewart, who was one of my students, stopped her in the hallway to explain how grateful he was that the mobile site for online registration was accessible to the visually impaired. Stewart was thrilled that he was able to register from his phone in about a minute. After receiving permission and then petting Stewart's guide dog, Baron, Secretary Grimes told Stewart how much his comment meant to her. She was demonstrably proud.

Stories such as these, from individuals who actually benefit from electoral improvements, make the push for voter enhancements so worthwhile.

THE UNIQUE NEEDS OF VOTERS WITH DISABILITIES

While Stewart is just one voter, his need for an accessible voting process is not unique. According to one estimate, more than thirty-five million eligible voters in the United States have a disability, which represents over 15 percent of the voting population.[2] About a third of disabled voters in 2012 said they encountered a hurdle with the voting process.[3]

Individuals with disabilities face physical barriers when going to vote, such as a lack of accessible parking, steep ramps, narrow entrances, broken elevators, obstructed pathways, a lack of adequate signage, insufficient privacy, failure to have accessible voting technology, too few workers who can assist, and other problems that significantly inhibit their ability to participate in the democratic process. A survey by the group Disability Rights DC found, after studying various Washington, DC, precincts in the June 2016 presidential primary, that 19 percent of the polling places were "structurally inaccessible," meaning that even poll workers could not have fixed the barriers, while 48 percent of the precincts were "operationally inaccessible," in that poll workers could have, but didn't, remedy the issues.[4] Some of the precincts suffered from both problems. In total, 54 percent of the surveyed precincts presented a hurdle to voting for disabled individuals.[5]

These barriers create real-world effects on the right to vote. Michelle Bishop, a voting rights specialist at the National Disability Rights Network, explained to National Public Radio that "If your polling place is somewhere that you can't even get in, not only do you sometimes feel like your vote may not matter. But it also feels like people don't want you to vote, or don't care if you can."[6] Lisa Schur, a professor at Rutgers School of Management and Labor Relations, found that about three million more people would have voted in 2012 had they not faced accessibility barriers.[7] Professor Schur, along with her colleague Douglas Kruse, also reported that turnout among disabled voters in the 2016 election was 6 percent lower than it was for voters without disabilities.[8]

Quite simply, individuals with disabilities have a harder time participating in our democracy.

PRIME III: THE VOTING MACHINE FOR *ALL* VOTERS

Voting with a disability presents a problem from the moment an individual arrives at the polling place. In addition to navigating any physical hurdles to reach the precinct, these voters must request the accessible machine, immediately saddling them with the stigma of being disabled. Further, because the one accessible machine at each precinct is used less frequently than the others, poll workers often receive less training on how to use it or do not prioritize learning about its functionality. Chris Stewart, the blind Kentucky law student who registered online, voted on the single accessible polling machine at his precinct in 2016, but it took over forty-five minutes while the poll workers scrambled to figure out how to operate it. There was so much confusion that the poll workers had to call the county clerk's office to ask for the code to start the machine—all during regular polling hours! This delay harmed both Stewart and other voters who had to wait while the poll workers addressed Stewart's need for an accessible machine that actually worked.[9]

Imagine, instead, if every voter could use *any* machine in the precinct, such that no one has to request an accessible machine. That's the goal of Dr. Juan Gilbert, an engineering professor at the University of Florida, who created software for a universally accessible voting machine called Prime III. This is the future of voting technology. As Dr. Gilbert explained:

> With the Prime III, voters can mark their ballots using touch, voice or both. They can touch the computer screen directly, or use a keyboard, button switches, joysticks or other input devices to interact with the voting interface. Other voters can use a microphone and headset to respond to verbal prompts. These options allow people who cannot read, cannot hear and even lack arms to all vote on the same machine as someone with perfect sight, dexterity and hearing. It's one machine for everyone, independent of their ability or disability.[10]

Gilbert calls the system at most polling places in the United States—with only one accessible voting machine—"separate but equal," which is not really equal at all.[11] That's an obvious reference to the US Supreme Court's decision in *Plessy v. Ferguson*, the 1896 case solidifying the "separate but equal" concept for race until the Court finally overruled it as fundamentally unfair and unequal in *Brown v. Board of Education* in 1954. Gilbert believes that forcing disabled individuals to vote on a separate machine, which poll workers often don't even know how to operate, makes the voting process inherently unequal.

Ensuring that all voting machines are usable for all voters levels the playing field by giving everyone the same experience. It removes the stigma of having a disability while that individual engages in the civic duty of voting. As David Linn, a rehabilitation specialist at the Florida Division of Blind Services—who is himself blind—said with respect to Prime III, "It's always a good feeling to sort of be able to do what everyone else is doing without any real special attention being drawn to myself or to another person with a disability."[12] During the pilot studies for the Prime III system, Gilbert reported disabled voters making comments such as, "I have never been able to vote by myself until now" and "This makes voting so easy!"[13]

Dr. Juan Gilbert and his team using the Prime III voting system. [Photo courtesy of University of Florida.]

An election system with one machine that everyone can use, regardless of disability, also ensures that poll workers receive adequate training for all voters because they must learn only one machine. Gilbert has made the software open source, meaning that anyone can download the code and use it for free. A few states have tried the system in pilot programs, with much success.

In 2016, some disabled voters in New Hampshire used a version of Prime III, which the state called One4All. There were no noted problems and having a disability was no longer as much of a distinguishing characteristic.[14] At least one New Hampshire town has considered the equipment for its own local elections. The machines, which consist of a tablet, docking station, printer, and headset, cost about $600, which is extremely reasonable for voting technology, though other resources are required such as the need to program each machine for each election and ongoing maintenance.[15] Compare that to the several-thousand-dollars per machine needed to buy new voting equipment.[16] Voting rights activists—which, it should be obvious by now, include all of us—should call on more states and localities to consider this innovation for their own elections.

LEARNING FROM DISABLED VOTERS ON WHAT WORKS BEST

It is not enough for a state simply to adopt an accessible voting machine and leave it at that. That's what I learned from Jean Shiner and Dana Trahan, two blind voters in New Hampshire who have worked on accessibility issues, including the implementation of One4All in their state.[17] Trahan was visiting her friend Shiner when I called Shiner on a warm summer day, and both were delighted to share their experiences with the accessible voting machine. Shiner has been blind her entire life, while Trahan has been blind for about eight years. The two friends have worked together on voter accessibility issues, knowing that a lot can be done to ease the burdens of having a disability.

They explained to me that education, targeted to the disabled community as well as to all voters, is vital to increase voter participation. Shiner lamented that many of her friends thought it would be too much hassle to vote, not realizing that the state was actively trying to make polling machines more accessible. Shiner herself used to bring someone to the polls with her so she could vote. Now she can vote independently and in secret—all thanks to these technological advances. Trahan mentioned that even having poll workers simply say to everyone, "Do you know about our accessible voting machines?" can be extremely helpful.[18] This outreach is needed not just for the disabled community but for all voters. Nondisabled people should try out the machines. Trahan explained that to achieve widespread adoption, the general public must understand "that it exists, that it's not scary, but that it actually works."[19] Doing so in a way that helps all voters, not just a subset of voters, will make a big difference. As Shiner said, "Having a system that everyone can use is really the key. There shouldn't be a system that is just for blind people to use. It should be for everyone. That will improve the entire voting experience."[20]

Jean Shiner with her guide dog, Lady. [Photo by Victor Lachance.]

ENCOURAGING ELECTION OFFICIALS
TO GO THE EXTRA MILE

Those who run our elections should strive to go beyond the mandates of federal and state law and work proactively to ensure accessibility.[21] That was the message from Mike Haas, the former administrator and head of the Wisconsin Elections Commission.[22] Haas and I enjoyed lunch on a crisp March day in Madison, Wisconsin, while chatting under the shadow of the state capitol building. Over salad and bread sticks, Haas told me about his commission's Accessibility Advisory Committee.[23] That committee includes representatives of numerous organizations that work on disability issues. The committee meets several times a year to discuss various aspects of the voting process. Experts on the committee help to educate election officials on issues facing individuals with disabilities and how these people interact with the voting process. The committee collaborates with advocacy groups to create and disseminate flyers that provide updates relevant to disabled voters.

In addition, the Wisconsin Elections Commission hires a staff of temporary workers for every Election Day to visit polling places throughout the state. Haas said that the commission wants to learn specific details about how actual voters experience the voting process, and the only way to do so is to monitor precincts themselves. The staff is trained on voter accessibility issues and then audits about 100 to 150 polling sites each Election Day. They take pictures and write a report on what they encounter. The commission then sends the findings to the state's county clerks, who must correct any problems and provide follow-up information to the commission.[24]

Often the fix is easy, simply requiring improved education for county clerks on why a particular setup made the precinct inaccessible for some voters—such as moving a trash can that was hindering the turning radius of a wheelchair. Other times, the results of these audits have been dramatic: one polling place added an elevator; another county in a rural area said that the report was the last straw and that it would now build a new accessible city hall. That action was particularly impressive and meaningful, as it would improve all of the local government's services for everyone.[25]

The commission visits every polling place in the state over a ten-year period specifically to monitor accessibility issues. Haas emphasized that understanding the needs of disabled voters is the first, vital step to ensure easy access to the polls. That means that election officials and everyday voters must speak up to make accessibility a priority. These proactive efforts in Wisconsin go a long way toward helping in that effort. Of course, no system is perfect. Some disabled voters in Wisconsin surely still face obstacles to voting—especially given the state's strict voter ID law, which voters with disabilities have a particularly harder time navigating.[26] But the initiatives of the Wisconsin Elections Commission are a valuable first step in the right direction.

A PROACTIVE APPROACH

Local election officials must be committed to ensure accessibility in all facets of the voting process. Take the example of the Los Angeles County Registrar-Recorder/County Clerk, which runs the city's elections. Its website indicates a lofty ambition: "The goal of the RR/CC is to have 100% participation of eligible voters in all elections, 100% polling place accessibility and options for all voters who seek independent and private voting."[27] The city starts with the laudable goal of 100 percent participation and 100 percent accessibility and publicizes it as a top priority. To help achieve this universal participation—particularly among disabled voters— the city employs a Voting Accessibility Advisory Consultant to assist elderly and disabled voters with any issues or questions they may have.[28]

North Carolina goes a step further with regard to auditing its polling places: it has photographs online of every polling site in the state.[29] This resource allows voters to view pathways, parking, and entrances to their precinct. For voters who have difficulty exiting a car, many states such as North Carolina and Wisconsin provide for curbside voting.[30] An election worker will physically bring the ballot to a voter's car and provide any assistance that is necessary.

Technological advances, particularly for voting machines, can make the voting process so much easier—not just for disabled voters, but for all voters. If we are going to have separate, accessible machines for disabled voters, then we must ensure that they function as easily as possible. Voting technology now allows individuals with disabilities to vote on machines that are wheelchair accessible but still provide privacy, have the ballot read to them through headphones, and facilitate the use of a sip-and-puff device for those who have mobility impairments.[31] Additionally, there are a variety of ways to mark the ballot, such as through a touch screen, with a wheel, or by a tool. Washington State produces accessible versions of all voter pamphlets and will mail this material in plain text or audio files on a CD or USB drive for those without internet access.[32] Other states, such as Louisiana, provide magnifying glasses, an audio voting touch pad, and Braille voting instructions at every polling place.[33] Iowa created an accessibility app for election workers that includes a checklist to ensure polling places are accessible.[34] Oregon has designed a website for voters with disabilities to mark a ballot, print it out, and then drop it off or mail it in.[35] Similarly, Maryland voters can download an absentee ballot, fill it out electronically using an online marking tool, and send it in. A federal court ruled that Maryland must ensure that this voting mechanism is accessible for blind individuals, meaning that the online marking system must be compatible with tools that blind people use every day such as text-to-Braille converters, magnifiers, and screen readers.[36]

We can also improve how we interact with disabled voters—and all voters—at the polls. In Santa Cruz County, California, for instance, poll workers tell all voters about the availability of accessible voting technology and the county assigns someone to that specific machine. That way, voters can decide for themselves whether they want to use the machine, and a dedicated individual is available to answer questions if needed.[37] Not all disabilities are obvious to others and some people may not want to disclose openly that they have a particular disability. Letting all voters know that they can use an accessible machine removes the stigma of having to disclose one's specific disability and makes the polling place more welcoming overall.

In addition to helping disabled voters, states and localities are making it easier for elderly individuals in nursing homes to cast a ballot, especially through the use of new technologies. Some counties in Oregon bring iPads and portable wireless printers to nursing homes so a voter can use the state's tablet technology to complete a ballot.[38] Overall, about half of the states allow "mobile polling," in which a bipartisan team of trained election workers go to nursing homes to assist residents fill out absentee ballots.[39] To ward off undue influence, some states require signage in nursing homes to remind people that coercing a voter is a crime.[40]

THE POWER OF ADVOCACY GROUPS

Organizations can help disabled voters—and all voters in the process. Every state has an organization focused on improving disability services, including voting.

Disability Rights California, a nonprofit advocacy group, has tried to combat the problem of misinformation and misallocated resources for individuals with disabilities. The organization has collaborated with the ACLU and the California Secretary of State's office to offer specific training to employees of government agencies that provide voter registration materials. The training includes best practices for interacting with individuals with disabilities, which the organization says helps to reduce both the stigma of having a disability and the barriers to voting opportunities. Another idea is to conduct local outreach before an election specifically targeted toward disabled voters. Local election officials can bring voting machines to community centers or other locations that disabled individuals tend to visit, such as independent living centers, so that the voters can understand the process they will encounter when they vote. These individuals also can ask questions of the county election workers, which eases the burden on poll workers come Election Day.[41]

Voter guides must be accessible and easy to understand for everyone. For instance, the nonpartisan League of Women Voters of California produces an *Easy Voter Guide*, printed in five languages, to help all voters understand the voting process. The guide identifies each of the races and propositions on the ballot in easy-to-comprehend, plain language.[42] Other states should use California's guide as a model for their own elections. In addition, as Disability Rights California suggests, states and localities should "beta test" their voter guides and other materials by asking individuals with a variety of disabilities to try them out and provide feedback before spending the money producing them on a wider scale.[43]

A common lesson underscores all of these positive voter enhancements: we need to increase public awareness of the changes that are possible for *all* voters. The adoption of voting machines that are truly accessible to all will help everyone, not only disabled voters. It will reduce lines and wait times at the polls. It will minimize poll worker errors because the use of one machine for everyone reduces the amount of differentiated training that is necessary. It will minimize the stigma of having a disability when voting. Most importantly, it will increase voter participation. That's the ultimate goal: to create a secure voting system that actually encourages participation, or at least removes systemic barriers to voting. A focus on voter accessibility in a way that promotes inclusivity is a meaningful strategy to improve turnout overall. Educating the public about these possibilities will go a long way toward achieving this goal.

Anyone can help those who might have a harder time participating in the election. Want to ensure that your polling place will be accessible for all voters? Go visit it before Election Day. If it is in a public building, just go and look around. If it is in a school or church, call ahead and tell the person that you are a voter who wants to ensure the polling station will be accessible on Election Day. Perhaps you will notice something that others have overlooked. A positive demeanor and a willingness to help can inspire others to make the necessary changes to enhance voting rights for many people. You can also tell your local election officials and legislators about the availability of Prime III, the single voting machine that is usable for all voters regardless of ability or disability. Collectively, we can make a difference, one voter and one polling place at a time.

AYUDANDO A TODOS A VOTAR[44]

Accessibility goes beyond helping individuals with physical disabilities, though that issue is obviously of vital importance. Non-English-speaking citizens are also entitled to vote. They are citizens, after all, and should have the same say in our democracy as everyone else. The federal Voting Rights Act requires that political subdivisions print voting materials in another language if at least 5 percent of its population (or ten thousand of its citizens) speak that language and have limited English proficiency.[45] This means that in some places, election officials must create registration forms and ballots in multiple languages. Precincts should have translators or other language assistance available.

But that's just the federal baseline. Localities can go further to make the voting process easy for all of their constituents. For example, New York City tripled the number of languages it uses for its voter registration

materials, adding more languages than federal law requires. As Mayor Bill
de Blasio said, "No one should be disenfranchised because of their language."[46] Some polling places in Philadelphia have cell phones available to
call a language assistance hotline that provides translation in over 170 languages.[47] Voters may also bring individuals to assist them at the polls if they
need a translator or cannot read or write. In Boston, the city places inter-
preters at polling places and also sets up a call center at city hall. Most of
the workers at the call center are immigrants who remember the difficulties
they first encountered when they came to the United States. The pay of
$9/hour is, they say, much less important than the pride they feel in helping
their country's democracy.[48] Minnesota has hired thousands of bilingual
election judges, in a variety of languages, for its polling places throughout
the state. Minnesota's secretary of state explained that "[a]s the son of an
immigrant, I know how important it is to provide our new Americans with
voter resources in their native language."[49]

Nonprofit advocacy groups are also stepping in to help non-English-
speaking voters. The organization 18 Million Rising, which focuses on
civic engagement for the approximately 18 million Asian Americans and
Pacific Islanders in the United States, set up an app called VoterVox, which
matches translators with voters.[50] The group helps voters request a mail-in
ballot (in states that allow one) and then finds a translator—often younger
people who speak both English and the voter's language. The translator
will meet with the voter in person to go over the ballot. Of course, the
translator cannot direct how the individual should vote, but he or she can
help the voter read the ballot. This matching of voters with translators can
effectively enfranchise millions of people who otherwise would not vote.

WE ALL HAVE A RESPONSIBILITY
TO ENSURE EASY ACCESS TO THE POLLS

The key to these reforms is to have election officials, technology experts,
advocacy groups, and the general public collaborate to figure out the best
ways to create an accessible voting experience for everyone. That kind of
brainstorming was the goal of a 2012 challenge sponsored by the Information Technology and Innovation Foundation. The nonprofit organiza-

tion partnered with the Los Angeles County Registrar-Recorder/County Clerk, various university researchers, and the National Federation of the Blind to identify best practices for voting accessibility. It used the online platform OpenIDEO to crowdsource ideas to improve election administration. The challenge asked, "How might we ensure that everyone—regardless of their physical, mental or psychological abilities—has equal access to the election process? How can we design for universal access, identify new technologies or develop new tools, so that everyone can use the same voting systems?"[51] There were 433 total contributions, which the general public helped to whittle down to eleven winners. The ideas included fostering election education on college campuses to better engage students, creating priority queues at polling places, and using voting vans equipped with electronic-voting machines to make scheduled stops at hospitals and rehab centers.[52] Now it is up to state and local election officials to study and try out these ideas.

The conversation on voter accessibility is ongoing, but it needs to expand. The various ideas for improving the voting system discussed above are important, yet they are not a regular part of our conversation when we discuss the right to vote. We can impact millions of people by making the registration and voting process easier to navigate. Stories from people like Jean Shiner and Dana Trahan, the blind New Hampshire voter advocates, and the efforts of Wisconsin election officials to audit every polling place, show that positive reforms are possible if we allocate enough resources and attention. Harnessing technology can enfranchise so many more people. This voter expansion could have a tangible effect on election outcomes. But more importantly, it will give a voice to millions of citizens who have difficulty voting through no fault of their own. The American ideal is to ensure that everyone has an equal voice in our democracy. We must make that ideal a reality by enhancing our efforts to improve the accessibility of the voting process.

Yet some voters without any physical disabilities still have a hard time voting due to onerous laws, such as strict voter ID requirements. There is no doubt that we should fight these laws in courts and legislatures. But is there a positive way to minimize the damaging effect of these laws, one voter at a time? Molly McGrath has the answer.

CHAPTER 6

THIS FORMER MISS WISCONSIN MAY SAVE YOUR VOTE

"**E**nough, already!" Molly McGrath thought. The energetic lawyer was back in New York City, having just helped with a political campaign in Kansas during the 2014 midterm elections. But trouble was brewing in her home state of Wisconsin. She felt like she needed to be involved, so she hopped on a flight back home and began an on-the-ground effort to combat the disenfranchisement that Wisconsin's new strict voter ID law was causing.[1]

McGrath and I met at a Colectivo Coffee in Madison in early 2017—mocha for me, tea for her. I found her at the back of the shop—"white sweater and long brown hair," she messaged me—poring over her computer, no doubt analyzing her next move in putting IDs into the hands of voters. Elections and voting, she quickly told me, are her passion. As Miss Wisconsin 2004, she traveled to 150 high schools across the state to speak with young people about the importance of participating in our democracy.[2] She even has the Twitter handle @VoterMolly. It's true: her face lights up when she talks about the individual voters she has helped. She knows that she is increasing voter participation one person at a time.[3]

McGrath made it her mission to serve as a counterweight to a Wisconsin law that makes it harder for some people to vote. In 2011, Wisconsin's Republican-controlled legislature passed, and conservative Governor Scott Walker signed, a strict photo identification requirement for voting. The Wisconsin League of Women Voters and other plaintiffs immediately challenged the law in court. In October 2014, the US Supreme Court held that Wisconsin could not use the law during the upcoming 2014 midterm elections, but that was a temporary order given that Election Day was so close.[4] With more time to implement the law, the courts would permit Wisconsin to require most voters to show a qualifying ID for the momentous 2016 presidential election.[5] The law had the potential to disenfranchise thousands of voters.

Molly McGrath felt like she just might be able to do something about that.

THE DIFFERENT FLAVORS OF VOTER ID LAWS

Thirty-four states require voters to show something at the polls, whether it's a photo ID, a non-photo ID like a bank statement or utility bill, or something else.[6] In the other states, election officials usually match the voter's signature with the signature on file from when the person registered to vote to verify the person's identity. Voter ID laws come in all shapes and sizes, from "strict" laws that limit the kinds of IDs that are permissible to milder forms that simply require that a voter show a document with his or her name and address. In Kentucky, I insist on presenting my credit card, which is one of the permissible forms of ID. (Leave it to the voting rights professor to be difficult at the polls!)

Wisconsin's photo identification requirement is of the strict variety. The law very specifically outlines the kinds of photo IDs that are allowed, meaning that voters must show one of these forms of identification (unless they fall under an exception like having a religious objection to being photographed) or they may not vote. Among the permissible IDs are a Wisconsin Department of Transportation–issued driver's license or identification card, a US military ID card, or a US passport. But most university-issued student IDs are insufficient. That's because the law counts a student ID as permissible *only* if it contains the student's photo, the date of issuance, the signature of the student, and an expiration date that is no more than two years after the date of issue. The regular University of Wisconsin ID cards do not comply with all of these requirements. In addition, voters using a special, compliant student identification card must also provide a separate document proving that the student is enrolled at the university at that time.[7] A federal court in 2014 estimated that around 300,000 valid Wisconsin voters did not have the necessary identification.[8] Voters without a valid ID are required to fill out a separate, provisional ballot and then take additional steps—such as traveling to the county clerk's office with the required ID within a few days after the election—to have their ballot count.[9] Other states also have strict ID requirements. In Texas, for example, a voter may use a gun license—but not a student ID card—though the courts have forced the state to accept a form signed under penalty of perjury if someone faces a "reasonable impediment" in obtaining an acceptable identification.[10]

Yet other states' laws are not as restrictive, allowing various types of IDs to suffice. Milder laws, of course, have less of an impact on voting rights. Most significantly, these states don't suffer from widespread voter fraud.

Many people support voter ID laws. They think it makes common sense. "I need an ID to board a plane or buy alcohol," they might say. What they may not fully realize is that not everyone has a photo ID—poor people typically can't afford to fly very often—while at the same time the requirement deters very little election fraud. Studies have unequivocally shown that voter identification requirements have few fraud-reducing benefits, while they do disenfranchise plenty of valid voters.[11] That's because a photo ID requirement for voting addresses only one kind of voter fraud: in-person impersonation, which rarely happens. The mandate merely prevents someone from pretending to be someone else while at the polls. That's a pretty ridiculous way to rig an election. You would need tons of people involved, and the more people who are part of the conspiracy, the more likely it will be uncovered. Maybe that's why a comprehensive study by Justin Levitt, a well-respected law professor, found only thirty-one potential instances of in-person impersonation in over one billion ballots cast over a twelve-year period.[12] In-person impersonation does not happen to any significant degree. Sure, preventing voter fraud is a worthy goal in the abstract, but not at the expense of disenfranchising valid voters. There is simply no reasonable justification for a *strict* voter ID law.

Most people reading this book probably have an ID in their wallet. The requirement to bring it to the polls seems like no big deal. But many other people quite simply don't need a photo ID in their day-to-day lives. Think of someone who lives in a city, works multiple jobs, and commutes by bus. They don't require a photo ID for their daily interactions. These laws make it harder for some valid voters to participate in an election—with a disproportionate impact on poor people, students, the elderly, transient populations, and racial minorities. It's no coincidence that, because these people tend to vote for Democratic candidates, Republican legislators are more supportive of voter ID requirements. That's why the debate over voter ID laws has become so partisan. But the political effects should be irrelevant. Instead, why should we accept the disenfranchisement of *any* valid voter for no good reason?

THE HARM TO ACTUAL VOTERS

Far from an abstract concern, real voters struggle to satisfy the requirements of a strict voter ID mandate. Ninety-year-old Christine Krucki, for instance, could not vote in the 2016 Wisconsin primary, missing her first election ever, after she was unable to obtain the required ID despite three trips to the DMV with various forms of documentation.[13] The problem was that her maiden name listed on her Illinois marriage certificate did not match the name on her Wisconsin birth certificate because she had adopted a non-Polish last name in her early twenties. She was persistent in trying to obtain a compliant ID, but the law's strict rules stood in the way.

Most voters are not as diligent as Krucki and many do not fully understand the intricacies of the law. Wisconsin election officials witnessed this problem firsthand. The city clerk in Madison said that ninety-eight voters went to the polls during the 2016 spring primary for local elections (which is on a different day than the presidential primary) either without any ID or lacking the proper ID under the state's new law.[14] That's almost one hundred people in just one county in a primary for local races who faced direct barriers to participation.[15] Imagine how many more individuals didn't go to the polls at all because they thought they wouldn't be allowed to vote.

The same thing happened in Texas. That state's strict voter ID rule sows immense confusion, especially in minority communities. A study in Texas showed that, of those surveyed, three out of five eligible citizens who did not vote in the 2016 presidential election did not fully understand the state's voter ID requirement.[16] That confusion was particularly pronounced for Latinos who did not cast a ballot; only 15 percent of eligible Latino nonvoters could correctly identify the state's rules. Around 15 percent of the nonvoters said they did not cast a ballot in part because they did not think they had the correct form of ID, with 2 percent saying it was the "principal" reason for their failure to participate.[17] In essence, many people disenfranchised themselves because of confusion over the voter ID requirement.

An ID law, however, should not prevent *any* valid voter from participating in our democracy. As we've discussed previously, a strong democracy requires full participation of the citizenry, and ID laws stand in the way with no corresponding benefits. If these voter ID laws are going to remain in effect, then we need to educate the public—and physically put IDs in the hands of every voter—so the requirements do not cause disenfranchisement.

Molly McGrath heard about these issues. Her friends back in Wisconsin told her that a significant number of the state's most marginalized voters would likely be shut out of the 2016 election because of the strict ID requirement. Pro-democracy advocates needed to provide outreach, education, and assistance to combat the disenfranchising effect of the law. The ongoing lawsuits were one thing—they were a defensive strategy to try to convince a court to toss out the requirement. But success in the courtroom was not guaranteed. The US Supreme Court had rejected a challenge to Indiana's similar voter ID law in 2008.[18] Lower courts have been mixed in their treatment of voter ID requirements, with most courts upholding the laws.[19] Courts have struck down only the strictest rules: a federal appeals court, for instance, found that North Carolina's harsh voting measures, including its voter ID law, intentionally targeted African American voters "with almost surgical precision."[20] But the Wisconsin courts had indicated that, with more time and outreach, the state could properly implement its new law.[21] Advocates needed to do something beyond the lawsuits.

How could McGrath, a socially conscientious woman who believes deeply in our democracy, sit on the sidelines while thousands of her fellow Wisconsinites faced potential disenfranchisement? What could she do to help?

VOTERIDERS: ONE OF THE MOST IMPORTANT DEMOCRACY GROUPS YOU'VE PROBABLY NEVER HEARD OF

McGrath moved back home to Wisconsin, finding a place in Madison, the state capital. She took a job with VoteRiders, a nonprofit advocacy organization focused on assisting people obtain the necessary identification for voting.[22] VoteRiders gave her a platform to work in various communities throughout the state.

Kathleen Unger, a California lawyer, founded VoteRiders in April 2012.[23] Unger had over a decade of experience volunteering with various organizations on election integrity and voter protection. She noticed, however, that no groups were focused on putting IDs into voters' hands, which was especially concerning given that more and more states were passing strict voter ID laws. After the Supreme Court refused to invalidate Indiana's voter ID rule in 2008, states all over the country began to enact even stricter laws—laws that further limited the kinds of allowable IDs required for voting.[24] Unger initially focused her group on Texas, holding a voter ID clinic in Houston in September 2013 to help citizens obtain the documents they needed under Texas's new restrictive voter ID requirement. Her group has since expanded to many other states, including Wisconsin.

The obstacles that a voter may face under a strict photo ID requirement come in many forms. Sometimes VoteRiders must help voters request the necessary underlying documentation, such as a birth certificate from another state.[25] VoteRiders will even cover the cost of these documents for needy voters. Other times, the work entails physically bringing voters to a DMV office and walking them through the steps of how to request an identification. As we will see, that can even mean educating the DMV workers as well!

It's a community-based effort to ensure that strict voter ID laws harm as few valid voters as possible. Yes, eliminating the laws in the first place, through litigation or legislation, is the better option, and we should continue to advocate against their passage and implementation. However, the reality is that voter ID laws are probably here to stay. They need not sully the electoral process if we can ensure that every valid voter actually has the necessary ID and that the electorate understands how to comply with the requirement. We can take a positive, proactive approach to a law that has the potential of voter suppression. In this way, we can flip the scourge of strict voter ID laws on its head. In fact, we can use the outreach and education required to increase voter participation.

That's one lesson of Molly McGrath's story.

McGRATH GOES HOME TO LIFT UP HER COMMUNITY

McGrath hails from Wisconsin Rapids, Wisconsin, a remote town of 18,000 residents that is located in the dead center of the state. She attended the University of Wisconsin, where she became interested in voting rights through various organizing activities. Her return home to Wisconsin to work on voter ID issues came after she earned her law degree from Brooklyn Law School and spent time in New York City and Kansas.

Molly McGrath, who helped Wisconsin voters obtain IDs. [Photo by Bobbie Harte.]

McGrath planted herself in Madison to head up VoteRiders' Wisconsin operation, arguably the most important of the 2016 election cycle. Wisconsin's voter ID requirement was in the limelight due to various judicial decisions that kept altering the rules on whether the state could use its voter ID law.[26] In addition, Wisconsin was becoming a battleground state: even though the Democratic nominee for president had won Wisconsin's electoral votes in every election since 1984, the governor and a majority of the state legislature were Republican.

As it turned out, Donald Trump won Wisconsin in 2016 by fewer than 23,000 votes out of about 2.7 million votes cast.[27] Yet virtually every political pundit had predicted that Hillary Clinton would win the state in 2016, along with the presidency. McGrath's work, however, wasn't about partisan politics. Indeed, VoteRiders is explicitly nonpartisan. Instead, McGrath's desire to ensure that people could vote in the face of the strict ID requirement had little to do with which side would benefit. It just did not seem fair that individuals who could vote in previous elections might be shut out of the process because the state had passed a law that would effectively disenfranchise thousands of voters. Given that the courts would not stop the requirement from going into effect, there was a need for people on the ground in Wisconsin to help voters comply with the law.

McGrath began by visiting churches, homeless shelters, and other community centers where marginalized voters were located. She gained the confidence of the people running these organizations, which made it easier to interact with individual voters. She then educated each person about the kind of identification they needed to vote. She opened a case file for each voter who indicated that they did not have a proper ID. McGrath and her volunteers then followed up to determine what, precisely, they needed to do to ensure that each person had the correct form of identification.[28]

McGrath also sought to maintain her visibility in the community as part of her voter outreach efforts. She and her staff went to county fairs, food pantries, schools, businesses—anywhere people may be—to interact with voters. For instance, each week McGrath and her VoteRiders volunteers set up at the local farmers market, asking voters who passed by if they had the proper form of voter identification. The goal was twofold: educate voters about the new voter ID requirement and help anyone who said they did not have the correct ID. Sometimes voters were quite surprised when

McGrath told them that their ID, such as an out-of-state driver's license or a University of Wisconsin student identification card, would not suffice. The voters had assumed that their picture ID would be enough. Had these individuals showed up on Election Day and tried to present the ID they had in their wallet, they would have been required to fill out a provisional ballot. Election officials ultimately would not have counted the ballot if the voter did not obtain the proper ID and go to the county clerk's office within seventy-two hours. McGrath's educational efforts thus prevented this sure disenfranchisement. It was like a voter registration drive, but for voter IDs. Wisconsin has same-day registration, meaning that valid voters may add their names to the voter rolls at their precincts on Election Day so long as they bring their ID and can prove their residency.[29] McGrath's voter outreach at the farmers market served a similar role as a voter registration drive, with an added twist: the effort often helped voters who thought they could vote—but were wrong—jump through the hoops of the state's new voter ID law.

There were two main aspects to the work. First, McGrath and her team assisted voters in obtaining the underlying documentation, like a birth certificate, that Wisconsin required before the state would issue a proper ID. This hurdle stymied many elderly voters in particular who were born in other states and who did not know how to request their birth certificates. Many voters also could not afford the associated fees for their birth certificate, so VoteRiders paid the cost when needed. Some voters required other documents, such as a change of name form or adoption records. Second, McGrath drove people to the DMV once they had obtained the proper documentation to actually request the ID. This was especially helpful for voters who did not drive or did not have the means to pay for their own transportation. As McGrath learned, "it takes a village" to help some people obtain a qualifying identification in a state like Wisconsin.[30]

Consider the example of Steve Pacewicz.[31] Pacewicz, who had driven a snowplow for a living among other odd jobs, had lost his Wisconsin driver's license. He had recently moved to Racine but had not yet received an updated license. He also said that he could not, at that time, afford the driver's license fee. So he sought a free voter ID, but the DMV clerk told him that requesting the free identification would void his DMV registration. He had planned to obtain a new driver's license eventually so he could begin working again, but the election was looming. Wisconsin law requires individuals to obtain a new driver's license within sixty days of moving, but it allows new residents to vote if they moved within ten days of Election Day. As reporter Zack Roth recounted, given that the free voter ID would cancel his DMV registration, Pacewicz faced a stark choice: "vote or drive."[32] Pacewicz lamented that "[m]y right to vote in this country is my right. And now I'm gonna exchange my driving privileges for this right. And it's hard enough to get a job as it is."[33] Why, McGrath thought, should Pacewicz suffer disenfranchisement because he had not yet updated his driver's license? McGrath helped Pacewicz, paying for the replacement license. Without her assistance, Steve Pacewicz probably would not have voted in the February 2016 primary.[34]

Or how about Margie Mueller, an eighty-five-year-old woman from Plymouth, Wisconsin, who had an expired state driver's license and did not need a new one because she did not drive. City officials told Mueller that to obtain a compliant ID, she would have to travel to the DMV office, which was about fifteen miles away. That seemed like too much trouble. McGrath tried to convince Mueller to go to the DMV, even offering her a ride, but Mueller found it offensive that state law was making her jump through these hoops to exercise her fundamental right to vote. She was also battling cancer and could not bear the hassle. Even though McGrath showed up at the Mueller's house on the Saturday before Election Day to try to help, both Margie and her husband Alvin decided they just could not deal with traveling and waiting in line. They ended up not voting. Margie Mueller died in March 2017, having not voted in 2016 after a lifetime of civic participation.[35]

Students also have a difficult time participating under the state's strict voter ID law. Alfonzo Noble, for instance, had just turned eighteen but did not have a driver's license. The young African American would have to travel forty-five minutes by bus to the nearest office for a special ID, but only after he could find his birth certificate, social security card, proof of address, and documentation of his name change from his adoption. McGrath eventually helped Noble gather the necessary documents and drove him to the DMV during his spring break.[36]

McGrath also set up shop at the University of Wisconsin, holding registration and voter ID events on campus. About a third of the voters she helped to register had an out-of-state ID and their university identification card would not suffice. McGrath explained to them what documents they needed and followed up with each one to ensure they had obtained the necessary ID. She also brought a printer to these events so students with the special student ID could print out the separate documentation the law required to prove their enrollment at the university. Many students, who otherwise would have been given a provisional ballot that would not count without further action, were able to vote thanks to these efforts.

These are not isolated stories. For every Steve Pacewicz, Margie Mueller, or Alfonzo Noble, thousands of others in Wisconsin also had a difficult time participating because of the voter ID law. A study conducted after the 2016 election estimated that between 16,800 and 23,250 eligible individuals in Madison and Milwaukee—the state's two largest cities and its Democratic strongholds—may not have voted due to the state's strict voter ID law.[37] Neil Albrecht, the executive director of Milwaukee's Election Commission, noted, "We saw some of the greatest declines [in voter turnout] were in the districts we projected would have the most trouble with voter ID requirements."[38] Extrapolating from the Madison and Milwaukee numbers, the voter ID law may have stymied as many as 45,000 voters statewide.[39] A disproportionate number of these voters were low income and racial minorities.[40] Milwaukee's county clerk, George Christenson, decried that "[a]s the clerk who serves the largest population of African-Americans in the state, I was shocked by the numbers and am furious to see that Jim Crow laws are alive and well."[41]

Some people may suggest that Wisconsin's voter ID law affected the result of the 2016 presidential election in the state, which Donald Trump won by fewer than 23,000 votes.[42] It's hard to say for sure. Yet regardless of the outcome, American democracy is weakened when valid voters cannot participate because of onerous laws that have no benefit in preventing actual fraud. Molly McGrath's work eased the burden on some voters, reducing the disenfranchising effect of the state's voter ID law. But we must do better. We have to join her efforts.

McGRATH TAKES IT TO THE MEDIA—AND THE COURTS

After hearing reports that DMV workers were giving voters inaccurate information about the new ID requirement, McGrath decided to go to the DMV with a voter who needed an ID and record the exchange. She wanted to experience firsthand what voters themselves were hearing. So she accompanied a thirty-four-year-old African American man named Zack Moore to the DMV. Moore had recently moved to Wisconsin from Chicago and was currently without a job after he had broken his leg. He met McGrath at a church breakfast, where she offered to help him obtain the required ID for voting. At the DMV, McGrath watched as an employee told Moore that he could not obtain an identification because he did not have a birth certificate with him—which was not actually a requirement under this circumstance. Because Moore had brought his out-of-state ID card, his social security card, and proof of Wisconsin residence, the DMV should have provided him with a temporary card that would suffice for voting while it processed his request. But instead, a DMV employee told Moore, "You don't get anything right away." Another DMV worker said that the way the state was handling IDs is "up in the air right now," which again was inaccurate—especially given Wisconsin attorney general Brad Schimel's declaration in court that DMV "field staff are now trained to ensure that anyone who fills out these forms will receive a photo ID, mailed to them within six days of their application."[43]

Curious if this wrong information was coming from just a few poorly trained DMV workers or was more widespread, McGrath enlisted her mother to visit DMV offices in another part of the state. Her seventy-two-year-old mom went to ten different DMV offices, offering herself as a voter who was interested in learning more about the ID requirement. McGrath's mom recorded the conversations. In seven of those ten interactions, her mom received incorrect information. The answers to her mom's questions were "all over the board," as McGrath put it.[44]

McGrath turned these audio recordings over to the national and local media, which published stories about the DMV's misinformation. As McGrath proudly explained to me, "No one was going to be denied the right to vote quietly under my watch."[45]

These news stories caught the attention of Judge James D. Peterson, who was hearing an ongoing lawsuit in federal court over Wisconsin's voter ID law.[46] Just a few weeks before Election Day, Judge Peterson issued an order, unprompted by any of the parties to the litigation, requiring the state to investigate whether the news reports were true. He gave the state a week to look into the allegations and report back to him. This was unprecedented. A court hardly ever acts without a request from one of the parties to the litigation, and it is even rarer still for a federal judge to issue an order, unprompted, stemming from a news report. But Judge Peterson found the media stories based on McGrath's recordings so disconcerting that he ordered the state to explain itself. The judge then issued a ruling saying that Wisconsin had not adequately educated the public about the voter ID requirement, telling the state to take specific steps to better inform voters as to how they could comply with the new mandate so as not to suffer disenfranchisement.[47]

Of course, McGrath could not do this work on her own. She relied on a stable of about one hundred volunteers across the state to meet voters, determine who needed help, and create a case file for each one. McGrath enfranchised hundreds if not thousands of voters on a shoestring budget. She likely could have had a much bigger impact if she had better funding and more paid staff members. If she has any regrets from her 2016 election experience in the battleground state, she says, it is this: she was not able to help even more voters.[48]

"SPREAD THE VOTE" ALL AROUND THE COUNTRY

Spread the Vote is another organization, similar to VoteRiders, that works tirelessly to help individuals obtain the necessary IDs to vote, with a particular focus on marginalized communities.[49] Kat Calvin, a lawyer and self-proclaimed social entrepreneur, started Spread the Vote after the 2016 election. I spoke with Calvin on the phone as she was passing through Nashville, opening up that city's Spread the Vote office before then heading to Texas to start new local chapters there. She's been all over the country during the past few years to promote the effort.

The 2016 election—when she heard numerous stories about people who suffered disenfranchisement due to strict voting laws—left Calvin feeling like she needed to do *something* in response. She thought about how she could have the most meaningful, positive impact on the electoral process. "I'm a practical person," she said. "I wanted a practical solution."[50] Noting the effect of voter ID laws on electoral participation—especially on minorities and students—she came up with a solution where she could truly make a difference: "The obvious answer was, 'let's just get IDs for people.'"[51]

Calvin quickly learned that those who are down-on-their-luck—unemployed, homeless, hungry—have difficulty navigating in today's society without proper identification, regardless of whether they can also vote. She found that people have a much easier time landing a job or even visiting a food bank or homeless shelter once they have an ID. "I've had people say to me that, 'without an ID, I'm not a person,'" she explained.[52] Voting is not high on their priority list when they are worried about the roof over their head or their next meal. Yet once these individuals have an ID and can take care of their necessities, they then want to participate through voting. Securing proper identification helps in their daily lives and also gives them a voice in our democracy. "We call it 365 plus one," she said. "We're helping them obtain an ID that they can use every day of the year and also on Election Day."[53]

Spread the Vote's model relies on local chapters and local volunteers. Calvin and her organization have trained hundreds of volunteers on how to help someone obtain an ID. The group gives the volunteers training, technology, and funding to work in local communities. Local chapters then partner with community organizations, connecting individuals who do not have an ID with a volunteer. The community groups love the help, as they typically don't have the resources to provide this kind of service. The volunteer does all of the legwork to ensure that the individual can secure a valid, state-issued identification, which can include obtaining the necessary documentation, driving the person to the DMV, and paying all costs. Then, during the election season, Spread the Vote's volunteers make sure these individuals are registered and offer rides to the polls.

Want to be inspired? Go to Spread the Vote's website and watch the videos of the actual voters Calvin and her organization have helped.[54] They are poor, predominately racial minorities, often with disabilities . . . and they just want to have a voice in our democracy. The videos all end in smiles (and sometimes tears) as the voters explain how meaningful it is for them to now have an ID.

This is about more than just giving people IDs: it's about breaking down barriers that impede civic engagement. Once a person has an ID, which will be valid for several years, they are much more likely to vote in future elections. Calvin's group is ultimately a voter turnout organization, helping to improve participation among people who otherwise probably wouldn't show up on Election Day. By using local volunteers, the group exemplifies the power of person-to-person grassroots activism to enhance the ability of thousands of people to have a say in our democracy.

Students from all over are also joining the effort. Much like Molly McGrath and Kat Calvin, Valencia Richardson played an important role in making it easier for students to vote in her home state of Louisiana.[55] An undergraduate student herself at Louisiana State University, Richardson was conducting a voter registration drive on campus when she learned that a university ID card would not suffice for voting because it did not include the individual's signature, which the state's voter ID law required. She heard from many students who had come to LSU from other states and now felt that Louisiana was their home. They wanted to vote in their new state, but these students did not have a state-issued ID that would comply with the state's voting law. Richardson thought that was bizarre and unfair. Shouldn't student IDs, issued by the state's flagship public university, serve as an acceptable ID for voting? So Richardson took it upon herself to change the law. She founded Geaux Vote LSU, a group to pressure lawmakers to require state universities to modify their student IDs. The effort worked. State Representative Randal Gaines sponsored successful legislation to require university IDs to include both a picture and a signature. Although the mandate does not go into effect until 2019, some universities began complying early: LSU issued over one thousand of the new voter-friendly ID cards before the 2016 election. As Richardson told the Baton Rouge newspaper the *Advocate*, "This isn't extremely groundbreaking. A lot of other states already have laws where students can use their IDs. We felt this was an easy way to raise voter turnout numbers for students."[56] It just took the initiative of someone on the ground who wanted to improve the voting process.

TURNING VOTER SUPPRESSION LAWS ON THEIR HEAD TO PROMOTE VOTER ENGAGEMENT

People like Molly McGrath, Kat Calvin, and Valencia Richardson, who simply want to make a difference in their communities, exist everywhere. Instead of just protesting restrictive voting laws, they are actively working to improve the election process in a positive way. McGrath is now part of the ACLU's People Power initiative, helping to organize its "grassroots army" throughout the nation. Kat Calvin has traveled the country facilitating Spread the Vote's local chapters. Other organizations, like local chapters of the League of Women Voters, are also instrumental in providing education and outreach. Collectively, by making a small impact for some voters, we can have a huge impact nationwide.

All of these efforts require boots on the ground. Individuals who are most likely to suffer the burdens of a voter ID law—the poor, elderly, students, minorities, those who are transient—are not necessarily going to find us. We must reach them where they are, in their own communities. Advocates and volunteers must show up at community organizations, food banks, homeless shelters, churches, and neighborhoods to help individuals wade through the intricacies of a state's election law.

It actually works. VoteRiders reported that turnout in six majority-Latino precincts in Houston was up almost 9 percent after it provided information cards about Texas's voter ID law to another organization, Mi Familia Vota, to distribute door-to-door.[57] VoteRiders also staffed a bilingual hotline to answer questions from voters. Direct outreach with easy-to-understand educational material helped some voters meet the requirements of Texas law.

Imagine if we had hundreds or thousands of Molly McGraths and Kat Calvins around the country, walking voters through the often-Byzantine procedures of new state laws that make it harder to vote. Think of the impact. You need not quit your job and focus on this issue full time, like McGrath did. What if every voter who already possesses a valid ID ensures that two other voters have the necessary documents, drives them to the DMV, or assists them in another way? It would take a single day. What if we put greater resources—money, time, and effort—into actively helping individual voters where they need it the most? Photo ID requirements impose unnecessary burdens with few, if any, corresponding benefits to election integrity. But if we collectively work to ensure everyone has an ID, we can eradicate their disenfranchising effect.

Think of it as playing defense through offense. We are often so focused on fighting voter suppression measures in court or opposing new legislation that we sometimes lose sight of how to make a positive impact on the ground for individual voters. We need to harness the energy we use protesting these laws to find ways to actually help people vote. This does not mean that we should give up the fight against burdensome voter suppression tactics. But it does mean that we should allocate our resources appropriately to leave ample room to assist voters as they wade through the process.

People on the ground like Molly McGrath and Kat Calvin are doing so in a positive way, helping to ensure voters do not suffer disenfranchisement. Organizations such as VoteRiders and Spread the Vote are always looking for volunteers. Local chapters of these national organizations are the key to their success. Want to help the cause of voting rights? Join these organizations in the fight. Each of us can enfranchise voters in a positive way, one person at a time.

Of course, once we remove the barriers to participation, voters themselves must be motivated to show up. Too many people feel like they face an unpalatable choice on Election Day, having to decide between what they deem as the lesser of two evils. In a state where one party always wins, they might think that their vote won't really make a difference, and they may decide not to turn out at all. What structural changes can we make to our voting process to ensure that *every* voter believes that his or her vote actually counts?

Perhaps the way the Academy Awards selects the Oscar winner for Best Picture can benefit our electoral politics. Let's find out in the next chapter.

CHAPTER 7

FORGET ABOUT THE
LESSER OF TWO EVILS

My favorite ice cream flavor is mint chocolate chip. It's my standard go-to whenever I visit the ice cream shop. But what if the ice cream parlor were out of mint chocolate chip that day? Would I just refuse ice cream altogether? Of course not! I would go to my second choice (maybe mocha chip or chocolate chip cookie dough).

We all have preferences. Why can't we express those preferences among numerous choices when we vote?

Almost every election presents a similar tale: many people just don't like either of the two major-party candidates. They feel like they have to choose between the lesser of two evils.[1] This happens in elections for US President all the way down to city council. Voting one's conscience can often feel like a wasted vote. Does my vote really "count" if I vote for the Democratic presidential nominee in Texas or the Republican nominee in California, where the outcome already seems preordained? Or what if I'm in a battleground state and I favor the Libertarian Party candidate? If I vote for the Libertarian instead of my second choice, the Republican, does that just effectively help the Democrat? Have I just been a spoiler? Why even bother voting at all?

These are not trivial questions. Al Gore lost Florida in 2000 to George W. Bush by 537 votes, yet over 97,000 people voted for Green Party candidate Ralph Nader.[2] In 2016, Hillary Clinton narrowly lost Michigan, Pennsylvania, and Wisconsin, yet Donald Trump's margin of victory in each of these states was less than the vote totals for Green Party nominee Jill Stein.[3] Many Green Party voters, if forced to choose between Clinton and Trump, probably would have selected the Democrat (though of course some may have just stayed home). Instead, by voting for Stein and not Clinton, at least some of these voters effectively helped Trump.

There's a better way to structure our elections so that the Nader or Stein voter can express a preference for the Green Party candidate while also influencing the outcome between the two major-party nominees. It's called Ranked Choice Voting (RCV) and it has the potential to fundamentally change American elections. Perhaps most importantly, it already works well in cities (and one state!) across the country. Its continued adoption and implementation relies on the power of grassroots activism.

HOW RANKED CHOICE VOTING WORKS

In the traditional election system, which most of us use, voters choose one candidate and the winner is whoever has the most votes, *even if that person does not gain a majority*. Winning with only a plurality, not a majority, is a common occurrence when there are more than two candidates, which is why election scholars often refer to this system as "first-past-the-post." In fact, if the winner received only a plurality of the votes, then by definition a majority of people actually voted for someone else.

In Ranked Choice Voting, by contrast, voters "rank-order" their preferences among some or all of the candidates, selecting who they would want first, second, third, and so on. If none of the candidates win a majority of first place votes, then the rankings come into play. Voters whose first choice comes in last overall have their second preference count instead. The process is repeated until a candidate receives a majority. It's a step toward proportional representation, a system used in many other countries, though it's not exactly the same. Instead, the eventual winner under RCV will have the broadest possible support, while still giving voters the opportunity to indicate their true preferences among all of the candidates.

Let's say that there are four candidates for a single seat. A voter could rank one, two, three, or all four candidates in order of preference. If a candidate receives 50 percent of first-place rankings, that candidate is the winner. But if there is no outright winner, then the counting system looks at the voter preferences. The candidate who received the fewest first-place rankings is eliminated, and everyone who chose that candidate has their second choice count instead. Importantly, each voter has only one selection count in the end, whether it's their first, second, third, or subsequent ranking. Eventually, a candidate will have majority support.[4]

The Maine Sample Ballot from June 2018 shows how Ranked Choice Voting works. [Photo courtesy of Maine Department of the Secretary of State.]

An example will help to illustrate the process and its potential impact. Let's pretend that Michigan used Ranked Choice Voting for the 2016 presidential election and that there were only four candidates: Donald Trump, Hillary Clinton, Gary Johnson, and Jill Stein. Trump won the state over Clinton by about 10,700 votes out of millions cast.[5] But well over 200,000 votes were for other candidates. The candidate in fourth (last) place was Green Party nominee Jill Stein, with about 51,000 votes. Let's assume that under a Ranked Choice Voting system, everyone who chose Stein as number 1 would have put Clinton as number 2 on their ballot. This means that, as neither Trump nor Clinton won 50 percent initially, Stein—having come in last—would be eliminated, and everyone who chose Stein would have their second choice, Clinton, count instead. Adding Stein's 51,000 voters to Clinton's column still does not put Clinton over the top as having more than 50 percent, but it's close. Gary Johnson, the Libertarian Party nominee (and a Republican when he was New Mexico's governor), was in third place with 172,000 votes. Since the RCV system eliminated Stein, Johnson is now in last place, so he is eliminated as well. Now, let's assume that half of Johnson's voters would have put Trump as number 2 and half would have chosen Clinton as number 2. Allocating these voters' second choices would have tipped the balance to Clinton.

Of course, this example uses various hypotheticals that we cannot prove. Perhaps many Stein or Johnson voters would have listed only their first choice candidate instead of putting either Clinton or Trump as number two. Surely some Stein voters would have selected Trump as their second choice. Maybe more Johnson voters would have ranked Trump second. The point is not that RCV will always change election outcomes. Instead, it has the potential to give *every* voter an actual voice in the election. No longer would a voter have to choose between voting his or her conscience for a third-party nominee and selecting who they perceive to be the lesser of two evils. Moreover, RCV provides a better sense of the electorate's overall preferences. A candidate cannot win without eventually securing majority support, even if he or she was not some voters' first choice. Lest you think this exercise is purely academic, consider all of the Ralph Nader voters in Florida in 2000, when the election came down to 537 votes, or the thousands of voters who chose independent Ross Perot in 1992, when Bill Clinton won the presidency with only 43 percent of the vote.[6] Would those elections have come out differently if these voters could have indicated a second choice?

As its name implies, Ranked Choice Voting gives voters more choices because it allows them to rank multiple candidates. Very few people like solely one ice cream flavor or kind of beer; we all have preferences. The same is almost always the case when there are multiple candidates in an election, especially for local races. We might truly prefer the Green Party or Libertarian Party nominee, but we know that choosing that person in a normal election will have little effect on the outcome if there are also Democratic and Republican nominees who will garner most of the vote. RCV allows voters to indicate those preferences, giving full support to their first choice but ensuring that they can influence who wins if their first selection does not come out on top. Democrats and Republicans would surely like the second-choice support for their candidates as well. The likelihood of having preferences among multiple candidates is even more significant in nonpartisan elections, where several individuals may be satisfactory to a particular voter. RCV also can reduce negative advertising. Candidates are less likely to throw mud at an opponent because they want their opponents' supporters to choose them as a second choice. And RCV saves money, especially when it replaces a low-turnout primary or a two-round system where the top two vote recipients move to a runoff.[7]

RCV offers great potential to reform state and local elections. Want proof that it actually works, even in a non-electoral setting? The Academy Awards uses it to determine who wins the Oscar for Best Picture.

THE BEST PICTURE GOES TO . . .

That's right: the Academy Awards has used Ranked Choice Voting for a decade for its top award. The reason? It provides a better sense of the Academy's overall preferences.

When the Academy expanded the Best Picture nominees from five to ten in 2009, it also adopted RCV to choose the winner. The Academy's six thousand voters rank-order the nominated films from first to last. The vote tabulators—PricewaterhouseCoopers in this instance—then run the ballots through the RCV metric: assuming that no movie has over 50 percent initially, the film with the fewest first place votes is eliminated, and the voters who chose that film first have their second choice count instead. The process repeats itself until a film has over 50 percent of the vote. In this way, the plurality winner at the first count may not win once voters' preferences are factored in, especially if there was more of a consensus on the second choice. The winning movie has the most fans throughout the Academy.[8]

The Academy of Motion Picture Arts and Sciences made this change in 2009 because it was worried that, with double the number of Best Picture nominees, a winner might receive only a small fraction of the vote.[9] In fact, it had already been using a preferential voting model for years to determine the nominees. The change put RCV in the spotlight, at least in the movie industry. As the Academy's executive director, Bruce Davis, told the website TheWrap.com, "You could really get a fragmentation to the point where a picture with 18 or 20 percent of the vote could win, and the board didn't want that to happen."[10] The system, he said, will uncover the "the picture that has the most support from the entire membership."[11] Or as the Academy itself put it when announcing the change, "the preferential system is one that best allows the collective judgment of all voting members to be most accurately represented."[12]

That's great for selecting the best movie of the year. Shouldn't that also be the goal for political elections, which have much starker consequences? Don't we want someone who sets policies to be the person that, in society's collective judgment, has the most support overall?

THIS IS NOT A NEW IDEA

In the 1850s, Thomas Hare of England and Carl Andræ of Denmark created a system known as Single Transferrable Vote to elect multiple members of a legislative body. Under that method, each district elects multiple people and voters can rank-order multiple candidates. Once a candidate either has enough votes to win or has no chance at election, voters who listed that candidate first have their second choice count instead. Essentially, Single Transferrable Vote is a way to achieve proportional representation, where the number of seats awarded in a legislative body is proportional to the overall vote.[13] In 1861, the noted British political theorist John Stuart Mill promoted this variation of Ranked Choice Voting as the best way to select members of a legislature.[14]

Then, around 1870, a professor at the Massachusetts Institute of Technology named W. R. Ware modified the idea for American elections.[15] Meanwhile, Australia started electing people with a form of RCV in the late 1890s. The first use of RCV in the United States was in 1912 for party primaries in Florida, Indiana, Maryland, and Minnesota.[16] Several municipalities began using it as well. But other election systems eventually took hold, in part because new voting equipment was not compatible with Ranked Choice Voting. Jurisdictions instead used primaries in which the top two vote-recipients move on to a runoff. RCV mostly stood dormant until the current reform effort, led by an innovative thinker named Rob Richie.

FAIRVOTE TAKES THE LEAD

Rob Richie has dedicated his career to fixing American elections. He looks the part: studious demeanor, wire-rimmed oval glasses, bald(ing). We met Richie back in chapter 1 in relation to Takoma Park, Maryland, lowering the voting age to sixteen for local elections. I've known Richie for several years through my work on election reform, but I sat down with him specifically to discuss Ranked Choice Voting at an event called the Unrig the System Summit in New Orleans in February 2018. He's popular among this crowd: several big names in the Democracy Movement stopped by our table to say hello. With Mardi Gras decorations surrounding us, we delved into the history of RCV and Richie's organization that promotes it, FairVote.[17]

Richie's advocacy for Ranked Choice Voting and his cofounding of the group FairVote derive from his interest in an electoral system of proportional representation. In a proportional representation democracy, seats in the legislature are allocated by political party in proportion to the votes cast. Richie and his wife, Cynthia Terrell, started a "Citizens for Proportional Representation" group in Washington State in the early 1990s. Through that group, they met Steven Hill, who had formed a similar Seattle-based organization. Their overall goal was to "resuscitat[e] democracy."[18]

Richie and Terrell then went to Cincinnati in 1991 to work on a campaign to bring back RCV for the city's elections. Cincinnati had used RCV from 1927–1957, so the prospects of employing it again seemed strong. The campaign ultimately failed, but it gave Richie and Terrell new allies for the cause, planting the early seeds for a larger organization to advocate for electoral reform.[19]

In June 1992, the reformers held a conference in Cincinnati to discuss the next steps in the effort. More than sixty people from seventeen states attended, with the goal of creating a national group to advocate for proportional representation. Cincinnati Mayor Ted Berry, the city's first African American mayor, gave a memorable speech to open the gathering.[20] The new national Citizens for Proportional Representation formed a board and Richie became its director.

The group quickly gained a prominent backer. Former Republican congressman John Anderson, who had run for president as an independent in 1980, came on as the national advisory board chair. Anderson wrote an op-ed for the *New York Times* in July 1992 to promote Ranked Choice Voting, which was particularly relevant given the insurgent presidential campaign of independent Ross Perot that was gaining steam that summer.[21] Anderson's op-ed spurred a national conversation. The movement was on.

In 1993, Richie and his fellow reformers changed the name of the organization to the Center for Voting and Democracy to reflect its broader interest in electoral reform. The organization released a research report called "Dubious Democracy" that analyzed the election systems of all fifty states.[22] The group strategized on how best to promote pro-voter reforms like Ranked Choice Voting. In the late 1990s, as the organization was growing, it created a website that it dubbed fairvote.org. The name stuck.[23]

But change takes time. Although some places debated the issue—the New Mexico state Senate supported legislation to use RCV for congressional elections in the late 1990s, and Santa Clara, California, approved it as a permissible option for city races in 1998—the first real action of the modern era came in San Francisco in 2002. The reform is now spreading across the country.

SAN FRANCISCO IMPROVES ITS ELECTION SYSTEM

San Francisco is a city long known for political activism and innovative ideas. In 1996, organizers like Steven Hill—who cofounded FairVote with Rob Richie and became its western regional director, and who a *New York Times* columnist once called "the guru of ranked-choice voting"[24]—pushed for the city to use Single Transferable Vote for its local elections. Although Hill lost the 1996 referendum to implement that change, he forged ahead undeterred. He finally saw success in 2002 with RCV, which supporters at the time dubbed "Instant Runoff Voting."[25]

Previously, San Francisco used a two-step process to elect its mayor and board of supervisors (its city council): the top two vote recipients in the November election moved on to a December runoff. Yet that December runoff had woefully low turnout and was expensive for candidates and the city. RCV would solve these problems. The reform would open the process to more candidates, eliminate the need for a low-turnout and high-cost runoff election, and provide a better sense of the electorate's overall preferences.

Before starting the formal campaign, Hill and his San Francisco-based colleague Caleb Kleppner focused on laying the groundwork through local groups. They convinced local organizations, such as the Harvey Milk Club and the Sierra Club, to use RCV to elect their officers. High school students agreed to employ RCV to elect their nonvoting delegate to the school board. A local alternative weekly newspaper used RCV to determine its "Best of the Bay" winners in various categories. These efforts demonstrated that RCV can easily aggregate voter preferences and that the system is not that complicated.[26]

But Hill had to translate these organizations' use of RCV for their internal operations into convincing everyday voters that RCV made sense for the city's elections. As Hill explained to me, campaigns are run on "three m's": message, messenger, and money.[27] The 2002 referendum campaign to adopt RCV was no different, and it provides a blueprint for future local ballot initiatives on electoral reform.

Regarding the message, the key was to explain how the new electoral system solved a problem for voters. The problem? A December runoff that no one really liked. RCV would save money by eliminating that second election. That meant cost savings for the city by not having to run another election, but it also meant that candidates would not need to raise money for a second election in a short time frame, especially as the holiday season geared up. Advocates used the slogan "one election, not two."[28] In addition, RCV would liberate voters by giving them more options. No longer would voters feel like they had to choose between the lesser of two evils or that they might act as a spoiler when selecting the candidate they truly favored. Finally, RCV would reduce negative campaigning, as candidates would fear turning off voters who otherwise might list them as a second or third choice.

The method of spreading this message—the messenger—was also vitally important. The proponents faced a problem: a perception that RCV is harder to understand than the traditional voting method where a voter simply chooses one candidate. They needed to explain RCV in a way that was accessible and credible. So Hill and his team came up with some innovative solutions.

Hill, Kleppner, and their fellow campaigners went to local clubs to give presentations about RCV. Volunteers walked neighborhood streets to educate voters. The local Public Interest Research Group (PIRG) chapter donated an employee to visit neighborhoods and explain how RCV would improve the city's elections. The advocates conducted phone banks. They highlighted the benefits in the voter guide that all voters receive.[29] In all, Hill estimates that over two hundred volunteers dedicated themselves to the effort. Perhaps most innovatively, Hill found a way to relate to voters where they were. He went to taverns at night, gathered the attention of the crowd, and said, "OK, let's rank our favorite beers," to demonstrate how RCV works. "That was a lot of fun," he gleefully told me. "It showed, in a tangible way, how RCV is not that complicated."[30] People have preferences in many areas of their lives. The same is often the case with elections.

The final "m" in the campaign formulation is money, and here Hill faced a disadvantage. The opponents of RCV outspent his campaign. The biggest opponents were the "political campaign class," as he put it: political consultants and print shops that benefitted financially from a runoff election in December. These groups ran ads and sent mailings saying that RCV would take away people's right to vote. That was false, of course. RCV gives voters *more* choices, not fewer. Hill's experience shows that money does not always win the day. Of course, Hill and his supporters would have preferred having more money than their opponents, but that ultimately was unnecessary because of the power of their message. As they explained to voters, RCV can make elections simpler and more affordable, especially because it consolidated two elections into one.

In 2002, San Francisco voters endorsed the use of Ranked Choice Voting for city elections by 55 to 45 percent.[31] Under the system, voters can rank up to three candidates for each position, though voters are not forced to list three preferences; they can choose just one if they want.[32]

As Hill wrote in his 2006 book, *10 Steps to Repair American Democracy*:

> Waiting for the initial results that election night, I reflected on the fact that no ranked ballot system like [RCV] had been enacted in the United States in 40 years. Americans are used to thinking that we are the paragon of democracy, that the way we elect our representatives is the best— indeed, the only way. . . . Yet against all those odds and more, we in San Francisco had been audacious enough to believe that we could convince an entire city to take a chance on an advanced method such as [Ranked Choice Voting]. Such hopeless dreamers![33]

San Francisco employed RCV for the first time in November 2004 to elect seven seats on its board of supervisors. In four of those seven elections, where the top candidate did not receive a majority of votes in the first round, RCV avoided the need for a separate runoff election.[34] Voters expressed overwhelmingly positive support for the system, finding it easy to use.[35] Candidates sought to build coalitions, recognizing the benefits of being listed second or third even if they were not a voter's first choice. This realization led to less negative campaigning. Moreover, given that the city used to hold a runoff election in December between the top two vote recipients from the November election, RCV saved money for candidates and the city: there was no longer a need for a runoff that usually had low turnout and created avenues for big campaign spending to affect the outcome.[36]

The first citywide election using RCV was in November 2005. A Fair-Vote analysis showed that turnout in that election was significantly higher than it would have been in a December runoff.[37] Turnout was particularly stronger than originally projected in neighborhoods that were racially diverse and socioeconomically disadvantaged, suggesting that RCV can help to increase participation among diverse populations.[38]

The long-term effects have been impressive. The city's board of supervisors has become more diverse under RCV.[39] Voter turnout in decisive elections has improved. Wealthy interests have diminished influence. As Hill wrote in 2011, "under RCV, old-fashioned door-to-door politics and coalition-building have given grassroots candidates a better chance against big money. Voters aren't stuck anymore with a single shot vote for the lesser of two evils, instead they are liberated to rank their . . . favorite candidates. With RCV, voter choice is king."[40]

IMPLEMENTING RANKED CHOICE VOTING: MINNEAPOLIS EDITION

Since November 2004, cities all around the country have adopted Ranked Choice Voting for their local elections. Places such as Minneapolis and St. Paul, Minnesota, Santa Fe and Las Cruces, New Mexico, Oakland, California, Portland, Maine, and Amherst, Massachusetts, have all jumped on board.[41] In November 2018, Memphis voters reaffirmed their desire to use

RCV when they rejected a proposal to repeal the city's prior approval.[42] The popularity of this electoral system is growing. But it's one thing to adopt RCV; it's quite another to actually put it into practice.

Consider the story from Minneapolis. FairVote Minnesota, a wing of the national organization, launched a campaign to bring RCV to the city's elections, and the measure passed by a two-to-one margin in November 2006.[43] Opponents challenged the law in court, but in 2009 the Minnesota Supreme Court issued a unanimous opinion upholding its constitutionality.[44] The city used the system for its elections that year.[45] Its first major test, however, came four years later in the 2013 mayoral election, when the incumbent decided not to run for reelection and thirty-five candidates registered for the ballot.[46]

Most voters and candidates praised the system. As the winner of the mayoral election, Betsy Hodges, explained, "With RCV, you can leave no voter unturned, you can leave no voter unasked, because you can't just play to your base and leave that alone. You have to go everywhere, and so we were going to mount that kind of campaign regardless but Ranked Choice Voting really rewarded that method."[47] The campaign was also a lot less negative. "The tenor of the campaigns was far more positive than usual, we literally sang 'Kumbaya' at the end of our last forum," Hodges said.[48] That's because candidates did not want to risk alienating voters who—although preferring an opponent for their first choice—might list the candidate second or third. Many of the losing candidates still praised the system for giving them a chance, saying they likely would not have run in the prior runoff system, which tended to favor the candidate endorsed by the dominant Democratic-Farmer-Labor (DFL) Party.[49]

Jeanne Massey, the executive director of FairVote Minnesota and a driving force for RCV in her state, explained that "ranked choice voting would not just foster civility in the campaign process, but foster the kind of compromise and consensus building in the governing process because candidates would need to reach beyond their narrow base, appeal to a broad majority, not just to be elected but to be re-elected in the process. So they go in with a much broader mandate of a majority of voters and that creates a new kind of environment for governing."[50]

Once again, voters said that they loved the system. In exit polls from that 2013 election, 87 percent said that they found RCV easy to navigate,

68 percent indicated that they wanted the city to continue using it, and 61 percent favored the process for statewide elections as well.[51]

The 2017 elections in Minneapolis and St. Paul (which approved RCV in 2009) once again revealed that candidates and voters overwhelmingly support RCV. FairVote Minnesota focused on education during that election, teaching candidates how to ask for second- and third-choice support and explaining to voters that "[t]he more you rank, the more powerful your ballot becomes."[52] The group also directed outreach specifically toward African American, Latino, Hmong, and Somali communities.[53] The efforts worked. Over 85 percent of voters in both cities ranked multiple candidates on their ballots and similar numbers indicated that they found RCV easy to use.[54] The message seems clear: the more people who use RCV, the stronger support it enjoys.

MAINE USES RANKED CHOICE VOTING FOR A STATEWIDE ELECTION

The largest success for Ranked Choice Voting so far has been in Maine, where voters have adopted the system for certain statewide elections. In fact, Maine voters have *twice* approved RCV. This result demonstrates that an idea that began small, for local elections, has the ability to spread and transform our democracy on a large scale.

Starting in the early 2000s, various groups, such as the League of Women Voters, studied the feasibility of using RCV for Maine elections. The state's largest city, Portland, employed RCV for its mayoral election in 2011, with glowing reviews from the local paper.[55] This local reform planted the seeds for statewide adoption. That effort took off in November 2014, when advocates began to collect more than 73,000 signatures to put a referendum on the ballot to approve RCV for all Maine elections.[56] Dick Woodbury, who was an independent state senator at the time, recalls organizing hundreds of volunteers for the effort.[57] Maine has a strong history of independent candidates, which frequently leads to a split vote among the major party nominees. Before 2018, nine of the previous eleven governors had won without a majority, and five of those governors had received less than 40 percent of the vote—including Tea Party favorite Paul LePage, a

Republican who garnered only 38 percent in 2010.[58] Maine citizens faced another election in which whoever won the governor's race would likely not enjoy a majority of the vote. Maine voters were frustrated. Woodbury recalls voters coming up to signature gatherers, hugging them, and saying "thank you for being here."[59] The desire for change was palpable.

Once the measure qualified for the ballot, the campaign for the referendum to adopt RCV began in earnest. Woodbury explained that campaigns like these start small and then snowball. A few energetic and committed people volunteered. They planned a field operation. Then a few dozen people showed up at the campaign office to help out. That turned into hundreds of volunteers. Individuals held house parties across the state; they spoke at rotary clubs and chambers of commerce; they went door-to-door. All of a sudden, what started with monthly strategy meetings years earlier became a major effort that required significant resources.

They won. In November 2016, Maine voters passed a referendum to adopt RCV for elections in the state.

Litigation ensued, and the Maine Supreme Court issued an advisory opinion saying that the use of RCV for gubernatorial and state legislative general elections would violate the state constitution.[60] The state legislature then voted to delay the implementation of RCV until 2021 and ultimately repeal it altogether if there wasn't a state constitutional amendment by then to address the legal concerns. The advocates of RCV, however, were persistent. They gathered signatures throughout the 2017–18 winter to launch what's known in Maine as a "People's Veto," allowing Maine voters to override the legislature's delay and repeal of RCV. Sixteen hundred volunteers spread across the state in subzero temperatures to collect over 66,000 signatures to put another measure on the ballot. As a result of these efforts, in June 2018 voters used RCV for the primary election and then, in a ballot question on the same day, also determined whether to retain it for future federal elections.[61] RCV again won the day, with over 54 percent of the vote. The upshot: by twice approving RCV, Maine voters indicated their continuing support for this electoral system, which they then used in the November 2018 congressional midterms.[62] By most accounts, the 2018 midterm election using RCV was a huge success, with the result of one of the congressional races coming down to the ranking system.[63]

Individual advocacy made a big difference to convince voters to adopt this reform. Kyle Bailey, the campaign manager for both ballot initiatives, described the "150,000 one-on-one conversations" he and his team conducted with Maine voters throughout the state, first on the initial adoption of RCV in 2016 and then to override the legislature's delay and repeal in 2018.[64] Hundreds of volunteers collected signatures and spoke with their fellow Maine residents about how RCV would improve elections. The message resonated: RCV would finally let Maine voters have a voice. "Vote your hopes, not your fears" became a rallying cry, because voters no longer would have to vote for the lesser of two evils.[65] Scrolling through the website of the Committee for Ranked Choice Voting, a grassroots organization that coordinated the effort, reveals an impressive number of individuals and groups involved in the campaign: students and teachers, business leaders, faith leaders, Democrats, Republicans, independents, and third-party members.[66] Supporters wrote letters to the editor.[67] They cajoled their neighbors and engaged in spirited debate. The success was a tribute to hard work and boots on the ground of everyday Maine residents who simply sought to reform Maine elections to ensure that they better reflected the will of the electorate.

The stories of the regular people who became involved are inspiring. Bailey proudly recalled individuals like Abby, a young woman with a four-year-old son who worked retail at the mall and volunteered her time to the campaign. She couldn't believe that a friend of hers didn't vote because the friend was apathetic about the choices on the ballot and didn't think her vote would make a difference. Abby eventually quit her job at the mall and worked on the referendum full time. She didn't want her son growing up in a world where he might believe his voice did not matter. Nicole, from Hancock County, had never been involved in politics, but she took off two weeks from work to gather signatures for the petition. Ron, a middle school teacher in Brewer, volunteered for the People's Veto because he was flabbergasted that the legislature had repealed a law that the voters initially approved. When he was not in the classroom, he was writing letters to the editor and attending community events to gather signatures. Phil, a retired senior citizen, was at the campaign headquarters all day, every day, doing whatever needed to be done. The list goes on and on. As Bailey noted, the volunteers epitomized the best of Maine: "They were men and women of every age, race, sexual orientation, and political affiliation from every corner of the state."[68] They simply wanted to improve our democracy.

SPREADING THE EFFORT, ONE LOCALITY AT A TIME

What, then, can regular people do to help bring Ranked Choice Voting to more places? Few of us are city council members, election officials, or experts like Rob Richie or Steven Hill. Is there a role—even a minor one—for each of us to help this innovation spread?

In fact, there's more than just a role; RCV cannot become a reality without the efforts of everyday Americans advocating for the reform in their local communities. The first job is to spread the message on why RCV solves a real problem. RCV gives voters more choices and opens up the political system, helping people understand that their vote really counts. This voting method can improve turnout and invigorate democracy. Apathy can be a thing of the past. This is not about implementing a pure proportional representation system or letting third parties take over. Instead, voters will have the flexibility to indicate the choices they really want, with the added benefit of reducing the negativity that surrounds campaigns.

Anyone can bring this message to their local communities. You can write a short column for your local neighborhood association's newsletter or your church pamphlet. It need not be long. A few hundred words can introduce the system and explain how it works well in other places. You can write a letter to the editor in your local newspaper to tout the idea. You can go to meetings of your local AARP or Sierra Club and discuss the system. Fair-Vote, the organization most active in promoting RCV, can provide materials and talking points—its main goal today is to identify and support state and local activists who wish to lead education and advocacy campaigns.[69] You might convince a local organization or school to use RCV for its own elections. There's a domino effect once one entity uses Ranked Choice Voting. Even the smallest of elections—or a family debate about ice cream choices—can help people understand its benefits. Civic activity at the local level can be a lot of fun. You will meet new people, foster a sense of belonging, and help improve democracy, all in just a few minutes.

Ranked Choice Voting has worked in a few places, so it's the innovation that makes the most sense to spread to other jurisdictions. But that should not stop conversations about other voting methods that may be useful to a particular community. For instance, in 2018, residents of Fargo, North

Dakota, passed an "approval voting" system, where voters may select more than one candidate, without ranking them, and the person with the most total votes wins.[70] Amarillo, Texas, is one of a handful of localities that uses "cumulative voting." Under cumulative voting, individuals can spread their votes among several candidates or give all of their votes to one person. If the school board has five seats, for example, a voter will have five votes to use. He or she can cast one vote each for five different candidates, give all five votes to one candidate, or something in between. This system often provides better representation to minority groups because they can allocate all of their votes to one candidate.[71] Localities can also experiment with ballot design and voting equipment, using technological innovations to ensure that the ballots best reflect voters' choices while also enhancing security.[72] Local reform efforts can help to improve choices for voters. Everyday Americans must be at the forefront of this advocacy.

Maria Perez of FairVote Santa Fe, who was instrumental in bringing RCV to that city as well as Las Cruces, New Mexico, explained that change is possible by starting at the local level. "Don't feel overwhelmed," she said. "Not everyone is an organizer, but everyone can be organized."[73] She suggests various possible activities: speak with your neighbors, give presentations, write a letter to the editor, and make others feel they are part of the process. That's what worked in both Santa Fe and Las Cruces. Momentum will then spread.

We cannot wait for our politicians to enact change to our electoral system. We have to do it ourselves. The success stories from this chapter occurred only because numerous volunteers took to the streets to convince their elected officials and their fellow citizens. It requires all of us to make it happen.

One person, sitting at his or her computer, can influence thousands and spark a movement, whether it's for RCV or another positive electoral reform. One person can completely change the structural forces that allow entrenched politicians to shape the rules of the game. One sentence can change the world. That's the lesson from Katie Fahey of Michigan, whose simple Facebook post may just have revamped redistricting in her state—our next topic.

CHAPTER 8

OVERTHROWING THE GOVERNMENT . . . PEACEFULLY

K atie Fahey was fed up. It was November 10, 2016, two days after the presidential election, and the twenty-seven-year-old Michigan resident felt like the country was more divided than ever. Many of her friends were in despair. Her family disagreed on politics: some were Bernie Sanders supporters during the primary while others voted for Donald Trump.[1] She was afraid to go to her family's Thanksgiving dinner later that month because she feared the tumultuous conversations that would occur.[2] "I just can't deal with that," she thought.[3] It felt like the country, her state, and her community were in an unprecedented period of turmoil.

But instead of wallowing in her unease, she decided to do something about it. What could bring everyone together, she wondered? What does everyone, besides the political elite, most hate about our electoral system? Two days after the election, she took to Facebook and wrote a one-sentence post that has sparked an overhaul of Michigan elections: "I'd like to take on gerrymandering in Michigan, if you're interested in doing this as well, please let me know ☺"[4]

THE DILEMMA OF GERRYMANDERING

It's a problem that plagues the electoral system of every state. Every ten years, states and localities must redraw their legislative boundaries in a process known as redistricting.[5] First, the US government conducts the census to count every person in America. States then take this data to draw their legislative maps for Congress and state legislature, and local governments do

the same for their own boundaries. The underlying constitutional requirement is equal population among districts.[6] That is, every district in a state
must have about the same number of people. That requirement is known as
"one person, one vote." It essentially means that the value of each person's
vote is the same—it should take roughly the same number of voters in a
city to elect someone to the legislature as it does in the suburbs or out in the
country. In addition to population equality, districts generally should be con-
tiguous—in that the lines of one district aren't broken by another district—
geographically compact, and strive not to unnecessarily divide political subdivisions such as counties. At least in theory. In practice, many maps violate
these guidelines.[7] Finally, the maps must not dilute the strength of minority
communities or intentionally discriminate on the basis of race.[8]

That's about it. Although complying with these mandates is certainly
complex, there are few other legal constraints on those who draw the maps.
So long as they start with population equality as the baseline and do not
discriminate on the basis of race, they can generally draw the lines however
they want.

Who draws the lines? Traditionally it is the politicians themselves.
Under the US Constitution, state legislatures have the authority to regulate the "Times, Places, and Manner" of federal elections, which includes
the power to redraw congressional lines in the state every ten years.[9] The
majority of state legislatures have kept that power for themselves, although
a few states have created independent redistricting commissions.[10] Most
state legislatures also redraw their own state legislative lines every ten years.
Hopefully you can see the problem: if politicians are charged with drawing
the very districts under which they and their political friends will run for
office, they will seek to maximize their political advantage when doing so.
It's only human. People want to stay in office, so if they can find a legal way
to manipulate the process to increase their chances of reelection, they have
an inherent incentive to do so. When politicians draw districts for political
gain, that's called partisan gerrymandering.[11]

Gerrymandering has a long and storied pedigree in the United States.
The Founding Fathers themselves partook in the practice. In 1788, Patrick
Henry of Virginia convinced the state legislature to draw the map in a
way that would harm James Madison, attempting to gerrymander him out
of the first Congress (it didn't work).[12] The word "gerrymander" derives

from the efforts of Massachusetts governor Elbridge Gerry, who signed the Declaration of Independence. In 1812, Gerry convinced the Massachusetts legislature to pass a map that strongly favored his own Democratic-Republican Party and harmed the competing Federalists by using irregular shapes for the districts. A political cartoonist likened one district to a salamander. It's perhaps the first political mash-up: Governor Gerry and the word salamander became "gerrymander." Governor Gerry pronounced his name with a hard *g*, as in golf, so the word gerrymander initially was pronounced with a hard *g* as well. Over the years the term morphed into using a soft *g*, as in giraffe.[13] The term gerrymander was born.

And my, how it's flourished! Gerrymandering is unfortunately a routine part of the redistricting process. Both parties do it. The goal is to protect incumbents and ensure that a political party can entrench itself in power, even if its candidates don't win a majority of the votes across the state. That's why just voting out those who engage in this practice is difficult: the map already stacks the deck in their favor. These days, Democrats in Illinois and Maryland draw maps, sometimes with irregular shapes, to harm Republicans in their states. Republicans, for their part, have drawn egregious maps in places like North Carolina, Pennsylvania, Texas, and Wisconsin. The strategy is to draw the lines so that as many of the other side's supporters are "packed" into as few districts as possible. That way, they will win a supermajority in those few districts, and the party controlling the process can win the majority of the other districts in the state. Another strategy is to "crack" up areas of one-party dominance—drawing the lines directly through those areas—so they can't win any seats there.

Assume, for instance, that a state has roughly 60 percent Democrats and 40 percent Republicans based on historical voting patterns. Also imagine that voters cluster themselves geographically—most Democrats live in the cities and most Republicans live in the suburbs. Finally, assume that this hypothetical state has five districts. There are lots of ways to draw the lines to create different outcomes while still complying with the one person, one vote requirement that each district has the same number of people. It's possible to "crack" the Republicans into all different districts so that each of the five districts has a 60 D/40 R split—meaning that the Democrats would win all five. Or, by packing as many Democrats as possible into just two districts, Republicans could win a bare majority in three of them, making the state go from five-zero Democrat to three-two Republican.

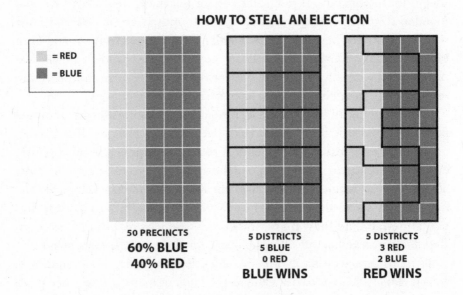

HOW TO STEAL AN ELECTION

= RED

= BLUE

50 PRECINCTS	5 DISTRICTS	5 DISTRICTS
60% BLUE	5 BLUE	3 RED
40% RED	0 RED	2 BLUE
	BLUE WINS	**RED WINS**

This gerrymandering diagram shows different ways to draw a map to affect the outcome of an election. [Wikimedia Creative Commons, author: Steve Nass; licensed under CC BY-SA 4.0.]

Using the strategies of packing and cracking, along with sophisticated redistricting software, those who draw the maps can fine-tune the districts even more to perform essentially as they want. For example, in Wisconsin, Republicans in charge of redistricting after the 2010 census drew a state legislative map that would perform well for Republicans even if their candidates did not receive a majority of the votes statewide. They were quite successful: in the 2012 election, Republicans won sixty of the ninety-nine seats even though their candidates garnered only 48.6 percent of the statewide vote. They won just over a majority of the votes in 2014, at 52 percent, yet secured sixty-three of the ninety-nine seats.[14] In North Carolina, Republicans won about 53 percent of the total votes for congressional candidates throughout the state in 2016, yet the map gave them ten of the thirteen seats.[15] North Carolina Republicans were even explicit about what they were doing: when challenged for making unlawful racial classifications in the map, they brazenly insisted that race had nothing to do with it because they were actually focused on maximizing their political advantage. Luckily, the US Supreme Court rejected this defense in 2017 as unlawful racial discrimination, saying that line drawers cannot make racial distinctions in the name of politics even if race and party affiliation strongly correlate.[16] Yet the Republicans' explicit acknowledgment of their political motivations shows how this isn't even an open secret anymore— it's just plain for all to see.

This is a bipartisan problem. Although Republicans generally have been more successful in recent years in gerrymandering to help their side, that's only because Republicans controlled more state houses in the latest round of redistricting.[17] Democrats do it too when they have the power. In Maryland, for instance, Democrats redrew one district to change it from majority-Republican to majority-Democrat.[18] The politicians are choosing their voters, instead of the other way around.

The Supreme Court has pretty much let this practice run rampant. Recall that the only legal mandates for redistricting are that the districts be of roughly equal population and that they cannot dilute minority voting strength or consider race too much, with other requirements of compactness, contiguity, and following political subdivision lines sometimes coming into play as well. Although there is robust case law on racial gerrymandering—drawing the lines based on the racial demographics of certain areas—the courts have generally failed to police partisan gerrymandering. Plaintiffs have asked the Supreme Court, on several occasions, to prevent the most egregious partisan gerrymanders, but the Court has refused to strike down unfair maps, saying there is no discernable legal standard to do so.[19] A new effort in 2018 to have the Court stop extreme gerrymanders in Wisconsin—done by Republicans—and Maryland—perpetuated by Democrats—resulted in the Court punting on the legal issues and failing to provide any guidance to lower courts on whether they can rule the practice unlawful.[20] The Court is hearing two new cases on partisan gerrymandering in 2019, out of Maryland and North Carolina, but it's quite possible that the Court will either punt again or rule the problem not one for judicial resolution. A few state courts, most notably in Pennsylvania, have stopped the worst abuses by saying that partisan gerrymandering violates the state constitution, but not all state courts agree.[21] This means that politicians have a ton of leeway to draw the lines consistently with these legal requirements yet also in a way that manipulates the districts' political performance. Not surprisingly, they do it all the time.

VOTERS NOT POLITICIANS

People like Katie Fahey are justifiably fed up with how politicians rig the system to favor themselves. That's why Fahey posted that Facebook status a few days after the 2016 election. "Redistricting is this systematic problem, yet we don't seem to do anything about it," she exclaimed.[22] In Michigan, as in most states, the governor and legislature control the redistricting process, and in the past two redistricting cycles (after the 2000 and 2010 censuses) the Republicans had used their advantage to draw favorable maps to entrench their power.[23] In 2016, voters were split about 50–50 between Republican and Democratic candidates for the state House, yet Republicans won sixty-three seats while Democrats won only forty-seven.[24] By posting on Facebook, Fahey simply wanted to see if this was an issue that could bring together a few of her friends and family members who otherwise disagreed on politics. Maybe a couple of people would respond and they could all join a group to work on the issue.

A funny thing happened. Although few people commented on Fahey's original post, several strangers shared it in various Facebook groups. Then more and more individuals responded. People began to send her messages asking how they could help. Fahey, who was working as a program officer for the Michigan Recycling Coalition, recalled turning to her coworker, Kelly Schalter, and saying, "I had this crazy idea and it seems like it's taking off."[25] Schalter helped Fahey create a Facebook group—which they originally called Michiganers for Nonpartisan Redistricting Reform—for the issue. Out of nowhere, a movement was born.

Fahey then set up a new organization, Voters Not Politicians, to advocate for a ballot initiative to amend the Michigan Constitution and reform redistricting in the state. The moniker Voters Not Politicians conveys the basic idea: voters should elect their politicians, not the other way around. The name itself came from a URL that one of the early volunteers had reserved years ago—giving the campaign a compelling message from the start.[26]

Fahey quickly realized that any effort would fail unless it was truly non-partisan, voter-centric, and results oriented. So she came up with three ground rules for the group:

1. Anyone who joined had to represent only themselves, not politicians, lobbyists, or special interests.
2. The focus must be on a solution that did not advantage or disadvantage anyone based on their political party.
3. There must be basic respect and privacy for everyone in the group.[27]

As people kept joining the Facebook group and contacting Fahey, she recognized that she needed some sort of structure or organization so that these people could actually do something, while keeping in mind her goal of crafting a real solution. She created a Google spreadsheet with a list of committees and asked people to indicate which committees most interested them. "We used technology to connect people, but it was fairly primitive at the beginning," she said.[28]

People from all walks of life saw Fahey's original Facebook post and wanted to join the effort. Strangers were meeting online. Jamie Lyons-Eddy, though a generation older than Fahey, is now one of her best friends because of their collaboration on redistricting reform. Lyons-Eddy had worked for General Motors, left GM to raise her kids, and then spent fourteen years as a middle and high school math teacher before retiring to care for her elderly parents.[29] She contacted Fahey in November 2016 and asked how she could help. After discussing various paths forward, Lyons-Eddy agreed to lead a field program in Michigan to generate support for changing how the state draws its maps.[30]

Fahey also created a policy committee to study various reform ideas. As she recalled, this committee included "a veterinarian, a brain surgeon, a birthing doula, lawyers, a retired mailman, and several others."[31] Fahey noted that "these individuals had very strong beliefs and different political persuasions, but everyone was committed to finding a solution that made sense for all voters."[32] They researched the possibility of sponsoring a lawsuit or advocating for new legislation, but those tactics had failed previously. They looked at what reformers in other states had done. The group landed on direct democracy as the best answer, seeking grassroots change from the voters themselves through a referendum.

But what precisely should go into a ballot initiative on redistricting reform? That's when Fahey had another epiphany. She was driving to work one morning when it hit her: why don't we just ask the people of Michigan what they want? Her goal was to end gerrymandering from *all* political parties, but she didn't have a specific agenda on how to do it. She decided that the group should host a few town-hall-style meetings around the state to ask voters what they wanted. Who should be on a commission to draw the maps and who should be excluded? What was more important in delineating a community: school district lines or county lines? How much input should the public have in the final maps?[33] If all of these people wanted to take redistricting away from self-interested politicians, then shouldn't the people themselves determine what process is better? That, after all, is the essence of democracy.

Fahey and her team held a press conference to announce the plan: six to eight town halls in a few places in Michigan. The response was overwhelming. People from all over the state called her, asking for a town hall meeting in their community and saying that they would help to organize it. Suddenly the plan had to expand. They hosted thirty-three town hall meetings in thirty-three days all across the state.[34]

Fahey and the other initial volunteers began in the town of Marquette, which is in the Upper Peninsula—the portion of Michigan north of Wisconsin. The group chose the "U.P." because, as Fahey said, politicians normally ignore that part of the state, and the organizers wanted to demonstrate that their plan was as inclusive as possible. They announced the meeting with only three days' notice in the middle of winter. Fahey was amazed when she showed up at the event, which was held at the public library: it was standing room only. "That showed me that this could happen," Fahey marveled.[35] The fervor in the room that day also gave her a renewed purpose: "I felt a newfound civic duty. If people are that excited to participate in this effort, then we have to find a way to make it work."[36]

Katie Fahey, who formed Voters Not Politicians, speaks at a rally.
[Photo courtesy of Voters Not Politicians.]

Her experience in the Upper Peninsula was not unique. The crowd was standing room only everywhere she went. On many Saturdays, she would wake up at 5:00 a.m. to start driving from her home in Caledonia, which is outside of Grand Rapids, to another part of the state. She would hold the town hall at 9:00 or 10:00 a.m., where people filled the rooms to hear her speak and wrote checks to her new anti-gerrymandering organization, and then she would travel to another part of the state to do it again. People were energized in part because they said that politicians had rarely even visited them before. They wanted change.

Most significantly, this was a volunteer effort the entire way. One member of the team spent time on Google figuring out where the local public meeting places were located and calling to reserve them. Another person was in charge of marketing, which essentially meant making posters and creating an event listing on Facebook. Someone else searched through the Google spreadsheet of individuals who had signed up to find local volunteers. Four team members rotated as presenters at the forums. Someone else would gather the surveys that attendees filled out and compile the data.[37]

The survey data told them that Michigan voters were clamoring for meaningful action on redistricting. They also learned a few other important details: the members of a redistricting commission had to come from all parts of the state, there must be true bipartisanship, and politicians and lobbyists must not play any role in the process.[38]

The group then drafted language for a ballot initiative to amend the state constitution to create an independent commission of thirteen people to draw the lines every ten years. The commission would include four members who self-identify as Democrats, four who self-identify as Republicans, and five more who declare that they are nonaffiliated.[39] The secretary of state would have to send applications to voters at random throughout the state to encourage people from all over Michigan to participate.[40] No commissioner could have been a candidate, elected official, or lobbyist within the past six years.[41] The commission would have to hold numerous public hearings throughout the state and create a map that does "not provide a disproportionate advantage to any political party."[42]

The reformers went to the secretary of state's office for approval of the ballot language. Although that office had said that review of the language usually takes just a few days, they heard nothing for weeks. On July 17, 2017—Elbridge Gerry's birthday—Voters Not Politicians held a press conference. They didn't have political connections, but they had a compelling message: "We would like the Bureau of Elections to make the people of Michigan a priority and follow through on the expectations they set," they exclaimed.[43]

That worked; the state finally approved the ballot language. Then the process of signature gathering began. They needed to collect about 315,000 signatures in 180 days to put the measure on the 2018 ballot. Normally this would require paid canvassers and a highly organized campaign. Voters Not Politicians had little money. Instead, they had thousands of dedicated volunteers.

Fahey and her team appeared at parades and county fairs. They went to college football games. Advocates in Ohio, too, were promoting redistricting reform, so at the rivalry game between Michigan and Ohio State they put up a sign saying "Wolverines and Buckeyes agree, voters should choose their politicians and not the other way around."[44] Volunteers appeared at rest stops along the highway. One day, a volunteer posted a picture in the group's internal Facebook page of him gathering signatures next to a cow pasture in a rural area; that same day someone else posted a picture of volunteers gathering signatures at the Detroit Jazz Festival.[45] What a contrast! All told, about four thousand volunteers gathered an astonishing 425,000 signatures from all eighty-three Michigan counties.[46] The signature gatherers came from all walks of life and all political persuasions. Even Fahey's mom, who had never been part of a political campaign and who normally disagrees with Fahey on politics, gathered 600 signatures.[47]

Fahey made sure to take advantage of the strengths of each of the volunteers, no matter how irrelevant those skills might have seemed. One woman named Rebecca contacted Fahey to say that she wanted to help but didn't know how. After chatting about Rebecca's interests, Fahey learned that her hobby is woodcarving. So Rebecca and other volunteers custom made about five thousand clipboards for signature gatherers to use, which included carvings of oddly shaped gerrymandered districts on the back to help volunteers educate voters about the problem. Instead of having to buy clipboards at over $5 a pop, the group armed their volunteers with unique clipboards for under 10 cents each.[48]

The all-volunteer effort impressed professional campaign operatives. Bob LaBrant, a Republican strategist, told the *U.S. News and World Report*, "They're making the petition management industry look bad. They've done for seemingly free what outfits charge a substantial amount of money to do. Their grassroots effort has been remarkable."[49] In fact, Fahey told me that she had to beg the volunteers to *stop* gathering signatures, as they would be paying a company to verify each one and they already had plenty.[50]

The next steps were to have the state certify the question for the ballot and to convince the state's voters to back the reform. Throughout the summer of 2018, the group fought the board of state canvassers, which was dragging its feet in approving the initiative for the November ballot.[51] There was also an unsuccessful lawsuit against the measure in a futile attempt by opponents to prevent it from going before the voters.[52] While defending against that lawsuit, Voters Not Politicians also continued to hold town hall meetings across the state, went door-to-door to educate voters, and encouraged volunteers to write op-eds for local newspapers.[53]

Remember: volunteers were doing all of the work. Stay-at-home parents, school teachers, restaurant owners, lawyers, marketing analysts, home builders, lots of students, and so many others felt the call to action. Redistricting reform consumed Fahey's mornings, nights, and weekends, while during the day she focused on her regular job. Her employer was supportive of her "extracurricular" activity; her supervisor even became a field captain and eventually encouraged Fahey to make redistricting reform her full-time job. Fahey finally left her position at the Michigan Recycling Coalition in spring 2018 and, for several months, was Voters Not Politician's sole paid employee.[54]

The initiative to create an independent redistricting commission went before the voters in November 2018. Voters overwhelmingly supported the measure, which passed with over 60 percent of the vote.[55] Fahey and her group are now working on implementation and combatting further attacks on the commission's legitimacy. Indeed, there may be additional lawsuits, and some scholars think the Supreme Court might eventually strike down independent redistricting commissions as unconstitutional, at least for congressional maps.[56] But even if that occurs—which is not a foregone conclusion given that the Court previously upheld Arizona's commission in 2015[57]—that doesn't mean people such as Fahey and her supporters should stop their advocacy efforts.

"You don't need a political background to change the state," she told me. "I was in the waste and recycling industry. I had no background in political organizing. But lots of everyday skills are translatable to political activism. So many people didn't believe we could do this. But it *is* possible. I've been so inspired by people who want to come together to do what's right."[58] Before this effort, she and someone like Jamie Lyons-Eddy, the retired math teacher, would have passed each other on the street without acknowledging one another. Now they are close personal friends, connected by an amazing bond: "We are overthrowing our government in a peaceful way together."[59]

A GRASSROOTS EFFORT IN PENNSYLVANIA

Most states have their own version of Katie Fahey, just looking for an opportunity to make a difference. A writer for the *New York Times* profiled Rose Reeder, a retired teacher in rural Clinton County in central Pennsylvania.[60] That's an area that overwhelmingly supported Donald Trump in the 2016 presidential election (ironic, given the county's name!). Reeder heard a presentation at her local library about redistricting and thought that maybe she could do something about it. Redistricting in Pennsylvania has been particularly contentious, with a case challenging the Republican's 2001 gerrymander dividing the US Supreme Court in 2004[61] and the Pennsylvania Supreme Court throwing out a congressional map in 2018 under the state constitution.[62] Litigation will likely continue to be part of the story of Pennsylvania redistricting unless the process is changed.

After hearing the presentation, Reeder asked to meet with her local board of county commissioners to discuss the issue. "I prepared visuals—just as if I was back in the classroom," she said.[63] After the meeting, the two Republicans and one Democrat on the commission unanimously passed a resolution to support an independent redistricting commission for the state. That success spurred Reeder to visit all of the municipalities in her county. Traveling at night, in some cases two hours away, she noted that "The hardest part was finding some of these places. I'd go in, and they were looking tired and thinking 'I hope she hurries up.' As I presented, I could see them sitting a little straighter, more attentive. I could see that they changed their attitude."[64] Eventually, all thirty governing bodies in her county endorsed resolutions to ask the Pennsylvania legislature to adopt an independent redistricting commission.[65] The grassroots organization Fair Districts PA celebrated with a rally on the county courthouse steps. In addition, the group March on Harrisburg conducted a hundred-mile march from Philadelphia to Harrisburg over nine days to raise awareness and, once they arrived, lobby legislators on redistricting reform and other pro-democracy measures—all as volunteers.[66] This advocacy produced positive results: in May 2018, a state Senate committee unanimously endorsed a plan to create an independent redistricting commission for Pennsylvania, though the issue became more contentious once it hit the full Senate.[67] The battle to win statewide support continues.

REDISTRICTING REFORM AT THE LOCAL LEVEL

As we've seen in other chapters, local reform is often easier to achieve than statewide reform. There are fewer people to convince, constituents feel closer to their local governments, and small changes can lead to more widespread adoption. That's certainly the case with redistricting reform as well.

In addition to the six states that, as of 2018, had already implemented independent redistricting commissions (Alaska, Arizona, California, Idaho, Montana, and Washington),[68] a handful of localities use independent commissions to draw the lines for local governmental units such as city councils. The list of localities with independent redistricting commissions includes Austin, Berkeley, Madison, Minneapolis, Oakland, and San Diego, among others. In California, San Diego was a leader in the effort, adopting an independent redistricting commission in 1992 to draw its local lines.[69] Other California cities, such as Berkeley,[70] approved independent redistricting mechanisms later, after California voters passed a proposition in November 2008 to create a statewide Citizens Redistricting Commission.[71] This shows how reform can trickle both up and down: from city implementation, to statewide adoption, and then back to additional cities.

Consider what happened in Sacramento. The California city had a well-known mayor, former NBA star Kevin Johnson, who in 2014 had proposed a "strong mayor" form of government that would give him additional authority over city affairs.[72] Part of the measure included language mentioning ethics, transparency, and independent redistricting, but Paula Lee, the local League of Women Voters president, described these words as "sweeteners" without any real substance.[73] The League successfully opposed the mayor's attempt to strengthen his powers—the voters defeated it by a large margin—but out of that effort came a renewed push for redistricting reform.

The League of Women Voters hosted public forums throughout the city to discuss the ethics and redistricting ideas that the strong mayor initiative had mentioned. They went to every council district in the city. They built relationships with various other organizations, such as the nonpartisan advocacy groups Common Cause and the League of United Latin American Citizens (LULAC). They also sought buy-in from neighborhood associations.[74]

During these meetings, they found a willing audience of individuals who wanted change, especially given the last round of redistricting in Sacramento, which was particularly contentious. In 2011, two council members rejected the suggestion of an advisory committee and drew the lines for their own districts.[75] That redistricting had split up Sacramento's largest Latino community into three different districts, resulting in zero Latinos elected to the city council even though Latinos comprised about a quarter of the city's population.[76] The politics of that 2011 redistricting were vitriolic, to say the least.

Sacramento's citizens were ready for something different. That's when Nicolas Heidorn became involved. He was working for the California Environmental Protection Agency, so he began his redistricting advocacy as a volunteer, but he then took a job with Common Cause specifically to focus on local redistricting. In fact, Heidorn was the only person who received any pay during the effort; everyone else was a volunteer. Heidorn, Paula Lee of the League of Women Voters, and others listened to Sacramento's citizens during the neighborhood meetings, which they hosted in every part of the city. Many of these neighborhoods, the people said, had rarely received attention from politicians. But they knew that they had a voice. Finally, someone was listening.[77]

Stemming from these meetings, Heidorn crafted a proposal for redistricting reform. Everything that went into the proposal came directly from the neighborhood meetings. The advocates wanted this to be a public-led effort. The neighborhood support was particularly significant because the 2011 redistricting had split up various neighborhoods into different districts. Under their proposal, a new thirteen-member independent redistricting commission would draw the lines for Sacramento's city council. There would be one person from each of the eight districts, selected by a screening panel that would follow various rules to ensure the commissioners' impartiality, and those eight people would choose the other five members of the commission. According to the measure, "The commissioner selection process is designed to produce a commission that is independent and that reasonably reflects the diversity of the city."[78] The new law also listed various rules for redistricting: in addition to complying with federal and state laws, the maps should consider, in order of priority, "existing neighborhoods and community boundaries," "communities of

interest," "integrity and compactness of territory," as well as other mandates.[79] The city council unanimously approved the measure for the ballot.[80]
That's significant: the council itself agreed to give up its own power to
draw the lines in favor of an independent commission because that's what
their constituents wanted.[81] In November 2016, Sacramento voters supported the initiative with over 52 percent of the vote—and that's with little
formal campaigning.[82] The new independent commission will draw the
city council map after the 2020 census. The focus now is on implementation. That's also important: the work isn't done once a measure passes.
Reformers must see it through to implement the change in a way that
fosters an open, fair, and inclusive democracy.

As Heidorn recounted, they had little money for a sophisticated campaign. Instead, they had the sheer willpower of their grassroots organization. "We took an issue that might seem esoteric and explained why
everyday people could be part of the process and make a difference," he
said.[83] Heidorn—who with the support of Common Cause and the University of the Pacific, McGeorge School of Law created an online tool,
www.localredistricting.org, to help other communities consider redistricting reform—also touted the power of local movements. "People often
forget the importance of local government and its effect on people's lives,"
he told me. "Yet this is a battle that's winnable by using a people-powered
campaign."[84]

A VOTER-CENTRIC MOVEMENT

Activity on redistricting reform is occurring all over the country at both the
state and local levels, with Democrats, Republicans, and independents all
on board. In 2018 alone, voters in five states—Colorado, Michigan, Missouri, Ohio, and Utah—decided whether to adopt redistricting commissions for their states—and every single measure passed![85] That's particularly significant given that only five states had ballot initiatives on the issue
during the previous ten years.[86]

There has also been legislative action. Maryland politicians have
debated the creation of an independent redistricting commission, with
a retired federal judge leading the charge.[87] That would help to prevent

another egregious gerrymander by the Democratic-led state legislature. The Maryland Redistricting Reform Commission, which Republican governor Larry Hogan created to study the issue, held hearings throughout the state and found that voters understood the problem and sought a real solution. As the retired judge noted, "They called out gerrymandering for fueling voter apathy and increasing partisanship. They were angry at the disenfranchisement caused by partisan redistricting, and even more angered at what one attendee described as 'bizarrely shaped' congressional districts."[88] Indiana legislators have considered a bill to create an independent redistricting commission, but the law died because a Republican legislator wouldn't even give it a hearing.[89] That didn't stop the Whiting City Council from unanimously passing a resolution to call on the state legislature to adopt comprehensive redistricting reform.[90] Whiting's mayor, Joe Stahura, noted that "[i]t's a bipartisan effort across the whole United States to kind of make the districts less gerrymandered and more fair."[91] A legislator in Broward County, Florida, is supporting an independent commission for her state.[92] In 2011, residents of New Rochelle, New York, who felt they were being shut out of the city's redistricting process, formed a new group, Concerned New Rochelle Citizens for Redistricting Committee, to present their own map to the city council.[93] The residents were particularly upset at the Democratic mayor and Democratic-controlled city council for their refusal to create an official independent commission—so they did it themselves. The process in that city was quite contentious, and the mayor and city council eventually passed their own plan, but the citizens' activism brought the issues to the forefront.

What's the lesson here? First, wins won't come easily and they may take time. We must be persistent. But that does not mean the effort is futile. Little by little, we can take the redistricting process away from politicians who seek to rig it for their own benefit. Second, advocating for local reform is often the best place to start. Over a dozen localities now use an independent or bipartisan redistricting commission to draw their lines.[94] If more localities come on board, then the reform has a better chance to spread to states as well. Third, on-the-ground grassroots advocacy can make a big difference. The League of Women Voters, for instance, engaged in various outreach efforts during the 2011 redistricting cycle in numerous states. In Georgia, local League chapters "organized 27 community programs and sent more than 39,000 emails to activists, directly reaching voters in all of the state's 13 congressional districts and resulting in widespread media coverage."[95] As the League explained, "the key to each of these successes was a well-planned, resourced, on-the-ground operation."[96] That operation, in turn, requires people to become involved. It would be nice if the courts prevented the worst partisan gerrymanders or if politicians were not so self-interested, but neither seem likely to happen anytime soon. We have to do it ourselves.

Individuals—many of whom had never been politically active before—are at the forefront of reforming the redistricting process. Katie Fahey didn't set out to fundamentally change her state's elections when she publicly vented on Facebook about our political system. The thousands of volunteers who joined her effort in Michigan just wanted change, and collectively they realized they could make it happen. Neighborhood leaders in Sacramento understood that they could have a big impact by becoming involved in local government. Partisan gerrymandering is not an intractable problem with zero solutions. Of course, independent redistricting commissions may have their own issues. It's probably impossible to eliminate politics from all consideration when drawing district lines. Even so, removing entrenched politicians from their self-interested gamesmanship is surely better than letting them draw maps that primarily favor their own reelection. To take back our elections, we must all join the effort in our local communities.

The details of how to structure an independent redistricting commission, at either the state or local level, are themselves up for debate, and they may legitimately vary among different places depending on the local political climate. Recall that the specifics of both the Michigan and Sacramento initiatives were themselves a product of public input from multiple meetings in each place. There are, however, a few universal truths that we should promote.[97] Any independent redistricting commission should be just that—independent. This requirement means that politicians, political actors, or those intimately involved in lobbying or campaigning should not be part of the process. Or, if it is more amenable to that jurisdiction, the commission should at least have an equal number of partisans on both sides, though none who would benefit directly from how the commission draws the lines. Further, members of the commission must be diverse in all facets, including race, gender, ethnicity, age, and geography. Austin, Texas, for instance, requires at least one member of its commission to be a community college or university student, which is a great example of a way to foster inclusivity for a city with a sizeable student population.[98] A commission will have legitimacy only if it is both truly independent and representative of the entire constituency. The lines themselves should take into account the area's racial history and geographic patterns, consistent with legal doctrine. The commission's work must be transparent and open to public debate. Of course, the commission will probably need the assistance of lawyers or other redistricting experts to wade through the myriad federal and state requirements for drawing a map. That's perfectly legitimate so long as it does not impede the independent nature of the commission. Regardless of the details, independence from the very politicians who will run in those districts must be the guiding principle. As one scholar notes, "Redistricting should be a periodic process that changes the boundaries of voting districts to reflect population changes and does so in accordance with express requirements that define the public interest. Nothing more! No political party or faction, individual or incumbent should be allowed to use the process to further their own self-interest."[99]

Minimizing gerrymandering is a worthy goal and its success depends on all of us speaking up and demanding action.

Gerrymandering is one of the biggest structural problems that plague our elections, as every ten years politicians essentially select their constituents based on political affiliation. But it's not the only structural problem with our democracy. Big money in campaigns is its ugly stepsister. Money drives our democracy such that only wealthy interests seem to have a say and only rich candidates have a chance to win. If individual advocacy and grassroots movements can ameliorate partisan gerrymandering, can it also reduce the influence of big money on our elections? By now you won't be surprised to learn that the answer is yes. To see how, let's meet an inspiring woman named Alison Smith who never imagined she would become the face of campaign finance reform.

CHAPTER 9

THE SECRET SAUCE
OF DEMOCRACY

Alison Smith was focused on raising her three kids, not sustaining our democracy. "I didn't set out to work on campaign finance reform," she said. "That was the furthest thing from my mind. You could have knocked me over with a feather if you told me 30 years ago that it would be my life's work."[1]

Yet a series of fortuitous events made Smith one of the public faces of a movement that has changed Maine elections and become a model for the nation. Sometimes it just takes a regular person to make a big difference.

THE INFLUENCE OF BIG MONEY ON CAMPAIGNS

Virtually everyone recognizes that our campaign finance system is in disarray. You can't mount a successful campaign, even for local office, without thousands of dollars. This means that wealthy individuals or those connected to wealthy donors have the most viable shot at winning. Campaigns cost money: yard signs and television commercials are expensive.

Several important Supreme Court decisions on campaign finance have resulted in an avalanche of money in elections. In the seminal 1976 case *Buckley v. Valeo*, the Court said that spending money on campaigns is a form of free speech that falls under the protection of the First Amendment.[2] The Court ruled that although Congress may limit the size of a donation given directly to a candidate (up to a reasonable amount) to ward off corruption, the government may not restrict people from spending their own money—at whatever amount—on their own electioneering. According to the Court, an "independent expenditure"—defined as money spent to support or oppose a candidate but not donated to or coordinated with the campaign—can never corrupt, because technically it occurs without the candidate's direction or formal approval. (You can decide if that seems likely in practice.) Essentially, the Court held that the First Amendment protects a ton of money in elections as campaign speech.

The Court has continued to fine-tune this formulation even while some legislators have tried to regulate the amount of money in politics. The Court has said that governments may not attempt to level the financial playing field among candidates.[3] Governments also cannot restrict the total amount of money campaigns may spend, as spending money on campaigns equals free speech.[4] Corporations and unions have the same First Amendment rights as individuals to spend money on elections.[5] Yes, that last one is the famous *Citizens United* decision.

Here's the practical result of the Supreme Court's rulings: money reigns supreme in elections. Want to run for Congress? You'll need to raise $1 million at a minimum.[6] A statewide campaign in Texas would require at least $20 million.[7] That's crazy, right?! So how about a smaller race, like for state representative, in the Lone Star State? A cool half million may do the trick.[8] The 2016 election for president and all congressional races cost about $6.4 billion in total.[9] That's billion with a *b*. That number has risen dramatically over the past two decades.

Candidates who win remember who gave money to them or spent "independently" to support their campaign, especially if they hope to garner that same support when it comes time for reelection. That can affect their policy choices. Imagine you are a member of Congress and each night your staff gives you a call sheet—a list of people you need to call back—that is several pages long. Who are you going to call first? The person who gave to your previous campaign and will likely do so again for the next election—so long as you legislate the way they want—or the constituent you have never heard of? Although we'd like to think we'd call the constituent, in reality most of us would probably call the wealthy donor first so we can try to stay in office. That's also why it's likely that an elected official will vote for policies that their donors support, keeping the money flowing for their reelection. Mick Mulvaney, a former Republican member of Congress from South Carolina who, among other positions, became the Acting White House Chief of Staff under President Trump, chillingly admitted how much politicians operate under a "pay-to-play" system, where money is essentially a requirement for any real action: "We had a hierarchy in my office in Congress. If you're a lobbyist who never gave us money, I didn't talk to you. If you're a lobbyist who gave us money, I might talk to you."[10] Mulvaney acknowledged that he would also meet with constituents from "back home" regardless of whether they had donated to him. But his candid remarks revealed an open secret in DC: money talks.

Indeed, the political parties expect members of Congress to spend at least four hours every day on "call time," where they quite literally dial for dollars by calling wealthy donors. The Democratic Congressional Campaign Committee—the Democratic party's fund-raising wing—told incoming freshmen members of Congress that every day they should spend at least four hours on "call time" and another four hours doing "strategic outreach," which includes fund-raisers and media relations.[11] That doesn't leave much time for their actual jobs of legislating.

I once had lunch with a candidate who had just won his first race for Congress. It was December, so this person was in his transition office. I asked him what he had been doing to prepare for his time in DC. His answer surprised me, and I study these things: he told me that he was spending much of his time making calls to potential donors for his reelection. He had not even taken the oath of office yet and he was already fund-raising for the next campaign in two years!

No wonder so many people think that our campaign finance system is broken. As Supreme Court Justice John Paul Stevens wrote in his stinging dissent in *Citizens United*, "While American democracy is imperfect, few outside the majority of this Court would have thought its flaws included a dearth of corporate money in politics."[12]

FEDERAL PUBLIC FINANCING, BUT ONLY FOR PRESIDENT

How can we unshackle the stranglehold of wealthy interests in our elections? Public financing of campaigns is one answer. Congress began a federal public financing scheme in the 1970s as part of its Watergate-era reforms. Ever notice that $3 checkoff on your federal tax form? It allows you to allocate $3 of your taxes to the Presidential Election Campaign Fund. Your taxes do not go up by $3. Instead, checking the box just tells the government to use $3 of your tax money to fund the public financing system. (I always do it.) Candidates can opt in to the program—it must be voluntary under the First Amendment—where they agree to various limits on how much private money they will raise and spend in exchange for public funds for their campaign.[13]

Under the federal system, only presidential candidates, not those running for Congress, are eligible for public financing—and fewer of them are even asking for the money, preferring instead to raise unlimited sums from private donors. Part of the problem is that Congress has not updated or modernized the program to increase the available funds (beyond accounting for inflation) or otherwise respond to the realities of today's presidential campaigns. Barack Obama was the first major party nominee to refuse the funds for the general election, saying that agreeing to the fund-raising limits in 2008 would hamstring his ability to compete with wealthy Republican-leaning PACs (political action committees, or political groups set up to support a candidate or cause).[14] Neither of the Democratic or Republican presidential nominees in either 2012 or 2016 sought public funds. Donald Trump raised over $333 million for his successful presidential bid in 2016, with a quarter of that money coming from "small" donors who gave less than $200 and almost 20 percent coming from his own pocket.[15] Hillary Clinton raised over $560 million, with over 50 percent coming from donors who gave more than $200 each, and she lost the race.[16] Those numbers don't include "outside" groups (like PACs) that do not contribute directly to the candidate but still spend money on campaign ads. Suffice to say, presidential elections are awash with money.

State races also require a lot of money. The cost of a campaign for state office in a place like Maine is a lot lower than for a federal race, but the numbers are still staggering for anyone who is not independently wealthy.[17] Most people don't have thousands of dollars readily available to run for office.

How can we bring democracy back to the people? Alison Smith saw a way to give everyday citizens a chance to run for office: public financing of elections.

MAINE'S RECIPE FOR THE "SECRET SAUCE" OF DEMOCRACY

It began, quite literally, in Smith's backyard. She was raising her young family in Redding, Connecticut, when a developer illegally drained water from a marsh that was next to her yard. Upset at what seemed like a violation of the wetland regulations, Smith went to a town meeting to learn more. After no one else said anything about what had happened, she found herself speaking out: "I voiced my opinions as best I could, red-faced, hesitant, and embarrassed. I found all these other people were thinking the same thing."[18]

Some of the town residents who were there that day encouraged Smith to join the local League of Women Voters. "I'm not much of a joiner, but thanks anyway," she replied.[19] But they were persistent, so she agreed to go to a meeting. That's where she learned a lot about local government. "I came of age during Watergate, when there were a lot of reasons to be apathetic about our government and democracy," she told me.[20] She was impressed with how many people were involved and engaged in making their local community better. She had an "environmental awakening," as she put it, serving on a local conservation commission and working with the League of Women Voters to promote recycling.[21]

Smith and her family then moved to Portland, Maine. As a going-away present, her friends in Redding bought her a membership to the Portland League of Women Voters. At the time, the League was working with a coalition of groups to promote a Clean Election referendum that would create a public financing system for Maine elections. Smith received a call from an organizer looking for people to gather signatures. Sure, she said, she could help. All of a sudden, she became the captain for her precinct. On a rainy Election Day in 1995, she stood at the polls and asked voters if they wanted to take big money out of politics. Virtually everyone said yes. Statewide, over 1,100 volunteers like Smith gathered enough signatures in a single day to send the measure to the ballot.[22]

The individuals who signed her petition, Smith recalled, fully understood how Maine could serve as a model for the rest of the country. Most people who spoke with her actually wanted to fix Congress and had not really considered the problems of money in politics for state gubernatorial and legislative elections. The measure that Smith was promoting, however, would apply only to Maine's state elections. But people were still encouraged. "If this will help pave the way and eventually lead to real reform in federal and presidential elections, then I'm for it," they told her.[23]

Once the measure qualified for the ballot, the next task was to convince the state's citizens to vote for it. Smith became a prime spokesperson. "The public wanted to hear from regular people, not polished public relations experts or politicians in suits," she told me. "Here I was, a regular old person, and the coalition of groups supporting this measure thought *I'd* be a credible spokesperson!"[24] Polls also indicated that the public trusted and respected the League of Women Voters, who Smith represented, giving her enhanced credence. Smith went to speak at various community meetings. She visited newspaper editorial boards. She cut a radio ad. She appeared on television talk shows—even though she hasn't owned a TV since Ronald Reagan became president! "That was like going to another planet for me," she said bemusedly.[25]

Alison Smith, who became a prime spokesperson for public financing in Maine. [Photo courtesy of Alison P. Smith.]

The message was really quite simple: public financing is the single campaign finance measure that provides greater—not fewer—opportunities for participation. Most campaign finance rules restrict who may give money or how the money can be spent. But public financing opens the door to nonwealthy candidates to enter politics by making funds available to anyone. "It's a very hopeful, open door for democracy," Smith explained. "We can help our friends and colleagues run for office instead of having people self-select because they have enough money or have wealthy friends."[26]

The measure to adopt a public financing system in Maine passed in 1996, earning over 56 percent of the vote.[27] There were lawsuits and legislative pushbacks, but the system eventually went into effect for the 2000 election. The policy provides public funds to candidates for governor and state legislative office who opt in once they raise a certain number of donations of $5 or more from individual Maine voters. To receive public funds, today's candidates for state House must obtain 60 "qualifying contributions" from registered voters of that district, candidates for state Senate must receive at least 175 contributions, and candidates for governor must obtain 3,200 contributions. These donations don't go to the candidate's campaign fund but instead are sent to the Maine Clean Election Act program, which administers the public financing system.[28] Once they qualify, candidates may not accept any private contributions whatsoever. This makes volunteers even more important for publicly funded candidates. The law exempts volunteer activities and house parties that cost $250 or less from the definition of a "contribution." All other campaign expenditures must come from public funds.

Candidates flocked to the system. In 2000, the first election when the state offered public financing, about one-third of the candidates used it. By 2008 that number had soared to 81 percent.[29] Two candidates—a Republican and a Democrat—who used the program wrote about how public financing offered them greater freedom: "We are happy to say that public funding has given us the freedom to spend more time with our constituents discussing important issues. We are no longer stuck in the 'dialing for dollars' game, in which we would need to spend long hours on the phone asking special interest donors and lobbyists to contribute to our campaigns."[30]

Former Maine Speaker of the House Hannah Pingree—who used

public financing all four times she ran for office—gave me a great example of when the Clean Election program really made a difference: "The legislature was considering a bill to regulate toxic chemicals in household products, an issue that really concerned me. The chemical industry brought in tons of lobbyists from out of state to try to convince legislators not to support the bill. They flooded the airwaves and bought tons of newspaper ads. They sent voters direct mail and did lots of robocalls. But it didn't work."[31] Why not? Many legislators were not that concerned about the viewpoints of the out-of-state chemical industry, at least as compared to the wishes of their Maine constituents. "Clean Elections made them not have to worry about lobbyist funding in their next election," she said.[32] She also remembered "countless debates during my time in the legislature that were so focused on what the constituents wanted, as compared to paid lobbyists. My friends who were legislators in other states felt differently—they *had* to pay more attention to lobbyists," or otherwise they might not receive adequate funding for their next campaign.[33]

While the program worked well for a decade, it soon faced a major roadblock. In 2011, the US Supreme Court struck down a program in Arizona that provided additional "matching" funds to publicly financed candidates who faced very wealthy opponents.[34] Maine had the same matching-funds feature, which, because of the Court's decision, was also now unconstitutional. So advocates in Maine like Alison Smith—who has been on the board of Maine Citizens for Clean Elections for years—went back to the voters, who in 2015 reapproved the public financing system and tweaked it to include the opportunity for candidates to receive "supplemental funds" if they obtain additional qualifying contributions.[35] The voters passed the 2015 update to Maine's Clean Election law with 55 percent of the vote.[36] The number of candidates who used public financing had dipped, especially after the Supreme Court's ruling on Arizona's law that took away the matching-funds option. But 2016 saw an uptick once again: 64 percent of the incoming legislators won their races with money from the Clean Election fund.[37] As Smith told me, vigilance is everything: passing a law like public financing is just the first step. Reformers must be willing to work on its implementation, protect it, and be there to tweak it when necessary.[38] The process of enhancing our democracy never ends.

In 2018, three candidates for governor—a Democrat, a Republican, and an independent—used Clean Election money for their campaigns.[39] John Brautigam, who had worked as a lawyer defending the law and then used Clean Election funds in his own winning campaign for the state legislature, marveled at how support for public financing crosses party lines: "It's kind of amazing at a time when it's so hard to find bipartisan approval for any issue that there has been strong participation from Democrats, Republicans, and independents. This is an issue that bridges the partisan divide."[40] To be sure, some Republicans have put up roadblocks, such as in summer 2018, when Governor Paul LePage refused to release some of the public funds and Republicans in the state House obstructed the legislature's attempt to fix a drafting error in the state budget that put the system in limbo.[41] Lawsuits predictably ensued and publicly funded candidates eventually received their campaign money. All this shows is that, though lots of Mainers support the program, it takes vigilance and sustained advocacy to make it actually work.

Hannah Pingree, the former Maine Speaker of the House, points to another benefit of Clean Elections: they make it easier for a wider and more diverse group of citizens to run for office.[42] Retired people, younger individuals, parents with kids—they all have a chance to win under the system even if they don't have ties to wealthy interests. People such as Deb Simpson, a waitress, Rob Hunt, a schoolteacher, and Andy O'Brien, a housepainter and caretaker, never would have even tried to run for office without the Clean Election system of public financing.[43] They all served in the Maine legislature. As Hunt said, "I don't owe anything to anybody at this point, except my constituents, and that's really what politics should be about. Clean Elections really took the money equation out of running for political office."[44] Instead, campaigns consist of knocking on doors and actually talking to voters about what matters to them, devoid of the pressure to raise money at the same time.

Of course, public financing will not eliminate all moneyed interests in campaigns, especially after court rulings that have limited the scope of various campaign finance restrictions. Deb Simpson, the waitress, lost reelection after she faced opposition from a tide of out-of-state money from interest groups.[45] But that's not a reason to abandon public financing. The system still opens opportunities for many who otherwise would not even attempt to enter politics.

Alison Smith was raising her kids when she unwittingly embarked on a journey to reform Maine elections through public financing. Reflecting on her efforts that began over two decades ago, she noted that "regular people" can make all the difference. That's the "secret sauce" of democracy, as she put it:

> One of the things I learned is that it's not enough to have experts. It takes regular folks creating a grassroots effort around the policy. It's about people getting off the couch and deciding that yeah, they worked all day and brought their kids to piano lessons and doctor's offices, but they are going to show up to meetings anyway because it's important. None of these people needed to do this, but they were all really committed. A diverse group of people from all walks of life can make a big difference. Seeing all of these people from all over the state and from all different backgrounds—it helped me realize that so many people care about the same thing. So many people were willing to drop everything and pitch in.[46]

SEATTLE'S VOTERS ARE NOT SLEEPLESS

Three thousand miles away from Maine's success, Seattle embarked on its own innovative public financing system to give elections back to the people. The first-in-the-nation program of Democracy Vouchers provides another model to democratize the influence of money in politics and could transform the city's elections.

Here's how it works: the city sends each Seattle resident four Democracy Vouchers worth $25 each. Voters can give those vouchers to any candidate who has qualified for the program. Candidates turn in the vouchers to the city to receive their funds. Instead of merely campaigning for votes, then, candidates also campaign for vouchers, with a cap on the total amount each candidate may receive. The city pays for the program through a small property tax, which costs the average homeowner about $11.50 per year.[47]

To qualify for Democracy Vouchers, a candidate must secure a certain number of small donations from Seattle residents, essentially as seed money. This requirement ensures that public funds go only to viable candidates. For instance, to run for a city council seat in a particular district, a candidate must obtain at least 150 donations—including 75 from within the district itself—of between $10 and $250. The candidate must also pledge not to accept any donations of more than $250 from a single person and to participate in at least three public debates. Finally, the candidate must agree not to personally solicit any money from a political party or PAC.[48] At that point, voters can give their Democracy Vouchers to qualifying candidates, which the candidates then cash in to the city. The city offers support and training on the program for any individual who plans to run for office.

Seattle actually used to have a public financing system in the 1980s and early 1990s, but a statewide voter initiative in 1992 banned all public financing of campaigns in Washington State.[49] In 2008, the state legislature enacted a law that once again let localities pass public financing for local elections if the voters approved.[50] In 2013, some Seattle residents and members of the city council put forth a standard public financing measure that would offer candidates public money matched to the amount of their small private donations. The measure went before the voters, and even though the campaign was not particularly robust, it still garnered just under 50 percent of the vote—though not enough to win.[51] That loss planted the seeds for a new push in 2015, but with a major twist: instead of a typical public match, the proponents would try for Democracy Vouchers.

Alan Durning was a major player in that effort. Durning founded the Sightline Institute, a Seattle-based think tank, in 1993 to focus on sustainability and the environment.[52] After that failed 2013 vote on public financing, Durning attended meetings with various organizations to discuss what to do next.[53] Proponents approached the Seattle City Council in 2014 to try for public matching again, but the council rejected the effort. According to Estevan Muñoz-Howard, who chaired the nonprofit volunteer group Fair Elections Seattle, the city council's action made the advocates realize that their effort should come from the ground up. There was no need to appease city leaders to improve local democracy.[54]

Durning then helped to coordinate a policy team with representatives from other groups to consider various proposals, including Democracy Vouchers. Academics like Harvard Law professor Lawrence Lessig had floated the idea of Democracy Vouchers for years,[55] and the local advocates thought that Seattle might be a good place to try them out. The policy group, composed of citizen volunteers, studied the topic. They spent nights and weekends discussing different aspects of the proposal in small groups. They wrote memos and emails back and forth. They strategized on the best ways to encourage candidates to opt in to a new public financing system. As Durning told me, the group felt confident in the idea because Seattle has a culture of civic engagement, and Democracy Vouchers would play into that culture by "giving every resident of the city a ticket to play in politics."[56] Muñoz-Howard concurred, noting that Democracy Vouchers seemed "more equitable," "added a new tool to the toolbox for other cities and states to fight the influence of money in politics," and had already polled well among Seattle residents.[57]

They were right: Seattle voters overwhelmingly supported the measure in 2015, with 63 percent of the vote.[58] The reason for the success? A broad coalition that expanded its reach beyond the constituencies that are typically involved in democracy reform.

Alissa Haslam is the executive director of the Win/Win Network, a Seattle-based nonprofit that brings together various organizations to work on issues of equality and democracy.[59] Her group was deeply involved in strategy and organization for the 2015 campaign to pass Democracy Vouchers. She explained to me that one key part of the campaign was to reach out to groups and individuals who had not normally been part of the Democracy Movement.[60] Historically, she said, "older white progressives" had been the main advocates for campaign finance reform, focusing on a message of good government. For 2015, her organization actively sought to bring younger individuals and people of color into the fold. "This movement cannot be won by traditional actors who have been doing it before—the democracy reformers who are white and older and who do not resonate with the community that needs to be convinced," she noted.[61] She focused her part of the campaign on reaching out to previously marginalized populations. Another organization, Washington CAN (Community Action Network), also worked on grassroots canvassing targeted toward minority communities.

The other strategy that worked was to campaign on a positive, value-based message. Instead of focusing on what they were fighting against—the corrupting influence of big money in politics—the advocates shaped their message around what they were fighting *for*: greater inclusivity in the voices heard in a campaign. That positive message resonated better with people who otherwise may not pay much attention to politics.[62]

Seattle used its Democracy Vouchers program for the first time in the 2017 election. Candidates in three races—two citywide council seats and the city attorney—were eligible for Democracy Vouchers. (The city waited to implement Democracy Vouchers for the mayoral election until it could learn how the program fared in these lower-profile races.) On various measures, Democracy Vouchers were a resounding success. Three candidates for council position 8, two candidates for council position 9, and one city attorney candidate received public funds through Democracy Vouchers.[63] All of the winners were participants in the program.[64] The number of Seattle residents who turned in vouchers—at 20,727—was about double the number who gave cash contributions to local political candidates.[65] In 2015, by contrast, only about 3,100 Seattle residents gave donations to candidates.[66] Almost 90 percent of voucher users had never previously contributed to a local candidate before.[67] Perhaps most significantly, the number and percentage of donations from outside the city decreased substantially: in 2015, without Democracy Vouchers, about 29 percent of individual donations to local candidates came from outside of the city, while in 2017 that number fell to 7 percent.[68] This means that Seattle constituents, not outside interests, were primarily funding the city's campaigns. In addition, while white, wealthy, and older voters were more likely to use vouchers than their minority, poor, and younger counterparts, those who returned vouchers were still more representative of the electorate than those who gave cash contributions.[69] People from all over the city turned in vouchers for their preferred candidates. Further, those who used their vouchers were more likely to vote, suggesting that the program may also improve turnout.[70]

Real people felt the impact. Voters such as Gina Owens, an African American woman affiliated with the group Washington CAN, wrote that even though she didn't have a lot of money, "Because of the vouchers, I've been able to contribute more than I ever have before. I know I still can't support candidates in a way that wealthy people can, but this program helps fight the appearance of corruption in our election system."[71] Susan Russell, who was formerly homeless, said that being able to use Democracy Vouchers made her feel like part of the community: "I had never donated to a campaign before, but vouchers gave me an opportunity to participate. Those little things that still keep you connected to the community as a whole is [*sic*] everything."[72] Leaders of the campaign noted that people like Owens and Russell were vitally important to their success, particularly to convince minority communities to support the measure.[73]

To be sure, Democracy Vouchers did not reduce overall campaign spending in the 2017 election, as some proponents had hoped. As one study found, Democracy Vouchers can make elections more competitive, which then incentivizes outside groups to spend even more money on running advertisements in these campaigns.[74] Nevertheless, Democracy Vouchers still opened the process to more people to become involved. Josh Silver of RepresentUs, a nonpartisan group dedicated to removing the influence of money in politics, points out that Democracy Vouchers are "a one-two punch. [Candidates] become more dependent on their constituents because their constituents become their funders, and . . . they're part of what I would call a 'dilution strategy'—you dilute the space with lots of small-dollar contributions to offset the undue influence of super PACs."[75]

Seattle might tweak the program to respond to issues that arose, but that's a feature, not a bug, of local electoral innovation. The city can provide valuable lessons for other jurisdictions that may wish to experiment with unique ways to mitigate the stranglehold of big money on our democracy. Congress, too, might consider a similar idea for federal elections.[76] As Wayne Barnett, the election official who oversaw Seattle's program, explained, "We know one thing for sure, which is that it brought a lot of new people into the process."[77]

CONTINUED LOCAL WINS

The stories from Maine and Seattle show how regular citizens can take on special interests and big money to give their elections back to the people through public financing. These are not isolated examples. Places all over the country have enacted their own versions of public financing or are currently debating the issue. New York City has enjoyed successful public financing of city elections since the late 1980s.[78] Candidates receive $6 in public money for every $1 they raise from private donations, up to $175 per contributor. Studies have shown that small-dollar donations given to candidates who participate in public funding come from a diverse group of constituents.[79] As the Brennan Center for Justice explains, "Candidates who have participated in both New York City and New York State elections agree. They have told us that by pumping up the value of small contributions, the New York City system gives them an incentive to reach out to their own constituents rather than focusing all their attention on wealthy out-of-district donors, leading them to attract more diverse donors into the political process. This is markedly different, they explained, from how they and other candidates conduct campaigns at the state level," where public financing is not available.[80] New York City residents like the system so much that in 2018 they voted, with 80 percent in favor, for a ballot measure that boosts the public match from $6 to $8 for every $1 raised and increases the cap on the total amount available for each publicly financed candidate.[81]

Several jurisdictions have adopted a traditional public financing system like New York City's that gives candidates a certain amount of public dollars for every small donation they receive, up to a limit, so long as they comply with various campaign finance rules like rejecting large donations. In 2016, Berkeley, California, voters adopted public financing for their city elections, with 65 percent of the vote.[82] As the proponents of the measure explained, their campaign had "national significance": "It show[ed] how a small group of activists, working with limited time and resources, can transform the way that local government works."[83] Portland, Oregon, which used to offer public financing, will once again have a public match available for its local elections beginning in 2020.[84] Montgomery County, Maryland, passed a public financing measure in 2014 that it implemented for the 2018 election; its neighbor, Howard County, will have public financing by 2022.[85] DC also passed a public financing bill in 2018, backed by a number of grassroots organizations that worked together through the DC Fair Elections Coalition.[86] The city will give participating local candidates a five-to-one match starting with the 2020 elections. Baltimore is on the path to use public financing by 2024; in 2018, the Baltimore City Council unanimously adopted a seven-to-one public match for local campaigns and the city's voters backed the measure with over 75 percent of the vote.[87] Denver voters also approved a campaign finance and ethics measure in 2018.[88]

Other places are thinking about using Democracy Vouchers instead of a traditional public matching program. A proposal in Albuquerque, New

Mexico, for "Burque Bucks" is gaining steam.[89] The Charter Review Commission in Austin, Texas, recommended that the city follow Seattle's lead and adopt Democracy Vouchers for its own elections. As Frances McIntyre of the local League of Women Voters told the commission, "We believe that this is the time for Austin to join Seattle. The proof is in the pudding and Seattle has proved that it's yummy and it works."[90]

It's not just voters in "blue," Democratic-leaning states who are clamoring for change. Missouri voters overwhelmingly passed a campaign finance amendment to their state constitution in 2016, which garnered almost 70 percent of the vote.[91] A federal court struck down parts of the law, but the portion limiting individual contributions to candidates at $2,600 remained.[92] In 2018, voters once again amended their state constitution to impose further campaign finance and ethics rules in a measure backed by the group Clean Missouri.[93] South Dakota voters passed a ballot initiative in 2016 to adopt a Democracy Voucher system and impose other campaign finance and ethics reforms.[94] The Republican-controlled legislature then repealed the law, thwarting the voters' will.[95] Josh Silver of RepresentUs noted that the fight will go on: "The state motto in South Dakota is 'Under God, The People Rule.' The fight against corruption will not end until elected leaders abide by that principle."[96] Tempe, Arizona, voters passed a campaign finance disclosure law by an astonishing 91 percent of the vote, requiring political nonprofits that spend more than $1,000 in a local campaign to reveal their financial backers. The goal is to uncover "dark money," or campaign funds spent without disclosure of who is behind them. But Arizona's Republican governor Doug Ducey then signed a state law that prohibited cities in the state from enforcing local campaign finance rules such as the new Tempe measure. As Tempe councilwoman Lauren Kuby said, "It is a direct poke in the eye to not just Tempe voters, but residents throughout the state."[97]

The examples from South Dakota and Arizona reveal a troubling trend: voters want reforms, but entrenched politicians who benefit from the current system have overruled the voters' wishes. When the people themselves seek to change our system to remove entrenched interests, it is incumbent upon elected officials, of whatever political party, to abide by their direction. Otherwise, we must vote them out.

These efforts from across the country demonstrate how voters are acting to reduce the influence of large political donations. Many of the reforms face various hurdles—lawsuits, legislative vetoes, and the like—but that just shows that change is not easy. Perseverance is vitally important. Little by little, win by win, we can take back our democracy from special interests and wealthy donors. People like Alison Smith, Alan Durning, and countless others who helped on these campaigns have shown the way.

Only fourteen states have any kind of public financing for any state elections.[98] The organization Dēmos counts twenty-seven total state and local jurisdictions nationwide that had a public financing option as of June 2017—though that number is growing.[99] Places that offer public financing typically see high voter participation rates. Public financing increases racial and class diversity among donors to campaigns, breaks down barriers for underrepresented groups such as women and minorities to enter politics, and allows candidates to actually connect with their constituents instead of their wealthy donors.[100] It's high time to add to the list of places that offer public financing. Maybe your jurisdiction is next?

CHAPTER 10

CLASS IS IN SESSION

I wish everyone in America could spend five minutes on the phone with Jen Hitchcock, a social studies teacher in Fairfax, Virginia. Her enthusiasm is infectious. She spends hours thinking about creative ways to instill a love of learning and democratic engagement in her students—"her" kids, as she lovingly refers to them.[1] She understands the importance of nurturing a lifelong practice of civic participation. When not teaching or course planning, she's a student of her own, working toward her master's degree in political science. All for paltry pay and too little recognition.

Ms. Hitchcock is just one example among thousands. Many of today's teachers engage students and foster meaningful debate through inspired, passionate, and respectful discussion on the current issues of the day. Of course, it's still not enough. We need to spend more time and resources creating a stronger culture of democratic participation. The examples of Ms. Hitchcock and many others like her show the way.

THIS ISN'T YOUR MOTHER'S CIVICS EDUCATION

Today's civics education, at least in many classrooms, looks nothing like what you might imagine, especially if you think about your own experiences from years ago. Civics education used to be, well, *boring*. There might have been a unit on separation of powers and another on checks and balances. The teacher probably lectured about the various roles of the executive, legislative, and judicial branches. Students would read from a textbook and memorize passages from the Declaration of Independence or the Gettysburg Address. You likely watched the *Schoolhouse Rock!* video "I'm Just a Bill." In the most innovative iteration for the time, the school might have held a mock election leading up to the real presidential election. And that's about it. Civics education was static. It was flat.[2]

That model, a memorization-based curriculum, emphasizes the wrong things. It's also not enough. The amount of civics education that students receive has declined from years ago. Federal and state funding for civics education has decreased, especially as schools focus more on reading and math—the tested subjects under the federal No Child Left Behind law.[3] One study found that between 2001–2007, 36 percent of school districts decreased the amount of time that elementary classes spent on social studies and civics, with underfunded schools—which disproportionately educate minority students—suffering the most.[4] Teachers are supposed to incorporate social studies education into their reading and math instruction. Go ask any teacher you know if that really works. Educators too often must "teach to the test," leaving behind the subjects that are not on standardized assessments. As education specialist Jonathan Kozol has said, "The civic education and engagement is being beaten out of kids by this tremendous emphasis on authoritarian instruction and [emphasis on] one right answer on the test. We need to empower young people to understand that the most important questions that we face in life have limitless numbers of answers and that some of those answers will be distressing to the status quo."[5]

No wonder surveys routinely show that Americans are painfully ignorant of many concepts that are vital to an engaged citizenry. Nearly a third of Americans can't identify the three branches of government (executive, legislative, and judiciary).[6] More Americans could name who wrote the songs "Beat It" and "Billie Jean" (Michael Jackson) than could identify the Bill of Rights as part of the US Constitution.[7] Forty percent thought that the Bill of Rights includes the right to vote, which it does not (though it probably should!).[8]

It should come as no surprise, then, that most people believe our current approach to civics education is a failure. They think that what little social studies curriculum is left is solely memorization of facts, not democratic engagement. The results seem to show it. At one point, more people voted for the American Idol winner than the president.[9] Can we really say that we have an engaged, informed citizenry?

Jen Hitchcock and thousands of other social studies teachers are out to prove that sentiment wrong. They are actively engaged in enlivening social studies and civics, even in spite of cuts to funding and the time allocated to these subjects. Their efforts will produce a more enlightened democracy. The key is to avoid rote memorization and passive, textbook learning. Active engagement with real-world problems will help young students learn how to think critically and debate respectfully.

"ACTION CIVICS"

Ms. Hitchcock has thought a lot about the best ways to engage students of all levels. She has taught government and civics for twelve years in Virginia and runs the website LovGov, which has resources and stories on teaching.[10] She moderates a Facebook group that includes over three thousand government teachers. She also participates in several online chats for social studies and civic educators: teachers gather on Twitter for #SSChat on Mondays and #HSGovChat on Sunday nights. As Ms. Hitchcock writes on her website, "Asking [my students] to see that civics education and engagement is perhaps not a career path, but is certainly an investment in each [of] their own future[s] is one of the most exciting parts of my profession."[11]

Jen Hitchcock, a social studies teacher in Fairfax, Virginia. [Photo by Mark Koenig, 2018.]

One of the first things Ms. Hitchcock impressed upon me during our conversation is the difference, as she sees it, between teaching "civics," at least in the traditional sense, and "government." Civics refers to the process of voting and how government works. It is procedural. Students have a hard time truly understanding how it relates directly to their everyday lives.[12]

Government, on the other hand, is innovative and exciting because it is about the substance of being an engaged citizen. To teach government, Ms. Hitchcock introduces constitutional law and philosophy. She asks her students big, relevant questions involving current events. For instance, just as Virginia's governor was easing the state's felon disenfranchisement rule in 2016 and the state's Republican legislators were objecting, Ms. Hitchcock tasked her students with researching both sides of the issue and presenting policy positions to support each argument. In another unit, Ms. Hitchcock had the students read Supreme Court majority and dissenting opinions on voter ID requirements. She then led a roundtable discussion where the students had to debate whether voter ID laws are an unconstitutional infringement on the right to vote or are a necessary and lawful means to root out voter fraud. Finally, the students wrote essays to flesh out the arguments in more detail. Ms. Hitchcock graded them solely on how well the students defended their theses with compelling evidence, not on which position they took.[13]

As Ms. Hitchcock explained to me, "today's students are really savvy in being able to form an argument. They are already doing this on social media all of the time."[14] She said that the students from Marjory Stoneman Douglas High School in Parkland, Florida, who were driving a national debate on gun rights at the time, "are like every student who I have ever had in class who knows how to do research, has a conviction, and can engage in respectful debate."[15] It's no coincidence that the Marjory Stoneman Douglas students were so articulate: their strong education had instilled skills and values they could draw upon in the wake of their tragic experience.[16]

Ms. Hitchcock is inspired daily by the stories she hears from her fellow teachers. She told me about a friend in Virginia Beach who invited the mayor, members of the Virginia House of Delegates, and the sheriff to visit her class for a bipartisan discussion on school safety and gun rights. The discussion was pointed, yet respectful. The exercise showed the students how to engage in civil discourse about a hot-button and emotional topic.

Education experts, like Professor Meira Levinson of Harvard, refer to this dynamic classroom engagement as "action civics."[17] Students ask compelling questions, look to history and evidence for ways to solve a problem, communicate the results in a meaningful way, and then take informed action. There are tons of examples. Harry Boyte, a professor at Ausburg University in Minneapolis, created an initiative called Public Achievement through a partnership with the mayor of St. Paul to engage students in solving real problems. As he wrote to me, through Public Achievement "young people are citizen co-creators, not citizens in waiting."[18]

YOUTH-LED CIVIC PROJECTS THAT CREATE REAL POLICY CHANGE

If you know anything about the Washington, DC, public schools, it's probably that they have a fairly poor reputation.[19] Yet the work of their social studies teachers is downright inspiring. They are showing students how to produce real change that has direct benefits for their schools and communities.

Scott Abbott is the Director of Social Studies for the Washington, DC, public schools. He spoke glowingly about the various initiatives of the district's social studies teachers, showing that even the most cash-strapped school can make a big difference.[20] DC completely revamped its social studies curriculum to adopt the C3 framework, which focuses on using social studies to instill values and skills for college, career, and civic life (the three Cs).[21] The program sets out desired competencies for all students, similar to the well-known Common Core curriculum but specifically for social studies. The guiding principle is that social studies should focus on the process of inquiry. Students must learn how to come up with a plan, gather sources and evidence, answer questions, communicate the conclusions, and—perhaps most importantly—take action. Kathy Swan, a professor in the College of Education at the University of Kentucky who was the lead writer for the C3 framework, explained that "what we are trying to do is create citizens who know how to approach the news and consume data and information."[22] Or as Scott Abbott told me, "Teaching social studies through an inquiry-based model will prepare students to engage critically and take action on issues that are important to them."[23]

Every social studies unit in the DC schools culminates in a perfor-mance task that the students must complete. Students are required to take action, such as going to speak with policy makers. The school district also partners with the Mikva Challenge, a nonprofit, nonpartisan organization that fosters youth engagement—its tagline is "democracy is a verb"—to foster an action civics approach, whereby students research a real problem and come up with a practical solution.[24]

Abbott is an administrator, so he helps to implement these policies from the top-down. How does that impact the teachers and students in classrooms all over the city? The stories, once again, are simply inspiring.

Abbott proudly told me about one school, Luke C. Moore High School, where students identified a significant problem among the school's popu-lation: many students were arriving late to school on a regular basis. The class decided to tackle the problem head-on. After researching the issue, they learned that some students simply had a hard time finding reliable transportation in the morning, especially because students at this school came from all over the city, not just the local neighborhood. So they went to school officials and the DC City Council to advocate for students to have free public transportation. They were successful. Every DC resident between the ages of five and twenty-one who attends school in the District can now obtain a Kids Ride Free card for the city's metro and bus system. Abbott said the move has helped more students arrive at school on time.[25]

At HD Woodson High, a teacher named Laura Fuchs used a program called "We the People: The Citizen and the Constitution" to simulate testi-mony before a legislative committee.[26] The teacher had her students research one of six constitutional problems and then prepare mock testimony about the issue. The students delivered that testimony and responded to questions before a panel of "legislators" drawn from the community. Finally, the students spoke before the real DC Board of Education. In another example, a teacher at Dunbar High School, Oumar Diallo, engaged students in a simulation in which they crafted a proposed law on gun safety in schools. That led to an invite from Mayor Muriel Bowser for a roundtable discussion on the topic.[27]

In all of these examples, students are tackling real problems while learning how to debate civilly with one another. They are quite literally practicing how to be engaged citizens.

Although these stories from DC involve high school classes, action civics education is important in elementary and middle schools as well. Many resources are available to foster engaged instruction. For instance, check out the "We the Civics Kids" fourth grade curriculum from the National Constitution Center.[28] The goal of the eight-lesson program is to allow students to "practice thinking and acting responsibly while participating in real-life problem solving situations and practicing democratic deliberation."[29] In the end, "each student will find his/her voice and work to be a change agent in his/her community."[30] What fun!

YES, IT'S OK FOR TEACHERS TO DISCUSS POLITICS

Jen Hitchcock engages her twelfth graders with the big issues of the day. They discuss whether it's good or bad for our country to be in a state of perpetual campaigns. They cover campaign finance and whether special interests have too much power over our elections, balanced with the right to free speech. They analyze gerrymandering. These are issues that face everyone, regardless of party or ideology. Ms. Hitchcock is ever vigilant not to impart her own political views, desiring solely to foster an open discussion. She frequently acts as a devil's advocate and counters whichever side her students take. She grades on how well students make their arguments, not on their outcomes or viewpoints. As she says, "these topics are skill-based. They need to know how to tackle real-world issues that are happening in front of them in a respectful way, even if they disagree."[31]

Teacher Brittany Marrs of Magnolia, Texas, is also not shy about invoking politics in her social studies curriculum. In addition to her regular teaching activities, Mrs. Marrs sponsors a group called the Student Leadership Program. The students in that group put together presentations for the high school's seniors about political participation and civic responsibility. The effort culminates in the school providing assistance to all eligible students to register to vote.[32] In 2016, the group helped to register about two hundred of the three hundred eligible students in the school. As Mrs. Marrs told the *Houston Chronicle*, "It's not just about voter registration, it's encouraging life-long citizen participation. That's what we strived for in this initiative, getting students excited to go register and starting those habits young to create a better Magnolia."[33]

Benjamin Fabian of Douglas S. Freeman High School in Henrico, Virginia, along with a coworker, developed a project for his students to simulate the legislative process. The students had to choose an interest group to research and then draft a law that the interest group would favor. Students could then contact lawmakers to see if the legislators would put the idea onto their agenda.[34]

Michael Martirone of Egg Harbor Township, New Jersey, invites judges, ambassadors, congressional candidates, and members of Congress to speak to his class, which, he says, allows his students "to more clearly develop their points of view and see a practical application of our content."[35] Trish Everett of Pine Crest School in Fort Lauderdale, Florida, also invites guest speakers, particularly alumni of the school who are involved in public and community service. She says that these speakers can inspire the next generation of leaders, especially to demonstrate "the value of persistence and personal connection [and] that the investment of energy and enthusiasm is worth it."[36]

These examples show why just teaching facts about American democracy—reciting the preamble to the Constitution, for instance—is woefully insufficient. As education expert Peter Levine of Tufts University explains, "[d]eliberation is one of the advanced skills necessary in a democracy. In courses and schools where 'civic education' devolves into learning a lot of facts about the official political system, students don't learn such skills. They may even forget the factual details that they have crammed for tests."[37]

Teachers in Scotland feel the same way. After Scotland lowered the voting age to sixteen, teachers of modern studies—the equivalent of civics or social studies—saw it as their responsibility to engage these new voters. Lessons went beyond bland lectures on how government works and instead engaged students in the political issues of the day. Political party leaders and candidates of all sides came into the schools to speak with students. The guiding principle was to invite candidates of all parties and to foster respectful debate.

Some teachers used their students' new political power to encourage registration and voting. One school tracked its success: at the beginning of the six-week curriculum, only eight out of forty-five 16- and 17-year-olds in the two modern studies classes were registered to vote. The modern studies teachers conducted a lesson on registration and then had the students register (if they wanted to). Right after registering, about half of them said they now planned to vote in the upcoming local elections. Then the instructors taught a six-week curriculum on the issues of the campaign. For example, one teacher brought in every piece of campaign mail he received and had the students analyze each one, debating its message, effect, and truthfulness. The teachers also conducted a mock election using real voting machines they borrowed from election officials. After the actual election, only eight students in an anonymous survey said they did *not* vote. Active classroom engagement on campaign issues flipped the numbers from only eight registered to only eight who did not participate.[38] I traveled to Scotland in 2017 to learn why lowering the voting age worked so well there. One person's comment said it all: "Democracy is a muscle, and you can't just learn about how it works; you have to actually use it, even in school."[39]

But what about political indoctrination in schools? There's little reason to worry. Teachers are not all Democrats or Republicans and they don't all have the same viewpoint. In one representative survey of K-12 teachers nationwide, 41 percent identified as Democrats, 27 percent said they are Republican, and 30 percent described themselves as independent.[40] Further, plenty of resources are available to ensure a robust inquiry without indoctrination. To highlight just one, a pair of education professors wrote about how to foster informed political debate in their book *The Political Classroom*.[41] I encourage every educator, parent, or interested citizen to check it out. The book provides resources and case studies to demonstrate how best to promote youth civic engagement in today's harried political times.

HER HONOR ORDERS CIVICS EDUCATION

Sandra Day O'Connor made history as the first woman to serve on the US Supreme Court. Although she stepped down from the bench in 2006, she did not slow down. In 2009, Justice O'Connor launched an interactive website, iCivics (www.icivics.org), to promote a fun way to reinvigorate civics education.[42] In recounting why she focused on civics education after she retired from the Supreme Court, she explained, "The only reason we have public school education in America is because in the early days of the country, our leaders thought we had to teach our young generation about citizenship . . . that obligation never ends. If we don't take every generation of young people and make sure they understand that they are an essential part of government, we won't survive."[43] Over 200,000 teachers in all fifty states use iCivics lessons and games in their classrooms. The website has an array of games for all ages and grade levels; interactive games include "Do I Have a Right?," "Argument Wars," "Court Quest," "People's Pie"—where players must control the federal government's budget—and my favorite: "Cast Your Vote."[44] Go play some of these games—they are fun!

The beauty of iCivics is that the games engage students through a medium that they fully understand. Video games are a common part of the lives of today's youth. Students *love* them. The iCivics lessons and games are easy for teachers to incorporate into their instruction. By changing the focus from rote memorization to interactive inquiry and by invoking new forms of technology, we can once again create a generation of engaged citizens.

Justice O'Connor's advocacy echoes another Supreme Court justice with an enduring legacy, Thurgood Marshall, who was the first African American to serve on the Court. In a case about public education, Justice Marshall wrote these compelling words (albeit in dissent):

> Of particular importance is the relationship between education and the political process. . . . Education serves the essential function of instilling in our young an understanding of and appreciation for the principles and operation of our governmental processes. Education may instill the interest and provide the tools necessary for political discourse and debate. Indeed, it has frequently been suggested that education is the dominant factor affecting political consciousness and participation.[45]

USING OUR SCHOOLS ON ELECTION DAY

Growing up, I remember Election Day well. Our school transformed into a polling place and adults would filter in throughout the day. We didn't have gym class because the town was using the gymnasium for a precinct. Besides missing gym, school went on as normal, but there was definitely a different vibe in the air. After school I would accompany my mom to the voting booth as she voted.

These days, several places close schools on Election Day so that election officials can use the facilities as polling places. Other jurisdictions use churches or community centers. Fewer and fewer schools even run mock elections, which should be a regular part of the curriculum.

Here's a better idea: let's use the schools and actually engage students during the voting process itself. This is the norm at the Democracy Prep Public Schools in New York, New Jersey, DC, Baton Rouge, and Las Vegas. On Election Day, elementary and middle school students run a Get Out the Vote campaign by standing on busy street corners near the school while wearing bright yellow T-shirts that say, "I can't vote, but you can!"[46] All schools should expand upon this example. Why not teach a civics class and then have high school students help out at polling sites, perhaps answering questions from voters as they wait in line? Orange County, California, allows high school students to work as poll workers.[47] So does Texas.[48] This is not to say that students should run the precincts without supervision, but we can certainly engage them in the process even before they are eligible to vote.

CIVICS EDUCATION IS NOT JUST FOR KIDS

Civics education should not stop at high school graduation. It's a lifelong commitment. We need more groups and organizations focused on educating adults. We also need adults to recognize the importance of fostering conversations about civics and democracy among their friends and families.

Since 2010, Orange County, California, has offered a free Election Academy for adults to teach them about the election process. The six-class program includes instruction on becoming a candidate, the ballot printing process, security issues, counting the vote, and certifying the winner. Although candidates and campaign workers obviously benefit from these classes, almost half of the participants in recent years have been interested members of the public with no other connection to politics. The cost to the county is minimal because the instructors are salaried members of the county's election office or outside speakers. To date, over 250 people have taken the class. That may sound like a small number, but imagine if counties all over the country replicated this model. Neal Kelly, from the Orange County Registrar of Voters, encourages other election officials to create a similar program: "The public is hungry for this info, and now, more than ever (in this climate) is the time ripe for us to push out as much 'fact based knowledge' as possible."[49]

The city of Staunton, Virginia, which is about forty-five minutes west of Charlottesville, takes a broader approach, offering a course that covers all aspects of local governance.[50] The twelve-week Citizen University, which meets for two hours each week, includes sessions on the city budget, voting and elections, the court system, tourism, community development, and more. Other cities should emulate this model.

Voter guides are also useful educational tools. Most chapters of the League of Women Voters issue nonpartisan voter guides that explain state and local elections. There is also a push to improve the language of ballot propositions. Rhode Island, for instance, has focused on simplifying ballot language so that average voters can better understand what they are deciding.[51] Hennepin County, Minnesota, has a "plain language coordinator," who reported that calls to the county's elections division dropped after the county revamped its online instructions for absentee voting to make them easier to understand.[52] Andrew Richter of Crystal, Minnesota, took on a similar task: cleaning up the city's code so that it was readable and understandable. He led a group of volunteers that culled through the code, chapter by chapter, to suggest revisions for the city council to adopt that would help everyday people understand the city's laws. Sure, the work was dry, he said, but it has produced meaningful policy changes and, according to the mayor, a "much more user-friendly city."[53]

We must also model good behavior for our children, bringing them with us to vote and talking to them about politics, policy, and civic engagement. My own kids have never missed an election. I hope I'm not outing them for voter fraud in admitting this, but they even "voted twice" one year, accompanying me in the morning and my wife in the afternoon! As Mrs. Marrs, the teacher from Magnolia, Texas, said, "teens participate more when their parents discuss politics at home. I think adults need to make more of an effort to concern themselves with local, state, and national politics."[54] Scott Abbott of the DC public schools echoes this sentiment: "If we want students to participate in active, civic engagement, then we need to model that behavior ourselves."[55] It may sound cliché, but we should have discussions about politics and civic issues at the dinner table; we should reach out to younger family members and include them in the conversation; we must show them why civic participation is so important. No age is too young—or too old—to start fostering an informed, engaged citizen.

WHAT CAN YOU DO?

"This sounds wonderful!" I hope you are thinking. "Look at these great examples of dedicated teachers and innovative strategies to better educate our young people and our overall citizenry about the importance of democratic participation!"

The point of this chapter, of course, is to highlight these positive developments in civics education. But it is not enough. In fact, social studies and civics education are under attack. There is woefully little funding. Education is unequal, such that schools with large minority populations tend to have inferior instruction and fewer opportunities to engage in action civics.[56] Test scores drive teacher accountability, which in turn requires a myopic focus on reading and math. The problem is the worst in elementary schools, arguably the time when we can most instill a culture of civics exploration and democratic participation. Indeed, few elementary school teachers have the time, resources, or encouragement from school officials to conduct separate civics lessons. Instead, they must incorporate the concepts within reading or math, and often all they can do is tell students about the three branches of government—which is plainly insufficient. Scott Abbott of the DC public schools thinks that most people don't even realize how much social studies is marginalized in elementary schools today. Yet declining social studies instruction, he notes, actually impacts reading scores as well.[57] He pointed me to numerous studies showing that when students have background knowledge of the topic of a text, they comprehend it at much higher levels.[58]

In addition, there's an active movement to devolve our high school civics education to a testing-based model that requires the memorization of facts, which comes at the expense of inquiry-based exploration. Several states now require high school students to pass the US naturalization test that immigrants must take to gain citizenship.[59] Having a basic understanding of our government is of course a noble cause. But that cannot be the only thing we do to improve civics education. There is a danger that legislatures will enact laws requiring students to pass this civics exam and think they have done enough to address the problem. That approach, however, would just incentivize teaching to the test and memorization instead of devoting meaningful resources to inquiry and debate.

Instead, we need to encourage civics education throughout the curriculum, from kindergarten all the way up through high school graduation, and beyond. There is room, even within our focus on reading and math or STEM (science, technology, engineering, and math), to add meaningful civics and government instruction. If states want to mandate better civics education, then they should follow Massachusetts's lead, which in 2018 passed a bill to require all students to complete a nonpartisan, inquiry-based civics project, either individually or in a group.[60] We must not lose sight of the main point of public education, which historically was to create an educated citizenry. Or as education expert Peter Levine explained, "The civics classroom is an excellent place to learn how to have a civil and responsible political conversation with people who disagree with you. And we know one way to boost young people's voting and their understanding of the political system is to teach them civics while they're still in high school."[61] That should be a primary goal, especially in today's political environment.

Improved civics education will produce a better-informed electorate and can lead to higher voter turnout. One researcher found that high schools with a "strong civic climate"—where at least 85 percent of the students listed voting as a component of good citizenship—sustained a higher voter turnout rate up to fifteen years after graduation.[62] That finding is particularly significant given that eighteen- to twenty-nine-year-olds have the lowest turnout rates among all age groups. As the researcher, Notre Dame professor David E. Campbell, explained, "What matters is that an adolescent's community, defined in this case as the high school, is populated with a high percentage of peers who express their belief that voting is an indicator of good citizenship."[63] Voting is a community-based activity, fostered through a value structure that emphasizes the importance of democratic participation.

Finally, we must trust our teachers and invest in our public schools. We must also trust our young citizens. Jessie Logan, a high school teacher in

Yorktown, Virginia, wrote to me that she wished the public "would recognize that our high school students do have something to say that matters. They often DO know what they're talking about, they have done their research, and they do think for themselves. So many people assume that our kids are just lazy teenagers, and most of them are anything but that. They're driven, focused, and they want to change the world. We as adults just need to listen and see where they want to go."[64]

What tangible action can you take? Call your school board member to learn about the kind of civics education that is happening in local classrooms. Write to your legislators to demand better funding for this curriculum. Share this chapter with them so they can see the kinds of innovative programs that are possible. Visit iCivics.org with your child and play one of the games together.

We have the tools. We have dedicated teachers. We have eager students. But we need the resources, the public will, and the fortitude to expand this push for a renewed culture of democratic participation. The benefits can reshape our democracy.

CHAPTER 11

HOW TO COMBAT "FAKE NEWS"

Patrick Marley does not have a law degree—at least formally. A reporter for the *Milwaukee Journal Sentinel* in Madison, Wisconsin, Marley has learned the law through baptism-by-fire, covering the state's various election disputes. That has entailed a deep dive into legal doctrine. Indeed, much of his work requires reading legislative text, legal briefs, and court orders. He must then figure out what is most important and translate it for a general audience, all under a tight deadline.

It's a job that Marley relishes, and here's why: he knows that he is actively helping to educate the public about the right to vote and our democratic process, providing accountability and transparency to our governmental institutions.[1] This is the exact opposite of "fake news." Reporters, particularly from local media, are vital to the protection and expansion of voting rights. The effect of their coverage is paramount to create a more inclusive and transparent democracy.

THE IMPACT OF LOCAL REPORTERS

The significance of media outlets to foster voting rights and a flourishing democracy is nothing new. Thomas Jefferson explained the importance of the media to the new government he helped to create: "[T]he basis of our governments being the opinion of the people, the very first object should be to keep that right; and were it left to me to decide whether we should have a government without newspapers, or newspapers without a government, I should not hesitate a moment to prefer the latter."[2] (To be fair, once he became president, Jefferson had a much different view of critical news coverage, writing in a letter, "Nothing can now be believed which is seen in a newspaper."[3]) The media are absolutely essential to democracy. That's why freedom of the press is a central component of the Bill of Rights, listed within the First Amendment to the US Constitution.

Media coverage can influence the public and affect policy. The Selma-to-Montgomery march in 1965 led to the passage of the Voting Rights Act, in part helped by news images and television clips of violence at the march that outraged the public and brought the issue of minority voting rights to the forefront.[4] Media scrutiny of the Florida recount during the 2000 presidential election led to greater transparency and a better understanding of how election law can influence electoral outcomes, ultimately prompting Congress to pass a new law (the Help America Vote Act) to improve the voting process. But these were big, sensational stories. The media also have an important—although less heralded—role in every election to illuminate issues surrounding voting rights within local communities.

Patrick Marley knows this well. Tall, clean shaven, with brown hair and a pleasant demeanor, Marley is one of the main storytellers of Wisconsin's political drama, from Republican governor Scott Walker's battle against unions and the failed recall effort against him to the ongoing debate over voter ID laws in the swing state. As Marley sees it, one of his most important roles is to educate voters. After Wisconsin enacted a new strict voter ID requirement, Marley chronicled the law's tortuous path through the court system and helped instruct voters on how to comply with the latest judicial interpretation. As Marley explained to me, bureaucrats aren't very good about breaking down a rule into its crucial elements so that nonexperts can understand them, and the courts' various decisions had made the situation even more complicated.[5] Many voters told Marley that they felt they had "entered a black hole" in their efforts to comply with the voter ID rule.[6] Marley recognized that he could serve the public by offering an easy-to-understand primer on what the law required. In this way, Marley is the ultimate translator.

There are few others who will do this crucial work. Although the national press covered the Wisconsin voter ID debate as part of an overall storyline on voter suppression across the country, few national reporters included in their stories the complicated details on the seven forms of identification allowed under state law, with its various exceptions and intricacies. The national media's primary audience, after all, is the entire country, not the just the voters on the ground in Wisconsin. A local reporter, by contrast, has the proper incentives and opportunity to wade through the nuances of the law and highlight the impact it will have on people throughout the community. They have relationships with the key players— election workers, local clerks, and individual voters. They serve a watchdog function, keeping a skeptical eye on government officials. Many people likely would not have understood how to comply with the state's new voter ID provision without Marley's careful reporting. By educating the public, Marley quite literally enfranchised voters.

Patrick Marley of the *Milwaukee Journal Sentinel*. [Photo by Andy Manis for the *Milwaukee Journal Sentinel*.]

Reporters also can help to ensure that a state is not erroneously preventing people from voting. In 2016, the Arkansas secretary of state sent a list of individuals flagged as felons to all of the state's county clerk offices and directed the county clerks to remove these individuals from the voter rolls. But many of these people had regained their right to vote after completing their prison sentences and parole. The list of felons the state had sent to the counties was wildly inaccurate and included people who had regained their voting rights or never lost them in the first place. In some counties, up to two-thirds of the names on the list were actually eligible voters.[7]

Benji Hardy of the *Arkansas Times* was one of the local reporters on the beat. He wrote an in-depth profile of various voters who received notices that they were no longer on the voter rolls, putting a personal face on the problem.[8] This was not an abstract issue: Hardy's story explained how valid voters like Bo Ingram of Cabot—who had regained his voting rights years earlier after finishing his sentence and parole—would face unnecessary hurdles and potential disenfranchisement because of the voter purge. "It came as a rude surprise," Hardy wrote, "for Ingram to be told almost a decade later that his rights were being rescinded again" after he had properly regained them.[9] *Arkansas Times* reporters then followed up with all seventy-five counties in the state to determine how they were responding to the inaccurate felon lists, leading many of these offices to recheck their records.[10] The local media coverage added pressure on Secretary of State Mark Martin to respond. He eventually wrote a letter to county clerks that "strongly recommended" they roll back any blanket deletions based on the previous faulty felon list. As Hardy and his colleague Max Brantley noted, "It's good the secretary of state's office is finally affirming what we've been saying all along: err on the side of the voter and don't disenfranchise anyone unless you're absolutely sure they should be removed."[11] In reflecting upon the impact of his work on this issue, Hardy wrote to me, "I do feel that local media coverage (both from the *Arkansas Times* and from other media outlets in the state) helped pressure the secretary of state to send the follow-up letter. Our staff also called every county clerk in the state, which I hope persuaded some they needed to vet their data more carefully."[12]

Local journalists are also vital to ensure a smooth Election Day. In particular, they can alert election officials to problems that are occurring while people are casting their votes. In 2016, six media organizations created Electionland, a virtual newsroom to cover voting rights issues across the country.[13] Partners, which included several news outlets, reporters, and journalism schools, shared tips of election issues through the platform, which local reporters then pursued. Over a thousand journalists and students participated in the project. They searched social media sites for various terms they thought people might use to describe their own voting experience, including common misspellings of those words. The team verified the accuracy of these reports and then sent tips to local reporters in that area. As *Houston Chronicle* reporter Matt Demsey explained, "To know what specific areas are having problems and to be able to send reporters to those specific areas is so much more effective and efficient than saying, 'Go out and go to a bunch of polling places and find voters who've had issues voting.' This way, you're starting with specifics. You're starting from the idea of voter complaints."[14]

During Texas's early voting period, for instance, Electionland received word that poll workers in Southeastern Houston were not allowing some people to vote based on the state's strict voter ID law. After receiving this tip, *Houston Chronicle* reporters went to the polling places and witnessed incorrect signage and poll workers giving incomplete information to voters about the ID requirement. Poll workers were telling voters waiting in line to take out their IDs without informing them of an alternative method available: under a recent court order, voters without a compliant identification could sign a "reasonable impediment" declaration saying that they faced a hurdle in obtaining an ID. The *Chronicle* published a story that highlighted these inaccuracies.[15] In the swirl of this activity, the county clerk sent a memo to poll workers advising them how they may ask for an ID so as to keep the "reasonable impediment" option open. This collective investigative journalism helped to streamline the process for the media and enhanced their ability to make a difference in ensuring voters did not face inappropriate barriers.

There are lots of reporters just like Patrick Marley (whose Twitter handle is @patrickdmarley), Benji Hardy (@unbenji) (now a freelancer in Arkansas), and the others I have mentioned already, dedicated to their craft and insistent upon accurate, timely election coverage that assists the public. Ari Berman (@AriBerman) of *Mother Jones*, Jessica Huseman (@JessicaHuseman) of *ProPublica*, Jonathan Lai (@Elaijuh) of the *Philadelphia Inquirer*, Sam Levine (@srl) of *Huffington Post*, Bryan Lowry (@BryanLowry3) of the *Kansas City Star*, Seema Mehta (@LATSeema) of the *Los Angeles Times*, Jonathan Oosting (@jonathanoosting) of the *Detroit News*, Jon Ralston (@RalstonReports) of the *Nevada Independent*, Max Smith (@amaxsmith) of *WTOP* in DC, and Sherman Smith (@sherman_news) of the *Topeka Capital-Journal* all come to mind. There are plenty of others, at publications of all sizes, who perform a vital service by impartially educating the public, calling out election officials for voting rights restrictions, and highlighting pro-voter policies.

COUNTERING LIES WITH THE TRUTH

The independent news media also can help to correct misstatements about policy or even the voting process itself. Donald Trump seems to think that if he says something enough times, people will believe it. Nonpartisan news organizations serve a vital role in correcting the record. PolitiFact, for example, exists specifically to fact-check politicians' statements. When Donald Trump said that there were three to five million illegal votes cast in the 2016 election, websites like PolitiFact were on top of the lie immediately.[16] Given that some politicians would use this false assertion to push restrictive voting laws for political gain, PolitiFact's analysis offered an important counterweight.[17] Trump's falsehoods breed distrust toward our electoral institutions, a dangerous attribute of a well-functioning democracy. Websites such as PolitiFact can therefore help, quite literally, to sustain our democratic processes. We need to trust and widely disseminate these truth-correcting stories.

Local media can serve the same role. As just one example, the *Florida Times-Union* editorial board wrote an article titled "Voter Fraud Claims are Often Based on Flawed Analysis," highlighting academic studies on voter fraud and concluding that "voter impersonation, which has led to so many state voter ID laws, is the least common type of fraud."[18] The general public usually does not read academic studies. Translating the findings for everyday people can facilitate an honest debate on how best to structure our elections.

Remember: we can and should trust local reporters. Few are overtly biased; in fact, most reporters I know make it a priority to remain as impartial as possible. I speak with many reporters throughout the year and I rarely think they are pushing their own agenda. It's also obvious when they are. Of course, most news anchors on MSNBC or Fox News have a particular partisan viewpoint, but that is their very role. Local mainstream print and television reporters, by contrast, pride themselves on their impartiality. We can trust them to tell us the truth.

Donald Trump may call news he dislikes "fake," but his attacks do nothing to change the transparency the media brings to his administration and our election process. On the contrary, the news media are indispensable. They shed light on difficulties voters may encounter. They put a public face on abstract problems buried in legislative nuance. They uncover situations in which voters may be turned away. They affirmatively encourage people to vote. In short, we could not run our elections fairly and freely without input, insight, and illumination from the media.

INADVERTENTLY INFLUENCING THE LAW

In addition to their role as educators and government watchdogs, sometimes reporters actually impact the law itself through their journalism, although that's rarely their goal. Instead, news reports on voting rights provide both transparency and information that can force officials to alter election processes for the better.

That was one of the results of Patrick Marley's reporting in 2016. Marley had heard from some voters that certain county election officials in Wisconsin had rejected numerous absentee ballots based on a strict interpretation of state law. The problem was that the witnesses to the absentee ballots had not listed their own complete address on the envelope, as Wisconsin law seemed to require. The legislature had added the address specification earlier in the year, tucked into a bigger piece of voting legislation, but many voters were unaware of this rule. Often witnesses to absentee ballots had put their street address but had failed to list a municipality—and many of the witnesses lived in the same household as the voter! Marley wrote a story about these voters, titled "Absentee Ballots at Risk of Being Tossed."[19] That story shed light on the problem, which was harming elderly voters the most. A week later, the state elections commission ruled that county clerks must add the witness's municipality to the envelope if they could determine that information.[20] Marley's reporting, then, helped to ensure that the state did not toss out hundreds if not thousands of votes. Without a local reporter highlighting the issue, which forced the elections commission to clarify the requirement, it is quite possible that county clerks would have too strictly construed the law and invalidated these ballots, ultimately disenfranchising valid voters.

In another instance, Marley's reporting helped to influence litigation over Wisconsin's voter ID law. As recounted in chapter 6, grassroots organizer Molly McGrath recorded her interactions with DMV workers as she helped voters comply with the state's new strict voter ID requirement. McGrath sent Marley these recordings, along with the ones her mom had made in other parts of the state. Marley then wrote a story to highlight the fact that DMV workers were giving voters inaccurate information.[21] The judge presiding over the case about the law saw the story and ordered the state to respond. This was extremely rare. Judges hardly ever issue an order based on news reporting, as opposed to legal arguments from the parties. Thanks to Marley's exposure of the problem, the judge ordered the state to provide more accurate information to the public.[22]

CHAMPIONING CIVIC ENGAGEMENT

One of the most important roles of the media is to educate voters and encourage citizens to become engaged in our democracy. Reporters, many of whom are local celebrities, have a platform in their community. Anastasiya Bolton understands this well. She was a television journalist for channel 9, the NBC affiliate in Denver (she's now a journalist in Houston). Bolton is from Russia and became an American citizen in 2008. She immediately registered and voted in her first US election that year. Eight years later, right before the 2016 election, she produced a video essay for channel 9 to highlight the importance of the right to vote.[23] She broke down into tears on camera as she explained,

> It makes me mad when people are cavalier with this privilege. When they say it's not important, or they won't participate because they're mad and nothing will change. I'm passionate about our democracy. I am excited to cast my ballot—because I can't wait to be heard. I know it matters. I'm certain it will count.[24]

No doubt her words inspired others. She received tons of messages of support, with people saying that her tears moved them to tears as well.[25] Numerous viewers told her that they would show the video essay to their relatives who didn't plan to vote in an effort to change their mind.[26]

The media also can help to promote ideas that will improve the voting process itself. For instance, one of the keys to success in the debate over online voter registration in Florida, discussed in chapter 3, was that the media portrayed the idea in a favorable light. That did not occur by happenstance. The nonpartisan Florida State Association of Supervisors of Elections—a group of all of the county election heads in the state—worked with the media to explain the merits of the reform. The county clerks articulated how online voter registration would make the registration process easier, more secure, and less costly. The media were able to tell that story to the public, leading legislators on both sides of the aisle to support the idea.[27]

Media outlets can partner with advocacy organizations to reach specific constituencies and encourage civic participation. For instance, both Houston-area Spanish language television stations, Telemundo and Univision, partnered with the organization Mi Familia Vota on voter outreach before the 2016 election. The stations sponsored billboards in Latino-majority neighborhoods, reaching over five million people.[28] Telemundo also helped with Mi Familia Vota's voter registration drives, sending TV personalities and providing trinkets as giveaways, making the events flashier than normal.[29] Once again, there was a tangible benefit: according to Carlos Duarte of Mi Familia Vota, five hundred young people registered in two days at a voter registration drive at the University of Houston, as compared to a typical yield of around thirty new registrants.[30] That's hundreds of new voters who can start the habit of voting early in their adulthood.

Newspapers also can promote voter registration through their own platforms. In August 2018, the *Ithaca Times*, a weekly publication available from newspaper boxes around town, printed a New York voter registration application on the front page of its paper that readers could complete, cut out, and mail in.[31] This service was particularly useful for students arriving in town to attend one of the area's three colleges. Marshall Hopkins, the Production Director/Designer for the *Ithaca Times*, explained that offering voter registration and promoting democratic engagement "matters more than having our newspaper's logo on the front for a week."[32] As the registration deadline nears, media outlets also can direct their online visitors to voter registration websites for their state.

Little by little, these efforts can have a significant impact. Collectively, they can reshape our democracy.

SOCIAL MEDIA HAS MADE US ALL JOURNALISTS

Although media outlets have the loudest microphones, there's a role for all of us to promote positive voting rights to our own listeners. In this age of social media, we are all citizen-journalists. We must take that responsibility seriously.

Molly Neck is a lawyer in San Antonio, Texas. She took advantage of Texas's early voting period, casting her ballot on October 24, 2016. As someone who follows both politics and law, she knew that a federal court had ordered the state to ease up on its voter ID requirement and provide an exception to voters who did not have an ID due to a reasonable impediment. But when Neck went to her polling place, she noticed outdated signs saying that all voters needed a photo ID, without exception. She took a picture of the sign and tweeted, "poll workers still using old sign the federal judge ruled against, officials telling everyone they need a photo ID."[33] She tagged the *Texas Tribune*. Other people then began to report similar issues at other polling places.

Neck's tweet led to local and national coverage of the issue. The *Texas Tribune* did a story, as did the *New York Times*.[34] The media explained how some polling stations were still not complying with judicial orders on the state's voter ID law. The result: greater exposure to the issue and the removal of the outdated signs. Indeed, the Texas secretary of state's official Twitter feed responded to Neck's tweet: "Posters were updated following judge's order. This one is being removed."[35] A state judge also formally ordered Texas to replace the signs.[36]

Similarly, Maria Taggert, also of Texas, took to social media to tell her story of poll worker intimidation while she voted. She explained in a lengthy Facebook post that the poll worker "was being extremely rude and physically in my face" as she requested the reasonable impediment declaration form for not having a Texas photo ID.[37] She said that the poll worker questioned her about why she did not have an ID and hovered over her shoulder as she filled out the form. The law does not direct poll workers to take either action. They are simply supposed to provide the form if the voter does not present a valid ID. They may not ask, as the poll worker did of Taggert, *why* she did not have a passport or other identification. This poll worker seemed to be trying to intimidate her, perhaps, she thought, because she is female and a minority. As she lamented, "How many people have been intimidated by this guy, and left without voting?"[38] A woman in line behind her said that this poll worker did the same thing to her the day before and didn't let her vote. Over five thousand people viewed the post and dozens shared it on their own Facebook pages. Taggert also filed complaints with the Texas secretary of state and the Department of Justice. A DOJ lawyer called her back within an hour of her complaint and opened an investigation, indicating that the poll worker would be removed or at least reprimanded.[39] This all occurred several days before Election Day, during the early voting period, so Taggert's wide dissemination of her story likely helped to reduce the impact of this rogue poll worker for hundreds of other voters.

Of course, if the 2016 election taught us anything, it's that we cannot believe everything we read on the internet. The rise of "fake news"—false reporting presented as legitimate information, often from non-reputable sources—is alarming. We must take what we read with a grain of salt and consider the trustworthiness of the source. But that does not mean we can denigrate any story as "fake news" simply because we disagree with it. We must train a skeptical eye on online news stories from unknown sources while still trusting the mainstream news media and our fellow citizens to inform us of what is happening as we vote. And we should provide tips to reporters so that they may follow-up and uncover issues on the ground when they occur.

WE MUST ALL BE PART OF THE SOLUTION

The media industry is struggling. Local newspapers' ad revenue and circulation are down.[40] So is viewership of local TV.[41] Layoffs and budget cuts are a common part of the trade. Although cable TV viewership has increased and more Americans receive their news from digital sources,[42] news organizations are hurting overall, especially at the local level.

This development should concern anyone who champions the ideals of the right to vote and our democratic process. As this chapter has recounted, local journalists are crucial to uncover and explain voting rights issues and encourage greater voter participation. But there are fewer reporters, with less time and limited resources, to do this work. That harms our democracy.

What can we do? For one, we must support both local and national journalism with our eyeballs and our wallets. Democracy depends on the news media. The *Washington Post*, recognizing this reality, adopted a new slogan soon after Donald Trump assumed the presidency: "Democracy Dies in Darkness." Reporters are people who need to earn a living. Media companies rely on money from subscriptions, as well as ad revenue, to fund their efforts. If we all spent a little more money on our local newspapers, they could flourish and continue to serve a significant public role for our communities. "No matter the tactics we pursue," says Joyce Dehli, the Pulitzer Prize board co-chair, "our starting point must be an affirmation of the importance of deeply reported, professional local journalism as an essential force in our democracy."[43]

Or as *New York Times* Executive Editor Dean Baquet said in explaining the importance of the media's watchdog function all over the country, "We have to figure out the Buffalos, the New Orleans, the Atlantas . . . so if a school board does something important in a suburb of New Orleans or Atlanta, it's covered."[44]

A recent study showed that individuals who regularly vote in local elections have stronger "local news habits" than nonvoters.[45] Although the study did not prove causation—it is not clear if voting makes someone pay attention to local news or if paying attention to local news encourages voting—the two are highly correlated. Local media play a crucial role in civic engagement. As the study found, "[a]ttachment to one's community and regular voting in local elections connect most strongly to local news habits."[46] To sustain our democracy, then, we need to double down on our commitment to local media, and in turn demand that the media focus on substantive, educational journalism.

In addition, journalists rely on individual voters to tell their stories. They do not necessarily know where problems are happening. On Election Day, many reporters wander around outside of polling places to see if there are any issues. That is not a particularly good use of their time. With budget cuts, there are fewer reporters to do this work. If they know where to go, who to talk to, and what to investigate, then they can report on issues much faster and more easily. Reporters are often looking for sources to tell them about their experience while voting. If you encounter an issue, contact your local reporter.

Our social media-dependent society also needs individuals to share their experiences. Use social media platforms to highlight how Election Day went for you—good or bad. Election officials pay attention. As former Denver county clerk Amber McReynolds explained, voters are their customers, and their goal is to improve the customer experience.[47] But they can do so only if they understand what that experience truly entails. Social media posts can highlight problems. They can also simply encourage people to go to the polls. Post a ballot selfie (if your state's law allows it)[48] or a picture of your "I voted" sticker to create a culture of participation among your friends. Democracy is noisy. Add your voice!

Another strategy is to write op-eds—short opinion articles—for your local paper. Parker Smith, a sophomore at a Lexington, Kentucky, high school, wrote a piece for his local newspaper, the *Lexington Herald-Leader*, on lowering the voting age to sixteen.[49] The article was well researched, with links to various studies that both promoted the reform and rebutted common objections. College students Shaan Merchant and Luke Kirkpatrick wrote an op-ed for the *Tennessean*, Nashville's primary paper, to highlight the problems students face under Tennessee's absentee balloting law when they register in Tennessee but leave for school out of state.[50] The article exposed this issue and encouraged more young people to vote. In 2016, Chase Thomas and Judi Hilman, two Utah advocates who work for local public interest organizations, wrote an article for the *Salt Lake Tribune* to encourage the state to adopt automatic voter registration.[51] Two years later, the state legislature passed an update to its voter registration laws, which included Election Day Registration and better opportunities to register prior to Election Day.[52]

Writing a piece like this does not take specialized expertise, although the more research the author does on the issue, the better. Newspapers are always looking for well-written content, about 500–800 words in length, that will spur a conversation. For some help, check out the Democracy Initiative's template for an op-ed about automatic voter registration.[53] Although newspapers generally will not pay for the submission, they allow community voices to influence the conversation. It simply takes a good, focused idea, a little time, and a desire to contribute to the local debate.

Newspapers will also publish shorter letters to the editor. As the group Let America Vote explains, "It may seem old-fashioned, but politicians (and their staffs) read the local newspapers every day."[54] These letters can influence both policy makers and the general public. For example, Phil Thompson of Priest River, Idaho, wrote a letter to the *Spokesman-Review* on the problem of money in politics: "This is supposed to be a democracy for the people by the people and if we the people do not get involved, the future is plain to see."[55] Deborah Zvosec of Minneapolis wrote to the *Star Tribune* about her concerns with gerrymandering: "We're watching. We recognize blatantly self-serving behavior when we see it. Minnesotans deserve a clean bill. We deserve fair and nonpartisan redistricting and clean elections that are fought fairly, not with behind-the-scenes machinations to stack the deck and undermine our democracy."[56] Tonya Lundahl penned a letter to the *Salt Lake Tribune* to cajole her fellow Utah voters into action: "I really hope Utahns will turn out in record numbers to vote in 2018. Special interest groups may have money, but we have votes."[57] These are just a few examples of many. Find an issue that concerns you and speak out as part of the public debate!

Individual voters feel the impact. They know what's on the ballot and are encouraged to vote because of news stories. They understand the state's particular requirements for voting based on the public education that reporters provide. They are allowed to vote without impediment thanks to local investigative journalism. They feel a call to action when they see their fellow citizens speak out. The media are vital players in the effort to expand voting opportunities. It's up to all of us to help out in that endeavor.

CHAPTER 12

THE PERILS OF ONLY PLAYING DEFENSE

This book has considered a fundamental question: how do we move forward in an era in which no one seems happy with our politics or our voting processes? I've heard it from all sides of the political spectrum and from every corner of the United States: our election system is in peril.

The sad reality is that this sentiment is partially correct. Think about the numerous voters turned away from the polls in places like Wisconsin and Texas because they did not have the exact form of identification that state law demanded. As we saw, people like eighty-five-year-old Margie Mueller of Plymouth, Wisconsin, didn't vote in 2016 for the first time in decades because of the voter ID law. Or how about someone who becomes interested in the election the weekend before Election Day but hadn't registered in time? She can't vote. Consider a nurse who works a twelve-hour shift on Election Day miles from her home precinct. She simply doesn't have time to make it to her polling place.

There are also serious structural problems with our elections. Politicians redraw legislative districts after the census ostensibly to reflect population shifts, but in reality they mostly favor their own interests, crafting oddly shaped districts that serve the main purpose of ensuring easy reelection for the incumbent. An influx of big money into campaigns produces a system in which wealthy interests have the largest influence, often serving as the gatekeepers to who can run for office. We fail to nurture a culture of participation among our youngest voters, with many people feeling it is not worth the effort. Civics education, which often focuses on what seems like the boring stuff such as checks and balances, is woefully inadequate.

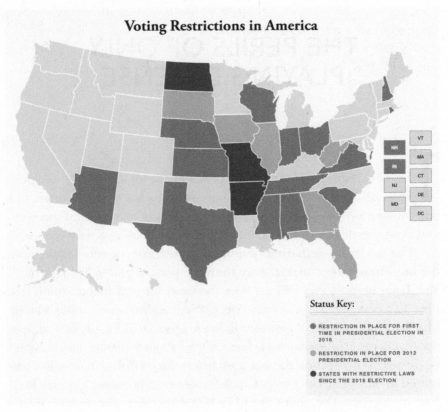

Voting Restrictions in America

Status Key:

● RESTRICTION IN PLACE FOR FIRST TIME IN PRESIDENTIAL ELECTION IN 2016

● RESTRICTION IN PLACE FOR 2012 PRESIDENTIAL ELECTION

● STATES WITH RESTRICTIVE LAWS SINCE THE 2016 ELECTION

A study by the Brennan Center shows states with the most restrictive election laws, including strict voter-ID requirements, barriers to voter registration, cutbacks on early voting days and hours, and new hurdles for felons to regain their voting rights. [Image by Brennan Center for Justice at NYU School of Law.]

The combined result is abysmal turnout, with only about 60 percent of eligible voters showing up for the presidential election.[1] Almost half of the country sits on the sidelines when we select the next commander in chief. The picture is even bleaker during off-year elections, when typically only 25 to 30 percent of voters turn out—meaning that any winner receives the votes of only a fraction of the population. The 2018 midterm elections, with closer to 50 percent turnout, was an anomaly in this regard, but even

50 percent participation is nothing to celebrate—it just means that half of the eligible electorate didn't show up.

In response, we try to fight back against the worst abuses in the voting process. We lament the doom-and-gloom that most of us think characterizes our elections. Both sides believe the system is "rigged" in some way or another.

That is, after all, what the media, our policy makers, and most commentators keep telling us. Consider some of the news headlines that appeared shortly after the 2016 election about the state of voting rights: "The Right to Vote Is Under Attack"; "Ballot Access and Voting Rights at Risk"; "Voting Rights Advocates Brace for 'Biggest Fight of Our Lifetime' During Trump Administration."[2]

This does not paint a pretty picture of American elections. No wonder, wherever I go, people say to me, "You should observe the elections *here*. They're terrible!"

ARE WE WINNING OR JUST NOT LOSING TOO BADLY?

In the face of constant bad news about voting rights, those who care about the fundamental right to vote sensibly fight back—but any successes seem to be fleeting, at best. We protest loudly when a legislature proposes a new voting rule in the guise of election integrity, knowing that the underlying goal is to maintain the current party's hold on its power. Voting rights attorneys file lawsuits to challenge these laws in court. Our Facebook and Twitter feeds are filled with people lamenting the current state of our democracy. Many of us are willing to join a cause—we might, for instance, wear T-shirts emblazoned with a catchy slogan or join a march against a new restrictive law.

This is all vitally important work that should continue. We must do everything we can to prevent a constant barrage of voter suppression measures. Many of today's new voter restrictions have a disproportionate impact on racial minorities, who continue to struggle for equal voting rights. Lots of organizations and individuals are engaged in laudable efforts to make it stop. Protesting and speaking out raises public awareness.

The problem is not that we engage in these activities; it's that the pushback is not enough, especially when is it focused primarily on fighting back, on resistance. For every battle we win against a particularly harsh measure that favors the powerful over everyday people, another one pops up in its place. We are playing Whack-a-Mole in an effort to stop the worst abuses. What do we have to show for it? A political system that produces apathy and shame.

NINETY PERCENT TURNOUT

What if we flip this narrative? Let's not just combat voter suppression. Let's also work on positive voting rights enhancements. As I've endeavored to show, there's actually a lot of good news these days about voting rights and democracy. Democracy Champions are fixing our system from the ground up. These local wins can bring so many more people into the democratic process.

Local, grassroots efforts are the key. Supreme Court Justice Louis Brandeis famously referred to the states as laboratories of democracy, noting that "a single courageous State may, if its citizens choose, serve as a laboratory; and try novel social and economic experiments without risk to the rest of the country."[3] We therefore have fifty potential laboratories to conduct different policy experiments with respect to elections and voting rights. Moreover, given that localities are so important to running our elections, we actually have thousands of potential laboratories to test out democratic innovations. If states are laboratories of democracy, then cities and counties can be "test tubes of democracy" that experiment with novel electoral reforms on an even smaller scale.[4]

Positive voting reforms will spread like wildfire. Once they work well in one community, other jurisdictions may well follow suit. The first movers can provide a blueprint for best practices on how to pass the reforms and make them actually work. Little by little, election by election, they can alter the scope of our democracy.

Indeed, state and local reforms can influence national policy. Once Democrats took over power of the House of Representatives in January 2019, their first proposed bill sought to fix our democratic processes, taking lessons from many of the success stories profiled in this book. H.R. 1, the

For the People Act of 2019, would improve voter access through measures such as automatic voter registration and felon re-enfranchisement, impose campaign finance regulations and adopt public financing, require states to create independent redistricting commissions to draw congressional maps, and offer many other positive, pro-voter reforms that are part of the Democracy Movement.[5] Although there is little chance that this bill will actually become law anytime soon given the gridlock in Washington, the proposal provides a glimpse into what is possible in a different political environment. The ideas in the bill all derive from state and local successes, and they all have one goal in mind: "strengthen our democracy and return political power to the people."[6]

In fact, we shouldn't consider 60 percent turnout in presidential elections and even lower turnout in all other elections to be acceptable. Simply put, it's not. Why not strive for something bigger and bolder? Let's collectively work toward an almost unimaginable goal—something like 90 percent turnout! We could, of course, choose a slightly higher or lower number. There's nothing magical about 90 percent, except how different it would be from our current reality. Ninety percent turnout may seem like a lofty ideal. Sure, but shouldn't we aspire to something that bold when it comes to our democracy, which we think of as the envy of the world?

A common theory of democracy is that a government is legitimate only through the consent of the governed; the Declaration of Independence even espouses this ideal.[7] Higher participation is better for our democracy because it means that more people will feel they have a stake in the election, that our democracy is truly theirs, and that they have properly consented to the government and its leaders. Higher turnout would make our governmental officials and our overall democracy more legitimate. Our politicians, and the policies they adopt, are more likely to reflect the actual will of the people when more people participate and express their preferences at the ballot box. This is especially important given the current underrepresentation of racial minorities and women in the halls of our local, state, and federal governments. We must strive to increase turnout substantially, thereby giving our democracy back to the people. At the same time, we must vastly improve civics education so that current and future voters fully appreciate their civic responsibility to engage in our democracy.

A much higher turnout rate is not out of reach. Australia, with a compulsory voting rule that imposes a small fine on those who don't vote, regularly sees turnout of over 90 percent.[8] Almost 85 percent of voters in Scotland participated in its 2014 referendum to gain independence from Great Britain (it narrowly failed).[9] Many other countries typically see turnout of 75 percent or higher. In fact, voter participation in the United States is regularly much lower than turnout in most other developed countries.[10]

To be sure, 100 percent turnout with a fully informed electorate would be ideal, but even countries with mandatory voting laws, like Australia, fail to reach universal participation. Some people simply will never choose to vote. Yet we shouldn't need a mandatory voting rule to achieve higher turnout. Citizens should embrace their right to vote as a form of community pride and civic responsibility. Our electoral policies should foster robust participation. Ninety percent is an aspiration, but it's attainable if we adopt all of the voting enhancements nationwide that some places are already trying, as discussed in this book. And if we reach for that 90 percent level and only make it to, say, 75 percent turnout? Well, that's still quite an improvement.

Yet even if none of the reforms discussed in this book lead to higher turnout, they are still important to adopt to improve the overall strength of our democracy. The reforms are inherently positive because they will open up the process to more people and have the potential to break the stranglehold of entrenched politicians and moneyed interests dictating the rules of the game. Making the voting process easier and more convenient, ensuring that individuals do not face unnecessary hurdles, and focusing on the community-based nature of democratic participation are all positive developments, regardless of the ultimate effects. These reforms, if widely adopted, will signal the health of our democracy.

We must move past the apathy about our elections that has invaded the American psyche. There is a feeling that the system truly is rigged against the average person—that the elites control the strings of power and that there is little everyday Americans can do about it. "My vote won't make a difference" is a common refrain. That sentiment immobilizes too many of us into not acting at all. As Frances Moore Lappé and Adam Eichen persuasively argue in their book *Daring Democracy*, "what most defeats us is feeling useless—that we have nothing to say, nothing to contribute, that we don't count. A sense of futility is what destroys us. And it's precisely this emotional plague that today afflicts too many Americans across all political lines."[11]

We think we're powerless, so we remain paralyzed. We are on our heels, always playing defense. Is a different, bolder, and better path available?

As I've tried to show in this book, here's the million-dollar answer: positive, practical solutions, already working in some localities, can reform our system and take our democracy to a place it has never been before.

EPILOGUE

It's a hot summer day and I'm sitting on my back porch, listening to the squeals of my kids, age seven and three, as they run through the sprinkler. My mind can't help but wander to a fundamental thought: what kind of society are we leaving them? What will they think of our democracy when they become voters?

We have two possible paths. We can accept that voter suppression is a routine aspect of our democracy, that entrenched interests will rule the day, and that we, as regular Americans, can't do anything about it. "We'll never win," according to this defeatist mentality, "so why even bother?" We presume that we can't make a difference unless we have tons of money or big-name connections, and in any event, today's political realities often make it seem like our votes and our voices don't really matter.

Or we can take a positive, proactive approach. We can recognize that reform *is* possible. We have seen it in communities throughout the country. It may seem cliché, but it's one of the fundamental truths of American democracy: a few courageous individuals can spark a movement that changes our country for the better.

The worst thing we can do is nothing. We can't stay paralyzed, thinking that we won't make a difference. That's particularly important when our inevitable setbacks seem like insurmountable losses. In June 2018, the Supreme Court issued several unfavorable rulings on voting rights, giving politicians even greater leeway to run elections to entrench their own interests.[1] President Trump has placed two conservatives on the Court who will impact the law and social policy for decades to come. State legislatures continue to enact stricter voting rules. An easy answer is to throw up our hands in despair. All of the cards are stacked against us. Why even bother? Isn't it easier to just go on living our daily lives and let the chips fall where they may?

No.

Complacency is not the answer.

That's one reason we are in this mess. When we sit on the sidelines and think our votes and our voices don't matter, then we allow entrenched, wealthy interests to take over. Who wins an election has a huge impact, both locally and nationally. It can mean the difference between continued favoritism or equality for all. It's a choice between having our country run by the few or the many. This is not about Democrats versus Republicans. It's about the people versus the powerful. The people can win.

That's the main message I hope you will take from this book. All aspects of the voting process are up for grabs. From who may vote to how we cast ballots to the way we draw the lines and fund our campaigns, reform is happening all over. Democracy Champions are everywhere. But they didn't start out as Democracy Champions and they would probably scoff at that label. They just wanted to make a difference in their own communities. These small efforts can snowball into bigger reforms.

This all begins with turning out, with voting, with taking a stand. Even more importantly, that process must begin at the local level. Too often we overlook local elections and community-based reforms. But as the stories in this book have shown, change often comes from the bottom up. One place tries something new. It works really well. Another place takes notice. All of a sudden a movement is born. We can't all lobby Congress or donate lots of money to presidential candidates. But all of us can attend town meetings, join local advocacy groups, write letters to our local newspapers, or speak with our neighbors about electoral reform. The appendix lists numerous organizations in every state that can help. Feel free to contact me as you embark on your own journey to reform our democracy—I'd love to hear your stories.

So what's the message for my kids, and hopefully you and your kids as well? I hope you're inspired. I hope you know that your voice makes a difference. I hope you recognize the change you can create. I'm sure you will become regular voters, but I hope you will go beyond that, working in your own communities to seek positive change and promote an inclusive democracy. *You* can take back our elections and change the future of voting.

★

In addition to the local-based reforms that I have discussed, advocates are also working on bigger and bolder movements to change the very structure of our democracy. I chose not to highlight them earlier in this book for two main reasons. First, most of them would require sweeping changes like constitutional amendments, which is quite a tall order given that a new amendment requires the agreement of two-thirds of both houses of Congress and three-fourths of the states. (The last time that happened was in 1992, and before that, 1971!) The focus of this book, however, is on concrete reforms that we can enact in our own communities today. Second, many of these broader efforts deal with the entire structure of our constitutional system. They are different in kind than enfranchising more people or making Election Day more convenient.

That said, several of these movements are worthy of a few words to show how reformers are working on even bigger changes to improve American democracy.

ABOLISH THE ELECTORAL COLLEGE

America's strange brew of democracy includes a unique twist for how we elect the president: the winner need not secure the most votes nationwide. Instead, under the Electoral College, each state has a certain number of electoral votes that it awards to the statewide winner (though Maine and Nebraska split their Electoral College votes, giving two to the statewide winner and the others based on the winner in each congressional district). The number of Electoral College votes in each state is equal to the number of their members of Congress and US senators.[2] My state of Kentucky, for example, has eight Electoral College votes because we have six members of Congress and (like every other state) two senators.

Although the Electoral College winner and the popular vote winner are often the same, that has not been the case four times in our history. In 1876, 1888, 2000, and 2016, the person elected president won the most Electoral College votes but not the popular vote.[3] That includes two of the past five presidential elections, in 2000 and 2016. After George W. Bush beat Al Gore in 2000 despite losing the popular vote, various reformers, mostly Democrats, began looking at ways to do away with the Electoral College.[4]

That effort gained steam after Donald Trump beat Hillary Clinton in the Electoral College in 2016 despite receiving almost 3 million fewer votes nationwide.[5]

To abolish the Electoral College, we would need either a constitutional amendment or a workaround that would pass constitutional muster. Today, the biggest movement to reform the Electoral College is through the National Popular Vote Interstate Compact. Under the US Constitution, states can decide how they want to allocate their Electoral College votes. States that have signed on to the National Popular Vote plan have agreed to award their Electoral College votes to the winner of the popular vote nationwide, regardless of who wins their state. For instance, Connecticut, which passed a law adopting this idea in 2018, would give its seven Electoral College votes to whoever wins the nationwide popular vote, irrespective of who wins Connecticut.[6] If, for example, the Republican wins the nationwide popular vote, Connecticut would award its Electoral College votes to that candidate even if the Democrat wins Connecticut. The agreement does not go into effect until enough states have signed on to equal 270 Electoral College votes—the number needed to win the presidency. As of early 2019, eleven states and DC have agreed to the plan (representing 172 Electoral College votes) and legislation is pending in a handful of other places.[7]

There are numerous obstacles to this reform. First, some question its constitutionality, especially given that it is a blatant attempt to deviate from the Constitution.[8] Second, the idea has passed only a handful of mostly Democratic-controlled states. For political success, it would probably require some Republican-controlled states to sign on. That likely won't happen unless a Republican presidential candidate wins the popular vote but not the Electoral College. That almost occurred in 2004: Republican George W. Bush beat Democrat John Kerry in Ohio by just over 118,000 votes, but had Kerry won that state, he would have secured the presidency but lost the national popular vote.[9] Many people also think the Electoral College serves an important role in ensuring that smaller states matter for the nationwide election, although a counterargument is that it grants small states too much say given their smaller population.[10]

In any event, this kind of reform requires a long-term strategy. Direct election of the president seems more, well, democratic (in the small *d* sense of the word, not in that it would necessarily help the Democratic Party).

But we are probably a ways off from seeing this reform actually implemented. Sustained advocacy for this idea is crucial.

CHANGE CONGRESS

A similar proposed reform is to increase the size of the US House of Representatives or change Senate rules to eliminate the current small-state bias.[11] One modest idea is to give DC a voting member of Congress—who would likely be a Democrat given the city's voting patterns—while adding a representative from a conservative state such as Utah (which based on census data was next in line for another member of Congress at the time of the proposal) to balance the change politically.[12] It's only fair that the 700,000 residents of DC have the same representation in Congress as anyone else living in the United States. That's why DC license plates have the slogan "Taxation Without Representation." There's also a movement for statehood and congressional representation for Puerto Rico.[13] Others seek to amend the Senate filibuster rule, which allows a single senator to hold up legislation; indeed, the Senate already went for the "nuclear option" and eliminated the filibuster for judicial nominees, including for Supreme Court justices.[14]

If these sound like inside baseball (or inside-the-Beltway) reforms, it's because they are. Yet the various rules for the makeup and operation of Congress are vitally important to the resulting policies it implements. It is worthwhile to consider these bolder rules even while we also reform our elections at the state and local levels.

TERM LIMITS FOR SUPREME COURT JUSTICES

A vacancy on the US Supreme Court is one of the most significant and cataclysmic events in American politics today. Under the Constitution, the president may nominate a justice and the Senate must provide its "advice and consent."[15] That justice serves for life. When Justice Antonin Scalia died in February 2016, Republican Senate Majority Leader Mitch McConnell immediately said that he wouldn't let the Senate consider any nominee that President Obama might put forward until after the November presidential election.[16] True to his word, McConnell and other Senate Republicans refused to hold any hearings for Obama's choice, Judge Merrick Garland, who was eminently qualified. The nomination fight over President Trump's first pick, Judge Neil Gorsuch, was heated and vitriolic, but that paled in comparison to the battle during the summer and fall of 2018 over Judge Brett Kavanaugh, Trump's choice to replace Justice Anthony Kennedy. The reason it's so contentious is that whoever sits on the Supreme Court can have an enormous impact on all aspects of American society for decades.

Fix the Court is a nonprofit grassroots organization that seeks to change the way we select justices and improve the operation of the Court itself.[17] The biggest idea is to impose an eighteen-year term limit on each justice. That would allow for regular rotation of justices, with a vacancy every two years. Each president would have the same number of nominees. Many scholars and policy thinkers have also floated this reform.[18] In addition, Fix the Court has called for greater media and public access to the Court, including video coverage of its hearings. Others have sought to amend the confirmation process and mandate strong ethics and recusal rules on the justices.[19]

Again, these are bold reforms that will likely face significant opposition because they require large-scale changes to the status quo. Even if we can't achieve success now, they should still be part of our national discourse.

CHANGE THE PRIMARY AND NOMINATION PROCESS

Many people are fed up with how the political parties choose their nominees. In states that have "closed" primaries, only affiliated party members may vote in a party primary. New York's closed primary, for instance, made it impossible for numerous Bernie Sanders supporters who were independents to vote for him during the 2016 Democratic nomination battle.[20] Donald Trump's children, Eric and Ivanka, could not vote for their dad in New York because they did not change their registration to Republican in time.[21] In fact, more than 3 million New Yorkers could not vote in the 2016 primary because they were not registered with a political party.[22] Closed primaries are the norm in nine states (Delaware, Florida, Kentucky, Maryland, Nevada, New Mexico, New York, Pennsylvania, and Oregon), while another seven states (Alaska, Connecticut, Idaho, North Carolina, Oklahoma, South Dakota, and Utah) use a "partially closed" system, where a party can choose either to close its primary to only its own members or also allow independents to participate.[23] States may also differ in their processes for nominating a presidential candidate, with Iowa's caucus system, involving a meeting of voters instead of a typical primary, the most prominent example.

Not surprisingly, movements are afoot to change many of these practices. The organization Open Primaries advocates for states and political parties to expand their primaries so that independents can participate.[24] Another option is the top-two system, used in California, Louisiana, and Washington, where all candidates appear on the same primary ballot regardless of political party and the top two vote recipients move on to the general election. The Democratic Party has reduced the influence of superdelegates—prominent party members who may vote at the party's national convention—in their presidential nomination process. These are all reforms to watch.

ELIMINATE FOREIGN INTERFERENCE IN OUR ELECTIONS

Almost everyone acknowledges that Russia interfered in the 2016 US election. The only question is to what extent? We'll probably never know the full answer.

At a minimum, the evidence suggests that Russia undertook two devastating and sophisticated actions to undermine the 2016 election. First, Russian operatives targeted over twenty states and successfully hacked into the voter databases in at least Illinois and probably other states as well.[25] Thankfully, hackers apparently did not alter any of the voter registration rolls. Further, there is no evidence that anyone hacked voting machines or otherwise interfered directly on Election Day. Still, this episode shows that we must shore up our security. Congress and states must invest in securing our election infrastructure, which includes making sure there is a paper record for every vote. Paper backups are inherently not hackable, at least electronically. In 2018, Congress allocated $380 million for states to upgrade their election security.[26] That's a good start, but more money and greater vigilance is required.

Second, Russia engaged in an incredibly successful cyberwar, using social media to sow discord among the US population, all in an effort to harm Hillary Clinton's chances at the presidency and help Donald Trump.[27] This is the true meaning of "fake news"—blatantly false (but seemingly believable) stories shared on social media platforms like Facebook and Twitter that were actually propaganda intended to create a false narrative to influence voters, especially in swing states. Facebook estimated that fraudulent Russian posts reached over 126 million Americans.[28] An indictment against thirteen Russians and three companies for interfering in the US election provided this example, showing how Russia sought to increase racial tensions as the election neared: "On or about October 16, 2016, Defendants and their co-conspirators used the Instagram account 'Woke Blacks' to post the following message: 'Particular hype and hatred for Trump is misleading the people and forcing Blacks to vote Killary. We cannot resort to the lesser of two devils. Then we'd surely be better off without voting AT ALL.'"[29] As Director of National Intelligence, Dan Coats, told Congress in 2018, "the United States is under attack."[30]

We must prevent this same distortion of our campaigns in future years. A bipartisan group of senators introduced the Honest Ads Act, a proposed federal law that would require disclosure of who funds online political ads.[31] Facebook then voluntarily imposed a disclosure regime for political ads purchased on its platform.[32] Twitter followed suit. Twitter also implemented a verification process for campaign ads and created an Ads Transparency Center to give more information to the public.[33] Of course, the devil is in the details, so as users we must demand that Facebook, Twitter, and other social media companies follow through on a strict regime to eliminate false information on their services. Congress should also pass legislation that more clearly prevents the kind of misinformation we saw in 2016.

The best defense, however, is all of us. Approach a news story—especially one shared on social media—with cautious skepticism. Dive in deeply to understand the sources that are spreading information. Use the transparency measures that social media companies have created. Trust respected news outlets. Counter fake news with the truth.

EMBRACE NEW TECHNOLOGIES

I don't understand much about blockchain, the newfangled technology behind the Bitcoin cryptocurrency that those "in the know" tell me will revolutionize our society. But whether it's through blockchain or some other technological innovation, I do know that we must modernize our elections.

Many people speak of blockchain as the wave of the future, which will soon impact our daily lives in the same way the internet and smartphones do now. At its most basic, blockchain is essentially a decentralized accounting of every interaction with a particular system or database. No longer will one entity have control over the contents of the system. There's no centralized computer. Instead, everyone who touches it has a piece, making it impossible to hack.[34] As two researchers note, "Using blockchain, all data of the election process can be recorded on a publicly verifiable ledger while maintaining the anonymity of voters, with results available instantly."[35]

In the 2018 primary and general elections, West Virginia used block-chain technology to allow overseas military voters and their families from two counties to vote via their mobile phones.[36] The goal was to test out this technology with an eye toward adopting it on a wider scale. All indications were that the pilot program was a success.[37] Proponents say that using blockchain for mobile voting will increase convenience and flexibility for voters while making elections as secure as possible, eliminating the concern of hacking. Skeptics worry about whether the system truly is secure, especially with ongoing concerns about Russian interference in our elections.

Voatz, a Boston-based start-up, created the technology that West Virginia used. Its goal is to "change how the world votes," moving the election process online.[38] It is raising money, seeking certification from the US Election Assistance Commission, and expanding its reach. The company was proud of the success of the West Virginia pilot program: "One particular overseas voter voted for the first time in over 15 years, so that was particularly heartening for us and a small indicator of the potential impact of this new platform."[39]

Blockchain, and the Bitcoin currency stemming from it, may also change how candidates finance their campaigns. The Federal Election Commission, which administers the country's campaign finance laws, already has guidelines for campaigns to receive contributions via Bitcoins.[40]

This recommendation, to harness new technologies for voting, is somewhat at odds with the previous one, on the necessity of a paper trail to ward off hacking. At present, having a paper backup is the best way to ensure the integrity of our electoral infrastructure. But that does not mean we should cease to explore innovative ways to run our elections. In ten or twenty years—if not sooner—our elections may look completely different thanks to blockchain or another technological advancement.

A book on voting rights and democracy reform would be incomplete without a reference to *Hamilton: An American Musical*, the Broadway smash hit by Lin-Manuel Miranda. Can't see the connection? Yes, I'm obsessed with the musical, but to me the link is clear.

Hamilton: An American Musical chronicles the founding of our country and the commencement of our democracy through the eyes of Alexander Hamilton and his contemporaries, those revolutionaries who were "young, scrappy, and hungry" for change.[41] Hamilton came from nothing—no money, no family in this new country, no vaunted pedigree. He simply had a desire to "rise up" to create a new democracy.[42] He was bold, with a sharp pen and a quick wit, refusing to "throw away his shot" when opportunities for change arose.[43] Along with the other Founders, he quite literally created this more perfect union that we now must sustain.

That struggle continues today, connecting Hamilton to ourselves. The Founding Fathers had the same basic attributes as the Democracy Champions I profiled in this book and the thousands of others working on similar efforts throughout the country. They won a revolution and created an enduring Constitution by sheer force of will and intellect. They were bold, refusing to back down when challenges mounted. They knew that they could create a better society by persuading their fellow citizens. That also describes the people I interviewed for this book. Each generation has made our union a little more perfect. The fight for positive voting rights is a winnable battle. It's now our turn to continue their legacy. We can't throw away our shot either.

(Finally, I'd be remiss without asking—Lin: assuming you are reading this, want to collaborate on *Vote for US: The Musical?*!)

When I was speaking with some friends about a title for this book, one of them suggested *Get Off Your Butt*. That seemed a little too pointed for the cover, but the sentiment is exactly correct. If we don't engage, then we'll be stuck with the same entrenched interests running the game, where those few in power craft rules that benefit only themselves and keep them in control. We have a stark choice: is our democracy truly "of the people, by the people, and for the people,"[44] or are we resigned to a system that few of us actually support? If we do nothing, if we keep throwing up our hands, if we focus only on combating the latest abuses—well, you already know what kind of democracy we'll have.

We must recognize that change is possible in our own communities if we all do just a little bit more to promote democracy reform. Collectively, those changes will add up to something big. Can each of us spend just an hour a week on improving our system? Might we all become Democracy Champions in our own communities? Can we all step up to create the kind of democracy and society that truly makes us proud?

I'm confident that the answer is yes. I'm secure in knowing that our future is bright if we all pitch in and do our part in a positive, proactive way. I'm sure that small wins will lead to larger victories. And I'm so excited to join you in that effort.

See you on the streets.

ACKNOWLEDGMENTS

Whenever I finish reading a book, I flip to the acknowledgments section to see who the author thanks—and I'm always amazed at the sheer number of names on the list. How does writing a book require that many people?

Now I know.

Although I am the author—and any errors are mine alone—this book is a product of numerous people's dedication and hard work. I am forever in their debt.

My agent, Lucy Cleland, and the entire team at Kneerim & Williams, believed in this project from its inception and guided me through the early writing process. Thanks, Lucy, for recognizing the power of positive stories. I'm so glad to have you by my side.

My sincere thanks to Will Carroll, Rowan Reid, and Jordan Shewmaker, my incredible team of research assistants, who looked up sources, drafted endnotes, worked on the appendix, and edited every part of this book. Your efforts made this book significantly better. I'm impressed how each of you took on an incredible amount of work for this book while still excelling in your law school classes. I am proud you were my students and I know that you will all be excellent lawyers. Thanks also to the UK College of Law for funding this research.

Thanks to Jake Bonar, Bruce Carle, Hanna Etu, Mark Hall, Jill Maxick, Steven L. Mitchell, Cate Roberts-Abel, Jade Zora Scibilia, Nicole Sommer-Lecht, and the entire team at Prometheus Books for focusing my arguments, improving my prose, and making the book ready for publication. Thanks also to Denise Roeper of Eloquent Edits for her copyediting expertise.

Numerous friends and acquaintances read chapters, discussed ideas with me, sent me leads of individuals to contact, and provided valuable feedback. I'm so flattered that people from all walks of my life became engaged in this work. Thanks to Aidan Ackerman, Matt Alford, Scott Bauries, Keith Blasing, Tanya Boulmetis, Joshua Cardenas, Tim Crosby, Matt Douglas, Irma Fallon (hi Mom!), Brian Frye, Roz Heise, Ashley Hinzman, Jen Hitchcock, Marni Karlin, Phil Keisling, Tim Lytton, Tim Male, Patrick Marley, Estevan Muñoz-Howard, Laurie Nichols, Chris O'Brien, Joe Oliveri, Mike Pitts, Mosh Prederick, Rob Richie, Zack Roth, Jean Shiner, Alison Smith, Beau Steenken, Chris Stewart, Steve Trout, Ramsi Woodcock, Rob Yablon, and Bill Zapf. Special thanks to Chris Bradley and Adam Eichen, who each reviewed a rough version of the entire manuscript and provided helpful insights. I'm so honored that all of you took the time to read early drafts and give me so much useful guidance.

I gained valuable feedback when I presented my ideas to the faculty of the Georgia State University College of Law, at the Unrig the System Summit in New Orleans, to the *Journal of Law & Public Affairs* at the University of Pennsylvania Law School, and to my own Election Law students at the University of Kentucky College of Law. Thanks to everyone who shared their thoughts with me. I'm especially grateful to my UK Law students, who are among the best in the nation.

Many people spent hours to meet with me, either in person or on the phone, to relay their stories of positive, grassroots activism in their local communities. I'm so grateful to have learned about your efforts and I have been honored to tell your stories in this book. Thanks to Scott Abbott, Julie Archer, John Avalos, Kyle Bailey, Elizabeth Battiste, Anastasiya Bolton, Harry Boyte, John Brautigam, Bill Bystricky, Kat Calvin, Joshua Cardenas, Adele Carpenter, Brian Corley, Josh Daniels, Scott Doyle, Carlos Duarte, Alan Durning, Trish Everett, Benjamin Fabian, Katie Fahey, Chuck Flannery, Eli Frankel, Juan Gilbert, Michael Haas, Benjamin Hardy, Alissa Haslam, Nicolas Heidorn, Steven Hill, Jenifer Hitchcock, Andres Idarraga, Phil Keisling, Paula Lee, Jessie Logan, Tim Male, Patrick Marley, Brittany Marrs, Michael Martirone, Molly McGrath, Andy McLaughlin, Amber McReynolds, Estevan Muñoz-Howard, Tammy Patrick, Maria Perez, Hannah Pingree, West Powell, Rob Richie, Denver Schimming, Jean Shiner, Alison Smith, Craig Stender, Chris Stewart, Willie Sullivan, Kathy Swan, Dana Trahan, Steve Trout, Whitney Westerfield, Dick Woodbury, and Gina Zejdlik. There's a reason I've called you all "Democracy Champions."

Numerous people helped me understand the publication process for a trade book. In particular, I'm grateful to Ari Berman, Emma Berry, Adam Eichen, and Zack Roth for their guidance.

My family is my rock and I am continually humbled by their love and support. My wife, Bari, will always be the light of my life. Thanks for enduring late nights and long weekends while I wrote, and for finding key typos before publication. My kids, Caitlyn and Harrison, are my every-thing. Thanks for bringing me so much joy. A quick story: I'll never forget the day that Caitlyn and I spent at a coffee shop while I edited this book. She read her own book for a little while but then asked if she could read the draft chapter I was reviewing. She read it diligently and with tons of interest—and she was only seven! At one point she asked me what "disen-franchisement" means, but otherwise she seemed to understand most of it. Thanks to my "twin" for showing so much interest. Harrison, at three years old, your biggest contribution was interrupting me with a big, goofy smile while I wrote or asking if we could go to the backyard to play baseball. I sure needed those breaks! The baseball references I put in this book were mainly for you.

Finally, I want to thank all readers of this book for considering how to improve our democracy through positive reforms. I firmly believe that academics need to engage the public to make their work have true meaning. I hope that this book helps in that effort.

Now go vote!

ORGANIZATIONS WORKING ON VOTING RIGHTS, ELECTION REFORM, AND CIVIC ENGAGEMENT

This appendix lists various organizations working on issues discussed in this book: voting rights, election law, redistricting reform, campaign finance reform, voter engagement, civic education, and other relevant topics. The first section lists organizations from every state and the second section lists national organizations grouped by their main focus. I have included mostly nonpartisan organizations, though I have indicated where a group may have a clear partisan agenda. Many of the national organizations, such as the ACLU, Common Cause, FairVote, and the League of Women Voters, have chapters in each state. I have listed some of those local chapters in states where the chapters have been particularly active in recent years.

No list of organizations can be comprehensive, as new groups are formed every year and others may go dormant. The information presented here is accurate as of this writing. Hopefully this list will give you a place to start your own advocacy for positive enhancements to our democracy. Please contact me if there are organizations in your state that I should include in a future edition.*

---

*Special thanks to my research assistant, Rowan Reid, for her help in locating many of these organizations. This appendix would not be possible without her hard work.

STATE ORGANIZATIONS

Alabama

ACLU Alabama | aclualabama.org | @ACLUAlabama | P.O. Box 6179, Montgomery, AL 36106 | (334) 265-2754

This chapter of the ACLU is involved in a myriad of campaigns to protect voting rights. One of these campaigns, the Voting Rights Restoration Clinic, provides assistance to people with felony convictions to restore their right to vote. To find upcoming clinic dates or to volunteer, visit aclualabama .org/en/campaigns/voting-rights-restoration-clinics.

Alabama Rights Restoration Coalition | alabamarrc.com | alrightsrestoration@gmail.com

This newly established organization lobbies for the automatic restoration of voting rights for individuals convicted of felonies. It emphasizes the importance of civic engagement to reduce recidivism rates. It has a contact form for individuals who want to have their voting rights restored.

Alabama Voting Rights Project | alabamavotingrights.com | (334) 235-7479

This project, a collaboration between the Campaign Legal Center and the Southern Poverty Law Center, seeks to re-enfranchise thousands of Alabama voters who are eligible to regain their rights. There are three regional representatives to cover the entire state.

Alaska

Alaska Center | akcenter.org | @AKCenter | 921 W 6th Ave., Suite 200, Anchorage, AK 99501 | (907) 274-3621

The Alaska Center seeks to promote positive change and mobilizes citizens to invest their time to state and local issues. On electoral reform, the group champions automatic voter registration, vote-by-mail, and voter education.

Arizona

*Arizona Advocacy Network | azadvocacy.org |
@AZadvocacy | 1 N 1st St., Suite 649, Phoenix, AZ 85004 |
(602) 899-3332*

This organization works to expand access to the polls, in part by asking for volunteers to participate in Election Protection. These volunteers observe the voting process and give advice to individuals who are having trouble voting. The group also defends Arizona's Clean Elections system.

*One Arizona | onearizona.org | @OneArizona |
345 E Palm Ln., Phoenix, AZ 85004 | (602) 393-0690*

This Latino-focused organization initially formed as a response to SB1070, a state law that some say allows the state to target illegal immigrants. The group now works to represent the growing number of Latino voters in Arizona, especially through its campaign, "Viva The Vote!"

*Outlaw Dirty Money | outlawdirtymoney.com |
@OutlawDirty | 747 W Roosevelt, Phoenix, AZ 85007 | (602)
633-5146*

This Arizona group works toward passing a state constitutional amendment to require the disclosure of campaign donations so that citizens can see what groups or individuals are funding candidates.

*Promise Arizona | promiseaz.org | @PromiseAZAction |
701 S 1st St., Phoenix, AZ 85004 | (602) 288-3663*

This faith-based organization works on immigration issues and seeks to create young community leaders. It runs the Promise Arizona Leadership Institute to train new leaders. It also focuses on registering new voters and promoting civic engagement.

Arkansas

ACLU Arkansas | acluarkansas.org | @ArkansasACLU | 904 West 2nd St., Little Rock, AR 72201 | (501) 374-2660

This local chapter of the American Civil Liberties Union works on issues of free speech, racial justice, and campaign finance reform. It has legislative tracking reports to educate individuals on the decisions local representatives are making. The resource section of its website also provides helpful information on how to speak with representatives in its *Guide to Being an Effective Citizen Lobbyist in Arkansas*.

Arkansas Public Policy Panel | arpanel.org | 1308 West 2nd St., Little Rock, AR 72201 | (501) 376-7913

This organization helps groups that are focused on public policy, ranging from improving the public school system to prison reform. Its Citizens First Congress coalition teaches and mobilizes citizens to lobby the Arkansas legislature.

California

ACCE Institute | acceinstitute.org | 3655 S Grand Ave., Suite 250, Los Angeles, CA 90007 | losangeles@calorganize.org | (213) 863-4548

This group assists traditionally underserved residents in California, including communities of color, low-income and working families, and the undocumented population. One of its major campaigns is civic engagement. Volunteers knock on doors and engage in phone banking to encourage stronger voter turnout among underserved individuals.

*California Clean Money Campaign | caclean.org |
@CACleanMoney | 3916 Sepulveda Blvd., Suite 208,
Culver City, CA 90230 | (310) 390-6025*

This campaign is focused on removing the influence of wealthy interests in California elections. The group supports a Clean Money initiative, lobbying for ballot measures focused on campaign finance disclosure and educating the public at local meetings. There are Working Groups that meet monthly throughout the state.

*California Local Redistricting Project | localredistricting.org |
nheidorn@pacific.edu | (916) 443-1792*

This initiative, a joint effort of California Common Cause and the University of the Pacific McGeorge School of Law, provides resources and assistance to help local jurisdictions reform their redistricting processes. The website offers best practices and guidance for those in charge of redistricting.

*California Voter Foundation | calvoter.org | @CalVoterFdn |
P.O. Box 189277, Sacramento, CA 95818 | (916) 441-2494*

A nonprofit, nonpartisan initiative, this group aims to use technology to improve the voting process. It publishes the California Online Voter Guide, providing valuable information to California voters on state and local issues for each election.

*Disability Rights California | disabilityrightsca.org |
@DisabilityCA | 1831 K St., Sacramento, CA 95811*

This nonprofit group—the largest disability rights group in the nation—advocates for individuals with disabilities. Its Voting Rights Unit ensures that polling places are accessible and educates election officials on best practices.

Future of California Elections | futureofcaelections.org | @FutureCAElect | 1000 N. Alameda St., Suite 240, Los Angeles, CA 90012 | (213) 346-3274

This organization is a collaboration between election officials, civil rights organizations, and election reform advocates with the aim of improving California's election administration. It advocates for policies and practices that will improve turnout.

Initiate Justice | initiatejustice.org | @InitiateJustice | P.O. Box 4962, Oakland, CA 94605 | initiatejustice@gmail.com

This organization's main focus is to reduce mass incarceration. One of its campaigns is Free The Vote, which seeks to pass the Voting Restoration and Democracy Act in California, a measure that would restore felons' right to vote. The campaign's Twitter handle is @FreeTheVoteCA.

Power California | powercalifornia.org | @PowerCANow | 436 14th St., Suite 500, Oakland, CA 94612

This group—an alliance of numerous community-based organizations across the state—works toward mobilizing younger people of color in California. A major focus is registering individuals and turning them out to vote. Its New Majority Fellows program trains young people to become leaders in their community.

Voter Access Project | voteraccess.org | @VoterAccess

This website, run by an air force vet who previously served as the Voter Access Coordinator for the California Secretary of State's Elections Division, aims to increase civic engagement by discussing trends in underserved communities regarding election access. The goal is to educate and encourage underserved communities to participate in our democracy.

Colorado

Fair Maps Colorado | @fairmapscolo |
820 South Monaco Pkwy. #284, Denver, CO 80224

This organization supported ballot measures to create independent redistricting commissions to draw maps for both Congress and the state legislature in Colorado. The ballot measures passed in November 2018.

Just Vote! Colorado Election Protection |
justvotecolorado.org | @JustVoteCO | (303) 292-2163

This group provides information to voters and monitors Colorado's election process. Its website has numerous resources about Colorado's election rules. It also runs telephone hotlines in English and Spanish to answer questions from voters.

New Era Colorado Foundation | neweracolorado.org |
@neweracolorado | 907 Acoma St., Denver, CO 80204 |
(720) 565-9317

This youth voting organization encourages young people to invest their time into local elections and policy issues. Its creative messaging is targeted toward voters in their twenties to register them and encourage them to vote.

Connecticut

Connecticut Citizen Election Audit | ctelectionaudit.org |
334 Hollister Way West, Glastonbury, CT 06033 |
(860) 918-2115

This organization performs private audits of Connecticut's elections to ensure their integrity. It produces citizen audit reports that describe Connecticut's election processes and highlights the positive improvements that occur. The website includes a form to sign up for a mailing list.

Common Cause Connecticut | commoncause.org/ connecticut | 65 Hungerford St., Hartford, CT 06106 | (860) 549-1220

This local chapter focuses on early voting, automatic voter registration, and electing the president through a national popular vote. In May 2018, the state adopted the National Popular Vote Interstate Compact, which would bind the Electoral College voters in the state to vote for the winner of the popular vote (see the epilogue for a brief discussion of this reform).

League of Women Voters of Connecticut | my.lwv.org/ Connecticut | @lwvct | 1890 Dixwell Ave., Suite 203, Hamden, CT 06514-3183 | (203) 288-7996

The Connecticut chapter of the League of Women Voters promotes early voting, campaign finance reform, and other pro-democracy initiatives. The website provides information on how to become involved.

Delaware

Common Cause Delaware | commoncause.org/delaware | @CommonCauseDE | P.O. Box 342, Newark, DE 19715 | (302) 293-8682

This Common Cause chapter works toward fair redistricting, advocating for a law to establish an independent redistricting commission to draw legislative districts in the state. Its Voting and Elections campaign promotes easy voter registration, secure ballots, and early voting.

Delaware Coalition for Open Government | delcog.org | 1012 Kent Rd., Wilmington, DE 19807 | (302) 319-1213

This organization works toward transparent governance by ensuring that local and state governments comply with the Freedom of Information Act. Its website provides resources to educate the public about open government.

League of Women Voters of Delaware | lwvdelaware.org | 2400 W 17th St., Clash Wing, Room 1, Lower Level, Wilmington, DE 19806 | (302) 571-8948

The Delaware chapter of the League has three local affiliates, in Kent County, New Castle County, and Sussex County. The group focuses on various voting and campaign finance issues. There are numerous opportunities to volunteer.

District of Columbia

DC Vote | dcvote.org | @DC_Vote | 1111 14th St. NW, Suite 1000, Washington, DC 20005 | (202) 462-6000

DC Vote is a bipartisan group focused on gaining representation for DC residents in Congress and securing local control over the District's budgets and laws.

VoteDC16 | vote16dc.org | @Vote16DC

VoteDC16 hopes to extend voting rights to sixteen- and seventeen-year-olds in the nation's capital. Its three main goals are to create lifelong voters, ensure youth voices are heard, and strengthen civic learning. See Vote16USA in the list of national organizations for more information.

Florida

Access Democracy | accessdemocracy.us | @accessdemocracy

This organization has programs in Florida, Pennsylvania, and Wisconsin that focus on administrative issues that can discourage citizens from voting. In Florida, the group channels its work into making polling places more accessible and effectively implementing Florida's new online voter registration system.

Engage Miami | engage.miami | @EngageMIA |
8325 NE 2nd Ave., Suite 205, Miami, FL 33138 |
(305) 204-3292

This group of young individuals is committed to improving civics education in Miami and registering young voters. Organizers on college campuses and in the Miami community foster civic engagement through its numerous activities. It is an affiliate of the Alliance for Youth Organizing.

Florida Initiative for Electoral Reform |
floridaelectoralreform.org | @FLIEReform | (561) 921-5309

This nonpartisan group works to achieve electoral reform on numerous issues, including redistricting, campaign finance, and Ranked Choice Voting, among others.

Florida RRC | floridarrc.com | @FLRightsRestore |
info@Floridarrc.org | (407) 901-3749

Florida RRC works on extending voting rights to previously convicted felons. Its website provides helpful resources to assist individuals in restoring their rights and information regarding the ballot initiative, which passed in November 2018, to reform Florida's felon disenfranchisement law.

Georgia

Fair Districts GA | fairdistrictsga.org | @FairDistrictsGA |
P.O. Box 1482, Decatur, GA 30031

Fair Districts GA champions redistricting reform in Georgia and connects volunteers to local events, rallies, and trainings to assist in lobbying for this issue. It also provides resources to educate voters about gerrymandering and its effects on democracy.

Fair Fight Action | fairfightgeorgia.com | @fairfightaction

Democrat Stacey Abrams created this organization after she lost the 2018 gubernatorial election in Georgia amidst allegations of voting irregularities. The group collects stories of individuals denied the right to vote and is challenging various aspects of Georgia's election laws in court.

Georgia Votes | gavotes.org | info@progeorgia.com

This organization's website provides easy directions for Georgia citizens to register to vote online. It also works toward ending gerrymandering and provides concrete steps individuals can take to assist in creating a fairer redistricting process. The project is a collaboration of numerous Georgia-based organizations, which are listed on the "privacy policy" section of its website.

New Georgia Project | newgeorgiaproject.org | @NewGAProject | 165 Courtland St., Suite A-231, Atlanta, GA 30303 | (404) 996-6621

This organization takes a "meet voters where they are" approach and seeks to register all eligible citizens of color in Georgia by 2020. It holds a five-week civics program that emphasizes the importance of participation in local elections.

ProGeorgia | progeorgia.org | 1530 Dekalb Ave., Suite A, Atlanta, GA 30307 | (404) 317-3563

This is a progressive-oriented civic engagement organization that works with various grassroots partners. A major focus is voter engagement, especially among traditionally underrepresented populations.

Hawaii

*Common Cause Hawaii I commoncause.org/hawaii I
@CommonCauseHI I 307A Kamani St., Honolulu, HI 96813 I
(808) 275-6275*

In addition to promoting positive voting rights reforms such as automatic voter registration, Ranked Choice Voting, and Vote by Mail, this local chapter of Common Cause works on increasing accountability in local government through its campaign for a Maui Council-Manager System. The goal is to change Maui's Council-Mayor system to a Council-Manager approach, where the city council would report to a professional city manager who would act as a connector between the council and the mayor. According to Common Cause Hawaii, this mechanism would promote accountability and stop the council and the mayor from blocking each other's initiatives.

Modern Elections Hawaii I modernelectionshi.org

This project of Common Cause Hawaii supports automatic voter registration, Ranked Choice Voting, Vote by Mail, and citizen funded elections. The website contains various resources on how to become involved, such as tips on writing an op-ed and ways to communicate with lawmakers.

Idaho

*League of Women Voters of Idaho I lwvid.org I
P.O. Box 324, Boise, ID 83701*

This League has a number of local chapters that can be found through its main website. It publishes online voter guides prior to each election to present nonpartisan information about candidates running for state and federal office.

United Vision for Idaho | uvidaho.org |
1912 W. Jefferson St., Boise, ID 83702 | (208) 869-3131

This explicitly progressive group works to build a movement toward social, economic, and environmental justice. The organization provides training and workshops throughout the state to build coalitions and create progressive leaders. While the focus is partisan, the group also advocates to improve election policies for all.

Illinois

Better Government Association | bettergov.org/backstory/
redistricting | @BetterGov

This organization is self-described as a "nonpartisan watchdog" that attempts to keep politicians focused on serving the people they represent. Its website provides a wealth of information regarding gerrymandering in Illinois and the redistricting process. There is a place to sign up for its newsletter.

Change Illinois | changeil.org | @CHANGEIL |
205 W. Randolph, Suite 510, Chicago, IL 60606 |
(312) 265-9067

This group works to change the culture of democracy and government in Illinois, focusing in particular on campaign finance and redistricting reform. Its goal is to create a transparent, accountable, and responsive government in the state.

Chicago Lawyers' Committee for Civil Rights | clccrul.org |
100 North LaSalle St., Suite 600, Chicago, IL 60602-2400 |
(312) 630-9744

The Voting Rights Project of this affiliate of the national organization advocates for policies that improve participation among minority groups and fights voter suppression. There is a place to sign up for a newsletter.

Chicago Votes | chicagovotes.com | @ChicagoVotes |
234 S Wabash, 6th Floor, Chicago, IL 60604 | (317) 910-9566

This millennial-led voting rights organization is known for its "Parade to the Polls," in which the group rents vans and drives young people to go vote. It also provides a DemocracyCorps Program that helps young people learn organizing skills that will allow them to impact local politics.

Just Democracy Illinois | justdemocracyillinois.org

This coalition of numerous organizations works on electoral reform in the state, such as automatic voter registration. There is a form to sign up for more information.

Illinois Ballot Integrity Project | ballot-integrity.org | 1433 W. Thome, Chicago, IL 60660 | (773) 338-3564

The Illinois Ballot Integrity Project seeks to educate the public and implement solutions to provide more security and reliability in the voting process. For instance, it advocates for independent hand-count audits for at least 10 percent of all ballots cast. It also supports the establishment of Election Day as a holiday.

Independent Voters of Illinois Independent Precinct Organization | iviipo.org | 1325 S. Wabash Ave., Suite 105, Chicago, IL 60605 | info@iviipo.org

This "good government" group is political in nature and advocates for various reforms, including Ranked Choice Voting and lowering the threshold for independent candidates to run for office. It also hosts candidate forums and endorses candidates who share its ideals.

Indiana

ACLU of Indiana | aclu-in.org | @ACLUIndiana |
1031 East Washington St., Indianapolis, IN 46202 |
(317) 635-4059

The Indiana chapter of the ACLU was involved in challenging the state's voter ID law. It now focuses on redistricting reform, Election Day Registration, no-fault absentee voting, and other pro-democracy measures.

All In For Democracy | allinfordemocracy.org |
@ALLIN4DEMOCRACY | admin@allinfordemocracy.org

All In For Democracy champions redistricting reform for Indiana, advocating for an independent, bipartisan redistricting commission. The website has information on the perils of the current system of partisan redistricting.

Indiana Local Government Redistricting |
indianalocalredistricting.com

This website provides research from a DePauw University professor and her students on local redistricting in Indiana for city councils and school boards. The researchers found that, after the 2010 census, many localities either did not redistrict as required or did not draw districts that were nearly equal in population, compact, and comprised of whole precincts, as the law requires. The site includes recommended legislation to fix the problem.

Iowa

Disability Rights IOWA | disabilityrightsiowa.org |
400 E. Court Ave., Suite 300, Des Moines, IA 50309 |
(515) 278-2502

This organization assists individuals with physical or mental disabilities in Iowa. It has a page specifically dedicated to voting, with a focus on eliminating inaccessible caucus sites.

Let Iowa Vote | facebook.com/groups/letiowavote

Iowa's chapter of the national organization, Let America Vote, works against voter suppression and promotes greater inclusivity in the election process. Its Facebook page helps organize Iowa volunteers by providing information on local events and volunteer opportunities.

LULAC Iowa | lulaciowa.org | @LulacIowa |
4618 Ashcraft Ct., Davenport, IA 52806 | (800) 293-9576

The Iowa chapter of this Latino-rights group has challenged Iowa's voter ID law and is involved in other advocacy to support minority voting rights.

Restore Fair Voting Rights in Iowa | restorevotesiowa.com |
505 Fifth Ave., Ste. 901, Des Moines, IA 50309 |
restorevotesiowa@gmail.com

This site, managed by the ACLU of Iowa, advocates for the elimination of Iowa's felon disenfranchisement law, which is among the harshest in the nation. The website has various facts on felon disenfranchisement and links to the ACLU's guide on how to restore one's voting rights.

Kansas

*ACLU of Kansas | aclukansas.org | @aclukansas |
6701 W. 64th St., Suite 210, Overland Park, KS 66202 |
(913) 490-4100*

This local chapter of the ACLU emphasizes the importance of voting rights and ensures elected officials are protecting these rights. It has brought several lawsuits against the Kansas secretary of state on various voting rights issues.

*KS Votes/Blueprint Kansas | ksvotes.org |
contact@blueprintkansas.org | (785) 414-9678*

This group focuses on voter registration and participation. Its website provides links to register to vote, find your polling place, and check your voter registration status.

*League of Women Voters of Kansas | lwvk.org |
515 S. Kansas Ave., Suite C, Topeka, KS 66603 |
(785) 234-5152*

With nine local chapters across Kansas, this organization provides numerous locations and opportunities to volunteer. The chapters work toward educating individuals about civic participation and registering voters. It also publishes a monthly newsletter aimed at keeping the electorate informed.

*Loud Light | loudlight.org | @loud_light |
P.O. Box 4045, Topeka, KS 66604*

Loud Light's mission is to increase civic participation among Kansas's young population. To do so, it targets social media and college campuses with messages about the importance of civic engagement. It also provides weekly "wrap up" videos of the Kansas legislature's session.

Kentucky

*Kentuckians for the Commonwealth | kftc.org | @kftc |
P.O. Box 1450, London, KY 40743 | (606) 878-2161*

Kentuckians for the Commonwealth is a progressive grassroots social justice organization that emphasizes the importance of new solutions to economic, political, and energy issues in Kentucky. Among its main foci is restoring voting rights for felons after their release from prison.

*League of Women Voters of Kentucky | lwvky.org |
115 S. Ewing Ave., Louisville, KY 40206 | (502) 875-6481 |
kentuckylwv@gmail.com*

The Kentucky chapter of the League is very active in election education and outreach. It publishes a quarterly newsletter called *The Kentucky Voter*. The local chapter in Lexington is also quite active, hosting candidate forums and engaging in get-out-the-vote efforts.

*Together Frankfort | togetherfrankfort.org |
P.O. Box 870, Frankfort, KY 40602-0870 |
togetherfrankfort2017@gmail.com*

This group advocates for civic engagement in elections and transparency in local government. One of its initiatives is to shed light on the impact of money in politics.

Louisiana

*Advocacy Center of Louisiana | advocacyla.org |
@advocacyla | 8325 Oak St., New Orleans, LA 70118 |
(800) 960-7705*

This group advocates for people with disabilities in Louisiana, with one focus to ensure they have easy access to the ballot. There are various ways to become involved.

Voice of the Experienced (VOTE) | vote-nola.org | @FIPVOTENOLA | P.O. Box 13622, New Orleans, LA 70185 | (504) 571-9599

Voice of the Experienced is an organization run by formerly incarcerated people (FIP) focused on restoring human and civil rights to those who have spent time in prison. The group offers resources to help restore voting rights and provides employment and housing assistance. VOTE also encourages FIP to turn out in local elections once they have regained their right to vote.

Maine

Committee for Ranked Choice Voting | rcvmaine.com | @rcvmaine | P.O. Box 928, Gorham, ME 04038 | (207) 370-7685

The Committee for Ranked Choice Voting focuses on passing and implementing a new voting system, where voters can rank candidates in order of preference. This group has its local team leaders' names directly on its website, making it easy to become involved.

Disability Rights Maine | drme.org | @DRightsMaine | 24 Stone St., Suite 204, Augusta, ME 04330 | (800) 452-1948

This agency protects the rights of disabled people in Maine. It has a page specifically dedicated to voter access. The organization provides volunteer opportunities for those who want to become involved.

Kids Consortium | kidsconsortiumarchives.com | 1300 Old Country Rd., Waldoboro, ME 04572 | (207) 740-2638

This nonprofit organization created an educational model based on service learning, which involves students in their communities. Its "living democracy" initiative develops students to become actively engaged participants in government.

Maine Citizens for Clean Elections |
mainecleanelections.org | @MECleanElection |
565 Congress St., Ste. 206A, Portland, ME 04101 |
(207) 831-6223

This organization facilitates Maine's Clean Election Act, which provides public financing for campaigns for state office.

Maryland

Common Cause Maryland | commoncause.org/maryland |
@CommonCauseMD | P.O. Box 942, Annapolis, MD 21404 |
(443) 906-0442

This local chapter of Common Cause promotes a number of local campaigns, including increasing access to elections, creating an independent redistricting system, and eliminating the power of money in elections. It also campaigns for free and open internet access to increase civic education and participation.

Communities United | marylandcu.org |
2221 Maryland Ave., 2nd Floor, Baltimore, MD 21218
director@communitiesunite.org | (410) 775-6673

This membership group of low- and moderate-income citizens tackles policy issues mostly related to social justice. It supported legislation to expand voting rights for individuals with a felony after being released from prison.

Fair Elections MD | fairelectionsmaryland.org |
@FairElectionsMD

This coalition works to enact public financing measures for local and state elections. It has seen success in a number of localities that have enacted public matching programs, including Montgomery County, Howard County, and Baltimore. Coalition partners include Common Cause Maryland, Progressive Maryland, Maryland PIRG, Maryland League of Conservation Voters, Every Voice, and Democracy Initiative.

League of Women Voters of Maryland | lwvmd.org | 111 Cathedral St., Suite 201, Annapolis, MD 21401 | (410) 269-0232

This group supplies a wealth of information regarding voting procedures and requirements in Maryland. It emphasizes collaboration among groups focused on increasing civic participation. There are twenty-four local chapters across the state.

Maryland PIRG | marylandpirg.org | 3121 St. Paul St., Ste. 26, Baltimore, MD 21218 | (410) 467-9389

This organization's "Democracy for the People" initiative works to decrease the influence of money in local politics. It places an emphasis on Fair Elections legislation, which would provide public financing of elections.

Our Voices Matter | ourvoicesmattermd.org | @OurVoicesMD | 9800 Georgia Ave., Suite 202, Silver Spring, MD 20902 | (240) 270-1360

This Montgomery County organization provides information to local voters regarding candidates running for office. It also offers training programs aimed at teaching advocacy skills.

Massachusetts

ACLU Massachusetts | aclum.org | @ACLU_Mass | 211 Congress St., Boston, MA 02110 | (617) 482-3170

The Massachusetts chapter of the ACLU has been involved in litigation that seeks to improve the registration and voting process in the state. There are numerous ways to become involved.

*Emancipation Initiative | emancipationinitiative.org |
@VoiceofEI | emancipationinitiative@gmail.com |
(413) 686-2083*

This organization's "Ballots Over Bars" campaign targets Massachusetts' policies regarding criminal disenfranchisement. One of the campaign's major goals is to restore the right to vote to incarcerated individuals.

*MassVote | massvote.org | @MassVOTE | 41 West St., #700,
Boston, MA 02111 | (617) 542-8683*

MassVote, a nonpartisan group, works to register and mobilize voters from historically underrepresented populations. It also supports various pro-democracy voting reforms. Its website provides a wealth of resources and opportunities to volunteer to register fellow citizens.

*Voter Choice Massachusetts | voterchoicema.org |
@voterchoiceMA | 14 Beacon St., #604, Boston, MA 02108 |
(617) 906-8166*

This Boston-based group champions Ranked Choice Voting in Massachusetts. Its website provides resources and research materials that explain Ranked Choice Voting and ways to support it.

Michigan

*Michigan Campaign Finance Network | mcfn.org |
@MichiganCFN | 600 W. St. Joseph, Ste. 3G, Lansing, MI
48933 | (517) 482-7198*

This nonpartisan organization offers a wealth of information about campaign expenditures in Michigan elections. Its Follow the Money page provides campaign finance information on every candidate running for office. There is also a place to sign up for a mailing list.

Michigan Election Reform Alliance | michiganelectionreformalliance.org | P.O. Box 981246, Ypsilanti, MI 48198-1246

This is a grassroots organization of individuals working toward positive voting rights reforms, including independent redistricting in Michigan. Its website provides resources to inform citizens about the voting rights measures that the state government is debating.

Promote the Vote MI | promotethevotemi.com | @Promote_VoteMI | 2966 Woodward Ave., Detroit, MI 48201

This initiative seeks an amendment to the Michigan Constitution that would promote and protect the right to vote. The coalition includes a long list of partners, including the ACLU and numerous Michigan organizations and residents.

Voters Not Politicians | votersnotpoliticians.com | @NotPoliticians | P.O. Box 8362, Grand Rapids, MI 49518 | (616) 227 0576

This is the grassroots organization, highlighted in chapter 8, that worked toward independent redistricting in Michigan. Its website provides a trove of campaign materials for people to advocate for an independent redistricting process.

Minnesota

Clean Elections Minnesota | cleanelectionsmn.org | mncce1@gmail.com

This nonpartisan Minnesota group champions fair redistricting, public financing of campaigns, and automatic voter registration. The organization furthers these initiatives by encouraging citizens to speak at town hall meetings and emailing their legislators. Its website lists dates and locations of public meetings.

FairVote Minnesota | fairvotemn.org | @FairVoteMN |
550 Vandalia St., St. Paul, MN 55114 | (763) 807-2550

FairVote Minnesota advocates for the adoption of Ranked Choice Voting in communities across the state. Its volunteer opportunities are varied, from staffing booths at local events to volunteering from home by assisting with research.

Restore the Vote Minnesota | restorethevotemn.org

This coalition of groups works on felon re-enfranchisement in the state. There are numerous ways to become involved. The website lists a large number of organizations who are part of the coalition.

Your Vote Your Voice | yourvoteyourvoicemn.org |
550 Rice St., Saint Paul, MN 55103 | (651) 224-5445

This website, from the League of Women Voters Minnesota, provides information about the past, present, and future of voting rights in Minnesota. There are eleven partner organizations that assisted with the project.

Mississippi

ACLU of Mississippi | aclu-ms.org/en/issues/voter-rights |
@ACLU_MS | P.O. Box 2242, Jackson, MS 39225 |
(601) 354-3408

This local chapter of the ACLU includes voting rights as one of its main platforms. The organization works to improve access to the polls, specifically by advocating for online voter registration, no-excuse early voting, solutions for voter ID problems, and other issues in Mississippi.

Common Cause Mississippi | commoncause.org/mississippi | P.O. Box 13651, Jackson, MS 39236 | (601) 366-9373

Among other voting rights and election issues, the Mississippi Common Cause chapter is working to pass legislation that would provide for online voter registration and adopt early voting.

Mississippi Rising Coalition | msrising.com | @MississippiRise | P.O. Box 1077, Ocean Springs, MS 39566 | (601) 345-3259

A civil rights and social justice organization, this group works on voter registration and voter education. It holds a series of Know Your Rights workshops along the Gulf Coast. There are easy ways to volunteer.

Southern Echo | southernecho.org | @SouEcho | 1350 Livingston Ln., Jackson, MS 39213 | (601) 982-6400

This organization seeks to empower African American individuals through community organizing. One of its policy areas is redistricting so that low-income minorities have fair representation.

Southern Poverty Law Center Mississippi | splcenter.org/state-offices/mississippi | @splcenter | (601) 948-8882

This organization, made up of lawyers and community advocates, focuses on social justice, combating racism, children's rights, and LGBT rights, among other issues. The Mississippi office has a particular focus on issues affecting children. In the past, SPLC has brought lawsuits to restore voting rights to felons.

Missouri

ACLU of Missouri | aclu-mo.org | @aclu_mo | 906 Olive St., Suite 113, St. Louis, MO 63101 | (314) 652-3114

The Missouri chapter of the ACLU has been very active in voting rights. In particular, it has fought against Missouri's voter ID law.

Clean Missouri | cleanmissouri.org | @CleanMissouri | 510 East 115th Ter., Kansas City, MO 64131 | (816) 663-9882

Clean Missouri concentrates on promoting transparency in the legislature, limiting campaign contributions to candidates, and ensuring a fair redistricting process where no party is given an advantage. This group is also focused on ethics reform, such as advocating that politicians should not become lobbyists for two years after the end of their term.

Missouri Faith Voices | missourifaithvoices.org | @MOFaithVoices | 301 E Capitol Ave., Jefferson City, MO 65101 | (855) 835-1538

This faith-based organization has four chapters within Missouri. It has worked on a ballot initiative to limit campaign donations to ensure fairer elections.

Montana

Montana Public Interest Research Group (MontPIRG) | montpirg.org | @MontPIRG | P.O. Box 505, Missoula, MT 59806 | (406) 437-9686

This consumer protection group champions a variety of issues, such as reducing the influence of money in state and federal elections. Its "Democracy for the People" campaign seeks to overturn the US Supreme Court's *Citizens United* decision by passing a constitutional amendment that clarifies that money does not qualify as speech and that corporations are not "people."

Montana Women Vote | *montanawomenvote.org* | *@MT_WomenVote* | *725 W. Alder St., Suite 21, Missoula, MT 59802* | *(406) 317-1504*

This group seeks to empower low-income women in Montana. Its website has a useful section with voter resources.

National Institute on Money in Politics | *followthemoney.org* | *@MoneyInPolitics* | *833 N. Last Chance Gulch, Helena, MT 59601* | *(406) 449-2480*

This organization is based in Helena, Montana, but has a nationwide focus. See the National Organization's section for more details.

Nebraska

Civic Nebraska | *civicnebraska.org* | *@CivicNE* | *1111 Lincoln Mall, Suite 350, Lincoln, NE 68508* | *(402) 904-5191*

Civic Nebraska stresses the importance of civic involvement and modern, fair elections. Its activities include civic leadership programs in K-12 schools, civic health programs—including one focused specifically on engaging rural voters—and a voting rights initiative that seeks to protect and promote the right to vote.

Common Cause Nebraska | *commoncause.org/nebraska* | *@CommonCauseNE* | *P.O. Box 94662, Lincoln, NE 68509* | *(402) 710-0583*

With respect to elections, this state chapter of Common Cause is focused on creating an independent redistricting commission and bringing back public financing of campaigns.

Nebraska Appleseed | neappleseed.org | @neappleseed |
941 O St., Suite 920, Lincoln, NE 68508 | (402) 438-8853

This community-based social justice organization seeks to improve the lives of poor people and promote civic engagement. Its Building Democracy page has various resources on voting and lists organizations in the state working on these issues.

Nevada

ACLU of Nevada | aclunv.org | @ACLUNV |
601 S. Rancho Dr., Suite B-11, Las Vegas, NV 89106 |
(702) 366-1226

This Nevada chapter has offices in Las Vegas and Reno and focuses on civil rights and civil liberties. One successful effort was an agreement with Nevada election officials to modernize the state's voter registration system.

Let Nevada Vote | facebook.com/groups/letnevadavote

This is the Nevada-based Facebook group for the national organization, Let America Vote. See the National Organization section for more information.

Nevadans For Election Reform |
nevadansforelectionreform.org | @nvelectionreform |
1740 Desert Mountain Dr., Sparks, NV 89436

This group, created by a military veteran, advocates for the adoption of Ranked Choice Voting for Nevada elections. It works with candidates and legislators who champion the reform while also gathering public support.

New Hampshire

*New Hampshire Campaign for Voting Rights |
facebook.com/NHVotingRights | @NHVotingRights |
(603) 361-2685*

This group is part of America Votes, a progressive organization, and works to promote voting rights in New Hampshire, including the adoption of online voter registration.

*Open Democracy | opendemocracynh.org |
@OpenDemocracyNH | 4 Park St., Suite 301,
Concord, NH 03301 | info@opendemocracy.me |
(603) 715-8197*

Open Democracy focuses on campaign finance reform in the wake of the Supreme Court's decision in *Citizens United*. Its goal is to make connections with independents, Democrats, Republicans, and everyone in between to create citizen-funded elections and keep big money out of campaigns.

*Rights and Democracy | radnh.org | @RightsNH |
83 Hanover St., Suite 26, Manchester, NH 03101 |
(802) 448-0326*

This progressive-oriented group works to promote policies that impact the community, such as securing a living wage and promoting health care for all. It also seeks to counter the influence of big money in politics. It has offices in both New Hampshire and Vermont.

New Jersey

*New Jersey Citizen Action | njcitizenaction.org |
@NJCitizenAction | 625 Broad St., Suite 270,
Newark, NJ 07102 | (973) 643-8800*

This progressive-oriented statewide organization focuses on social, racial, and economic justice. On democracy issues, it fights for voter education, expanded access to voting, campaign finance reform, and an independent judiciary.

*New Jersey Institute for Social Justice | njisj.org |
@NJ_ISJ | 60 Park Place, Suite 511, Newark, NJ 07102 |
(973) 624-9400*

This social justice organization has a number of initiatives focused on urban citizens. Its civic engagement initiative works to increase access to the polls, especially for people of color, and helps to restore the right to vote to previously incarcerated individuals.

New Mexico

*Center for Civic Policy | civicpolicy.com | @ClearlyNM |
P.O. Box 27616, Albuquerque, NM 87125 | (505) 842-5539*

This group provides information and resources to New Mexico citizens on numerous public policy issues. Its goal is to promote transparency and an accountable government. One focus has been fair elections and voting rights.

*FairVote New Mexico | fairvote.org/fairvote_newmexico |
@FairVoteNM*

This local affiliate of FairVote's national organization is very active in championing Ranked Choice Voting. Santa Fe used RCV to elect its mayor and city council in 2018. The data and resources collected from this election provide an expansive overview of how Ranked Choice Voting operates.

New York

*Brennan Center for Justice | brennancenter.org |
@BrennanCenter | 120 Broadway, Suite 1750,
New York, NY 10271 | (646) 292-8310*

See the National Organizations section for more details on this national group based in New York City.

*Citizen Action of New York | citizenactionny.org |
@citizenactionny | 94 Central Ave., Albany, NY 12206 |
(518) 465-4600*

A grassroots organization with a progressive focus, this group seeks big changes on numerous policy issues such as education and health care. It supports public financing of campaigns.

*Common Cause New York | commoncause.org/new-york |
@commoncauseny | 80 Broad St., Suite 2703,
New York, NY 10004 | (212) 691-6421*

This New York chapter represents thousands of New Yorkers to promote voting rights and electoral reform. It has several campaigns to reform New York elections, including a focus on ethics rules, money in politics, gerrymandering, and Election Day convenience.

*League of Women Voters of the City of New York |
lwvnyc.org | @LWVNYC | 4 West 43rd St., Suite 615,
New York, NY 10036 | (212) 725-3541*

The New York City chapter of the League of Women Voters holds a telephone hotline for citizens to call with questions about government, publishes educational materials, hosts candidate debates, and provides numerous other resources for voters.

Let NY Vote | letnyvote.org | @LetNYvote | (347) 342-5492

This coalition of numerous New York voting organizations champions five voting rights issues: early voting, flexibility to change party affiliation, electronic poll books, automatic voter registration, and restoration of felon voting rights. The website has a place to sign up for the group's newsletter.

New York Civil Liberties Union | nyclu.org | @NYCLU | 125 Broad St., 19th Floor, New York, NY 10004 | (212) 607-3300

The New York chapter of the ACLU promotes and protects voting rights and an inclusive democracy through various initiatives in the courts, the legislature, and the community. A major focus has been the restoration of felon voting rights.

NY PIRG | nypirg.org/vote | @NYPIRG | 9 Murray St., Lower Level, New York, NY 10007 | (212) 349-6460

NY PIRG has offices in both NYC and Albany and works to educate the public on numerous issues. Its voting rights and voter mobilization efforts focus on improved voter registration, reforming voter ID requirements, monitoring polling sites, and other nonpartisan election-related activities.

Youth Progressive Policy Group | yppg.org | @YPPGOfficial | YPPG.NY@gmail.com

Started by three high school students, this organization engages young voters in their local and state governmental processes. In particular, the group advocates for expanded civics education and to lower the voting age.

North Carolina

*Democracy North Carolina | democracync.org |
@democracync | 1821 Green St., Durham, NC 27705 |
(919) 286-6000*

Democracy North Carolina is a nonpartisan organization working on voting rights, redistricting reform, and money in politics. The Take Action page provides various resources to become involved.

*End Gerrymandering Now | endgerrymanderingnow.org |
@CommonCauseNC | 907 Glenwood Ave.,
Raleigh, NC 27605 | (919) 836-0027*

End Gerrymandering Now is a project of Common Cause North Carolina. This specific project advocates for nonpartisan redistricting and encourages citizens to contact their state lawmakers. Its interactive Take Action! page provides simple steps to become involved from your computer.

*NC Coalition for Lobbying & Government Reform |
nclobbyreform.org | @ncethiclobby | 907 Glenwood Ave.,
Raleigh, NC 27605 | (919) 833-0092*

This nonpartisan organization focuses on government policies that allow citizens to have a larger voice in the legislature. The group advocates for fair and independent redistricting, stricter lobbying and ethics laws, and keeping legislators accountable. There are numerous coalition partners who are part of the group.

*North Carolina Voters for Clean Elections | ncvce.org |
1821 Green St., Suite 104, Durham, NC 27705 |
(919) 371-VOTE*

NCVCE advocates for public financing of campaigns for state elections to create a fairer system, with the goal of reducing the influence of special interests.

Southern Coalition for Social Justice |
southerncoalition.org | @scsj | 1415 West Highway 54,
Suite 101, Durham, NC 27707 | (919) 323-3380

This group focuses on empowering people of color and securing voting rights for all. It works on redistricting reform and combating voter suppression, among other initiatives. Its efforts extend throughout the South.

Stronger North Carolina | strongernc.org | @StrongerNC |
(919) 670-0019

This nonpartisan group with a progressive lean formed after the 2016 election. It seeks to improve civic engagement in the state. The organization's website has "toolkits" and "calls to action" on various issues that face the electorate.

North Dakota

Reform Fargo | reformfargo.org | @ReformFargo |
reformfargo@gmail.com

This initiative focused on reforming local elections in Fargo, North Dakota, including elections for mayor, commissioners, and municipal judges. The goal, which voters approved in November 2018, was to institute approval voting, where voters can indicate approval for as many individuals as they want and the candidate who receives the most votes will win.

Represent North Dakota | volunteer.represent.us/
north_dakota | representnd@gmail.com

RepresentUs is a national organization focused on ethics and campaign finance reform for local and national politics. North Dakota's chapter (as well as other local chapters) works to enact the American Anti-Corruption Act for local elections, which would institute restrictions on special interest donations and require greater disclosure of donations to political campaigns.

Ohio

*ACLU of Ohio | acluohio.org/vote-center |
Max Wohl Civil Liberties Center, 4506 Chester Ave.,
Cleveland, OH 44103 | (216) 472-2200*

This state chapter has an extremely useful Vote Center guide on its website that provides information and resources on voting and elections. There is also a Voter Complaint Form for voters who encounter issues at the polls.

*Fair Districts = Fair Elections | fairdistrictsohio.org |
@OhFairDistricts | 35 E. Gay St., Suite 404, Columbus, OH
43215 | ohiofairdistricts@gmail.com | (614) 259-8388*

An initiative of the League of Women Voters, this group advocated for a ballot measure to create an independent redistricting commission, which the voters passed in 2018. The organization remains active in supporting independent redistricting.

*Northeast Ohio Voter Advocates (NOVA) | nova-ohio.org |
contact.nova.ohio@gmail.com*

NOVA focuses on voter registration, research, and advocacy to enhance voting accessibility. Its mission is to increase registration and turnout in underrepresented areas of Northeast Ohio and improve Ohio's election process. Its website has a place to sign up for a newsletter.

*Ohio Uprising | americanpromise.net/ohio |
ellen.greene.bush@gmail.com or twknapke@gmail.com*

This is the Ohio chapter of American Promise, an organization that seeks to enact a Twenty-Eighth Amendment to the US Constitution to overturn the Supreme Court's decision in *Citizens United*.

*Ohio Voter Rights Coalition | ohiovrc.blogspot.com |
@votercoalition | ohiovoterrightscoalition@gmail.com |
(614) 682-9145*

This coalition of nonprofit groups provides information and resources on voting rights protection. The website includes a list of volunteer opportunities. As of the publication of this book, the website has not been updated in a while, but the group appears active on Twitter.

Oklahoma

*Let's Fix This OK | letsfixthisok.org | @LetsFixThisOK |
(405) 361-2027*

Let's Fix This OK educates Oklahoma citizens on policies that will directly affect them and encourages them to engage with their government. Its website offers easy tools and advice on how to contact legislators.

*Represent OK | representok.com | @RepresentOK |
P.O. Box 2711, Oklahoma City, OK 73101 | (405) 309-9102*

Represent OK advocates for the establishment of a nonpartisan redistricting commission to stop political gerrymandering. The goal is to pass a ballot initiative to enact this reform.

*The Oklahoma Academy | okacademy.org |
@OKAcademy | P.O. Box 968, Norman, OK 73070 |
(405) 307-0986*

This group researches issues facing Oklahoma and provides an avenue for citizens to meet and discuss pertinent problems through its yearly town hall event (the 2017 topic was Oklahoma Votes, which focused on access to voting and turnout rates). It also plans events where citizens can interact with their legislators.

Together OK | togetherok.org | 907 S Detroit Ave., Suite 1005, Tulsa, OK 74120 | (918) 794-3944

This nonpartisan grassroots advocacy group seeks to influence Oklahoma's budget choices through education and outreach. It speaks with lawmakers and the media, connects individuals to local chapters, and educates the public about the relevant issues of the day.

Oregon

City Club of Portland | pdxcityclub.org | 901 SW Washington St., Portland, OR 97205 | (503) 228-7231

City Club is a nonpartisan education and research group dedicated to improving the lives of those who live and work in Portland and the rest of Oregon. Its Civic Scholars Program helps high school students learn to become better advocates. The group also provides numerous opportunities for individuals to interact with civic leaders in the community.

Honest Elections | honest-elections.com | (503) 427-8771

Honest Elections is an Oregon-based organization focused on campaign finance reform. It seeks to limit the influence of large donations in local elections. It has worked on passing legislation to cap donations to political candidates and promotes a state constitutional amendment to ensure that local laws will pass constitutional muster.

The Bus Project | busproject.org | @busproject | 333 SE 2nd Ave., Portland, OR 97214 | (503) 233-3018

The Bus Project mobilizes young voters by focusing on voter and civic engagement. It has promoted reforms like automatic voter registration and has worked to register voters. It also holds PolitiCorps, a training program for young leaders aged eighteen to twenty-five.

Pennsylvania

Access Democracy | accessdemocracy.us | @accessdemocracy

This organization's work in Pennsylvania seeks to improve the voting process, particularly with respect to voter registration, old voting machines, and long lines at the polls. The group, a project of the Leadership Conference Education Fund, works with local election officials to ensure all eligible citizens have easy access to the ballot.

Committee of Seventy | seventy.org | @Committeeof70 | 123 South Broad St., Suite 1800, Philadelphia, PA 19109 | (215) 557-3600

This Philadelphia-focused good government organization publishes a voter guide with information about candidates and issues. It also promotes various reforms to the election system and has advocated for Philadelphia to create a Department of Elections administered by a professionally accredited Election Director.

Draw the Lines PA | drawthelinespa.org | @DrawTheLinesPA

Draw the Lines PA holds a digital mapping competition to engage Pennsylvania voters in actually drawing district lines. The competition aims to educate citizens on gerrymandering and provide a model for other states to follow.

Fair Districts PA | fairdistrictspa.com | @fairdistrictsPA | 226 Forster St., Harrisburg, PA 17102 | (800) 313-1597

This group focuses on preventing partisan gerrymandering. It promotes a state constitutional amendment to create a citizens redistricting commission. There are dozens of affiliated local groups throughout the state that provide volunteer opportunities at the grassroots level.

March on Harrisburg | mohpa.org | @EndPACorruption |
4700 Wissahickon Ave., Philadelphia, PA 19144 |
(240) 338-3093

This organization of grassroots activists marches to bring attention to the problems it sees with Pennsylvania's political system. It advocates legislation to ban most gifts to politicians and promotes an independent redistricting commission.

Rhode Island

ACLU of Rhode Island | riaclu.org | @RIACLU |
128 Dorrance St., Suite 400, Providence, RI 02903 |
(401) 831-7171

The Rhode Island chapter of this national organization has a wealth of information on voting and elections on its website, including a detailed voting rights guide. It also advocates for positive voting reforms such as early voting.

Open Doors Rhode Island | opendoorsri.org |
485 Plainfield St., Providence, RI 02909 | (401) 781-5808

This organization focuses on supporting formerly incarcerated members of the Rhode Island community. It successfully championed the Rhode Island law that eased felon disfranchisement so that those on probation or parole may now vote.

Rhode Island Disability Law Center | ridlc.org |
275 Westminster St., Suite 401, Providence, RI 02903 |
(401) 831-3150

This is a nonprofit law office that advocates for individuals with disabilities. It helps those with disabilities wade through Rhode Island's election process, including obtaining IDs and ensuring accessible polling places. It also operates a Voting Rights Hotline on Election Day.

South Carolina

*League of Women Voters of South Carolina | lwvsc.org |
P.O. Box 8453, Columbia, SC 29202 | (803) 251-2726*

This local chapter of the national League of Women Voters is very active in election issues. It champions voter access, election audits, redistricting, and improved voter technology. It holds an annual "League Education and Advocacy Day" (a past topic in South Carolina was redistricting).

*Palmetto Project | palmettoproject.org | @PalmettoProject
| 6296 Rivers Ave., Suite 100, North Charleston, SC 29406 |
(843) 577-4122*

This organization works on a myriad of social and economic issues, including two civic engagement programs. The Palmetto Voter Project seeks to restore public confidence in voting systems and encourage higher voter turnout. The Young Voters Initiative helps people as young as sixteen work as poll managers, leading to civic participation before they can even vote.

*South Carolina Progressive Network | scpronet.com/
democracy-project | @SCProNet | (803) 808-3384*

This organization, while focused on progressive social and economic policy, has a Democracy Project aimed at increasing voter engagement and eliminating partisan redistricting. Its website tracks legislation to create a Citizens Redistricting Commission and provides other useful resources. The organization holds monthly meetings; check the website's calendar page for current times and locations.

South Dakota

*ACLU of South Dakota | aclusd.org | @ACLUSouthDakota |
P.O. Box 1170, Sioux Falls, SD 57101 | (605) 332-2508*

This local chapter has been extremely involved in both legislation and lit-igation over South Dakota election rules. For instance, it won a lawsuit requiring the state to accept tribal identification cards as valid voter IDs.

*Four Directions | fourdirectionsvote.com | P.O. Box 194,
Mission, SD 57555 | (605) 828-1422*

This organization advocates for full voting rights for Native Americans. The name "Four Directions" comes from Lakota culture. Adapted for elec-tions, the four directions of this group are "voting rights, voter empower-ment, voter protection, and voter engagement."

*League of Women Voters of South Dakota |
my.lwv.org/south-dakota | P.O. Box 1572, Sioux Falls, SD
57101-1572 | lwvsouthdakota@gmail.com*

This chapter of the League of Women Voters educates voters and advo-cates for policy changes, all based on grassroots input. The chapter has five local leagues in South Dakota.

Tennessee

*ACLU Tennessee | aclu-tn.org | @aclutn | P.O. Box 120160,
Nashville, TN 37212 | (615) 320-7142*

The Voting Rights Resource Center of this ACLU chapter provides a lot of information about voting and elections. The group has fought Tennes-see's voter ID law and advocated for students who may not have a proper ID. ACLU Tennessee also focuses on felon re-enfranchisement and mod-ernizing the state's election system. The "No Barriers to the Ballot Box" initiative includes a Voting Rights Toolkit that offers resources and suggests specific action items.

BriteHeart | briteheart.org | @BriteHeartNow | 41 Peabody St., Nashville, TN 37210 | connect@briteheart.org

This civics-minded organization seeks to empower Tennessee citizens by connecting them to organizations focused on democratic engagement. Its #GetCivic effort helps users find their "civic match."

Center for Civic Engagement | tennesseeyig.org | @TNCCE | 1000 Church St., Nashville, TN 37203 | (615) 743-6237

This is an initiative of the YMCA to run Model United Nations and Youth in Government programs for students aged eleven to nineteen. The goal is to teach young people about government in a hands-on way. Students participate in mock governments at the state, national, and international levels.

CivicTN | civictn.org and proudvoter.org

Financially backed by the Southern Alliance for Clean Energy, this non-profit organization engages Tennessee voters by helping coalition partners on voter registration, turnout, protection, and research. Its Proud Voter Challenge (proudvoter.org) seeks to improve voter registration and turnout among people of color, single women, and those under thirty years old, who are traditionally underrepresented.

Restore My Rights | restoremyrights.com | restoremyrightshelp@gmail.com

This website provides resources and a step-by-step guide for Tennessee citizens looking to restore their voting rights after a felony conviction.

**Tennessee Center for Civic Learning and Engagement |
tccle.org | 203 Rocky Rd., Dunlap, TN 37327 |
tccle111@gmail.com**

This nonprofit organization works to educate Tennesseans on law and policy. The website has various resources and links to foster civic education.

**Think Tennessee | thinktennessee.org | @ThinkTN |
1033 Demombreun St., #300, Nashville, TN 37203 |
Info@thinktn.org**

This nonpartisan research organization focuses on shaping public policy by using the power of data. With respect to elections, it found that Tennessee voters want stronger election security and a modern election infrastructure.

Texas

**ACLU of Texas | aclutx.org | @ACLUTx | P.O. Box 8306,
Houston, TX 77288 | (713) 942-8146**

The Texas chapter of the ACLU has been intimately involved in various legal challenges and advocacy efforts regarding voting rights and redistricting in Texas, particularly as they affect minority voters.

**Go Vote Texas | govotetexas.org | @ProgressTX |
501 N. IH 35, Austin, TX 78702 | (512) 730-0819**

The website govotetexas.org is run by a progressive, left-leaning organization called Progress Texas. Though partisan, the website itself has neutral information for voters about the registration and voting process in Texas.

**MOVE San Antonio/MOVE Texas | movesanantonio.org |
@MOVE_texas | 110 E Houston, 7th Floor,
San Antonio, TX 78205 | (210) 396-0845**

This progressive-oriented group engages young Texans in political participation. Volunteers register voters and encourage people to vote. The organization runs a leadership program to create a new generation of citizen-lobbyists. It also advocates for various policies, including accessible elections.

Texas Civil Rights Project | texascivilrightsproject.org | @TXCivilRights | 1405 Montopolis Dr., Austin, TX 78741 | (512) 474-5073

This group of lawyers and advocates uses litigation to promote the cause of voting rights. Volunteers can assist with its various initiatives. The organization's Voter Protection Task Force provides counsel to organizations and individuals involved in voter registration drives or get-out-the-vote efforts.

Texas Organizing Project | organizetexas.org | @OrganizeTexas | 2404 Caroline St., Houston, TX 77004 | (832) 582-0061

This organization focuses on civic and electoral participation for low-income and working-class Texas families. Its Voting campaign seeks to improve turnout among low-income individuals, particularly people of color. It has offices in Houston, Dallas, and San Antonio.

Texas Rising | tfn.org/category/tx-rising | @texrising | P.O. Box 1624, Austin, TX 78767 | (512) 322-0545

An outgrowth of the Texas Freedom Network—an organization dedicated to religious freedom, individual liberty, and public education—Texas Rising focuses on engaging young people in civic advocacy. It works on various electoral issues, such as combating voter suppression.

Texas State LULAC | texasstatelulac.com | 635 W. Woodlawn, San Antonio, TX 78212 | (210) 391-3274

The Texas chapters of the League of United Latino American Citizens work on a variety of topics affecting Hispanic Americans, including civic participation, education, and voting rights. The organization has also been involved in voting rights and redistricting litigation in the state. There are over 200 local councils in Texas, which are all listed on LULAC's national website, lulac.org.

Utah

Alliance for a Better Utah | betterutah.org | @betterutah | P.O. Box 521847, Salt Lake City, UT 84152 | (801) 893-2281

This progressive-leaning group works to ensure that there is a balance of viewpoints, transparency, and accountability in Utah's government. The main goal is to keep public officials accountable to the public. It hosts election debates between candidates for the state legislature during the election season. It also provides scorecards for elected officials in Utah to help voters make more educated decisions.

Better Boundaries | betterboundaries.org | @BBforUtah | 4609 South 2300 East Ste. #103b, Holladay, UT 84117

The group Utahns for Responsive Government started the Better Boundaries initiative to advocate for a ballot measure to create an independent redistricting commission for Utah—which passed in November 2018. The website provides a wealth of news about its efforts and a sign-up form to volunteer.

Voterise | voterise.org | @voterise_ | 307 West 200 South, Suite 5002, Salt Lake City, UT 84101 | (855) 725-VOTE ext. 505

This organization, based in Utah but with a national reach, focuses on turnout among younger voters and other underrepresented populations. Its website assists individuals in registering to vote and offers resources for volunteers to register others or serve as "Social Media Ambassadors" to promote democratic engagement.

Vermont

Disability Rights Vermont | disabilityrightsvt.org |
141 Main St., Ste. 7, Montpelier, VT 05602 | (802) 229-1355

This organization promotes policies to assist disabled people in all aspects of their lives and advocates for their full voting rights.

League of Women Voters of Vermont | my.lwv.org/vermont |
@LWV_VT | P.O. Box 1391, Montpelier, VT 05601 |
league@lwvvt.org

The Vermont chapter of this national organization has four local Leagues. It issues a nonpartisan voter guide and advocates for pro-voter policies like Ranked Choice Voting.

Rights and Democracy | radvt.org | @RightsVT |
241 N. Winooski Ave., Burlington, VT 05401 | (802) 448-0326

This progressive-oriented group works on promoting policies that impact the community, such as securing a living wage and promoting health care for all. It also seeks to counter the influence of big money in politics. It has offices in both New Hampshire and Vermont.

Virginia

New Virginia Majority | newvirginiamajority.org |
@NewVAMajority | 3801 Mt. Vernon Ave., Alexandria, VA
22305 | (571) 699-3139

A progressive-oriented civic engagement organization, this group focuses on economic and social justice issues. Volunteers are encouraged to register voters using the resources available on its website. Volunteers may even participate from home through phone banks and social media.

One Virginia 2021 | onevirginia2021.org | @1VA2021 |
1100 W Clay St., Unit A, Richmond, VA 23220 |
(804) 240-9933

This Virginia group, started by residents of Charlottesville in 2013, seeks to enact nonpartisan redistricting for the state. The organization hopes to establish an independent redistricting commission following the 2020 census to draw new lines.

Virginia Civic Engagement Table | engageva.org |
P.O. Box 8586, Richmond, VA 23226

This progressive-oriented group seeks to improve voter turnout and enact redistricting reform in Virginia. Its network includes over thirty allied groups that promote civic engagement. The group holds a Citizens Training Academy with various courses to train new local leaders.

Virginia Organizing | virginia-organizing.org |
@VAOrganizing | 703 Concord Ave., Charlottesville, VA
22903 | (434) 984-4655

This nonpartisan, grassroots organization operates within local communities to fight injustice. In particular, it focuses on empowering those who are traditionally underrepresented. The group works on various substantive issues, including civic engagement. The website lists numerous partners in Virginia.

Washington

Fix Democracy First | fixdemocracyfirst.org |
@fixdemocracy1st | 1402 Third Ave., #201, Seattle, WA
98101 | (206) 552-3287

This group's goal is to facilitate fair elections in Washington. It supports public campaign financing, transparent elections, Ranked Choice Voting, and protection of voting rights. It has a number of projects that need volunteers.

Honest Elections Seattle | honestelectionsseattle.org | @HonestSEA | (206) 727-8855

This coalition of groups and individuals successfully campaigned for a local ballot initiative to adopt Democracy Vouchers in Seattle. It now focuses on implementing this form of public financing.

Municipal Research and Services Center | mrsc.org | @MRSC_WA | 2601 4th Ave., Suite 800, Seattle, WA 98121 | (206) 625-1300

This nonprofit organization focuses on informing local governments in Washington about various policy issues. The website has a section on governance that provides a wealth of resources for becoming involved in local policy.

Washington CAN | washingtoncan.org | @WashingtonCAN | 1806 E Yesler Way, Seattle, WA 98122

This grassroots social justice organization champions a number of civic engagement initiatives, including expanded access to the polls for immigrants and incarcerated individuals. It also supports a Democracy Voucher system for campaign finance.

Washington Voting Justice | wavotingjustice.org | @wavotingjustice

This coalition of numerous community organizations champions voting rights and improved turnout. Its policy objectives include increasing online access to voting for individuals with disabilities, preregistration for sixteen- and seventeen-year-olds, and encouraging felons to vote after completion of their sentence.

Win/Win Network | winwinnetwork.org | 1402 Third Ave., Suite 201, Seattle, WA 98101 | (206) 436-0830

This group brings together various organizations to work on social, racial, and economic equality in Washington State. Its network of groups and organizations focuses on specific ways to improve democracy and society overall.

West Virginia

West Virginia Citizen Action Group | wvcag.org | 1500 Dixie St., Charleston, WV 25311 | (304) 346-5891

This group works on public policy issues and seeks greater government accountability and transparency. Its Clean Elections initiative promotes public financing of campaigns.

West Virginia Citizens for Clean Elections | wvoter-owned.org | @WVCleanElection | P.O. Box 6753, Huntington, WV 25773-6753 | (304) 346-5891

An outgrowth of the West Virginia Citizen Action Group, this organization works toward "clean elections" in West Virginia, advocating for public financing of campaigns. The website has petition forms so that individuals can become involved.

Wisconsin

Access Democracy | accessdemocracy.us | @accessdemocracy |

In Wisconsin, this organization, an initiative of the Leadership Conference Education Fund, promotes early voting and switching to electronic poll books to improve the election process.

One Wisconsin Institute/One Wisconsin Now |
onewisconsininstitute.org | @onewisconsinnow |
152 W. Johnson St., #214, Madison, WI 53703 |
(608) 204-0677

A progressive-leaning research organization, this group works against voter suppression measures such as the state's strict voter ID law. It provides advocacy and education to the state's citizens on important issues that affect Wisconsin's government, such as voting rights and why courts matter.

Wisconsin Voices | wisconsinvoices.org | @WisVoices |
633 S. Hawley Rd., Suite 112, Milwaukee, WI 53214 |
(414) 226-4289

This progressive-oriented organization's Our Democracy 2020 coalition works toward accessible elections, fair voting district maps, campaign finance reform, and restoring voting rights to felons. Through programming, it helps its member organizations and individuals improve their organizing capabilities.

Wisconsin United to Amend | wiuta.org | @WI_UTA |
P.O. Box 3392, Madison, WI 53704 | (608) 316-1792

This group seeks to amend the US Constitution to undo the effects of the Supreme Court's decision in *Citizens United*. The "Get Involved" section of the website lists numerous local affiliates across the state.

Wyoming

Equality State Policy Center | equalitystate.org |
@EqualityState | 419 South 5th St., Suite #1,
Laramie, WY 82070 | (307) 228-4163

This organization works toward transparency in state government and promotes fair elections in Wyoming. A major focus is civic engagement. The group puts on a program called SHAPE WY that teaches effective ways to communicate with the legislature. Graduates of this program are then encouraged to start ENGAGE WY chapters to encourage civic participation in their own communities.

*Wyoming Promise | wyomingpromise.org |
info@wyomingpromise.org | P.O. Box 511,
Laramie, WY 82073*

This is a nonpartisan grassroots organization working on a constitutional amendment to overturn the Supreme Court's decision in *Citizens United* and more broadly to support campaign finance reform. The goal is to have a citizens' initiative on the 2020 ballot. Plenty of volunteer opportunities are available.

NATIONAL ORGANIZATIONS

I have listed national organizations grouped by category based on their primary focus: voter access and voting rights, campaign finance reform, Ranked Choice Voting, voter mobilization and protection of traditionally underrepresented groups, and youth mobilization. Many of these organizations work on multiple issues; indeed, although there is not a separate section for redistricting reform, many of the voting rights groups also work on this issue. I have not, however, included groups that are affiliated with the national political parties. A lot of the organizations have state-specific chapters, found easily on the national group's website. The best idea is simply to contact the organization working on an issue that most interests you.

Voter Access and Voting Rights

*American Civil Liberties Union | aclu.org | @ACLU |
125 Broad St., 18th Floor, New York, NY 10004 |
(212) 549-2500*

The ACLU is widely recognized for its continuing fight for civil liberties. The organization has chapters across the nation so that individuals can become involved close to home. The group is involved in litigation to combat voter suppression measures and promotes legislation on positive voting rights reforms.

America Votes | americavotes.org | @AmericaVotes | 1155 Connecticut Ave. NW, Suite 600, Washington, DC 20036 | (202) 962-7240

America Votes is a progressive coalition of national and state organizations committed to equal access in elections. There are numerous state affiliates. The group focuses on combating voter suppression and promoting easier access to the ballot.

Brennan Center for Justice | brennancenter.org | @BrennanCenter | 120 Broadway, Suite 1750, New York, NY 10271 | (646) 292-8310

This research and policy organization is involved in voting rights, redistricting, and campaign finance reform. Its election-specific research areas include automatic voter registration, redistricting best practices, public financing of elections, and many more. It also works to promote fair courts.

Campaign Legal Center | campaignlegalcenter.org | @CampaignLegal | 1411 K St. NW, Suite 1400, Washington, DC 20005 | (202) 736-2200

The Campaign Legal Center works to improve and strengthen the democratic process by reforming voting rights, campaign finance, redistricting, and ethics rules. Though originally its main focus was campaign finance reform, it has now expanded its work to all aspects of our democracy. Trevor Potter, best known as Stephen Colbert's election lawyer for the Colbert Super PAC, is the founder and president.

Common Cause | commoncause.org | @CommonCause |
805 15th St. NW, 8th Floor, Washington, DC 20005 |
(202) 833-1200

Common Cause focuses on voting rights, electoral reform, and a stronger democracy. It addresses issues such as redistricting, voter suppression, and money in politics, among others. There are chapters in thirty states.

Democracy Fund | democracyfund.org | @democracyfund |
1200 17th St. NW, Suite 300, Washington, DC 20036

This explicitly bipartisan organization funds groups that are working to improve US democracy. Grants are awarded to groups that will have a large impact and offer creative solutions to democratic issues, such as enhancing election administration.

Democracy Initiative | democracyinitiative.org |
@Unite4Democracy

This progressive-oriented organization is a coalition of groups that works toward a stronger democratic process. Its main initiatives are campaign finance reform, the promotion of voting rights, and changing current US Senate rules. It has also partnered on a website, to be launched in spring 2019, focused on the Democracy Movement: democracymovement.us.

Democracy Works | democracy.works | @demworksinc |
20 Jay St., Suite 840, Brooklyn, NY 11201 |
INFO@DEMOCRACY.WORKS

Democracy Works is dedicated to using technology to improve the democratic process and ensure that everyone has access to the ballot. The goal is to increase turnout by making voting "fit the way we live."

Demos | demos.org | @Demos_Org | 220 Fifth Ave., 2nd Floor, New York, NY 10001 | (212) 633-1405

This national policy organization focuses on empowering individuals from all different backgrounds. Its research and advocacy help to inform citizens on a variety of issues, including campaign finance reform, voting rights and registration, redistricting, and civic engagement.

League of Women Voters | lwv.org | @LWV | 1730 M St. NW, Suite 1000, Washington, DC 20036 | (202) 429-1965

The League of Women Voters organizes volunteers to focus on expanding voting rights, eliminating voter suppression laws, and fighting partisan redistricting, among other topics. With over seven hundred local Leagues, there are numerous opportunities to become involved close to home.

Let America Vote | letamericavote.org | @letamericavote | 611 Pennsylvania Ave. SE, Suite 143, Washington, DC 20003

This organization, founded by Democrat and former Missouri secretary of state Jason Kander, fights voter suppression. The website highlights various ways to volunteer, such as by hosting a voting rights house party or going door-to-door to promote stronger turnout. In 2018, the organization opened field offices in Georgia, Iowa, Nevada, New Hampshire, and Tennessee, and it expanded its reach to even more states in 2019.

Local Progress | localprogress.org | @LocalProgress | (202) 464-7375

This progressive organization, a project of the Center for Popular Democracy, includes a coalition of hundreds of local elected officials from across the country. The group addresses the lack of civic participation in the United States by advocating for universal voter registration, no-fault absentee statutes, and same-day voter registration.

National Vote at Home Institute | voteathome.org | @voteathome

This organization promotes vote-at-home/vote-by-mail policies. While the group favors universal vote-at-home/vote-by-mail, it also advocates for more incremental reforms like no-excuse absentee voting.

Nonprofit VOTE | nonprofitvote.org | @npvote | 2464 Massachusetts Ave., Suite 210, Cambridge, MA 02140

This organization partners with nonprofits to promote voter participation among the communities that the nonprofits serve. It provides resources for nonprofit groups on how to engage in election activities like voter registration drives.

Overseas Vote | overseasvotefoundation.org | @overseasvote | 4325 Old Glebe Rd., Arlington, VA 22207 | voterhelpdesk@usvotefoundation.org

Overseas Vote is an initiative of the US Vote Foundation that ensures that uniformed service members and US citizens living abroad can participate in elections at home. It provides resources, applicable deadlines, and information to guide these citizens through the process of voting while overseas. Voters with questions can email voterhelpdesk@usvotefoundation.org or call 1-866-687-8683.

Spread The Vote | spreadthevote.org | @SpreadTheVoteUS

This organization, run through state and local chapters, focuses on combating voter identification laws by providing individuals with help in obtaining the necessary identification to vote. Its website hosts an interactive page to submit your information if you need help securing identification.

VoteRiders | voteriders.org | @VoteRiders | 171 Pier Ave. #313, Santa Monica, CA 90405 | (844) 338-8743

VoteRiders' mission is to ensure that no voter is disenfranchised because of a voter ID law. It provides comprehensive information about voter ID laws in each state and works in communities to secure IDs for individuals who need them.

When We All Vote | whenweallvote.org | @WhenWeAllVote | info@whenweallvote.org

This nonpartisan effort to increase voter registration and democratic participation across the country, begun in mid-2018, is co-chaired by various notable celebrities, including Michelle Obama, Tom Hanks, Lin-Manuel Miranda, Janelle Monáe, Chris Paul, Faith Hill, and Tim McGraw. The goal is to spark a movement surrounding the importance of registration and voting.

Campaign Finance Reform

Democracy 21 | democracy21.org | @FredWertheimer | 2000 Massachusetts Ave., NW, Washington, DC 20036 | (202) 355-9600

Democracy 21 works to eliminate the influence of money in politics by promoting campaign finance reform. In particular, it advocates for public financing of elections.

End Citizens United | endcitizensunited.org | @StopBigMoney | P.O. Box 66005, Washington, DC 20035 | (202) 798-5253

This progressive-oriented Political Action Committee works to limit the effects of the Supreme Court's decision in *Citizens United*. It funds pro-campaign finance reform candidates and hopes to create a national platform to discuss money in politics.

Every Voice | everyvoice.org | @EveryVoice |
1211 Connecticut Ave., NW, Suite 600, Washington, DC
20036 | (202) 640-5600

Every Voice focuses on combatting money in politics by creating "small-donor elections" programs throughout the country. Under this system, candidates agree to accept donations only up to a certain amount in exchange for matching public funds.

Free Speech for People | freespeechforpeople.org | @FSFP |
contact@freespeechforpeople.org

Free Speech for People wants to overturn the Supreme Court's decision in *Citizens United* and other precedents by amending the US Constitution. To achieve this goal, it organizes state and national leaders. Its website has an Organizer's Toolkit. Individuals can also sign a petition on its website.

National Institute on Money in Politics |
followthemoney.org | @MoneyInPolitics |
833 N. Last Chance Gulch, Helena, MT 59601 |
(406) 449-2480

This organization compiles information about donations, lobbying, and other money in politics issues and makes it available to the public on its website. Included are data on lobbyist expenditures, the competitiveness of specific races, and donations received by state and national officials.

RepresentUs | represent.us | @RepresentUs |
P.O. Box 60008, Florence, MA 01062 |
(855) 585-8100

This national organization, supported in states through local chapters, is focused on addressing political corruption in American elections. It lobbies local, state, and federal governments to enact the American Anti-Corruption Act, which has three main goals:

1. Fix the broken election system by adopting Ranked Choice Voting, ending partisan gerrymandering, and opening up primaries.
2. Stop political bribery through stringent fund-raising rules.
3. End secret money by requiring robust disclosure.

If there is not already a chapter near you, the website provides a sign-up form to start your own chapter.

Ranked Choice Voting

FairVote | fairvote.org | @fairvote | 6930 Carroll Ave., Suite 240, Takoma Park, MD 20912 | (301) 270-4616

FairVote works for electoral reforms on the local, state, and national levels and specifically champions Ranked Choice Voting and fair representation in the legislature. See chapter 7 for more details.

Voter Mobilization and Protection of Traditionally Underrepresented Groups

Advancement Project | advancementproject.org | @adv_project | 1220 L St. NW, Ste. 850, Washington, DC 20005 | (202) 728-9557

This organization works to ensure voters of color have easy access to the polls on Election Day. One focus is to restore voting rights for individuals who were formerly incarcerated. It also engages in legal battles to address unfair barriers to the polls, such as challenging voter ID laws across the country.

Asian and Pacific Islander American Vote | apiavote.org | @APIAVote | 1612 K St. NW, Suite 510, Washington, DC 20006 | (202) 223-9170

This national organization mobilizes Asian Americans and Pacific Islanders (APIA) to engage in the civic process. Its overarching goal is to have a larger

number of APIAs in elected positions in local, state, and federal governments. The website has a host of resources about the voting process.

Fair Elections Center | fairelectionscenter.org | @fairerelections | 1825 K St. NW, Suite 450, Washington DC 20006 | (202) 331-0114

This nonprofit, nonpartisan organization works toward removing barriers
to the voting process and improving election administration. Its affiliate,
the Fair Elections Legal Network (FELN) is made up of attorneys who
assist voter mobilization groups with legal and technical assistance, with a
special focus on student and minority voters.

Lawyers' Committee for Civil Rights Under Law | lawyerscommittee.org | @LawyersComm | 1401 New York Ave. NW #400, Washington, DC 20005 | (202) 662-8600

This national civil rights organization files lawsuits to protect the right
to vote and combat voter suppression, focusing in particular on minority
voting rights. There are affiliates in Boston, Chicago, Denver, Jackson (Mississippi), Los Angeles, Philadelphia, San Francisco, and Washington, DC.

League of United Latin American Citizens | lulac.org | @lulac | 1133 19th St. NW, Suite 1000, Washington, DC 20036

The oldest and largest organization focused on Hispanics in the United
States, LULAC strives for equality, political influence, and civic rights for
Hispanic Americans. It has over one thousand chapters nationwide. In
addition to education and outreach, the organization has been involved in
many lawsuits involving voting rights, particularly on redistricting.

Mexican American Legal Defense and Educational Fund | maldef.org | @MALDEF | 634 S. Spring St., Los Angeles, CA 90014 | (213) 629-2512

MALDEF is a Latino civil rights organization that champions a variety of issues, including voting rights for Latino citizens. The organization promotes policies and files lawsuits to protect voting rights, expand voter accessibility, and support legislation such as the Voting Rights Act.

Mi Familia Vota | mifamiliavota.org | @MiFamiliaVota | 1710 E Indian School Rd., Suite 100, Phoenix, AZ 85016 | (602) 263-2030

This national organization exists to promote political power among Latino communities. It has offices in Arizona, California, Colorado, Florida, Nevada, and Texas. On voting rights, it supports increased participation among Latinos and fights voter suppression.

National Association for the Advancement of Colored People (NAACP) | naacp.org | @NAACP | 4805 Mt. Hope Drive, Baltimore, MD 21215 | (410) 580-5777

This storied national organization has local chapters across the country to fight for equality and representation. It works to include minorities in the election process by registering voters, addressing redistricting, and ensuring that every individual can vote through its election protection initiative.

National Disability Rights Network | ndrn.org | @NDRNadvocates | 820 1st St. NE, Suite 740, Washington, DC 20002 | (202) 408-9514

This is the national membership organization for the federally mandated Protection and Advocacy (P&A) Systems and the Client Assistance Programs (CAP) for individuals with disabilities. Affiliates exist in each state. The national organization has a webpage specifically devoted to voters with disabilities.

Native Vote | nativevote.org | @nativevote

This organization seeks to improve turnout and representation of American Indian and Alaska Native voters. Volunteers can sign up to become Native Vote Coordinators to help register voters.

VoterVox | votervox.org | @votervox

VoterVox connects voters who speak a language other than English with translators to help fill out ballots. In particular, the group assists Asian American and Pacific Islanders. In 2016, the organization 18 Million Rising (18millionrising.org), which brings Asian American communities together through technology, used VoterVox to partner voters with translators.

Voto Latino | votolatino.org | @votolatino | P.O. Box 35608, Washington, DC 20033 | (202) 386-6374

This group aims to register young Latinos to vote, educate them about important issues, and develop young leaders in the Latino community. It also advocates for issues that are important to young Latinos.

Women's Voices Women Vote | wvwvaf.org | @Women_Vote | 1707 L St. NW, Suite 300, Washington, DC 20036 | (202) 659-9570

This organization focuses on elevating the voices of unmarried women, who comprise 25 percent of eligible voters. It attempts to highlight the growing population of unmarried women, minorities, and millennials so that elected officials will take their issues of concern seriously.

Youth Mobilization

Campus Vote Project | campusvoteproject.org |
@campusvote | (202) 331-0114

This organization, a part of the Fair Elections Center, focuses on college campuses, working with faculty, staff, and students at colleges and universities across the country to remove barriers to student voting. The goal is to educate students on registration, voter ID, and other potential hurdles to democratic participation.

Generation Citizen | generationcitizen.org | @gencitizen

Generation Citizen engages young voters through a civics curriculum provided to high school teachers and administrators. This interactive curriculum encourages students to create a strategic plan to address an issue they care about. The organization currently has offices in Austin, Boston, New York, Oakland, Oklahoma City, and Providence.

Head Count | headcount.org | @HeadCountOrg |
104 West 29th St., 11th Floor, New York, NY 10001 |
(866) OUR-VOTE (687-8683)

This voting registration organization partners with musicians to bring voter registration drives to concerts. It targets young people specifically and has registered almost 500,000 voters since 2004.

Inspire U.S. | inspire-usa.org | @inspire2vote |
(760) 839-6626

Inspire U.S. is a voter registration organization focused on increasing civic participation among younger generations. It provides volunteer opportunities to register voters at local high schools and in particular targets high school students to register their peers to vote.

*Rock the Vote | rockthevote.com | @RockTheVote |
1875 Connecticut Ave. NW, 10th Floor,
Washington, DC 20009 | (202) 719-9910*

This nonpartisan, youth voting organization aims to register as many young people to vote as possible. It offers a voter registration tool kit to assist you in hosting your own event. Although the group is mostly known for holding concerts, its website has abundant resources and information on the voting process.

*Vote16USA | vote16usa.org | @Vote16USA |
110 Wall St., New York, NY 10005*

Vote16USA is a project, run by Generation Citizen, to increase youth participation in elections by lowering the voting age in local elections to sixteen. It has a variety of campaigns in cities across the nation, including in Washington, DC, San Francisco, Boulder, Memphis, and many more.

NOTES

PROLOGUE

1. Jackie Robinson and Alfred Duckett, *I Never Had It Made: An Autobiography of Jackie Robinson* (New York: G. P. Putnam's Sons, 1972), p. 268.

2. Wesley Hood and Amina Doghri, "First Lady Michelle Obama Encourages Pitt Students and Community Members to Vote," *Pitt News*, September 28, 2016, https://pittnews.com/article/111564/featured/first-lady-michelle-obama-encourages-pitt-students-community-members-vote [https://perma.cc/SH6R-C9AW].

3. The law lists the specific felonies eligible for expungement, which includes crimes like theft and various drug offenses. For a full list, visit "Class D Felony Offenses Eligible for Expungement," Kentucky Court of Justice, https://courts.ky.gov/Expungement/Pages/eligibleoffenses.aspx [https://perma.cc/3MUT-USEA].

4. "West Powell's Felony Expungement Testimony," West Powell testifies at the Interim Joint Judiciary Committee meeting in Hopkinsville, October 2015, Clean Slate Kentucky, posted April 28, 2016, YouTube video, 4:05, https://www.youtube.com/watch?v=F6AM31p7qpQ&feature=youtu.be.

5. Ibid.

6. Whitney Westerfield, in discussion with the author, July 20, 2017.

7. Adam Beam, "Convict's Testimony Changes Republican Minds in Kentucky," *Washington Times* (Associated Press), April 10, 2016, https://www.washingtontimes.com/news/2016/apr/10/convicts-testimony-changes-republican-minds-in-ken [https://perma.cc/4PPU-WYEK]; "Felony Expungement Supporters Herald Bill Signed into Law as a Second Chance for Many Kentuckians," Spectrum News, April 12, 2016 [https://perma.cc/4BX5-CPK3].

8. West Powell, in discussion with the author, March 23, 2018.

9. Ibid.

CHAPTER 1: THE TALE OF A SIXTEEN-YEAR-OLD VOTER

1. Annys Shin, "Takoma Park 16-Year-Old Savors His History-Making Moment at the Polls," *Washington Post*, November 3, 2013, https://www.washingtonpost.com/local/takoma-park-16-year-old-savors-his-history-making-moment-at-the-polls/2013/11/03/89f00962-425c-11e3-b028-de922d7a3f47_story.html [https://perma.cc/Z24Y-DWX6].

2. TAKOMA PARK MUNICIPAL CHARTER § 601 (July 26, 2017), available at https://www.mdmunicipal.org/DocumentCenter/View/188/takomapark [https://perma.cc/7NEA-UNX8].

3. Tim Male, email message to author, February 19, 2018.

4. Seth Grimes, "Let's Enfranchise Takoma Park Renters and Strengthen the Right to Vote!" *One Takoma* (blog), February 21, 2013, http://www.onetakoma.com/2013/02/lets-enfranchise-takoma-park-renters.html [https://perma.cc/ZVT7-X5ZV].

5. Shin, "Tacoma Park 16-Year-Old."

6. Bill Bystricky, email message to author, July 15, 2017.

7. Shin, "Tacoma Park 16-Year-Old"; *see, e.g.*, Eva Zeglovits and Julian Aichholzer, "Are People More Inclined to Vote at 16 Than at 18? Evidence for the First-Time Voting Boost among 16- to 25-Year-Olds in Austria," *Journal of Elections, Public Opinion and Parties*, July 3, 2014, https://www.ncbi.nlm.nih.gov/pmc/articles/PMC4864896 [https://perma.cc/WH9L-7LL4].

8. Resolution No. 2013-25: Right to Vote, City of Tacoma Park, MD, May 13, 2013, available at http://www.promoteourvote.com/uploads/9/2/2/7/9227685/takoma_park_right_to_vote_resolution.pdf [https://perma.cc/RKE9-CXVJ].

9. Charter Amendment Resolution No. 2013-1: Voting and Elections, City of Takoma Park, MD, May 13, 2013, available at https://documents.takomaparkmd.gov/government/city-council/charter-amendment-resolutions/charter-amendment-resolution-2013-01.pdf [https://perma.cc/8A7Z-YR2V]; Lindsay A. Powers, "Takoma Park Grants 16-Year-Olds Right to Vote," *Washington Post*, May 14, 2013, https://www.washingtonpost.com/local/takoma-park-grants-16-year-olds-right-to-vote/2013/05/14/b27c52c4-bccd-11e2-89c9-3be8095fe767_story.html [https://perma.cc/9WAD-VL99].

10. J.B. Wogan, "Takoma Park Sees High Turnout among Teens after Election Reform," *Governing*, November 7, 2013, http://www.governing.com/news/headlines/gov-maryland-city-sees-high-turnout-among-teens-after-election-reform.html [https://perma.cc/L3M9-5Y2L].

11. Generation Citizen, *Lowering the Voting Age for Local Elections in Takoma Park and Hyattsville, MD: A Case Study* (New York: Vote16USA, October 2016), http://vote16usa.org/wp-content/uploads/2016/10/Final-MD-Case-Study.pdf [https://perma.cc/5ALW-MX4R].

12. Tim Male, email message to author, February 19, 2018.

13. HYATTSVILLE CHARTER AND CODE, art. IV, § C4-1, available at http://www.hyattsville.org/DocumentCenter/View/340/Section-2 [https://perma.cc/FA7H-D459]; Elena Schneider, "Students in Maryland Test Civic Participation and Win Right to Vote," *New York Times*, January 9, 2015, https://www.nytimes.com/2015/01/10/us/politics/students-in-maryland-test-civic-participation-and-win-right-to-vote.html.

14. Bill Bystricky, email message to author, July 15, 2017.

15. Ibid.

16. Emily Blackner, "Greenbelt Council Takes Steps Toward Lowering Voting Age," *Sentinel*, May 24, 2017, https://pgs.thesentinel.com/2017/05/24/greenbelt-council-takes-steps-toward-lowering-required-voting-age [https://perma.cc/3KQY-HC77].

17. Ibid.

18. University of Maryland Institute for Governmental Service and Research, *City of Greenbelt, Maryland: Results of 2015 Community Questionnaire* (College Park, MD: February 2016) [https://perma.cc/3WH6-JP6G].

19. Ema Smith, "How Young People Pushed Greenbelt, Maryland, to Lower the City's Voting Age," *Teen Vogue*, November 22, 2017, https://www.teenvogue.com/story/how-young-people-pushed-greenbelt-maryland-to-lower-the-citys-voting-age [https://perma.cc/3TVF-LP9A]; "Election Results 2017," City of Greenbelt, Maryland [https://perma.cc/3U5T-XG6N]; Charter Amendment Resolution No. 2017-1: Resolution No. 2057, City of Greenbelt, MD, December 11, 2017, available at [https://perma.cc/3E9W-KHQM].

20. Blackner, "Greenbelt Council Takes Steps."

21. Gibson Chu, "Measure Y1 Could Implement Lower Voting Age for Certain Elections in Berkeley," *Daily Californian*, October 27, 2016, http://www.dailycal.org/2016/10/27/measure-y1-could-implement-lower-voting-age-for-certain-elections-in-berkeley [https://perma.cc/PGT8-YQGR].

22. "Measure Y1 Passes to Lower Voting Age for School Board Elections," Vote16USA, http://vote16usa.org/project/berkeley-ca [https://perma.cc/A4UU-CRK5].

23. Stell Simonton, "Teens Push to Lower the Voting Age," *Youth Today*, January 17, 2017, https://youthtoday.org/2017/01/teens-push-to-lower-the-voting-age [https://perma.cc/R9PV-MD8D].

24. Josh Daniels, in discussion with the author, March 27, 2018.

25. Ibid.; "City of Berkeley Measure Y1 Election Results," Voters Edge California, http://votersedge.org/ca/en/ballot/election/area/42/measures/measure/2509?election_authority_id=1 [https://perma.cc/ST3T-RS5K].

26. Joshua Cardenas, in discussion with the author, March 23, 2017.

27. Laura Dudnick, "Youths Seek to Lower Voting Age to 16 in SF," *SF Examiner*, January 6, 2015, https://archives.sfexaminer.com/sanfrancisco/youths-seek-to-lower-voting-age-to-16-in-sf/Content?oid=2916012 [https://perma.cc/BA8G-JG26]; Carrie Kirby, "The Case for Letting Teens Vote in Local Elections," *City Lab*, October 6, 2015, https://www.citylab.com/equity/2015/10/the-case-for-letting-teens-vote-in-local-elections/408853 [https://perma.cc/C2TP-QW9A].

28. John Avalos, in discussion with the author, March 10, 2017.

29. Adele Carpenter, in discussion with the author, March 7, 2017.

30. John Avalos, in discussion with the author, March 10, 2017.

31. Zachary Crockett, "The Case for Allowing 16-Year-Olds to Vote," *Vox*, November 7, 2016, https://www.vox.com/policy-and-politics/2016/11/7/13347080/voting-age-election-16 [https://perma.cc/WBX9-33ZY].

32. Ibid.

33. Adele Carpenter, in discussion with the author, March 7, 2017.

34. Ibid.

35. Vote16USA, "Historic Measure Almost Passes: More Than 172,000 Vote to Extend Voting Rights to 16-Year-Olds for Municipal Elections," press release, November 28, 2016, http://vote16usa.org/press-release-historic-measure-almost-passes-more-than-172000-vote-to-extend-voting-rights-to-16-year-olds-for-municipal-elections [https://perma.cc/PCF3-YX8L].

36. Joshua Cardenas, in discussion with the author, March 23, 2017.

37. Joshua A. Douglas, "The Right to Vote Under Local Law," *George Washington Law Review* 85 (2017): 1039. The appendix to this article lists the laws in all fifty states with respect to the authority of localities to enact local-specific voting rules.

38. Youth Progressive Policy Group, https://yppg.org [https://perma.cc/P8WG-XRAX].

39. Eli Frankel, in discussion with the author, April 20, 2017.

40. Ibid.

41. Eli Frankel, "Give High Schoolers the Right to Vote—Young People Need a Voice," *New York Daily News*, May 5, 2017, http://www.nydailynews.com/opinion/give-high-schoolers-vote-young-people-voice-article-1.3137513 [https://perma.cc/EHW8-5LFF].

42. Joshua A. Douglas, "In Defense of Lowering the Voting Age," *University of Pennsylvania Law Review Online* 165 (2017): 65, https://www.pennlawreview.com/essays/index.php?id=48 [https://perma.cc/5BVQ-XMUW].

43. Much of the discussion in this section is derived from an unpublished manuscript: Jenny Diamond Cheng, "How Eighteen-Year-Olds Got the Vote," (unpublished manuscript available on SSRN, Vanderbilt University Law School, 2016), https://papers.ssrn.com/sol3/papers.cfm?abstract_id=2818730 [https://perma.cc/2UUJ-KDUF]; Alexander Keyssar, *The Right to Vote: The Contested History of Democracy in the United States* (New York: Basic Books, 2000), pp. 277–81.

44. U.S. CONST. art. I, §§ 2, 4.

45. Douglas, "The Right to Vote Under Local Law."

46. George Arnett, "Votes for 16- and 17-Year-Olds: Where Else Outside Scotland?" *Guardian*, June 18, 2015, https://www.theguardian.com/politics/datablog/2015/jun/18/votes-for-16--and-17-year-olds-where-else-outside-scotland [https://perma.cc/KS7G-J693].

47. James B. Raskin, "Legal Aliens, Local Citizens: The Historical, Constitutional, and Theoretical Meanings of Alien Suffrage," *University of Pennsylvania Law Review* 141 (1993): 1391, available at https://scholarship.law.upenn.edu/penn_law_review/vol141/iss4/3/ [https://perma.cc/68MH-DPZX].

48. Michael P. McDonald, "2016 November General Election Turnout Rates," United States Elections Project, last updated September 5, 2018, http://www.electproject.org/2016g [https://perma.cc/9ERE-V72A].

49. "Highlights of the French Presidential Vote," *New York Times*, May 7, 2017, https://www.nytimes.com/2017/05/07/world/europe/france-president-elections-le-pen-macron.html; Reiss Smith, "French Election Turnout 2017: How Many People Ruined Their Ballot Papers?" *Sunday Express*, May 8, 2017, https://www.express.co.uk/news/world/801656/French-election-turnout-2017-ruined-spoiler-ballot-papers [https://perma.cc/DR5V-55NW].

50. Michael P. McDonald, "Voter Turnout Demographics," United States Elections Project, http://www.electproject.org/home/voter-turnout/demographics [https://perma.cc/C3QM-ELBC]; William A. Galston and Clara Hendrickson, "How Millennials Voted This Election," Brookings, November 21, 2016, https://www.brookings.edu/blog/fixgov/2016/11/21/how-millennials-voted [https://perma.cc/CCJ4-2N5Q].

51. Thom File, *Young Adult Voting: An Analysis of Presidential Elections, 1964–2012* (Washington, DC: United States Census Bureau, April 2014), https://www.census.gov/prod/2014pubs/p20-573.pdf [https://perma.cc/G2Q9-J3PF].

52. Catherine Rampell, "Where Are All the Young Voters?" *Washington Post*, July 23, 2015, https://www.washingtonpost.com/opinions/where-are-the-young

-voters/2015/07/23/2781990e-316f-11e5-8f36-18d1d501920d_story.html [https://perma.cc/NX9H-7VMP].

53. Alan S. Gerber, Donald P. Green, and Ron Schachar, "Voting May Be Habit Forming: Evidence from a Randomized Field Experiment," *American Journal of Political Science* 47 (2003): 540.

54. Daniel Hart and Robert Atkins, "American Sixteen- and Seventeen-Year-Olds Are Ready to Vote," *Annals of the American Academy of Political and Social Science* 633 (2011): 207–208; Laurence Steinberg et al., "Are Adolescents Less Mature Than Adults? Minors' Access to Abortion, the Juvenile Death Penalty, and the Alleged APA 'Flip-Flop,'" *American Psychologist* 64 (2009): 583, 592; Laurence Steinberg, "A 16-Year-Old Is as Good as an 18-Year-Old—or a 40-Year-Old—at Voting," *Los Angeles Times*, November 3, 2014, https://www.latimes.com/opinion/op-ed/la-oe-steinberg-lower-voting-age -20141104-story.html [https://perma.cc/9SRV-X7DL]; Joshua Gans, "Why It's Time to Give Children the Right to Vote," *Forbes*, April 20, 2012, https://www.forbes.com/sites/joshuagans/2012/04/20/its-time-to-give-children-the-vote [https://perma.cc/AW3M-3CRA].

55. Douglas, "The Right to Vote Under Local Law."

56. American Sociological Association, "More Than Half of 'Children' Misperceive or Reject Parents' Political Party Affiliations," press release, November 17, 2015, http://www.asanet.org/sites/default/files/savvy/documents/press/pdfs/ASR_Dec_2015 _Ojeda_Hatemi_News_Release.pdf [https://perma.cc/GW3K-3WYZ].

57. "Millennials in Adulthood: Detached from Institutions, Networked with Friends," Pew Research Center, Washington, DC, March 7, 2014, http://www.pewsocial trends.org/2014/03/07/millennials-in-adulthood [https://perma.cc/CRU6-969E].

58. Emma Langman, "Scottish Independence: Research Finds Young Voters 'Don't Copy Parents,'" BBC News, March 4, 2014, http://www.bbc.com/news/uk-scotland -scotland-politics-26265299 [https://perma.cc/DK8S-P8J9]; Jan Eichhorn, *Will 16 and 17 Year Olds Make a Difference in the Referendum?* (Edinburgh: ScotCen Social Research, 2013), http://www.scotcen.org.uk/media/205540/131129_will-16-and-17-years-olds-make-a -difference.pdf [https://perma.cc/N5AV-3U3Z].

59. *Scottish Independence Referendum: Report on the Referendum Held on 18 September 2014* (London: Electoral Commission, December 2014), https://www.electoralcommission.org .uk/__data/assets/pdf_file/0010/179812/Scottish-independence-referendum-report.pdf [https://perma.cc/9C35-8EZT]. For information about the improved civics education in Scotland classrooms during this time, see chapter 10.

60. Ibid.; John Curtice, "So How Many 16 and 17 Year Olds Voted?" *What Scotland Thinks* (blog), December 16, 2014, http://blog.whatscotlandthinks.org/2014/12/many -16-17-year-olds-voted [https://perma.cc/G4NJ-7YX3].

61. Ruth Davidson, Sarah Wollaston, and David Fazakerley, *Giving 16 and 17 Year Olds the Vote: The Tory Case* (London: Tory Reform Group, 2016), https://www.trg.org.uk/ wp-content/uploads/2015/09/TRG_Giving-16-and-17-Year-Olds-the-Vote.pdf [https://perma.cc/96SF-UYLF].

62. David Denver, *The Scottish Parliament Elections of 2016: Report to the Electoral Commission* (London: Electoral Commission, 2016), https://www.electoralcommission.org.uk/__data/ assets/pdf_file/0003/214959/Report-Electoral-Data-May-2016-Scotland-Scottish -Parliament.pdf [https://perma.cc/G2NR-F6BC]. ("The Scottish electorate increased

from 3,950,626 in 2011 to 4,098,462 in 2016[,] an increase of 3.7%. More than half of the increase was due to 16- and 17-year olds being allowed to vote in these elections.").

63. Vote16USA, http://vote16usa.org [https://perma.cc/R3W5-W8S9].

64. I am a member of Vote16USA's advisory board, which is separate from the youth advisory board. Vote16USA: Advisory Board, http://vote16usa.org/about-us/advisory-board [https://perma.cc/9PDQ-V3YR].

65. Vote16USA, http://vote16usa.org [https://perma.cc/R3W5-W8S9].

66. Peggy Fox, "Washington, D.C., May Allow 16-Year-Olds to Vote for President in the 2020 Election," *USA Today*, April 17, 2018, https://www.usatoday.com/story/news/nation-now/2018/04/17/washington-d-c-may-allow-16-year-olds-vote-president-2020-election/523301002 [https://perma.cc/3QBT-53YX].

CHAPTER 2: SECOND CHANCES

1. "Denver Schimming," Sentencing Project, http://www.sentencingproject.org/stories/denver-schimming [https://perma.cc/J5TR-WZBD].

2. Denver Schimming, in discussion with the author, July 19, 2017.

3. Ibid.

4. For instance, the law requires former felons to pay all financial obligations such as legal fees and child support before they may regain their voting rights.

5. "Denver Schimming," Sentencing Project.

6. Denver Schimming, in discussion with the author, July 19, 2017.

7. "Voting as an Ex-Offender," Nonprofit VOTE, https://www.nonprofitvote.org/voting-in-your-state/special-circumstances/voting-as-an-ex-offender [https://perma.cc/7M2M-Q334].

8. Joseph "Jazz" Hayden and Lewis Webb Jr., "The State of Felony Disenfranchisement in America," MSNBC, January 17, 2015, http://www.msnbc.com/msnbc/the-state-felony-disenfranchisement-america [https://perma.cc/KV6U-Q3XH]; "Felon Disenfranchisement," FairVote, https://www.fairvote.org/felon_disenfranchisement [https://perma.cc/G4HV-P5ZK].

9. Christopher Uggen, Ryan Larson, and Sarah Shannon, "6 Million Lost Voters: State-Level Estimates of Felony Disenfranchisement, 2016," Sentencing Project, October 6, 2016, http://www.sentencingproject.org/publications/6-million-lost-voters-state-level-estimates-felony-disenfranchisement-2016 [https://perma.cc/LRK7-TGV7].

10. Nick Learned, "Wyoming House Passes Bill Which Would Automatically Restore Voting Rights of Some Nonviolent Felons," K2 Radio, January 26, 2017, http://k2radio.com/wyoming-house-passes-bill-which-would-automatically-restore-voting-rights-of-some-nonviolent-felons [https://perma.cc/2TGU-9G2U]; Ruth Kimata, "As of This Month Former Wyoming Felons Will Have the Right to Vote," KGWN, July 21, 2017, https://www.kgwn.tv/content/news/Former-Wyoming-felons-will-have-the-right-to-vote--435839693.html [https://perma.cc/SRQ3-2EN3].

11. "Voting Rights Restoration in Nevada," Brennan Center for Justice, April 20, 2018, https://www.brennancenter.org/analysis/voting-rights-restoration-efforts-nevada [https://perma.cc/P78J-XT87].

12. Restore the Vote: Minnesota, https://restorethevotemn.org [https://perma.cc/6NT6-T3LD]; Bobby Harrison, "Should Some Felons Regain Voting Rights?" *Daily Journal*, February 8, 2017, http://www.djournal.com/news/crime-law-enforcement/should-some-felons-regain-voting-rights/article_a3170594-7665-573b-8a18-1c7df15b0327.html [https://perma.cc/TNJ9-QDWH].

13. "Voting Rights Restoration Efforts in Nebraska," Brennan Center for Justice, May 10, 2017, https://www.brennancenter.org/analysis/voting-rights-restoration-efforts-nebraska [https://perma.cc/6C5B-LSV4].

14. Connor Sheets, "Gov. Ivey Signs Bill Restoring 'Thousands' of Alabama Felons' Right to Vote," *Birmingham News*, May 25, 2017, https://www.al.com/news/index.ssf/2017/05/gov_ivey_signs_bill_restoring.html [https://perma.cc/5W3Q-X2L3].

15. Sam Levine, "Roy Moore Criticizes Effort to Make Sure All Eligible Voters Can Vote in Alabama," *Huffington Post*, November 29, 2017, https://www.huffingtonpost.com/entry/roy-moore-alabama-voter-registration_us_5a1ef85ce4b017a311ebe308 [https://perma.cc/3FE9-8FHC].

16. "Andres Idarraga," Sentencing Project, http://www.sentencingproject.org/stories/andres-idarraga [https://perma.cc/58EN-LEPW].

17. Andres Idarraga, in discussion with the author, August 30, 2017.

18. "About OpenDoors," OpenDoors, http://www.opendoorsri.org/about [https://perma.cc/4S5K-57NS].

19. Brent Staples, "The Racist Origins of Felon Disenfranchisement," *New York Times*, November 18, 2014, https://www.nytimes.com/2014/11/19/opinion/the-racist-origins-of-felon-disenfranchisement.html; Janell Ross, "The Race-Infused History of Why Felons Aren't Allowed to Vote in a Dozen States," *Washington Post*, May 24, 2016, https://www.washingtonpost.com/news/the-fix/wp/2016/05/24/the-race-infused-history-of-why-felons-arent-allowed-to-vote-in-a-dozen-states [https://perma.cc/5DER-6UHM].

20. "Andres Idarraga," Sentencing Project.

21. Ibid.

22. Andres Idarraga, in discussion with the author, August 30, 2017.

23. "Andres Idarraga," Sentencing Project.

24. Andres Idarraga, in discussion with the author, August 30, 2017.

25. Camila DeChalus, "In Virginia, Ex-Felons Find Empowerment in the Voting Booth," CNN, November 5, 2016, https://www.cnn.com/2016/11/05/politics/virginia-felons-voting-rights [https://perma.cc/L79Y-MBK4].

26. Laura Barrón-López, Amber Ferguson, and Sam Levine, "67,000 Virginia Ex-Felons Just Got Their Voting Rights Back. This Man Wants to Make Sure They Keep Them," *Huffington Post*, October 20, 2016, https://www.huffingtonpost.com/entry/virginia-felons-voting-rights_us_5809292fe4b000d0b155b2cc [https://perma.cc/33NY-AQBX].

27. DeChalus, "In Virginia, Ex-Felons Find Empowerment."

28. Barrón-López, Ferguson, and Levine, "67,000 Virginia Ex-Felons."

29. Matt Ford, "Restoring Voting Rights for Felons in Maryland," *Atlantic*, February 9, 2016, https://www.theatlantic.com/politics/archive/2016/02/maryland-felon-voting/462000 [https://perma.cc/Z7Y8-JPG8].

30. Lindsay A. Powers, "Takoma Park Grants 16-Year-Olds Right to Vote," *Washington Post*, May 14, 2013, https://www.washingtonpost.com/local/takoma-park

-grants-16-year-olds-right-to-vote/2013/05/14/b27c52c4-bccd-11e2-89c9-3be8095fe767
_story.html [https://perma.cc/9WAD-VL99].

31. Etta Myers, "I'm Going to Cast My First Vote at 62: Column," *USA Today*, March 9, 2016, https://www.usatoday.com/story/opinion/2016/03/09/first-time-voter -felon-age-62-maryland-column/81535722 [https://perma.cc/TM6Z-LSGR].

32. Fenit Nirappil and Jenna Portnoy, "Va. High Court Invalidates McAuliffe's Order Restoring Felon Voting Rights," *Washington Post*, July 22, 2016, https://www .washingtonpost.com/local/virginia-politics/virginia-court-invalidates-gov-terry -mcauliffes-order-restoring-felon-voting-rights/2016/07/22/3e1d45f6-5058-11e6-a7d8 -13d06b37f256_story.html [https://perma.cc/H3GX-WDJ8].

33. VA. CONST. art. II, § 1, available at https://law.lis.virginia.gov/constitution/ article2/section1 [https://perma.cc/GJ3Z-7PJP].

34. Graham Moomaw, "Va. Supreme Court Strikes Down McAuliffe's Order on Felon Voting Rights," *Richmond Times-Dispatch*, July 23, 2016, http://www.richmond.com/ news/virginia/government-politics/va-supreme-court-strikes-down-mcauliffe-s-order -on-felon/article_718d04d8-70b2-5bfb-aa8c-0ff1ca108b8d.html [https://perma.cc/ W49B-FDNM].

35. Office of the Governor, "Governor McAuliffe Statement on the Virginia Supreme Court Decision on the Restoration of Civil Rights," news release, July 22, 2016, https://www.governor.virginia.gov/newsroom/all-releases/2017/mcauliffe -administration/headline-826617-en.html [https://perma.cc/B9A9-F7KF].

36. Laura Vozella, "McAuliffe Restores Voting Rights to 13,000 Felons," *Washington Post*, August 22, 2016, https://www.washingtonpost.com/local/virginia-politics/ mcauliffe-restores-voting-rights-to-13000-felons/2016/08/22/2372bb72-6878-11e6 -99bf-f0cf3a6449a6_story.html [https://perma.cc/NY97-62KL]; Laura Vozella "Va. Gov. McAuliffe Says He Has Broken U.S. Record for Restoring Voting Rights," *Washington Post*, April 27, 2017, https://www.washingtonpost.com/local/virginia-politics/va-gov -mcauliffe-says-he-has-broken-us-record-for-restoring-voting-rights/2017/04/27/ 55b5591a-2b8b-11e7-be51-b3fc6ff7faee_story.html [https://perma.cc/968A-TAXN].

37. Graham Moomaw, "McAuliffe Rights Restoration Official Will Stay on Under Northam," *Richmond Times-Dispatch*, December 28, 2017, https://www.richmond.com/ news/virginia/government-politics/mcauliffe-rights-restoration-official-will-stay-on -under-northam/article_bfdc6d2a-525b-56e5-a2df-02e0083be72e.html [https://perma .cc/B8TQ-YDSB].

38. "Legislative Update: Restore the Vote Scheduled for a Hearing!" Restore the Vote: Minnesota, March 20, 2018 [https://perma.cc/HEC7-99AC].

39. Joshua Lewis Berg, "The Case for Re-Enfranchisement," *Humanist*, October 25, 2016, https://thehumanist.com/magazine/november-december-2016/up-front/case -re-enfranchisement [https://perma.cc/UGQ6-25MY].

40. Dan Sweeney, "Florida's Felons Inch Closer to Regaining Right to Vote," *Sun Sentinel*, December 31, 2016, http://www.sun-sentinel.com/news/florida/fl-voting-rights -felons-20161231-story.html [https://perma.cc/K429-H9UV?type=image].

41. "Election 2016: Florida Results," CNN, http://edition.cnn.com/election/ results/states/florida.

42. "About Desmond Meade," Florida Rights Restoration Coalition, 2018, https:// floridarrc.com/desmond-meade [https://perma.cc/96F8-5D96].

43. "Florida Amendment 4, Voting Rights Restoration for Felons Initiative (2018)," *Ballotpedia*, https://ballotpedia.org/Florida_Amendment_4,_Voting_Rights_Restoration _for_Felons_Initiative_(2018) [https://perma.cc/HXY9-PJUP].

44. Guy Padraic Hamilton-Smith and Matt Vogel, "The Violence of Voicelessness: The Impact of Felony Disenfranchisement on Recidivism," *Berkeley La Raza Law Journal* 22 (2012): 407.

45. DeChalus, "In Virginia, Ex-Felons Find Empowerment."

46. Jeff Manza, Clem Brooks, and Christopher Uggen, "Public Attitudes Toward Felon Disenfranchisement in the United States," *Public Opinion Quarterly* 68 (2004): 275.

47. Joshua A. Douglas, "Virginia Is Proof That Every Vote Counts," CNN, December 20, 2017, https://www.cnn.com/2017/12/20/opinions/virginia-house-of -delegates-opinion-douglas/index.html [https://perma.cc/6PWT-RY6C].

48. Jeff Manza and Christopher Uggen, *Locked Out: Felon Disenfranchisement and American Democracy* (Oxford: Oxford University Press, 2006); Robert Farley, "Cruz on Violent Criminals and Democrats," FactCheck.org, December 1, 2015, https://www .factcheck.org/2015/12/cruz-on-violent-criminals-and-democrats [https://perma.cc/ Y2GN-BJGE].

49. However, some state courts have struck down portions of a felon disenfranchise-ment rule under their state constitution. See Joshua A. Douglas, "State Judges and the Right to Vote," *Ohio State Law Journal* 77 (2016): 21–24.

50. West Powell, in discussion with the author, March 23, 2018.

CHAPTER 3: WHAT DO TACO TRUCKS HAVE TO DO WITH VOTER REGISTRATION?

1. Gina Zejdlik, in discussion with the author, March 20, 2017.

2. Jeff Mapes, "Kate Brown Gets to Sign Her Own Bill, for Automatic Voter Registration in Oregon," *Oregonian*, March 16, 2015, https://www.oregonlive.com/ mapes/index.ssf/2015/03/kate_brown_gets_to_sign_her_ow.html [https://perma.cc/ E2A4-78ZM].

3. Steven Hill, *10 Steps to Repair American Democracy* (Sausalito, CA: PoliPointPress, 2006), pp. 36–37; Seth Grimes, "Let's Enfranchise Takoma Park Renters and Strengthen the Right to Vote!" *One Takoma* (blog), February 21, 2013, http://www.onetakoma.com/ 2013/02/lets-enfranchise-takoma-park-renters.html [https://perma.cc/ZVT7-X5ZV] (suggesting Election Day Registration for Takoma Park, Maryland).

4. Steve Trout, in discussion with the author, March 14, 2017.

5. Electronic Registration Information Center (ERIC), https://www.ericstates.org [https://perma.cc/3AR3-7L6Y].

6. Ibid.

7. Steve Trout, in discussion with the author, March 14, 2017.

8. Gina Zejdlik, in discussion with the author, March 20, 2017.

9. Ibid.

10. Steve Trout, in discussion with the author, March 14, 2017.

11. Rob Griffin, Paul Gronke, Tova Wang, and Liz Kennedy, "Who Votes with

Automatic Voter Registration?" Center for American Progress, June 7, 2017, https://www
.americanprogress.org/issues/democracy/reports/2017/06/07/433677/votes-automatic
-voter-registration [https://perma.cc/SCM5-Q8CZ].

12. Gina Zejdlik, in discussion with the author, March 20, 2017.

13. Mapes, "Kate Brown Gets to Sign Her Own Bill."

14. Gina Zejdlik, in discussion with the author, March 20, 2017.

15. National Voter Registration Act of 1993, 52 U.S.C. §§ 20501–20511.

16. Niraj Chokshi, "Automatic Voter Registration a 'Success' in Oregon," *New York Times*, December 2, 2016, https://www.nytimes.com/2016/12/02/us/politics/oregon-voter-registration.html; Ari Berman, "Automatic Voter Registration in Oregon Is Revolutionizing American Democracy," *Nation*, May 16, 2016, https://www.thenation.com/article/automatic-voter-registration-in-oregon-is-revolutionizing-american-democracy [https://perma.cc/6LJN-YYC9].

17. Griffin et al., "Who Votes with Automatic Voter Registration?"

18. Sean McElwee, Brian Schaffner, and Jesse Rhodes, "Oregon Automatic Voter Registration Methodology and Data," Dēmos, July 26, 2017, https://www.demos.org/publication/oregon-automatic-voter-registration [https://perma.cc/VAQ4-BWBB].

19. Paris Achen, "The Unrealized Potential of Nonaffiliated Voters," *Portland Tribune*, November 30, 2017, https://portlandtribune.com/pt/9-news/380100-267198-the-unrealized-potential-of-nonaffiliated-voters [https://perma.cc/R4LG-H7WJ].

20. Ibid.

21. For more on vote-by-mail, see chapter 4.

22. Sophie Schuit and Jonathan Brater, "West Virginia Third State to Pass Automatic Voter Registration," Brennan Center for Justice, April 4, 2016, https://www.brennancenter.org/blog/west-virginia-third-state-pass-automatic-voter-registration [https://perma.cc/GB5K-YADU]; Chuck Flannery, Chief of Staff for the West Virginia Secretary of State, in discussion with the author, March 13, 2017.

23. Julie Archer, in discussion with the author, March 20, 2017.

24. Chuck Flannery, in discussion with the author, March 13, 2017.

25. "Automatic Voter Registration," Brennan Center for Justice, April 9, 2018, https://www.brennancenter.org/analysis/automatic-voter-registration [https://perma.cc/JR33-XP4Y].

26. Josh Eidelson, "Alaska's Oil Cash Now Comes with Automatic Voter Registration," Bloomberg, November 10, 2016, https://www.bloomberg.com/news/articles/2016-11-10/alaska-s-oil-cash-now-comes-with-automatic-voter-registration [https://perma.cc/Y2PH-AQG3].

27. Sophia Tareen, "Illinois Governor Signs Automatic Voter Registration Law," Bloomberg, August 28, 2017, https://www.bloomberg.com/news/articles/2017-08-28/illinois-governor-signs-automatic-voter-registration-law [https://perma.cc/F6LL-JWXZ].

28. Jacqueline Tempera, "Raimondo Signs Automatic Voter Registration Bill into Law," *Providence Journal*, August 1, 2017, http://www.providencejournal.com/news/20170801/raimondo-signs-automatic-voter-registration-bill-into-law [https://perma.cc/BY7Q-5VA3]; "Automatic Voter Registration," Brennan Center for Justice.

29. Julia Manchester, "New Jersey Lawmakers Pass Automatic Voter Registration Bill," *Hill*, April 12, 2018, http://thehill.com/homenews/state-watch/382956-new-jersey-lawmakers-pass-automatic-voter-registration-bill [https://perma.cc/LA3C-GJ4T];

Joshua Miller, "Automatic Voter Registration May Be Coming to Mass.—and Bringing 500,000 New Voters with It," *Boston Globe*, June 27, 2018, https://www.bostonglobe.com/ metro/2018/06/27/automatic-voter-registration-may-coming-mass-and-bringing-new -voters-with/DPzH0vtwMWv0cKiS6mhkfO/story.html [https://perma.cc/7KPT-25X9].

30. "History of AVR & Implementation Dates," Brennan Center for Justice, November 7, 2018, https://www.brennancenter.org/analysis/history-avr-implementation -dates [https://perma.cc/KFW3-PUWR].

31. "Online Voter Registration," National Conference of State Legislatures, October 10, 2018, http://www.ncsl.org/research/elections-and-campaigns/electronic-or -online-voter-registration.aspx [https://perma.cc/96KJ-NDSX].

32. Help America Vote Act of 2002, 52 U.S.C. §§ 20901–21145.

33. Craig Stender, in discussion with the author, April 17, 2017.

34. Brian Corley, in discussion with the author, March 15, 2017.

35. Tammy Patrick, in discussion with the author, March 31, 2017; Presidential Commission on Election Administration, "Presidential Commission on Election Administration Presents Recommendations to President Obama," news release, January 22, 2014, http://web.mit.edu/supportthevoter/www/2014/01/22/presidential -commission-on-election-administration-presents-recommendations-to-president-obama [https://perma.cc/J8KK-Q3KP].

36. "The Many Benefits of Online Voter Registration," Scholars Strategy Network, February 27, 2014, https://scholars.org/brief/many-benefits-online-voter-registration [https://perma.cc/55JP-VZS3].

37. Brian Corley, in discussion with the author, March 15, 2017.

38. "Online Voter Registration Application," (position paper; Tallahassee, FL: Florida State Association of Supervisors of Elections, December 11, 2014), https://www .myfloridaelections.com/portals/fsase/documents/fsase__position_paperovr_application .pdf [https://perma.cc/6762-WJ4N].

39. "CS/CS/SB 228: Online Voter Application," Florida Senate, July 1, 2015, http://www.flsenate.gov/Session/Bill/2015/0228 [https://perma.cc/7BL2-3JE9]; Erin Ferns Lee, "Florida Adopts Online Registration, Effective 2017," Project Vote, May 30, 2015, http://www.projectvote.org/blog/florida-adopts-online-registration-effective-2017 [https://perma.cc/9LCT-TGQM].

40. Brian Corley, in discussion with the author, March 15, 2017.

41. "MyVote Unique URL," Washington Secretary of State, https://www.sos .wa.gov/elections/civics/myvote-unique-url.aspx [https://perma.cc/DY99-K2UF].

42. David Becker, "Online Voter Registration APIs—A New Trend?" Center for Election Innovation & Research, September 26, 2016, https://electioninnovation.org/ 2016/09/26/online-voter-registration-apis-a-new-trend [https://perma.cc/3KJB -JULW]; "Online Voter Registration Trends in Development and Implementation," Pew Charitable Trusts, May 2015, https://www.pewtrusts.org/~/media/assets/2015/05/ ovr_2015_brief.pdf [https://perma.cc/AWJ3-3VSM].

43. "Online Voter Registration | Tammy Patrick, Maricopa County, Ariz.," National Conference of State Legislatures, August 24, 2012, http://www.ncsl.org/ research/elections-and-campaigns/online-voter-registration-with-tammy-patrick.aspx [https://perma.cc/8LSA-A3TE].

44. "Interview with J. Alex Halderman on Cybersecurity for Online Voter Registration,"

National Conference of State Legislatures, March 2013, http://www.ncsl.org/research/ elections-and-campaigns/itnerview-j-alex-halderman-online-registration.aspx [https://perma .cc/3D9Q-XCTF]; "Understanding Online Voter Registration," Pew Charitable Trusts, January 2014, https://www.pewtrusts.org/~/media/legacy/uploadedfiles/pcs_assets/2013/ understandingonlinevoterregistrationpdf.pdf [https://perma.cc/F3CM-5LE5].

45. Kei Kawashima-Ginsberg, "Voter Registration among Young People in Midterm Elections," Center for Information & Research on Civic Learning & Engagement, June 2014, https://civicyouth.org/wp-content/uploads/2014/06/CIRCLE _FS2014_YouthRegistration.pdf [https://perma.cc/JRR2-Y3VE]; "Online Voter Registration (OLVR) Systems in Arizona and Washington: Evaluating Usage, Public Confidence and Implementation Processes," Pew Charitable Trusts, April 1, 2010, https://www.pewtrusts.org/~/media/legacy/uploadedfiles/pcs_assets/2010/ onlinevoterregpdf.pdf [https://perma.cc/FEM5-FUTY].

46. "Online Voter Registration," National Conference of State Legislatures.

47. "Same Day Voter Registration," National Conference of State Legislatures, March 27, 2018, http://www.ncsl.org/research/elections-and-campaigns/same-day -registration.aspx [https://perma.cc/NZF2-W75D].

48. Steven Carbo and Brenda Wright, "The Promise and Practice of Election Day Registration," Dēmos, https://www.demos.org/sites/default/files/publications/The -Promise-and%20Practice-of-Election-Day-Registration-copy.pdf [https://perma.cc/ 488G-24CS]; "Election Day Registration: FAQs," National Conference of State Legislatures, May 2013, http://www.ncsl.org/documents/legismgt/elect/Canvass _May_2013_No_40.pdf [https://perma.cc/AJC8-8LQ3].

49. Carbo and Wright, "The Promise and Practice."

50. Ibid.

51. "Same Day Voter Registration," National Conference of State Legislatures.

52. Ibid.

53. "Same-Day Registration," Dēmos, http://www.demos.org/sites/default/files/ publications/SameDayRegistration-2015.pdf [https://perma.cc/Z3WS-BDB2].

54. Lorraine C. Minnite, "An Analysis of Voter Fraud in the United States," Dēmos, http://www.demos.org/sites/default/files/publications/Analysis.pdf [https://perma.cc/ B8RA-FSDA]; Benjamin E. Griffith, ed., *America Votes!* (Chicago: American Bar Association 2008): 72.

55. "America Goes to the Polls: A Report on Voter Turnout," *NonprofitVOTE*, https://www.nonprofitvote.org/america-goes-to-the-polls-2016 [https://perma.cc/ TC4H-AUP4].

56. Ibid.

57. Carbo and Wright, "The Promise and Practice."

58. "Preregistration for Young Voters," National Conference of State Legislatures, March 28, 2018, http://www.ncsl.org/research/elections-and-campaigns/preregistration -for-young-voters.aspx [https://perma.cc/5XEN-XWJD].

59. Michael P. McDonald, "Voter Preregistration Programs," Comparative Study of Electoral Systems, http://www.cses.org/plancom/2009Toronto/CSES_2009Toronto _McDonald.pdf [https://perma.cc/QZ7H-NHKE].

60. "Voting Rights Lose in North Carolina," *New York Times*, April 27, 2016, https:// www.nytimes.com/2016/04/27/opinion/voting-rights-lose-in-north-carolina.html.

61. Rebecca Elliot, "Latino Political Participation Still Lags Population in the County," *Houston Chronicle*, November 27, 2016, https://www.houstonchronicle.com/news/houston-texas/houston/article/Latino-political-participation-still-lags-10639038.php [https://perma.cc/9QJ2-W2Q9].

62. Carlos Duarte, in discussion with the author, March 27, 2017.

63. "Big as Texas? Lone Star Election Turnout Is Minuscule," *Houston Chronicle*, January 6, 2018, https://www.houstonchronicle.com/opinion/editorials/article/Big-as-Texas-Lone-Star-election-turnout-is-12474905.php [https://perma.cc/9RAK-HXME].

64. Carlos Duarte, in discussion with the author, March 27, 2017.

65. Jeremy Schwartz and Dan Keemahill, "Number of Texas Latino Voters Climbed 29 Percent in 2016, Records Show," *Austin American-Statesman*, February 10, 2017, https://www.mystatesman.com/news/number-texas-latino-voters-climbed-percent-2016-records-show/O8b3mnjP20l3erCaH1xcFI [https://perma.cc/88H5-4GDS].

66. Alexa Ura and Ryan Murphy, "Despite High Expectations for 2016, No Surge in Texas Hispanic Voter Turnout," *Texas Tribune*, May 11, 2017, https://www.texastribune.org/2017/05/11/hispanic-turnout-2016-election [https://perma.cc/RXS2-FB7E].

67. "High School Students Participate in Voter Registration," Huntsville City Schools, https://www.huntsvillecityschools.org/schools/high-school-students-participate-voter-registration [https://perma.cc/Z886-ZB6R].

68. Daniel Beekman, "Seattle Landlords Must Give Voter-Registration Info to New Renters, City Council Decides," *Seattle Times*, June 20, 2017, https://www.seattletimes.com/seattle-news/politics/seattle-landlords-must-give-voter-registration-info-to-new-renters-city-council-decides [https://perma.cc/C98B-8M4K].

CHAPTER 4: HOW VOTING CAN BE AS EASY AS FOOD SHOPPING

1. "Vote Centers Come of Age," National Conference of State Legislatures, August 2011, http://www.ncsl.org/research/elections-and-campaigns/cnv-the-canvass-vol-xxii-aug-2011.aspx#Center [https://perma.cc/JK29-AURS].

2. Scott Doyle, in discussion with the author, November 7, 2017.

3. Ibid.

4. Help America Vote Act of 2002, 52 U.S.C. §§ 20901–21145.

5. John A. Straayer, Robert J. Duffy, and Courtenay W. Daum, eds., *State of Change: Colorado Politics in the Twenty-First Century* (Boulder: University Press of Colorado, 2011), p. 123.

6. Scott Doyle, in discussion with the author, November 7, 2017.

7. "Vote Centers and Election Costs: A Study of the Fiscal Impact of Vote Centers in Indiana," Indiana Fiscal Policy Institute, January 2010, http://www.in.gov/sos/elections/files/Full_Report.pdf [https://perma.cc/8CFR-ARPW]; Doug Chapin, "Vote Centers Turn 10," Election Academy, May 31, 2013, http://editions.lib.umn.edu/electionacademy/2013/05/31/vote-centers-turn-10 [https://perma.cc/U6JS-LS5L].

8. "Vote Center History," Larimer County, https://www.larimer.org/clerk/elections/resources/history-vote-centers/vote-center-history [https://perma.cc/Z32S-47W6]; Scott

Doyle, "Larimer County Clerk and Recorder," Larimer County, July 3, 2003, https://www
.larimer.org/sites/default/files/vote_centers.pdf [https://perma.cc/TXW7-R5JF].

9. "Vote Center History," Larimer County.

10. Monte Whaley, "Vote Centers 'a Total Fiasco,'" *Denver Post*, November 8, 2006,
http://www.denverpost.com/2006/11/08/vote-centers-a-total-fiasco [https://perma.cc/
Y5CB-FLLA].

11. Robert M. Stein and Greg Vonnahme, "Engaging the Unengaged Voter: Vote
Centers and Voter Turnout," *Journal of Politics* 70, no. 2 (April 2008): 487–97.

12. "Vote Centers Come of Age," National Conference of State Legislatures.

13. Straayer et al., *State of Change*, p. 120.

14. Scott Doyle, in discussion with the author, November 7, 2017.

15. Ibid.

16. Ibid.

17. "Civil Service Went Before Politics for Scott Doyle," *Reporter-Herald*, May 1,
2013, http://www.reporterherald.com/opinion/editorial/ci_23151083/civil-service
-went-before-politics-scott-doyle [https://perma.cc/4VQF-K92L].

18. "A Study of Vote Centers and their Applicability to the Hoosier Election
Process," Indiana Government, December 13, 2005, http://www.in.gov/sos/elections/
files/VoteCenters.pdf [https://perma.cc/9GFV-UCJJ]; "Where to Vote on Election
Day," Teton County, Wyoming, http://www.tetonwyo.org/283/Where-to-Vote-on
-Election-Day [https://perma.cc/PAK5-YXEL].

19. Chapin, "Vote Centers Turn 10"; "Do You Live in a Vote Center County?" Indiana
Government, http://www.in.gov/sos/elections/3574.htm [https://perma.cc/T66N-5W2F].

20. Straayer et al., *State of Change*, p. 125.

21. "Use of Vote Centers on the Rise Nationwide," Pew Charitable Trusts, January
15, 2015, http://www.pewtrusts.org/en/research-and-analysis/analysis/2015/01/15/
use-of-vote-centers-on-the-rise-nationwide [https://perma.cc/U8X2-MSSC];
"Introduction," National Conference of State Legislatures, http://www.ncsl.org/
research/elections-and-campaigns/vote-centers.aspx [https://perma.cc/AA6Q-KW8B].

22. "Voting Convenience Centers," Doña Ana County, https://donaanacounty.org/
elections/vcc [https://perma.cc/E67P-TULZ]; "Where to Vote On Election Day," Teton
County, Wyoming.

23. Phil Keisling, "Vote at Home and Save Our Democracy" (presentation, Unrig
the System Summit, New Orleans, LA, February 2, 2018).

24. "All-Mail Elections (AKA Vote-by-Mail)," National Conference of State
Legislatures, January 12, 2017, http://www.ncsl.org/research/elections-and-campaigns/
all-mail-elections.aspx [https://perma.cc/R3MX-4F5L].

25. Phil Keisling, "Vote from Home, Save Your Country," *Washington Monthly*,
January/February 2016, https://washingtonmonthly.com/magazine/janfeb-2016/vote
-from-home-save-your-country [https://perma.cc/TL2Y-PJTH].

26. Robert Lindsey, "Mailbox Replaces Voting Booth in San Diego Referendum,"
New York Times, April 25, 1981, https://www.nytimes.com/1981/04/25/us/mailbox
-replaces-voting-booth-in-san-diego-referendum.html; "The Origins of All-Mail Voting
Are Further South Than You May Think," U.S. Vote Foundation, https://www
.usvotefoundation.org/blog/domestic-voting/origins-all-mail-voting-are-further-south
-you-may-think [https://perma.cc/9CF6-UZCW].

27. Ibid.; "State Elections Performance," *Capitol Ideas*, September/October 2014, p. 22, https://www.csg.org/pubs/capitolideas/2014_sept_oct/2014_sept_oct_images/ SeptOctCI2014_Interactive.pdf [https://perma.cc/D5KU-F7E5].

28. "Oregon Vote-by-Mail," Oregon Secretary of State, http://sos.oregon.gov/ elections/Documents/statistics/vote-by-mail-timeline.pdf [https://perma.cc/ M6Z7-4HFU].

29. Much of the information in this section comes from an interview I conducted with Phil Keisling. Phil Keisling, in discussion with the author, October 31, 2017.

30. Keisling, "Vote from Home, Save Your Country."

31. Ibid.

32. Don Hamilton, "The Oregon Voting Revolution," *American Prospect*, April 16, 2006, http://prospect.org/article/oregon-voting-revolution [https://perma.cc/ DGF5-2K9V].

33. Ibid.

34. Phil Keisling, in discussion with the author, October 31, 2017.

35. Timothy Egan, "Oregon's Mail-In Election Brings Cheer to Democrats," *New York Times*, February 1, 1996, http://www.nytimes.com/1996/02/01/us/oregon-s-mail -in-election-brings-cheer-to-democrats.html.

36. Paul Gronke, "Ballot Integrity and Voting by Mail: The Oregon Experience," Early Voting Information Center at Reed College, June 15, 2005, https://people.reed .edu/~gronkep/docs/Carter%20Baker%20Report-publicrelease.pdf [https://perma.cc/ 8FJE-3D8W].

37. Ibid.

38. Hamilton, "The Oregon Voting Revolution."

39. Gronke, "Ballot Integrity and Voting by Mail."

40. Gilad Edelman and Paul Glastris, "Letting People Vote at Home Increases Voter Turnout. Here's Proof," *Washington Post*, January 26, 2018, https://www.washington post.com/outlook/letting-people-vote-at-home-increases-voter-turnout-heres-proof/ 2018/01/26/d637b9d2-017a-11e8-bb03-722769454f82_story.html [https://perma.cc/ P7MU-U296].

41. Ibid.

42. Ibid.

43. Ibid.

44. Phil Keisling, in discussion with the author, October 31, 2017; Phil Keisling, email message to author, June 14, 2018.

45. "About Us," National Vote at Home Institute, https://www.voteathome.org/ about [https://perma.cc/LQ5W-EXMX].

46. Ibid.

47. Phil Keisling, in discussion with the author, October 31, 2017.

48. "electionlineWeekly—March 2, 2017," *electionLine*, March 2, 2017, http://www .electionline.org/index.php/2017/2132-electionlineweekly-march-2-2017 [https:// perma.cc/6U93-77G5]; "King County Successfully Pilots Pre-Paid Postage: Voter Turnout Exceeds Projections," King County, February 24, 2017, http://www.kingcounty .gov/depts/elections/about-us/newsroom/news-releases/2017/february/24-pilot-results .aspx [https://perma.cc/Y48Y-CUKN].

49. Ibid; Sam Levine, "Washington Officials Say State Will Cover Postage for

Mail-In Ballots This Year," *HuffPost*, May 15, 2018, https://www.huffingtonpost.com/entry/washington-will-pay-postage-ballots_us_5afb4742e4b06a3fb50b8293?cll [https://perma.cc/BZG9-2KLL].

50. "All-Mail Elections (AKA Vote-by-Mail)," National Conference of State Legislatures.

51. "State Status—July 2018," National Vote at Home Institute, https://www.voteathome.org/about [https://perma.cc/QU8Q-WASZ?type=image].

52. The jurisdictions that allow permanent absentee ballot status for any voter are Arizona, California, DC, Hawaii, Minnesota, Montana, New Jersey, and Utah. "Absentee and Early Voting," National Conference of State Legislatures, January 3, 2019, http://www.ncsl.org/research/elections-and-campaigns/absentee-and-early-voting.aspx [https://perma.cc/8R3A-H3W3].

53. Ibid.

54. Keisling, "Vote at Home and Save Our Democracy."

55. Keisling, "Vote from Home, Save Your Country."

56. Paul W. Taylor, "Why Hasn't Voting by Mail Spread?" *Governing*, March 2011, http://www.governing.com/columns/dispatch/Why-Hasnt-Voting-by-Mail-Spread.html [https://perma.cc/APK9-U8XQ].

57. "The Misleading Myth of Voter Fraud in American Elections," Scholars Strategy Network, January 28, 2014, http://www.scholarsstrategynetwork.org/brief/misleading-myth-voter-fraud-american-elections [https://perma.cc/75M3-7S4V]; Adam Liptak, "Error and Fraud at Issue as Absentee Voting Rises," *New York Times*, October 6, 2012, http://www.nytimes.com/2012/10/07/us/politics/as-more-vote-by-mail-faulty-ballots-could-impact-elections.html.

58. Gronke, "Ballot Integrity and Voting by Mail"; Kate Brown, "Vote Fraud Is Extremely Rare and Always Unacceptable," *Oregonian*, April 20, 2010, http://www.oregonlive.com/opinion/index.ssf/2010/04/vote_fraud_is_extremely_rare_a.html [https://perma.cc/YH2W-KHLE].

59. Brown, "Vote Fraud Is Extremely Rare."

60. Keisling, "Vote from Home, Save Your Country."

61. Brown, "Vote Fraud Is Extremely Rare."

62. Gronke, "Ballot Integrity and Voting by Mail."

63. Keisling, "Vote at Home and Save Our Democracy."

64. "Voting Methods and Equipment by State," *Ballotpedia*, https://ballotpedia.org/Voting_methods_and_equipment_by_state [https://perma.cc/A534-FXMU].

65. "Vote by Mail Concerns, Part 1," Election Integrity Project, https://www.electionintegrityproject.com/education/voting/Vote_by_Mail_concerns1.pdf [https://perma.cc/ZZ7E-3EQP].

66. Charles H. Stewart, "Losing Votes by Mail," *New York University Journal of Legislation and Public Policy, Symposium Issue—Helping America Vote: The Past, Present, and Future of Election Administration* 13.3 (2010): 573–601; Liptak, "Error and Fraud at Issue."

67. "Electronic Transmission of Ballots," National Conference of State Legislatures, February 28, 2018, http://www.ncsl.org/research/elections-and-campaigns/internet-voting.aspx [https://perma.cc/F5M5-9QSA]; Sara Horwitz, "More Than 30 States Offer Online Voting, but Experts Warn It Isn't Secure," *Washington Post*, May 17, 2016, https://www.washingtonpost.com/news/post-nation/wp/2016/05/17/more-than-30-states-offer-online-voting-but-experts-warn-it-isnt-secure [https://perma.cc/MP6L-DQV4].

68. Horwitz, "More Than 30 States."

69. Cynthia McFadden, William M. Arkin, and Kevin Monahan, "Russians Penetrated U.S. Voter Systems, Top U.S. Official Says," NBC News, February 7, 2018, https://www.nbcnews.com/politics/elections/russians-penetrated-u-s-voter-systems-says -top-u-s-n845721 [https://perma.cc/SMD7-K7EB].

70. Horwitz, "More Than 30 States."

71. Ibid.

72. Scott Wolchok et al., "Attacking the Washington, D.C. Internet Voting System," *Proc. 16th Conference on Financial Cryptography & Data Security* (2012), https://jhalderm.com/ pub/papers/dcvoting-fc12.pdf [https://perma.cc/FQ8C-FPTD].

73. Ibid.; Richard L. Hasen, *The Voting Wars: From Florida 2000 to the Next Electoral Meltdown* (New Haven: Yale University Press, 2012): 163–64.

74. Hasen, *The Voting Wars*, p. 165.

75. Morgan Chalfant, "West Virginia Tests Secure Mobile Voting App for Military Personnel," *Hill*, March 28, 2018, http://thehill.com/policy/cybersecurity/380690 -west-virginia-tests-secure-mobile-voting-app-for-military-personnel [https://perma.cc/ QBN3-HMBS].

76. Casey Craiger, "Boyle One of 7 Counties Testing Paperless Polling Check-Ins," *Advocate-Messenger*, May 26, 2018, https://www.amnews.com/2018/05/26/boyle-one-of -7-counties-testing-paperless-polling-check-ins [https://perma.cc/LXW6-MJLU].

77. Brandon Smith, "Senate Panel Advances Bill to Allow No-Excuse Absentee Voting," Indiana Public Media, January 8, 2018, https://indianapublicmedia.org/ news/senate-panel-advances-bill-noexcuse-absentee-voting-136884 [https://perma.cc/ P45U-FKQQ].

78. Ibid.

79. Sam Levine, "Michigan Just Made It a Lot Easier to Vote," *Huffington Post*, November 6, 2018, https://www.huffingtonpost.com/entry/michigan-promote-the-vote _us_5bdcda50e4b09d43e31f00e9 [https://perma.cc/PQM8-KPDN].

80. Zoe Clark and Rick Pluta, "Who Wants to Make Absentee Voting Easier in Michigan?" Michigan Radio, March 20, 2017, http://michiganradio.org/post/who -wants-make-absentee-voting-easier-michigan [https://perma.cc/HA28-ZBG8].

81. Ann-Christine Diaz, "Boost Mobile Is Turning Its Storefronts into Polling Places on Election Day," *Ad Age*, October 5, 2016, http://adage.com/article/campaign-trail/ boost-mobile-turning-storefronts-polling-places/306175 [https://perma.cc/8NY5 -GU4F]; "Winners Announced for Ad Age's New Creativity Awards," *Ad Age*, http:// adage.com/article/news/winners-ad-age-s-creativity-awards/308729 [https://perma .cc/822J-44NL]; Michael Harriot, "This Is What Happened When Boost Mobile Came Up with a Solution to Voting Inequality," Root, April 27, 2017, http://www.theroot.com/ this-is-what-happened-when-boost-mobile-came-up-with-a-1794712712 [https://perma .cc/36AR-KEQE].

82. Blake Paterson, "First-Time Voters Get More Than a Sticker at This Poll," *Houston Chronicle*, November 3, 2016, http://www.houstonchronicle.com/news/politics/ houston/article/First-time-voters-get-more-than-a-sticker-at-this-10592053.php [https:// perma.cc/BZG9-2KLL].

CHAPTER 5: ALL FOR ONE AND ONE FOR ALL: VOTING MACHINE EDITION

1. "Online Voter Registration," National Conference of State Legislatures, December 6, 2017, http://www.ncsl.org/research/elections-and-campaigns/electronic-or-online-voter-registration.aspx [https://perma.cc/T4A3-D3FA].

2. Pam Fessler, "Voters with Disabilities Fight for More Accessible Polling Places," NPR, October 24, 2016, http://www.npr.org/2016/10/24/499177544/disabled-voters-fight-for-more-accessible-polling-places [https://perma.cc/YE8P-7P3R].

3. Ibid.

4. "DC Voting Access Report—the June 14, 2016 Presidential Primary Election," University Legal Services for the District of Columbia, June 14, 2016, http://www.uls-dc.org/DC%20Voting%20Access%20Report%20-%20June%2014,%202016%20Presidential%20Primary.pdf [https://perma.cc/E7P9-36LS].

5. Ibid.

6. Fessler, "Voters with Disabilities Fight."

7. Lisa Schur, "Reducing Obstacles to Voting for People with Disabilities," *White Paper prepared for Presidential Commission on Election Administration*, June 22, 2013, http://web.mit.edu/supportthevoter/www/files/2013/08/Disability-and-Voting-White-Paper-for-Presidential-Commission-Schur.docx_.pdf [https://perma.cc/SL5T-PNQW].

8. Lisa Schur and Douglas Kruse, "Fact sheet: Disability and Voter Turnout in the 2016 Elections," Rutgers School of Management and Labor Relations, https://smlr.rutgers.edu/sites/default/files/documents/PressReleases/kruse_and_schur_-_2016_disability_turnout.pdf [https://perma.cc/RU47-LZYM].

9. Chris Stewart, email message to author, April 28, 2017.

10. Juan Gilbert, "How Universal Design Can Help Every Voter Cast a Ballot," *University of Florida News*, May 5, 2016, http://news.ufl.edu/articles/2016/05/how-universal-design-can-help-every-voter-cast-a-ballot.php [https://perma.cc/R2B4-38RN].

11. Ibid.

12. Alexa Lorenzo, "UF-Developed Voting Machine for Disabled Used On Election Day," WUFT, November 16, 2016, https://www.wuft.org/news/2016/11/16/uf-developed-voting-machine-for-disabled-used-on-election-day [https://perma.cc/YSN9-9UT8].

13. Juan Gilbert, email message to author, April 30, 2017.

14. "Prime III," Verified Voting, https://www.verifiedvoting.org/one4all [https://perma.cc/XA3V-W3P2].

15. Hadley Barndollar, "Exeter to Fund Technology for Blind Voters," *Seacoast Online*, February 23, 2017, http://www.seacoastonline.com/news/20170223/exeter-to-fund-technology-for-blind-voters [https://perma.cc/ME7E-9BDE].

16. Sarah Breitenbach, "Aging Voting Machines Cost Local, State Governments," Pew Charitable Trusts, March 2, 2016, http://www.pewtrusts.org/en/research-and-analysis/blogs/stateline/2016/03/02/aging-voting-machines-cost-local-state-governments [https://perma.cc/PWH2-JJKZ].

17. Jean Shiner and Dana Trahan, in discussion with the author, July 5, 2017.

18. Ibid.

19. Ibid.

20. Ibid.

21. There are at least four federal laws that guarantee voters with disabilities equal access to the polls: the Voting Rights Act of 1965, the Voting Accessibility for the Elderly and Handicapped Act of 1984, the Americans with Disabilities Act of 1990, and the Help America Vote Act of 2002. Most state laws also include similar mandates. For example, Michigan law requires that electronic voting machines "[b]e compatible with or include at least 1 voting device that is accessible for an individual with disabilities to vote in a manner that provides the same opportunity for access and participation, including secrecy and independence, as provided for other voters. The voting device shall include nonvisual accessibility for the blind and visually impaired." MICH. COMP. LAWS § 168.795, available at http://www.legislature.mi.gov/(S(5b2vmj3tixysy0m5e0z23nk2))/mileg.aspx?page=get object&objectname=mcl-168-795 [https://perma.cc/8ZJP-FWL8].

22. Michael Haas, in discussion with the author, March 2, 2017.

23. "Voting Accessibility," Wisconsin Elections Commission, http://elections.wi .gov/voters/accessibility [https://perma.cc/AZP6-BPTU].

24. Michael Haas, in discussion with the author, March 2, 2017.

25. Ibid.

26. S. E. Smith, "Voting Is Already Hard for People with Disabilities. Voter ID Laws Make It Even Harder," *Vox*, April 1, 2016, https://www.vox.com/2016/4/1/11346714/ voter-id-laws-disabilities [https://perma.cc/RZE7-DLNK].

27. "Rights for Voters with Specific Needs," Los Angeles County Registrar-Recorder/County Clerk, https://www.lavote.net/home/voting-elections/voting-options/ voting-accessibility/rights-for-voters-with-specific-needs [https://perma.cc/H55T-D3U2].

28. Ibid.

29. "Voter Aid and Accessibility," North Carolina State Board of Elections & Ethics Enforcement, https://www.ncsbe.gov/voting-accessibility [https://perma.cc/TJ54-4JQK].

30. Ibid.; "Voting Accessibility," Wisconsin Elections Commission.

31. "Accessible Voting," Office of the Secretary of State—Washington, https:// wei.sos.wa.gov/agency/osos/en/Documents/accessible_voting.pdf [https://perma.cc/ M5U2-8B9T].

32. Ibid.

33. "Election Day: Louisiana Voter's Bill of Rights and Voting Information," Louisiana Secretary of State, https://www.sos.la.gov/ElectionsAndVoting/Published Documents/BillOfRights.pdf [https://perma.cc/J48T-4L3J].

34. Paul Pate, "Iowa Sec. of State Tweet," Twitter, April 5, 2017, https://twitter .com/iowasos/status/849723751394672640 [https://perma.cc/6YYZ-GXC8].

35. "Voting Instructions for Voters with a Disability," Oregon Secretary of State Dennis Richardson, http://sos.oregon.gov/voting/Pages/instructions-disabilities.aspx [https://perma.cc/2LXU-CJW8].

36. Nat'l Fed'n of the Blind v. Lamone, 813 F.3d 494, 498 (4th Cir. 2016); Andy Jones, "Court: Maryland Must Implement Online Ballot Marking Tool," Rooted in Rights, February 24, 2016, http://www.rootedinrights.org/court-maryland-must -implement-online-ballot-marking-tool [https://perma.cc/V3BC-MV7C].

37. "Best Processes to Reduce and Eliminate Accessibility Barriers for Voters with Disabilities: Presentation to the Presidential Commission on Election Administration," Disability Rights California, August 6, 2013, http://web.mit.edu/supportthevoter/www/

files/2013/06/FOCE.12-DRC-Barriers-and-Best-Processes-Voters-with-Disabilities.pdf [https://perma.cc/DBY2-JCB3].

38. Katherine Q. Seelye, "Oregon Tests iPads as Aid to Disabled Voters," *New York Times*, November 16, 2011, http://www.nytimes.com/2011/11/17/us/oregon-tries-out -voting-by-ipad-for-disabled.html.

39. "Voting for Residents of Long Term Care Facilities," National Conference of State Legislatures, December 16, 2013, http://www.ncsl.org/research/elections-and-campaigns/ voting-for-residents-of-long-term-care-facilities.aspx [https://perma.cc/M9M3-8KYZ].

40. Ibid.

41. "Best Processes to Reduce and Eliminate Accessibility Barriers for Voters with Disabilities," Disability Rights California.

42. "Welcome to the Easy Voter Guide Project!" *Easy Voter Guide*, http://www .easyvoterguide.org [https://perma.cc/939X-UVCA].

43. "Best Processes to Reduce and Eliminate Accessibility Barriers for Voters with Disabilities," Disability Rights California.

44. This is Spanish for "helping everyone vote."

45. 52 U.S.C. § 10503.

46. Michael D. Regan, "New Languages for NYC Voter Registration Could Expand Access for Immigrants," *PBS NewsHour*, October 9, 2016, http://www.pbs.org/ newshour/rundown/new-york-city-voter-registration-languages [https://perma.cc/ 9JPK-HAPT].

47. "Election Program: Election Ambassador Handbook," Committee of Seventy, November 17, 2017, https://seventy.org/uploads/files/5828008085284063-election -ambassador-handbook-nov-2017.pdf [https://perma.cc/G77Y-WHR3].

48. Gabrielle Emanuel, "How Boston Helps Its Non-English Speaking Voters Fill Out Their Ballots," Public Radio International, November 7, 2016, https://www.pri.org/ stories/2016-11-07/how-boston-helps-its-non-english-speaking-voters-fill-out-their-ballots [https://perma.cc/HH4S-JNS4].

49. Ibrahim Hirsi, "How Minnesota Has Tried to Make Voting More Accessible to New Americans," *Minnesota Post*, November 4, 2016, https://www.minnpost.com/new -americans/2016/11/how-minnesota-has-tried-make-voting-more-accessible-new -americans [https://perma.cc/VZ9W-K624].

50. Aysha Khan, "This New App Takes On Language Barriers Crippling the Asian American Vote," Medium, August 10, 2016, https://medium.com/umdplex/this -new-app-takes-on-language-barriers-crippling-the-asian-american-vote-2d68a8678a0d [https://perma.cc/9HV9-M2AY]; Frances Kai-Hwa Wang, "Can This New App Help More Asian Americans Vote in 2016?" NBC News, August 13, 2015, https://www .nbcnews.com/news/asian-america/can-new-app-help-more-asian-americans-vote -2016-n406021 [https://perma.cc/KSL5-NSY4].

51. "How Might We Design an Accessible Election Experience for Everyone?" OpenIDEO, https://challenges.openideo.com/challenge/voting/brief.html [https:// perma.cc/K92Z-ZJ64].

52. Ibid.

CHAPTER 6: THIS FORMER MISS WISCONSIN
MAY SAVE YOUR VOTE

1. Molly McGrath, in discussion with the author, March 1, 2017.

2. Ari Berman, "Rigged: How Voter Suppression Threw Wisconsin to Trump," *Mother Jones*, November/December 2017, https://www.motherjones.com/politics/2017/10/voter-suppression-wisconsin-election-2016 [https://perma.cc/BQ3M-C5VN].

3. Molly McGrath, in discussion with the author, March 1, 2017.

4. Richard Wolf, "Supreme Court Blocks Wisconsin's Voter ID Law," *USA Today*, October 9, 2014, https://www.usatoday.com/story/news/politics/2014/10/09/supreme-court-wisconsin-voter-id/16985963 [https://perma.cc/C5QK-KYLX]; Richard L. Hasen, "Reining in the Purcell Principle," *Florida State University Law Review* 43 (2016), p. 427.

5. "Wisconsin Voter Identification Requirements and History," *Ballotpedia*, https://ballotpedia.org/Wisconsin_voter_identification_requirements_and_history [https://perma.cc/J7WT-KMMD].

6. "Voter Identification Requirements | Voter ID Laws," National Conference of State Legislatures, October 31, 2018, http://www.ncsl.org/research/elections-and-campaigns/voter-id.aspx [https://perma.cc/D2VQ-2QBM].

7. Christina A. Cassidy and Ivan Moreno, "Wisconsin Voter ID Law Proved Insurmountable for Many," *Milwaukee Journal Sentinel*, May 14, 2017, https://www.jsonline.com/story/news/politics/2017/05/14/wisconsin-voter-id-law-proved-insurmountable-many/321680001 [https://perma.cc/6CMS-L86Q].

8. Frank v. Walker, No. 11-CV-01128 (E.D. Wisc. 2014), available at "Read the Judge's Ruling Striking Down Wisconsin's Voter ID Law," *Wisconsin State Journal*, April 29, 2014, http://host.madison.com/wsj/news/local/govt-and-politics/read-the-judge-s-ruling-striking-down-wisconsin-s-voter/pdf_f1a01292-a8e4-5ddc-90ed-0a5d75385a2b.html [https://perma.cc/76RE-TC85].

9. "Voter Identification Requirements | Voter ID Laws," National Conference of State Legislatures.

10. Paul Premack, "Court Order Relaxes Voter ID Requirements," *San Antonio Express-News*, August 29, 2016, https://www.mysanantonio.com/life/life_columnists/paul_premack/article/Court-Order-relaxes-Voter-ID-requirements-9191400.php [https://perma.cc/JB3Z-H6E7]; "Texas NAACP v. Steen (consolidated with Veasey v. Abbott)," Brennan Center for Justice, April 27, 2018, https://www.brennancenter.org/legal-work/naacp-v-steen [https://perma.cc/ZS5W-TQ36].

11. The Brennan Center has compiled a list of numerous papers demonstrating the effects of voter ID laws on voter participation and election integrity. "Research on Voter ID," Brennan Center for Justice, April 11, 2017, https://www.brennancenter.org/analysis/research-and-publications-voter-id [https://perma.cc/5GC5-F6B2].

12. Justin Levitt, "A Comprehensive Investigation of Voter Impersonation Finds 31 Credible Incidents out of One Billion Ballots Cast," *Washington Post*, August 6, 2014, https://www.washingtonpost.com/news/wonk/wp/2014/08/06/a-comprehensive-investigation-of-voter-impersonation-finds-31-credible-incidents-out-of-one-billion-ballots-cast [https://perma.cc/4YXE-PBZ6].

13. Ari Berman, "A 90-Year-Old Woman Who's Voted Since 1948 Was

Disenfranchised by Wisconsin's Voter-ID Law," *Nation*, October 5, 2016, https://www
.thenation.com/article/a-90-year-old-woman-whos-voted-since-1948-was-disenfranchised
-by-wisconsins-voter-id-law [https://perma.cc/KR52-NKRQ].

14. Shamane Mills, "National Group Steps in to Help Madison Voters with ID
Requirements," Wisconsin Public Radio, March 2, 2016, https://www.wpr.org/national
-group-steps-help-madison-voters-id-requirements [https://perma.cc/8EMJ-KGR8].

15. The spring primary involved nonpartisan judicial and local candidates.
Wisconsin held its presidential preference primary a few months later. "Spring Primary
Voter Turnout Estimated at 10 Percent," Wisconsin Elections Commission, February 12,
2016, http://elections.wi.gov/node/3873 [https://perma.cc/D7XP-NP9J].

16. Renée Cross, Jim Granato, and Mark P. Jones, "In Texas, Almost All Non-Voters
Have a Photo ID—but Few Understand the Voter Identification Rules," *Washington Post*,
May 8, 2017, https://www.washingtonpost.com/news/monkey-cage/wp/2017/05/08/
in-texas-almost-everyone-has-a-photo-id-but-few-understand-the-voting-rules [https://
perma.cc/G5T6-BHED].

17. Ibid.

18. Crawford v. Marion County Election Board, 553 U.S. 181 (2008).

19. Joshua A. Douglas, "The History of Voter ID Laws and the Story of *Crawford
v. Marion County Election Board*," *Election Law Stories* (Douglas and Mazo, eds., St. Paul:
Foundation Press, 2016), p. 457.

20. NC State Conference of NAACP v. McCrory, 831 F.3d 204, 214 (4th Cir. 2016).

21. "Wisconsin Voter Identification Requirements and History," *Ballotpedia*.

22. VoteRiders, https://www.voteriders.org [https://perma.cc/M5EN-HGLY].

23. Lane Florsheim, "VoteRiders President Kathleen Unger, Who Aims to Help
Disenfranchised Voters in States with Stringent Voter ID Laws," Bustle, September 16,
2013, https://www.bustle.com/articles/4676-voteriders-president-kathleen-unger-who
-aims-to-help-disenfranchised-voters-in-states-with-stringent-voter-id [https://perma.cc/
8U78-TDVR].

24. "History of Voter ID," National Conference of State Legislatures, May 31,
2017, http://www.ncsl.org/research/elections-and-campaigns/voter-id-history.aspx
[https://perma.cc/2MSV-TREU].

25. Dartunorro Clark, "Restrictive Voter ID Laws Are No Match for This Group,"
NBC News, https://www.nbcnews.com/politics/politics-news/restrictive-voter-id-laws
-are-no-match-group-n845291 [https://perma.cc/5UKA-CU4G].

26. Shawn Johnson and Laurel White, "The Timeline of Voter ID Rules in
Wisconsin," *Wiscontext*, September 26, 2015, https://www.wiscontext.org/timeline-voter
-id-rules-wisconsin [https://perma.cc/AR99-5N9H].

27. "Wisconsin Results," *New York Times*, August 1, 2017, https://www.nytimes.com/
elections/2016/results/wisconsin.

28. Molly McGrath, in discussion with the author, March 1, 2017.

29. "I'm a First-Time Voter and Want to Register," Wisconsin Elections
Commission, http://elections.wi.gov/voters/first-time [https://perma.cc/3TJ4-E37K].

30. Molly McGrath, in discussion with the author, March 1, 2017.

31. Mills, "National Group Steps in to Help"; Zachary Roth, "'Desperate Times for
Democracy' in Wisconsin," MSNBC, April 4, 2016, http://www.msnbc.com/msnbc/
desperate-times-democracy-wisconsin [https://perma.cc/J5MR-9XD3].

32. Roth, "'Desperate Times for Democracy.'"

33. Ibid.

34. Molly McGrath, in discussion with the author, March 1, 2017.

35. Ibid.; Cassidy and Moreno, "Wisconsin Voter ID Law Proved Insurmountable"; Ari Berman, "This 99-Year-Old Man Rode His Bike to the Polls. Wisconsin Republicans Turned Him Away," *Nation*, November 8, 2016, https://www.thenation.com/article/this -99-year-old-man-rode-his-bike-to-the-polls-republicans-turned-him-away [https://perma .cc/V5Z9-8G9N].

36. Roth, "'Desperate Times for Democracy.'"

37. Kenneth R. Mayer and Michael G. DeCrescenzo, "Supporting Information: Estimating the Effect of Voter ID on Nonvoters in Wisconsin in the 2016 Presidential Election," Elections Research Center, September 25, 2017, https://elections.wiscweb.wisc .edu/wp-content/uploads/sites/483/2018/02/Voter-ID-Study-Supporting-Info.pdf [https:// perma.cc/G6TP-QX76]; Ari Berman, "A New Study Shows Just How Many Americans Were Blocked from Voting in Wisconsin Last Year," *Mother Jones*, September 25, 2017, https:// www.motherjones.com/politics/2017/09/a-new-study-shows-just-how-many-americans-were -blocked-from-voting-in-wisconsin-last-year [https://perma.cc/G2H2-MHMY].

38. "Milwaukee Elections Chief: Voter ID Law Hurt the City's Turnout," *Chicago Tribune*, November 21, 2016, http://www.chicagotribune.com/news/nationworld/ midwest/ct-milwaukee-voter-id-law-20161112-story.html [https://perma.cc/ T6AL-435S?type=image].

39. Berman, "A New Study Shows."

40. Mayer and DeCrescenzo, "Supporting Information."

41. Patrick Marley and Jason Stein, "Wisconsin Voter ID Law Deterred Nearly 17,000 from Voting, UW Study Says," *Milwaukee Journal Sentinel*, September 25, 2017, https://www.jsonline.com/story/news/politics/2017/09/26/wisconsin-voter -id-law-deterred-nearly-17-000-voting-uw-study-says/702026001 [https://perma.cc/ 8MPH-UXK6].

42. Berman, "Rigged: How Voter Suppression."

43. Molly McGrath, in discussion with the author, March 1, 2017; Ari Berman, "Wisconsin Is Systematically Failing to Provide the Photo IDs Required to Vote in November," *Nation*, September 29, 2016, https://www.thenation.com/article/wisconsin -is-systematically-failing-to-provide-the-photo-ids-required-to-vote-in-november [https:// perma.cc/4XCM-2HYE]; Patrick Marley, "DMV Gives Wrong Information on Voter ID," *Milwaukee Journal Sentinel*, September 29, 2016, https://www.jsonline.com/story/ news/politics/elections/2016/09/29/dmv-gives-wrong-information-voter-id/91283462 [https://perma.cc/8Y2B-Q3K4]; Berman, "Rigged: How Voter Suppression."

44. Molly McGrath, in discussion with the author, March 1, 2017; Michael Wines, "As ID Laws Fall, Voters See New Barriers Rise," *New York Times*, October 25, 2016, https://www.nytimes.com/2016/10/26/us/elections/voter-id-laws.html.

45. Molly McGrath, in discussion with the author, March 1, 2017.

46. Mark Sommerhauser, "Judge Orders State to Probe Report That DMV Gave False Information on Voter ID," *Wisconsin State Journal*, October 1, 2016, http://host .madison.com/wsj/news/local/govt-and-politics/judge-orders-state-to-probe-report-that -dmv-gave-false/article_6230e9d4-8b75-5db1-b26d-4e80b62b50c2.html [https://perma .cc/N3PD-EMT7].

47. One Wisconsin Institute, Inc. v. Thomsen, No. 15-cv-324 (W.D. Wisc. Oct. 13, 2016), available at http://moritzlaw.osu.edu/electionlaw/litigation/documents/OneWisconsin-OpinionandOrder.pdf [https://perma.cc/9WS8-NNTR].

48. Molly McGrath, in discussion with the author, March 1, 2017.

49. Spread the Vote, https://www.spreadthevote.org [https://perma.cc/R6PX-VBGV].

50. Kat Calvin, in discussion with the author, March 6, 2018.

51. Ibid.

52. Ibid.

53. Ibid.

54. "Our Voters," Spread the Vote, https://www.spreadthevote.org/our-voters [https://perma.cc/X9T9-SSFE].

55. Terry L. Jones, "New LSU Student ID Cards Serve as Ticket to Voting Booth," *Advocate*, November 7, 2016, http://www.theadvocate.com/baton_rouge/news/politics/elections/article_91e9bed8-a11d-11e6-af59-8fbe354d7ea0.html [https://perma.cc/TVK6-JLBE].

56. Ibid.

57. Patt Morrison, "Disenfranchised Because of Voter ID Bureaucracy? VoteRiders and Kathleen Unger Can Help," *Los Angeles Times*, December 6, 2017, http://www.latimes.com/opinion/op-ed/la-ol-patt-morrison-unger-vote-riders-20171206-htmlstory.html [https://perma.cc/M5UR-VDJW].

CHAPTER 7: FORGET ABOUT THE LESSER OF TWO EVILS

1. Travis N. Rieder, "Is the 'Lesser of Two Evils' an Ethical Choice for Voters?" *Washington Post*, August 13, 2016, https://www.washingtonpost.com/posteverything/wp/2016/08/13/is-the-lesser-of-two-evils-an-ethical-choice-for-voters [https://perma.cc/3GJY-TK38].

2. "2000 Official Presidential General Election Results," Federal Election Commission, December 2001, https://transition.fec.gov/pubrec/2000presgeresults.htm [https://perma.cc/GG7Q-QE2F].

3. Brooke Seipel, "Trump's Victory Margin Smaller Than Total Stein Votes in Key Swing States," *Hill*, December 1, 2016, http://thehill.com/blogs/blog-briefing-room/news/308353-trump-won-by-smaller-margin-than-stein-votes-in-all-three [https://perma.cc/7SQF-3EMG].

4. "Ranked Choice Voting/Instant Runoff," FairVote, http://www.fairvote.org/rcv#how_rcv_works [https://perma.cc/W83B-C2UG].

5. "2016 Michigan Election Results," State of Michigan—Secretary of State, November 28, 2016, http://miboecfr.nictusa.com/election/results/2016GEN_CENR.html [https://perma.cc/T2EA-YTNF].

6. Nicholas Stephanopoulos, "Rank the Vote," *New Republic*, October 1, 2010, https://newrepublic.com/article/78043/instant-runoff-voting-elections-florida-2000 [https://perma.cc/DQ6M-LQL6]; Robin Toner, "The 1992 Elections: President—The Overview; Clinton Captures Presidency with Huge Electoral Margin; Wins a Democratic

Congress," *New York Times*, November 4, 1992, https://www.nytimes.com/1992/11/04/us/1992-elections-president-overview-clinton-captures-presidency-with-huge.html.

7. "Benefits of RCV," FairVote, http://www.fairvote.org/rcvbenefits [https://perma.cc/K6CG-7QUG].

8. Walt Hickey, "Here's How the Academy Chooses the Best Picture," FiveThirtyEight, February 22, 2015, https://fivethirtyeight.com/features/academy-awards-best-picture-instant-runoff [https://perma.cc/5MB9-Y572].

9. Steve Pond, "Academy Makes Big Changes in Best Picture Voting," Wrap, September 2, 2009, https://www.thewrap.com/academy-makes-big-changes-best-picture-voting-5700 [https://perma.cc/5W77-6UXQ]. The Academy actually used this preferential voting system from 1934–1945. Ibid.

10. Ibid.

11. Ibid.

12. Neil Nagraj, "Academy Awards Makes Change to Voting for 'Best Picture' Oscar; Members Will Rank 10 Nominees," *New York Daily News*, September 1, 2009, http://www.nydailynews.com/entertainment/tv-movies/academy-awards-change-voting-best-picture-oscar-members-rank-10-nominees-article-1.401972 [https://perma.cc/U5HQ-RM4K].

13. "The History of Instant Runoff Voting," FairVote Archive, http://archive.fairvote.org/irv/vt_lite/history.htm [https://perma.cc/VV5K-T58C].

14. John Stuart Mill, *Considerations on Representative Government* (London: Parker, Son, and Bourn, 1861), p. 143.

15. "The History of Instant Runoff Voting," FairVote Archive.

16. Ibid.

17. Rob Richie, in discussion with the author, February 3, 2018.

18. John Patrick Thomas, "The History of FairVote: The Founding Years," FairVote, October 18, 2017, http://www.fairvote.org/the_history_of_fairvote_the_founding_years [https://perma.cc/9WUC-3YQA].

19. Rob Richie, email message to author, July 4, 2018.

20. Thomas, "The History of FairVote."

21. John B. Anderson, "Break the Political Stranglehold," *New York Times*, July 24, 1992, http://www.nytimes.com/1992/07/24/opinion/break-the-political-stranglehold.html.

22. "Dubious Democracy," FairVote, http://www.fairvote.org/dubious_democracy [https://perma.cc/EEC2-KKXZ].

23. John Patrick Thomas, "The History of FairVote: The Middle Years," FairVote, October 24, 2017, http://www.fairvote.org/the_history_of_fairvote_the_middle_years [https://perma.cc/KDJ7-MRYD].

24. Scott James, "A Critical Spotlight Shines on Ranked-Choice Voting," *New York Times*, October 6, 2011, http://www.nytimes.com/2011/10/07/us/a-critical-spotlight-shines-on-ranked-choice-voting.html.

25. Steven Hill, in discussion with the author, March 15, 2018; Rob Richie, email message to author, July 4, 2018.

26. Steven Hill, in discussion with the author, March 15, 2018.

27. Ibid.

28. "San Francisco, IRV and You!" Voice for Democracy, November–December 2001, https://www.cfer.org/newsletter/vfd1201.htm [https://perma.cc/M3S7-435M].

29. "City and County of San Francisco Voter Information Pamphlet and Sample Ballot," RangeVoting.org, March 5, 2002, http://rangevoting.org/SF5march2002.pdf [https://perma.cc/DBW2-4SGS].

30. Steven Hill, in discussion with the author, March 15, 2018.

31. "Instant Runoff Voting Charter Amendment for San Francisco," FairVote Archive, http://archive.fairvote.org/sfrcv/irvleg.htm [https://perma.cc/TXZ8-QUZA].

32. "Marking Your Ballot," City and County of San Francisco: Department of Elections, https://sfgov.org/elections/marking-your-ballot [https://perma.cc/Y4B2 -TBZ3]. The city is now considering whether to adopt new voting machines that would allow voters to rank up to ten candidates. Dominic Fracassa, "Possible New Election Twist for Voters Who Want to Rank More Than 3 Choices: Try 10," *San Francisco Chronicle*, July 27, 2018, https://www.sfchronicle.com/bayarea/article/Possible-new-election-twist-for -voters-who-want-13109151.php [https://perma.cc/ZP5V-UMKE].

33. Steven Hill, *10 Steps to Repair American Democracy* (Sausalito, CA: PoliPoint Press, 2006), p. 51.

34. Christopher Jerdonek, "Ranked Choice Voting and Voter Turnout in San Francisco's 2005 Election," FairVote Archive, February 4, 2006, http://archive.fairvote.org/ rcv/brochures/SF_Research_IRV_and_Turnout.pdf [https://perma.cc/2L6Y-NQQ6].

35. "Exit Poll Data," InstantRunoff.com, http://instantrunoff.com/instant-runoff -home/in-action/exit-poll-data [https://perma.cc/85SB-8GRN].

36. Steven Hill and Robert Richie, "Success for Instant Runoff Voting in San Francisco," *National Civic Review*, March 28, 2005, http://onlinelibrary.wiley.com/ doi/10.1002/ncr.85/full [https://perma.cc/Q9HY-H5BZ]; "San Francisco Ethics Commission Resolution," FairVote Archive, June 23, 2003, http://archive.fairvote.org/ ?page=2352 [https://perma.cc/PFH7-LQRK] (showing the amount of campaign spending in San Francisco runoff elections).

37. Jerdonek, "San Francisco's 2005 Election."

38. Ibid.

39. Steven Hill, "Ranked Choice Voting Is Right for San Francisco," StevenHill .com, November 1, 2011, http://www.steven-hill.com/ranked-choice-voting-is-right -for-san-francisco [https://perma.cc/F3QW-C9VF].

40. Ibid.

41. "Ranked Choice Voting in US Elections," FairVote, http://www.fairvote.org/ rcv_in_us_elections [https://perma.cc/JL6N-YL4D].

42. Nancy Lavin, "Memphis Voters Reaffirm Ranked Choice Voting," FairVote, November 7, 2018 [https://perma.cc/EM87-VLTA].

43. "Our Story," FairVote Minnesota, http://www.fairvotemn.org/our-story [https://perma.cc/2HL2-CC6X].

44. Minnesota Voters Alliance v. City of Minneapolis, 766 N.W.2d 683, 688 (Minn. 2009).

45. "Minneapolis Ranked-Choice Voting History," Minneapolis: Your City, Your Vote, http://vote.minneapolismn.gov/rcv/RCV-HISTORY [https://perma.cc/6ZGG-E845].

46. "2013 Background Information and Data," Minneapolis: Your City, Your Vote, http://vote.minneapolismn.gov/rcv/WCMSP-193823 [https://perma.cc/U58A-V6ZZ].

47. Jeff Achen, "Special Report: Ranked Choice Voting—The Minneapolis Experiment," Uptake, November 25, 2014, http://theuptake.org/2014/11/25/special-report -ranked-choice-voting-the-minneapolis-experiment-2 [https://perma.cc/TZ94-8SSL].

48. Ibid.

49. Ibid.

50. Ibid.

51. Ibid.

52. "Ranked Choice Voting 2017 Elections Report," FairVote Minnesota, http://www.fairvotemn.org/ranked-choice-voting-2017-elections-report [https://perma.cc/M7H5-7BDJ].

53. Ibid.

54. Ibid.

55. "Ranked Choice Voting in Portland, Maine," FairVote Archive, http://archive3.fairvote.org/reforms/instant-runoff-voting/where-rcv-is-used-2/ranked-choice-voting-in-portland [https://perma.cc/NEU5-LAWW]; "Our View: Brennan, Ranked-Choice Voting Both Winners," *Portland Press Herald*, November 12, 2011, https://www.pressherald.com/2011/11/12/brennan-ranked-choice-voting-both-winners_2011-11-12 [https://perma.cc/V8LJ-DVUB].

56. Mario Moretto, "Maine Lawmakers Seek to End Strategic Voting, 'Spoilers' with Petition for Ranked-Choice Voting," *Bangor Daily News*, October 27, 2014, http://bangordailynews.com/2014/10/27/politics/elections/maine-lawmakers-seek-to-end-strategic-voting-spoilers-with-petition-for-ranked-choice-voting [https://perma.cc/TBC5-3VPZ].

57. Dick Woodbury, in discussion with the author, April 2, 2018.

58. Nik DeCosta-Klipa, "How Paul LePage Got Elected, and How Mainers Think They Can Fix a Broken Voting System," *Boston Globe*, September 1, 2016, https://www.boston.com/news/politics/2016/09/01/how-paul-lepage-got-elected-and-how-mainers-think-they-can-fix-a-broken-voting-system [https://perma.cc/9HKF-7U2A?type=image]. LePage won 48 percent of the vote in his successful reelection bid in 2014. Ibid.

59. Dick Woodbury, in discussion with the author, April 2, 2018.

60. *Opinion of the Justices*, 162 A.3d 188 (Me. May 23, 2017, revised September 19, 2017), available at http://www.courts.maine.gov/opinions_orders/supreme/lawcourt/2017/17me100.pdf [https://perma.cc/9F6Y-86G5]; Katharine Q. Seelye, "Ranked-Choice Voting System Violates Maine's Constitution, Court Says," *New York Times*, May 23, 2017, https://www.nytimes.com/2017/05/23/us/maine-ranked-choice-elections-voting.html.

61. "A Timeline of Ranked-Choice Voting in Maine," Maine Government, http://www.maine.gov/sos/cec/elec/upcoming/pdf/rcvtimeline.pdf [https://perma.cc/X5NN-3E5M]; Crystal Canney, "Timeline of Ranked Choice Voting Initiative in Maine," Knight Canney Group, January 16, 2018, https://www.knightcanney.com/timeline-ranked-choice-voting-initiative-maine [https://perma.cc/S49Z-RR9D].

62. "Spotlight: Maine," FairVote, http://www.fairvote.org/spotlight_maine [https://perma.cc/FGF5-DEK6].

63. Christopher Burns, "Maine Led the Nation with Ranked-Choice Voting. Will Others Follow?" *Bangor Daily News*, November 19, 2018 [https://perma.cc/6DMQ-H95H].

64. Kyle Bailey, in discussion with the author, April 24, 2018.

65. Ibid.

66. "Yes On 1: Protect Ranked Choice Voting," Committee for Ranked Choice Voting, http://www.rcvmaine.com [https://perma.cc/GV3Q-SPVB].

67. Peggy Bayliss, "Letter to the Editor: Voters Should Give Ranked-Choice a Try," *Press Herald*, March 20, 2018, https://www.pressherald.com/2018/03/20/letter-to-the -editor-voters-should-give-ranked-choice-a-try [https://perma.cc/WBK4-JH9D].

68. Kyle Bailey, in discussion with the author, April 24, 2018.

69. FairVote's website has plenty of resources to help, which you can find here: http://www.fairvote.org/rcv#rcvbenefits.

70. Helmut Schmidt, "Reform Fargo Gathering Signatures to Get 'Approval Voting' on Fall Ballot," *West Fargo Pioneer*, May 1, 2018, https://www.westfargopioneer.com/news/ government-and-politics/4439576-reform-fargo-gathering-signatures-get-approval-voting -fall [https://perma.cc/UX5M-2EDS]; Kelsey Piper, "This City Just Approved a New Election System Never Tried Before in America," *Vox*, November 15, 2018 [https:// perma.cc/8BR4-YEF3].

71. Maya Efrati, "Local Elections in Texas Demonstrate the Power—and Limits—of Cumulative Voting Rights," FairVote, May 19, 2017, http://www.fairvote.org/texas _cumulative_voting_rights [https://perma.cc/4B8U-SZAG].

72. Michael Byrne, "Designing Better Ballots," Conversation, November 13, 2017, http://theconversation.com/designing-better-ballots-82414 [https://perma.cc/6JLN -FGVJ]; Jacquelyn Bengfort, "Safer Elections Mean Newer Equipment, No Networks," *StateTech*, April 11, 2017, https://statetechmagazine.com/article/2017/04/safer-elections -mean-newer-equipment-no-networks [https://perma.cc/WNA3-X8PM].

73. Maria Perez, in discussion with the author, March 14, 2018.

CHAPTER 8: OVERTHROWING THE GOVERNMENT . . . PEACEFULLY

1. Katie Fahey, in discussion with the author, May 1, 2018.

2. Tina Rosenberg, "Putting the Voters in Charge of Fair Voting," *New York Times*, January 23, 2018, https://www.nytimes.com/2018/01/23/opinion/michigan -gerrymandering-fair-voting.html.

3. Katie Fahey, in discussion with the author, May 1, 2018.

4. Katie Fahey, Facebook, November 10, 2016, https://www.facebook.com/katie .rogala.3/posts/10153917724442633 [https://perma.cc/776Q-FLQV?type=image].

5. U.S. CONST. art. I, § 2.

6. Reynolds v. Sims, 377 U.S. 533 (1964).

7. Ibid.

8. Cooper v. Harris, 137 S. Ct. 1455 (2017); Johnson v. DeGrandy, 512 U.S. 997 (1994).

9. U.S. CONST. art. I, § 4.

10. Before the 2018 election, the states that had implemented redistricting commissions included Alaska, Arizona, California, Idaho, Montana, and Washington. The independent redistricting commissions in these states draw both federal and state legislative districts (though Alaska and Montana have only one congressional representative so do not draw congressional districts). "Who Draws the Lines?" Loyola Law School: All about Redistricting, http://redistricting.lls.edu/who.php [https://perma

.cc/GDP6-5YC5]. Several other states have "politician commissions," where elected officials can select members of the redistricting commission, with a requirement that the commission itself have partisan balance. Ibid.

11. Christopher Ingraham, "This Is the Best Explanation of Gerrymandering You Will Ever See," *Washington Post*, March 1, 2015, https://www.washingtonpost.com/news/wonk/wp/2015/03/01/this-is-the-best-explanation-of-gerrymandering-you-will-ever-see [https://perma.cc/RCS3-NWTT].

12. Vieth v. Jubelirer, 541 U.S. 267, 274 (2004); Robert Draper, "The League of Dangerous Mapmakers," *Atlantic*, October 2012, https://www.theatlantic.com/magazine/archive/2012/10/the-league-of/309084 [https://perma.cc/D64E-5RPG].

13. Jennifer Davis, "Elbridge Gerry and the Monstrous Gerrymander," Library of Congress, February 10, 2017, https://blogs.loc.gov/law/2017/02/elbridge-gerry-and-the-monstrous-gerrymander [https://perma.cc/3P8F-WGDV].

14. Michael Li and Thomas Wolf, "5 Things to Know about the Wisconsin Partisan Gerrymandering Case," Brennan Center for Justice, June 19, 2017, https://www.brennancenter.org/blog/5-things-know-about-wisconsin-partisan-gerrymandering-case [https://perma.cc/TSN3-PV7N].

15. Rosenberg, "Putting the Voters in Charge."

16. Cooper v. Harris, 137 S. Ct. 1455 (2017).

17. Draper, "The League of Dangerous Mapmakers"; David Daley, *Ratf**ked: Why Your Vote Doesn't Count* (New York: Liveright, 2016).

18. Thomas Wolf, "5 Things to Know about the Maryland Partisan-Gerrymandering Case," Brennan Center for Justice, March 22, 2018, https://www.brennancenter.org/blog/5-things-know-about-maryland-partisan-gerrymandering-case [https://perma.cc/94TD-ELD8].

19. Vieth v. Jubelirer, 541 U.S. 267, 274 (2004).

20. Gill v. Whitford, 138 S. Ct. 1916 (2018); Benisek v. Lamone, 138 S. Ct. 1942 (2018).

21. League of Women Voters v. Commonwealth, 178 A.3d 737 (Pa. 2018).

22. Katie Fahey, in discussion with the author, May 1, 2018.

23. Jonathan Oosting, "Federal Suit Alleges GOP 'Gerrymandering' in Michigan," *Detroit News*, December 22, 2017, https://www.detroitnews.com/story/news/politics/2017/12/22/lawsuit-gerrymandering-michigan/108856648 [https://perma.cc/TQ9P-FPSA].

24. David Eggert, "Anti-Gerrymandering Group Defies Odds with 2018 Ballot Drive," *U.S. News and World Report*, November 20, 2017, https://www.usnews.com/news/best-states/michigan/articles/2017-11-20/anti-gerrymandering-group-defies-odds-with-2018-ballot-drive.

25. Katie Fahey, in discussion with the author, May 1, 2018.

26. Elizabeth Battiste, account executive at the PR firm Martin Waymire, email message to author, May 25, 2018.

27. Katie Fahey, in discussion with the author, May 1, 2018.

28. Ibid.

29. "Jamie Lyons-Eddy—Canvassing and Field Team Director," Voters Not Politicians, https://www.votersnotpoliticians.com/jamie_lyons_eddy [https://perma.cc/P6BP-6ETL].

30. Katie Fahey, in discussion with the author, May 1, 2018.

31. Ibid.

32. Ibid.

33. Ibid.

34. Ibid.; Mark Tewksbury, "Redistricting Reform Ballot Proposal Town Hall Scheduled in Bay City," Michigan Live, October 7, 2017, http://www.mlive.com/news/bay-city/index.ssf/2017/10/redistricting_reform_ballot_pr.html [https://perma.cc/YLG5-QMFH].

35. Katie Fahey, in discussion with the author, May 1, 2018.

36. Ibid.

37. Ibid.

38. Ibid.

39. "Voters Not Politicians Constitutional Amendment Language," Voters Not Politicians, https://www.votersnotpoliticians.com/language [https://perma.cc/EA3W-6VLT].

40. Ibid.

41. Ibid.

42. Ibid. Jonathan Oosting, "Group Hits State for Delaying Gerrymandering Petitions," *Detroit News*, July 17, 2017, https://www.detroitnews.com/story/news/politics/2017/07/17/gerrymandering-michigan-voters-politicians-petitions/103782256 [https://perma.cc/Y5PP-SFMC].

43. Katie Fahey, in discussion with the author, May 1, 2018; Oosting, "Group Hits State for Delaying."

44. Rosenberg, "Putting the Voters in Charge."

45. Katie Fahey, in discussion with the author, May 1, 2018.

46. Rosenberg, "Putting the Voters in Charge."

47. Katie Fahey, in discussion with the author, May 1, 2018.

48. Ibid.

49. Eggert, "Anti-Gerrymandering Group Defies Odds."

50. Katie Fahey, in discussion with the author, May 1, 2018.

51. Oosting, "Group Hits State for Delaying."

52. Citizens Protecting Michigan's Constitution v. Secretary of State, No. 157925 (Mich. 2018), available at http://courts.mi.gov/Courts/MichiganSupremeCourt/Clerks/Recent%20Opinions/17-18%20Term%20Opinions/157925.pdf.

53. Katie Fahey, in discussion with the author, May 1, 2018.

54. Ibid. The group eventually hired a few more paid staff members to work on the November 2018 campaign.

55. Paul Egan, "Michigan's Anti-gerrymandering Proposal Is Approved. Now What?" *Detroit Free Press*, November 7, 2018 [https://perma.cc/F2SP-NNHQ].

56. Richard L. Hasen, "The Next Threat to Redistricting Reform," *Harvard Law Review Blog*, October 22, 2018, https://blog.harvardlawreview.org/the-next-threat-to-restricting-reform [https://perma.cc/RM24-3CJE].

57. Arizona State Legislature v. Arizona Independent Redistricting Commission, 135 S. Ct. 2652 (2015).

58. Katie Fahey, in discussion with the author, May 1, 2018.

59. Ibid.

60. Rosenberg, "Putting the Voters in Charge."

61. Vieth v. Jubelirer, 541 U.S. 267, 274 (2004).

62. League of Women Voters v. Commonwealth, 178 A.3d 737 (Pa. 2018).

63. Rosenberg, "Putting the Voters in Charge."

64. Ibid.

65. Kristina Papa, "Group Seeks End to Gerrymandering State Legislative Districts," WNEP, December 7, 2017, http://wnep.com/2017/12/07/group-seeks-end-to-gerrymandering-state-legislative-districts [https://perma.cc/9T7K-66R9].

66. Layla A. Jones, "Activists Plan 100-Mile March to Harrisburg," *Philadelphia Tribune*, May 5, 2017, http://www.phillytrib.com/news/activists-plan--mile-march-to-harrisburg/article_9a772a8a-4dc2-5c34-8796-2435946bdd73.html [https://perma.cc/P5QW-594G].

67. "Bill Would Revamp how Pennsylvania Draws District Boundaries," Penn Live, May 22, 2018, http://www.pennlive.com/news/2018/05/bill_would_revamp_how _pennsylv.html [https://perma.cc/A575-NVNZ]; Jonathan Lai, Gillian McGoldrick, and Liz Navratil, "Pa. Senate Passes Anti-Gerrymandering Bill with 'Poison Pill' Judicial Districting Amendment," *Philadelphia Inquirer*, June 13, 2018, http://www.philly.com/ philly/news/politics/state/pennsylvania-senate-gerrymandering-redistricting-reform-bill -sb22-judicial-district-20180613.html [https://perma.cc/LX6F-YA2L].

68. "Independent Redistricting Commissions," *Ballotpedia*, https://ballotpedia.org/ Independent_redistricting_commissions [https://perma.cc/36NX-K8PD]; "Who Draws the Lines?" Loyola Law School.

69. "2010 Redistricting of the City of San Diego," City of San Diego, October 25, 2011, https://www.sandiego.gov/sites/default/files/legacy/redistricting/pdf/2011/2011 RecomendationsDRAFT.pdf [https://perma.cc/ZF8P-ZY8E].

70. "Berkeley, California, City Council Redistricting Charter Amendment, Measure W1 (November 2016)," *Ballotpedia*, https://ballotpedia.org/Berkeley,_California,_City _Council_Redistricting_Charter_Amendment,_Measure_W1_ (November_2016) [https://perma.cc/USU6-J3PP].

71. "California Proposition 11, Creation of the California Citizens Redistricting Commission (2008)," *Ballotpedia*, https://ballotpedia.org/California_Proposition_11, _Creation_of_the_California_Citizens_Redistricting_Commission_(2008) [https://perma .cc/Z2T2-WD9C]; "Background on Commission," California Citizens Redistricting Commission, https://wedrawthelines.ca.gov/commission [https://perma.cc/42AG-QCYE].

72. Ryan Lillis, "Sacramento's Strong-Mayor Measure Defeated," *Sacramento Bee*, November 4, 2014, http://www.sacbee.com/news/politics-government/election/local -election/article3528468.html [https://perma.cc/W3XN-S6HB].

73. Paula Lee, in discussion with the author, April 26, 2018.

74. Ibid.

75. Bob Moffitt, "Sacramento Redistricting Commission One Step Closer to Reality," Capital Public Radio, May 24, 2016, http://www.capradio.org/articles/ 2016/05/24/sacramento-redistricting-commission-one-step-closer-to-reality [https:// perma.cc/F3VR-L9RA].

76. Scott Thomas Anderson, "Sacramento City Council Aims to Resolve Boundary Issues through New Redistricting Commission," *News Review*, August 4, 2016, https://www.newsreview.com/sacramento/sacramento-city-council-aims-to/

content?oid=21619578 [https://perma.cc/2UZT-X9CH]; Mariel Garza, "Where Have All the Latinos Gone? A Statistical Mystery in Local Politics," *Sacramento Bee*, December 20, 2014, http://www.sacbee.com/opinion/opn-columns-blogs/mariel-garza/article4660557.html [https://perma.cc/5TC4-XF2P].

77. Nicolas Heidorn, in discussion with the author, April 26, 2018.

78. Sacramento City Attorney, "City of Sacramento Measure L," Sacramento County, http://www.elections.saccounty.net/Documents/Measure%20L%20-%20 NOV16.pdf [https://perma.cc/MNZ6-37UJ].

79. "City of Sacramento, California, Independent Redistricting Commission, Measure L (November 2016)," *Ballotpedia*, https://ballotpedia.org/City_of_Sacramento, _California,_Independent_Redistricting_Commission,_Measure_L_(November_2016) [https://perma.cc/N295-YJLH].

80. Moffitt, "Sacramento Redistricting Commission."

81. Anderson, "Sacramento City Council Aims."

82. "City of Sacramento, California, Independent Redistricting Commission, Measure L," *Ballotpedia*.

83. Nicolas Heidorn, in discussion with the author, April 26, 2018.

84. Ibid.

85. Michael Wines, "Drive Against Gerrymandering Finds New Life in Ballot Initiatives," *New York Times*, July 23, 2018, https://www.nytimes.com/2018/07/23/us/gerrymandering -states.html; Pema Levy, "Utah—Yes, Utah—Has Approved a Ballot Initiative to Curb Gerry- mandering," *Mother Jones*, November 21, 2018 [https://perma.cc/TV4F-RDK6].

86. Wines, "Drive Against Gerrymandering."

87. Alexander Williams Jr., "Don't Wait for the Courts, Reform Redistricting Now," *Baltimore Sun*, March 30, 2018, http://www.baltimoresun.com/news/opinion/oped/ bs-ed-op-0401-redistricting-20180329-story.html [https://perma.cc/26ZU-73SB].

88. Ibid.

89. Kaitlin Lange, "Indiana Redistricting Reform Bill Dies Without a House Vote," *IndyStar*, February 23, 2018, https://www.indystar.com/story/news/politics/ 2018/02/23/indiana-redistricting-reform-bill-dies-without-house-vote/367894002 [https://perma.cc/X7DS-NXXA].

90. Paul Czapkowicz, "Whiting Council Endorses Legislative Redistricting Reform," *NWI Times*, April 30, 2018, http://www.nwitimes.com/news/local/lake/whiting -council-endorses-legislative-redistricting-reform/article_834673c2-640e-50ba-a395 -a73e41dbf4c7.html [https://perma.cc/3ZQP-ZU23].

91. Ibid.

92. Kate Payne, "State Lawmaker Wants Independent Redistricting Commission," WFSU News, December 1, 2016, http://news.wfsu.org/post/state-lawmaker-wants -independent-redistricting-commission [https://perma.cc/Z2QP-XKPU].

93. EHEZI, "New Rochelle Non-Partisan, Independent Group Forms after Mayor Bramson and City Council Refuse to Guarantee Independent Redistricting Process," *Yonkers Tribune*, March 22, 2011, http://www.yonkerstribune.com/2011/03/new-rochelle -non-partisan-independent-group-forms-after-mayor-bramson-and-city-council-refuse -to-guarantee-independent-redis [https://perma.cc/A4HC-SYR8]; "City Council Adopts Redistricting Plan," *Mayor Noam Bramson* (blog), May 11, 2011, https://noambramson .org/2011/05/city-council-adopts-redistricting-plan [https://perma.cc/FD3V-FTSK].

94. Steve Bickerstaff, "Making Local Redistricting Less Political: Independent Redistricting Commissions for U.S. Cities," *Election Law Journal* 13 (2014): 421–22.

95. "Shining a Light; Redistricting Lessons Learned in 2011," League of Women Voters Education Fund, January 2012, https://my.lwv.org/sites/default/files/Redistricting_Lessons_Learned.pdf [https://perma.cc/89M4-TVH4].

96. Ibid.

97. Bickerstaff, "Making Local Redistricting Less Political," pp. 425–30.

98. "Boards and Commissions Information Center—Independent Citizens Redistricting Commission," City of Austin, http://www.austintexas.gov/content/independent-citizens-redistricting-commission [https://perma.cc/DQM5-U935].

99. Bickerstaff, "Making Local Redistricting Less Political," p. 430.

CHAPTER 9: THE SECRET SAUCE OF DEMOCRACY

1. Alison Smith, in discussion with the author, April 24, 2018.

2. Buckley v. Valeo, 424 U.S. 1 (1976).

3. Arizona Free Enterprise Club's Freedom Club PAC v. Bennett, 564 U.S. 721 (2011).

4. Buckley v. Valeo, 424 U.S. 1 (1976).

5. Citizens United v. Federal Election Commission, 558 U.S. 310 (2010).

6. Soo Rin Kim, "The Price of Winning Just Got Higher, Especially in the Senate," Open Secrets, November 9, 2016, https://www.opensecrets.org/news/2016/11/the-price-of-winning-just-got-higher-especially-in-the-senate [https://perma.cc/2G3S-9DHA].

7. Alex Samuels, "Hey, Texplainer: How Much Does It Cost to Run for Office in Texas?" *Texas Tribune*, November 10, 2017, https://www.texastribune.org/2017/11/10/hey-texplainer-how-much-does-it-cost-run-office-texas [https://perma.cc/NA68-JSE7].

8. Ibid.

9. "Cost of Election," Open Secrets, https://www.opensecrets.org/overview/cost.php?display=T&infl=Y [https://perma.cc/9WVU-PC8Y].

10. Jim Puzzanghera, "CFPB's Mick Mulvaney Gives Lobbying Advice to Bankers, Further Infuriating Consumer Advocates," *Los Angeles Times*, April 25, 2018, http://www.latimes.com/business/la-fi-mulvaney-cfpb-lobbyists-20180425-story.html [https://perma.cc/4XZK-TZVH].

11. Ryan Grim and Sabrina Siddiqui, "Call Time for Congress Shows How Fundraising Dominates Bleak Work Life," *Huffington Post*, January 8, 2013, updated December 6, 2017, https://www.huffingtonpost.com/2013/01/08/call-time-congressional-fundraising_n_2427291.html [https://perma.cc/C4ZX-4SNJ].

12. Citizens United v. Federal Election Commission, 558 U.S. 310, 479 (2010) (Stevens, J., dissenting).

13. "Public Funding of Presidential Elections," Federal Election Commission, February 2017, https://transition.fec.gov/pages/brochures/pubfund.shtml [https://perma.cc/77HY-VWUW].

14. Libby Watson, "Why Did Only 1 Presidential Candidate Take Public Financing?" Sunlight Foundation, January 27, 2016, https://sunlightfoundation.com/

2016/01/27/why-did-only-1-presidential-candidate-take-public-financing [https://perma.cc/CJ8C-FT6Z].

15. "Donald Trump (R) Winner," Open Secrets, https://www.opensecrets.org/pres16/candidate?id=N00023864 [https://perma.cc/RNN5-5TCR].

16. "Hillary Clinton (D)," Open Secrets, https://www.opensecrets.org/pres16/candidate?id=N00000019 [https://perma.cc/TGZ8-BKX5].

17. "Maine House of Representatives Elections, 2016," *Ballotpedia*, https://ballotpedia.org/Maine_House_of_Representatives_elections,_2016#Campaign_contributions [https://perma.cc/2ND9-3C2J]; "Maine State Senate Elections, 2016," *Ballotpedia*, https://ballotpedia.org/Maine_State_Senate_elections,_2016#Campaign_contributions [https://perma.cc/PEC5-7YDS].

18. Paul Loeb, "Alison Smith: Elections Money Can't Buy," *Yes! Magazine*, January 26, 2012, http://www.yesmagazine.org/issues/the-yes-breakthrough-15/alison-smith-elections-money-cant-buy [https://perma.cc/3UE8-K9FK] (excerpted from Paul Rogat Loeb, *Soul of a Citizen: Living with Conviction in Challenging Times* [New York: St. Martin's Griffin, 2010]).

19. Alison Smith, in discussion with the author, April 24, 2018.

20. Ibid.

21. Ibid.

22. Ibid.

23. Ibid.

24. Ibid.

25. Ibid.

26. Ibid.

27. "Maine Public Campaign Financing, Question 3 (1996)," *Ballotpedia*, https://ballotpedia.org/Maine_Public_Campaign_Financing,_Question_3_(1996) [https://perma.cc/ZA7C-Q2D3].

28. "Qualifying Contributions," Maine Commission on Governmental Ethics & Election Practices, http://www.maine.gov/ethics/mcea/qualify.htm [https://perma.cc/E4XG-N2AQ].

29. "Maine Clean Election Act Overview of Participation Rates and Payments 2000–2008," Maine Commission on Governmental Ethics & Election Practices, https://www.maine.gov/ethics/pdf/publications/2008_mcea_overview.pdf [https://perma.cc/UWB2-XP5F].

30. "Clean Elections Works in Maine," Maine Citizens for Clean Elections, October 24, 2005, https://www.mainecleanelections.org/node/278 [https://perma.cc/ALL7-9EJK]. One of the former legislators, John Brautigam, echoed these same themes when I interviewed him for this book. John Brautigam, in discussion with the author, April 9, 2018.

31. Hannah Pingree, in discussion with the author, May 2, 2018; "Statement of Hannah Pingree to the U.S. Senate Environment and Public Works Committee and the Subcommittee on Superfund, Toxics and Environmental Health, Hearing: 'Oversight of the EPA Authorities and Actions to Control Exposures to Toxic Chemicals,'" U.S. Senate Committee on Environment and Public Works, July 24, 2012, https://www.epw.senate.gov/public/_cache/files/e/f/efdbf9be-6fd1-4d56-b8da-719d7485cb83/01AFD79733D77F24A71FEF9DAFCCB056.72412hearingwitnesstestimonypingree.pdf [https://perma.cc/9DWJ-LJGS].

32. Hannah Pingree, in discussion with the author, May 2, 2018.

33. Ibid.

34. Arizona Free Enterprise Club's Freedom Club PAC v. Bennett, 564 U.S. 721 (2011).

35. "Initial Distributions for Candidates in the 2018 Elections," Maine Commission on Governmental Ethics & Election Practices, http://www.maine.gov/ethics/mcea/initialdist.htm [https://perma.cc/8RS6-7XPA].

36. "Maine 'Clean Elections' Initiative, Question 1 (2015)," *Ballotpedia*, https://ballotpedia.org/Maine_%22Clean_Elections%22_Initiative,_Question_1_(2015) [https://perma.cc/7RZJ-NU3R].

37. "Money in Politics Project Report #14—Clean Election Participation Rates and Outcomes: 2016 Legislative Elections," Maine Citizens for Clean Elections, https://www.mainecleanelections.org/sites/default/files/web/Proof02%202016%20Legislative%20MCCE%20Report%2014%20Candidate%20MCEA%20Participation%20Analysis_0.pdf [https://perma.cc/6NVL-ZV6W].

38. Alison Smith, in discussion with the author, July 30, 2018.

39. Alex LaCasse, "3 Qualify as Clean Election Candidates in Maine Governor's Race," *Seacoast Online*, April 20, 2018, http://www.seacoastonline.com/news/20180415/3-qualify-as-clean-election-candidates-in-maine-governors-race [https://perma.cc/QPT2-9YSH].

40. John Brautigam, in discussion with the author, April 9, 2018.

41. Scott Thistle, "Legislative Candidates Ask Judge to Force LePage to Release Clean Elections Funds," *Portland Press Herald*, July 24, 2018, https://www.pressherald.com/2018/07/24/justice-hears-arguments-for-releasing-maine-clean-election-act-funding [https://perma.cc/4KUT-RKRM]; Christopher Cousins, "Maine Public Campaign Funding Hangs in Limbo as Lawmakers Keep Squabbling," *Bangor Daily News*, June 20, 2018, https://bangordailynews.com/2018/06/20/politics/maine-public-campaign-funding-hangs-in-limbo-as-lawmakers-keep-squabbling [https://perma.cc/QA3J-V525].

42. Hannah Pingree, in discussion with the author, May 2, 2018.

43. Brooke Jarvis, "Can't Buy My Vote: Maine's Fight for Fair Elections," *Yes! Magazine*, October 27, 2011, http://www.yesmagazine.org/people-power/keeping-it-clean-maines-fight-for-fair-elections [https://perma.cc/79W4-MEV9].

44. Ibid.

45. Ibid.

46. Alison Smith, in discussion with the author, April 24, 2018.

47. "Democracy Voucher Program," City of Seattle, https://www.seattle.gov/democracyvoucher/about-the-program [https://perma.cc/UQB2-NV3Y].

48. "Democracy Voucher Program: Information for Candidates," City of Seattle, http://www.seattle.gov/democracyvoucher/i-am-a-candidate [https://perma.cc/ZDN6-SAGY]; "Democracy Voucher Program: 2017 Candidate Pledge," City of Seattle, http://www.seattle.gov/Documents/Departments/EthicsElections/DemocracyVoucher/Democracy%20Voucher%20Program%202017%20Candidate%20Pledge.pdf [https://perma.cc/XW2T-WPKG].

49. "Washington Limit on Campaign Contributions, Initiative 134 (1992)," *Ballotpedia*, https://ballotpedia.org/Washington_Limit_on_Campaign_Contributions,

_Initiative_134_(1992) [https://perma.cc/9WZ5-FELS]; Goldy, "A Pictoral History of Public Campaign Financing in Seattle," *Stranger*, October 29, 2013, https://www .thestranger.com/slog/archives/2013/10/29/a-pictorial-history-of-public-campaign -financing-in-seattle [https://perma.cc/4WNE-828P].

50. WASH. REV. CODE § 42.17A.550—Use of Public Funds for Political Purposes, available at http://app.leg.wa.gov/RCW/default.aspx?cite=42.17A.550 [https://perma .cc/R9PJ-A4CQ].

51. "2013 Election Report," Seattle Ethics & Elections Commission, February 5, 2014, p. 24, http://www2.seattle.gov/ethics/elpub/2013Report.pdf [https://perma.cc/ M57W-SPXN].

52. "About Us," Sightline Institute, http://www.sightline.org/about [https://perma .cc/H2XG-CK9B].

53. Alan Durning, in discussion with the author, May 3, 2018.

54. Estevan Muñoz-Howard, email message to author, May 31, 2018.

55. Lawrence Lessing, "More Money Can Beat Big Money," *New York Times*, November 16, 2011, https://www.nytimes.com/2011/11/17/opinion/in-campaign -financing-more-money-can-beat-big-money.html.

56. Alan Durning, in discussion with the author, May 3, 2018.

57. Estevan Muñoz-Howard, email message to author, May 31, 2018.

58. "City of Seattle Restrictions on Campaign Finance and Elections, Initiative Measure No. 122 (November 2015)," *Ballotpedia*, https://ballotpedia.org/City_of_Seattle _Restrictions_on_Campaign_Finance_and_Elections,_Initiative_Measure_No._122 _(November_2015) [https://perma.cc/KJ9M-LH3X]; "Initiative 122," City of Seattle, November 24, 2015, http://www.seattle.gov/Documents/Departments/EthicsElections/ DemocracyVoucher/I-122%20Text-%20Master.pdf [https://perma.cc/K257-J6WJ].

59. "Our Staff," Win Win Network, http://winwinnetwork.org/about/staff [https://perma.cc/43JJ-J27S].

60. Alissa Haslam, in discussion with the author, May 11, 2018.

61. Ibid.

62. Ibid.

63. "Democracy Voucher Program: Program Data," City of Seattle, http://www .seattle.gov/democracyvoucher/program-data [https://perma.cc/M7KM-3VMW].

64. Bob Young, "M. Lorena González and Teresa Mosqueda Win Seattle City Council Seats," *Seattle Times*, November 7, 2017, https://www.seattletimes.com/seattle -news/politics/seattle-city-council-election-2017 [https://perma.cc/XN2K-V5CY]; Sara Jean Green, "Seattle City Attorney Pete Holmes Cruises to Re-Election Over Scott Lindsay," *Seattle Times*, November 7, 2017, https://www.seattletimes.com/seattle-news/ politics/seattle-city-attorney-pete-holmes-scott-lindsay [https://perma.cc/XFJ4-7CZ5].

65. "Expanding Participation in Municipal Elections: Assessing the Impact of Seattle's Democracy Voucher Program," University of Washington Center for Studies in Demography & Ecology, http://www.seattle.gov/Documents/Departments/EthicsElections/ DemocracyVoucher/UW_Seattle_Voucher_Final.pdf [https://perma.cc/F8UV-CME3].

66. Margaret Morales, "Seattle's Democracy Vouchers Are Changing the Campaign Trail for Candidates and City Residents," Sightline Institute, November 28, 2017, http:// www.sightline.org/2017/11/28/seattles-democracy-vouchers-are-changing-the -campaign-trail-for-candidates-and-city-residents [https://perma.cc/SXJ4-YMDV].

67. "Seattle Democracy Voucher Program Evaluation," City of Seattle Ethics and Elections Commission, April 20, 2018, http://www.seattle.gov/Documents/Departments/EthicsElections/DemocracyVoucher/DVP%20Evaluation%20Final%20 Report%20April%2025%202018.pdf [https://perma.cc/SJ5S-KDBH].

68. "2017 Election Report," Seattle Ethics & Elections Commission, March 9, 2018, http://www2.ci.seattle.wa.us/ethics/elpub/2017Report.pdf [https://perma.cc/5HK9 -TS9Z]; Ron Fein, "The Impact of Seattle's Democracy Voucher Program on Candidates' Ability to Rely on Constituents for Fundraising," Free Speech for People, May 2018, https://freespeechforpeople.org/wp-content/uploads/2018/05/FSFP-Issue -Report-2018_1.pdf [https://perma.cc/UST8-L4QJ].

69. "Expanding Participation in Municipal Elections," University of Washington Center for Studies in Demography & Ecology.

70. Ibid.

71. Gina Owens, "Democracy Vouchers Fight Corruption in Elections," Seattle Patch, September 8, 2017, https://patch.com/washington/seattle/democracy-vouchers -fight-corruption-elections [https://perma.cc/335V-WDAC].

72. Susan Russell, "Democracy Vouchers Gave This Seattle Resident a Voice," Washington CAN, March 12, 2018, https://www.washingtoncan.org/civic-engagement -stories/2018/3/12/democracy-vouchers-gave-this-seattle-resident-a-voice [https:// perma.cc/D689-6YVG].

73. Gene Balk, "Do Seattle's Democracy Vouchers Work? New Analysis Says Yes," *Seattle Times*, October 13, 2017, https://www.seattletimes.com/seattle-news/data/ do-seattles-democracy-vouchers-work-new-analysis-says-yes [https://perma.cc/YG4Y -KKYL]; Estevan Muñoz-Howard, email message to author, May 31, 2018.

74. "Seattle Democracy Voucher Program Evaluation," City of Seattle Ethics and Elections Commission.

75. Gregory Krieg, "A New Way to Reform: 'Democracy Vouchers' vs. Citizens United," CNN, November 10, 2015, https://www.cnn.com/2015/11/10/politics/ democracy-vouchers-seattle-honest-elections-finance-reform/index.html [https://perma .cc/AA7K-NHKW].

76. Russ Feingold and Ro Khanna, "A New Approach to Big Money in Politics," *Concord Monitor*, May 15, 2018, http://www.concordmonitor.com/Getting-big-money-out -of-politics-17448454 [https://perma.cc/AYS6-452P].

77. Hanna Brooks Olsen, "Seattle's Creative Campaign Finance Reform," *Democracy: A Journal of Ideas*, December 12, 2017, https://democracyjournal.org/arguments/seattles -creative-campaign-finance-reform [https://perma.cc/KB93-8974].

78. "History of the CFB," New York City Campaign Finance Board, https://www .nyccfb.info/about/history [https://perma.cc/4GWF-ZLGD].

79. Sundeep Iyer, Elisabeth Genn, Brendan Glavin, and Michael J. Malbin, "Donor Diversity through Public Matching Funds," Brennan Center for Justice, May 14, 2012, http://www.brennancenter.org/publication/donor-diversity-through-public-matching -funds [https://perma.cc/MG27-Z3AQ].

80. Ibid.

81. Hazel Millard, "Another Election Winner—Public Financing," Brennan Center for Justice, November 12, 2018 [https://perma.cc/9R27-3A4Y].

82. Hamsini Sridharan, "Bringing Fair Elections to Berkeley: A Case Study,"

MapLight, January 2018, https://s3-us-west-2.amazonaws.com/maplight.org/wp-content/uploads/20180118011356/Bringing+Fair+Elections+to+Berkeley_A+Case+Study.pdf [https://perma.cc/G5LC-GZZW].

83. Ibid.

84. Paul Blumenthal, "The Future of Campaign Finance Reform Is at the State and Local Level," *Huffington Post*, December 20, 2016, https://www.huffingtonpost.com/entry/campaign-finance-reform_us_5858569ae4b03904470a4d1b [https://perma.cc/A5MU-65A8].

85. Bill Turque, "Montgomery Council Approves Plan for Public Finance of Local Campaigns," *Washington Post*, September 30, 2014, https://www.washingtonpost.com/local/md-politics/montgomery-council-approves-plan-for-public-finance-of-local-campaigns/2014/09/30/b3e2b15c-482d-11e4-b72e-d60a9229cc10_story.html [https://perma.cc/6PZP-GDZ8]; Andrew Michaels, "Howard County Council Passes Small Donor Finance System to Begin in 2022 Election Cycle," *Baltimore Sun*, June 6, 2017, http://www.baltimoresun.com/news/maryland/howard/columbia/ph-ho-cf-council-campaign-funding-0608-20170606-story.html [https://perma.cc/SNG5-GGE6?type=image].

86. Peter Jamison, "D.C. Mayor, Reversing Course, Signs Law Creating Publicly Financed Campaigns," *Washington Post*, March 13, 2018, https://www.washingtonpost.com/local/dc-politics/dc-mayor-reversing-course-signs-law-creating-publicly-financed-campaigns/2018/03/13/699b6e90-26f5-11e8-b79d-f3d931db7f68_story.html [https://perma.cc/KG8K-EXEY].

87. Talia Richman, "Baltimore City Council Passes Public Financing Charter Amendment," *Baltimore Sun*, July 9, 2018, http://www.baltimoresun.com/news/maryland/baltimore-city/bs-md-ci-public-finance-20180709-story.html [https://perma.cc/4KT5-SGHB?type=image]; Millard, "Another Election Winner—Public Financing."

88. Millard, "Another Election Winner—Public Financing."

89. Tanvi Misra, "More Cities Want to Embrace 'Democracy Vouchers,'" CityLab, August 8, 2018, https://www.citylab.com/equity/2018/08/more-cities-want-to-embrace-democracy-dollars/566801 [https://perma.cc/V8WS-4DV6].

90. Mark Lisheron, "Controversial 'Democracy Voucher' Program May Be Coming to Austin Soon," *Texas Monitor*, February 22, 2018, https://texasmonitor.org/controversial-democracy-voucher-program-may-be-coming-to-austin-soon [https://perma.cc/DAM9-6LK5].

91. "Missouri State and Judicial Campaign Contribution Limits, Constitutional Amendment 2 (2016)," *Ballotpedia*, https://ballotpedia.org/Missouri_State_and_Judicial_Campaign_Contribution_Limits,_Constitutional_Amendment_2_(2016) [https://perma.cc/G2MR-M5D2].

92. Travis Zimpfer, "Campaign Contribution Amendment Largely Overturned in Federal Court," *Missouri Times*, May 5, 2017, http://themissouritimes.com/40402/campaign-contribution-amendment-largely-overturned-federal-court [https://perma.cc/48DE-F4R9].

93. Celeste Bott, "Voters Say Yes to 'Clean Missouri' Ethics Overhaul, $12 an Hour Minimum Wage by 2023," *St. Louis Post-Dispatch*, November 6, 2018 [https://perma.cc/3A48-CVVK].

94. Alan Greenblatt, "Voters in 4 States Limit Money's Role in U.S. Politics,"

Governing, November 9, 2016, http://www.governing.com/topics/elections/gov-campaign -finance-ballot-measures.html [https://perma.cc/8VLP-BAU4].

95. Gregory Krieg, "South Dakota GOP Uses 'Emergency' Rules to Repeal Anti-Corruption Law," CNN, February 2, 2017, https://www.cnn.com/2017/02/02/ politics/south-dakota-corruption-bill-republican-repeal/index.html [https://perma.cc/ KD4A-K4BC].

96. Ibid.

97. Jerod MacDonald-Evoy, "91% of Tempe Voters Saw a Problem. Arizona Just Outlawed a Fix," *Arizona Republic,* March 29, 2018, https://www.azcentral.com/story/ news/local/tempe/2018/03/29/arizona-lawmakers-favor-anonymity-political -spending/471081002 [https://perma.cc/MAK2-676T].

98. As of 2018, twelve states have a public financing option for candidates running for governor or lieutenant governor: Arizona, Connecticut, Florida, Hawaii, Maine, Maryland, Massachusetts, Michigan, Minnesota, New Jersey, Rhode Island, and Vermont. Only five states—Arizona, Connecticut, Hawaii, Maine, and Minnesota—provide public financing for state legislative candidates. Some candidates for judge can receive public financing in New Mexico and West Virginia. "Overview of State Laws on Public Financing," National Conference of State Legislatures, http://www.ncsl.org/research/ elections-and-campaigns/public-financing-of-campaigns-overview.aspx [https://perma .cc/6BYM-A964].

99. Juhem Navarro-Rivera and Emmanuel Caicedo, "Public Funding for Electoral Campaigns: How 27 States, Counties, and Municipalities Empower Small Donors and Curb the Power of Big Money in Politics," Dēmos, June 28, 2017, http://www .demos.org/publication/public-funding-electoral-campaigns-how-27-states-counties -and-municipalities-empower-sma [https://perma.cc/3T8Q-RV9T]. The full report is available at http://www.demos.org/sites/default/files/publications/Public_Financing _Factsheet_FA[5].pdf [https://perma.cc/J3BQ-3CAE].

100. Ibid.

CHAPTER 10: CLASS IS IN SESSION

1. Jenifer Hitchcock, in discussion with the author, April 2, 2018.

2. "The New Civics: Civic Learning Is Not Flat Learning," Education Commission of the States, April 2013, https://www.ecs.org/clearinghouse/01/06/96/10696.pdf [https://perma.cc/R6ZT-E4CH].

3. Kristina Rizga, "Why Teaching Civics in America's Classrooms Must Be a Trump-Era Priority," *Mother Jones,* January 2017, https://www.motherjones.com/ politics/2017/02/civics-education-trump-bullying [https://perma.cc/R7QR-VCBA].

4. Ibid.; Jennifer McMurrer, "NCLB Year 5: Choices, Changes, and Challenges: Curriculum and Instruction in the NCLB Era," Center on Education Policy, July 24, 2007, https://www.cep-dc.org//displayDocument.cfm?DocumentID=312 [https:// perma.cc/QLP8-6VWR].

5. Kristina Rizga, "'I Fight Back.' Jonathan Kozol's Plan to Stop Bigotry in Trump's America," *Mother Jones,* November 24, 2016, https://www.motherjones

.com/politics/2016/11/jonathan-kozol-trump-education-segregation [https://perma
.cc/8CWZ-C2BR] (alteration in original).

6. Valerie Strauss, "Many Americans Know Nothing about Their Government.
Here's a Bold Way Schools Can Fix That," *Washington Post*, September 27, 2016, https://
www.washingtonpost.com/news/answer-sheet/wp/2016/09/27/many-americans-know
-nothing-about-their-government-heres-a-bold-way-schools-can-fix-that [https://perma
.cc/J2YN-TSH9].

7. Max Fisher, "Americans vs. Basic Historical Knowledge," *Atlantic*, June 3, 2010,
https://www.theatlantic.com/politics/archive/2010/06/americans-vs-basic-historical
-knowledge/340761 [https://perma.cc/MK2M-AV7Z].

8. Ibid.

9. Hunter Schwarz, "RIP 'American Idol': The Show That Proved How Bad
Americans Are at Voting," *Washington Post*, May 11, 2015, https://www.washingtonpost
.com/news/the-fix/wp/2015/05/11/rip-american-idol-the-show-that-gave-us-an-easy
-shorthand-for-americans-not-voting [https://perma.cc/TW5N-FHRE].

10. "LovGov," *LovGov Education Government Blog*, http://lovgov.weebly.com [https://
perma.cc/W2HA-9A56].

11. "About," *LovGov Education Government Blog*, http://lovgov.weebly.com/about.html
[https://perma.cc/7VUT-L9T3].

12. Jenifer Hitchcock, in discussion with the author, April 2, 2018.

13. Ibid.

14. Ibid.

15. Ibid.

16. Dahlia Lithwick, "They Were Trained for This Moment: How the Student
Activists of Marjory Stoneman Douglas High Demonstrate the Power of a
Comprehensive Education," *Slate*, February 28, 2018, https://slate.com/news-and
-politics/2018/02/the-student-activists-of-marjory-stoneman-douglas-high-demonstrate
-the-power-of-a-full-education.html [https://perma.cc/D6MD-VSZ7].

17. Meira Levinson, *No Citizen Left Behind* (Cambridge: Harvard University Press,
2014), p. 224; Meira Levinson, "Action Civics in the Classroom," *Social Education* 78, no. 2
(2014): 68–70, http://www.c3teachers.org/wp-content/uploads/2016/09/Levinson.pdf
[https://perma.cc/8X5W-RRBN].

18. Harry Boyte, email message to author, March 30, 2018; "Work in Progress,"
Inside Augsburg, http://inside.augsburg.edu/publicachievement/work-in-progress
[https://perma.cc/V5D2-ZWCL].

19. WTOP Staff, "Study: D.C. Ranks Near Bottom of U.S. School Systems,"
WTOP, July 28, 2015, https://wtop.com/dc/2015/07/study-d-c-ranks-near-bottom-u-s
-school-systems [https://perma.cc/JST9-AGAK].

20. Scott Abbott, in discussion with the author, April 2, 2018.

21. "College, Career, and Civic Life (C3) Framework for Social Studies State
Standards," National Council for the Social Studies, https://www.socialstudies.org/c3
[https://perma.cc/YV6G-YGDV].

22. Kathy Swan, in discussion with the author, April 10, 2018.

23. Scott Abbott, in discussion with the author, April 2, 2018.

24. "Mikva Challenge DC," Mikva Challenge, https://www.mikvachallenge.org/dc
[https://perma.cc/KM93-4NBN].

25. Scott Abbott, in discussion with the author, April 2, 2018; Abigail Hauslohner, "D.C. Students Will Be Riding Metro for Free This Year," *Washington Post*, August 17, 2015, https://www.washingtonpost.com/local/dc-politics/dc-students-will-be-riding -metro-for-free-this-year/2015/08/17/e81027d2-44e6-11e5-8ab4-c73967a143d3_story .html [https://perma.cc/7LB9-3XTH].

26. "The We the People Program," Center for Civic Education, http://www.civiced .org/wtp-the-program [https://perma.cc/6HKH-5FWQ].

27. Scott Abbott, in discussion with the author, April 2, 2018; Fenit Nirappil, "Bowser—the 'Mayor Who Hates Guns'—champions March for Our Lives and Steps into National Spotlight," *Washington Post*, March 23, 2018, https://www.washingtonpost .com/local/dc-politics/bowser--proud-dc-mayor-who-hates-guns--champions-march -for-our-lives/2018/03/23/efbe4844-2e0c-11e8-8688-e053ba58f1e4_story.html [https:// perma.cc/8ZPL-3XWH].

28. "We the Civics Kids," National Constitution Center, https://constitutioncenter .org/learn/educational-resources/we-the-civics-kids [https://perma.cc/4TFA-4MR7].

29. Ibid.

30. Ibid.

31. Jenifer Hitchcock, in discussion with the author, April 2, 2018.

32. Brittany Marrs, personal communication with author via Google Forms, April 2, 2018.

33. Glynn A. Hill, "Magnolia Students Ready to Hit Polls in November," *Houston Chronicle*, October 12, 2016, https://www.chron.com/neighborhood/magnolia/schools/ article/Magnolia-students-ready-to-hit-polls-in-November-9967020.php [https://perma .cc/BUD4-T4DE].

34. Benjamin Fabian, personal communication with author via Google Forms, April 2, 2018.

35. Michael Martirone, personal communication with author via Google Forms, April 2, 2018.

36. Trish Everett, personal communication with author via Google Forms, April 2, 2018.

37. Matthew Lynch, "Explainer: What Is Wrong with America's Civic Education," Edvocate, http://www.theedadvocate.org/explainer-wrong-americas-civic-education [https://perma.cc/99SV-ARG5].

38. Andy McLaughlin—Scottish High School Teacher, in discussion with the author, May 24, 2017.

39. Willie Sullivan—Director, Scottish Electoral Reform Commission, in discussion with the author, May 22, 2017.

40. Alyson Klein, "Education Week Survey Paints Political Portrait of America's K-12 Educators," *Education Week*, December 12, 2017, https://www.edweek.org/ew/ articles/2017/12/13/survey-paints-political-portrait-of-americas-k-12.html [https:// perma.cc/73QB-NT2L].

41. Diana E. Hess and Paula McAvoy, *The Political Classroom: Evidence and Ethics in Democratic Education* (Abington: Routledge, 2014). You can learn more about the book here: http://thepoliticalclassroom.com [https://perma.cc/M24Y-PPG5].

42. "iCivics," iCivics, https://www.icivics.org [https://perma.cc/EN6L-LXQY].

43. Alexander Heffner, "Former Supreme Court Justice Sandra Day O'Connor on

the Importance of Civics Education," *Washington Post*, April 12, 2012, https://www
.washingtonpost.com/lifestyle/magazine/former-supreme-court-justice-sandra-day
-oconnor-on-the-importance-of-civics-education/2012/04/10/gIQA8aUnCT_story.html
[https://perma.cc/QJ5Y-QZP9].

44. "iCivics Games," iCivics, https://www.icivics.org/games [https://perma.cc/
G4MK-ED7C].

45. San Antonio Indep. Sch. Dist. v. Rodriguez, 411 U.S. 1, 113 (1973) (Marshall, J.,
dissenting).

46. "About Democracy Prep," Democracy Prep Public Schools, http://
democracyprep.org/about [https://perma.cc/3RBX-RK69].

47. "Student Poll Worker Program," Orange County Registrar of Voters, https://www
ocvote.com/volunteer/student-poll-worker-program [https://perma.cc/3HLL-2HFZ].

48. "Student Election Clerk Information," Texas Secretary of State David
Whitley, https://www.sos.state.tx.us/elections/pamphlets/seci.shtml [https://perma.cc/
HP6U-T84K].

49. "electionlineWeekly—February 8, 2018," *electionLine*, February 8, 2018, http://
www.electionline.org/index.php/2018/2415-electionlineweekly-february-8-2018 [https://
perma.cc/2FF4-LA49]; "Election Academy Course Descriptions: 2018 Session," Orange
County Registrar of Voters, https://www.ocvote.com/community/orange-county-election
-academy/election-academy-course-descriptions [https://perma.cc/LG55-99CE].

50. "Citizen University," Staunton, Virginia, https://www.ci.staunton.va.us/
departments/city-manager/citizen-university [https://perma.cc/8TGN-DYHR].

51. J.B. Wogan, "Studies Show Voters Need a Graduate-Level Education to
Understand Ballot Measures," *Governing*, November 6, 2017, http://www.governing.com/
topics/politics/gov-rhode-island-ballot-measures-language.html [https://perma.cc/
Q7Q3-NAYQ].

52. Hannah Covington, "Jargon Beware: More Language Warriors Join Local War
Against Government Goobledygook," *StarTribune*, March 13, 2018, http://www
.startribune.com/jargon-beware-more-language-warriors-join-local-war-against
-government-gobbledygook/478463363 [https://perma.cc/CD7X-GQ4R].

53. Ibid. For more on the plain language movement, check out the Center for Plain
Language: https://centerforplainlanguage.org.

54. Brittany Marrs, personal communication with author via Google Forms, April 2,
2018.

55. Scott Abbott, in discussion with the author, April 2, 2018.

56. Kei Kawashima-Ginsberg, "Do Discussion, Debate, and Simulations Boost
NAEP Civics Performance?" Circle: The Center for Information & Research on Learning
& Engagement, April 2013, http://civicyouth.org/wp-content/uploads/2013/04/
CIRCLE_NAEPBechtelFactSheetApril30.final_.pdf [https://perma.cc/WW3W-SQJ9].

57. Scott Abbott, in discussion with the author, April 2, 2018.

58. *See, e.g.*, Sarah J. Priebe, Janice M. Keenan, and Amanda C. Miller, "How
Prior Knowledge Affects Word Identification and Comprehension," *Reading and Writing*
7 (2011): 581, available at https://www.ncbi.nlm.nih.gov/pmc/articles/PMC3142886
[https://perma.cc/6G3S-WHA9]; Donna R. Recht and Lauren Leslie, "Effect of Prior
Knowledge on Good and Poor Readers' Memory of Text," *Journal of Educational Psychology*
80 (1998): 16, available at http://www.literacyhow.com/wp-content/uploads/2016/03/

Effect-of-Prior-Knowledge-on-Good-and-Poor-Readers-Memory-of-Text.pdf [https://perma.cc/96F5-GB2Z].

59. Tess Williams, "Lawmakers to Debate Testing Nebraska Students about Civics," *Washington Times* (Associated Press), March 29, 2018, https://www.washingtontimes.com/news/2018/mar/29/lawmakers-to-debate-testing-nebraska-students-abou [https://perma.cc/XL5G-9BNT].

60. Mass.gov, "Governor Baker Signs Bill to Promote Civics Education for Students," press release, November 8, 2018, https://www.mass.gov/news/governor-baker-signs-bill-to-promote-civic-education-for-students [https://perma.cc/A5H2-SDBG]; "Bill S.2375: An Act to Promote and Enhance Civic Engagement," The 190th General Court of the Commonwealth of Massachusetts, https://malegislature.gov/Bills/190/S2375 [https://perma.cc/G4HS-TP6K].

61. Christian M. Wade, "Civics Project May Be Required to Graduate High School," *Salem News*, March 21, 2018, http://www.salemnews.com/news/local_news/civics-project-may-be-required-to-graduate-high-school/article_6ecf6053-9579-52cd-9154-bbd0473cb5e4.html [https://perma.cc/9UPU-F8CZ].

62. David E. Campbell, "Vote Early, Vote Often," Education Next, Summer 2005, http://educationnext.org/voteearlyvoteoften [https://perma.cc/M5H7-4GEC].

63. Ibid.

64. Jessie Logan, personal communication with author via Google Forms, April 2, 2018.

CHAPTER 11: HOW TO COMBAT "FAKE NEWS"

1. Patrick Marley, in discussion with the author, March 2, 2017.

2. "Extract from Thomas Jefferson to Edward Carrington, Jan. 16, 1787," Thomas Jefferson Foundation, http://tjrs.monticello.org/letter/1289 [https://perma.cc/49SU-8K6B].

3. "Thomas Jefferson to John Norvell, June 11, 1807," Library of Congress, https://www.loc.gov/resource/mtj1.038_0592_0594/?sp=2&st=text [https://perma.cc/5X39-9FDJ].

4. Ari Berman, *Give Us the Ballot: The Modern Struggle for Voting Rights in America* (New York: Farrar, Straus, and Giroux, 2015), pp. 18–22.

5. Patrick Marley, in discussion with the author, March 2, 2017.

6. Ibid.

7. Benjamin Hardy, "Thousands of Arkansas Voters Flagged for Removal," *Arkansas Times*, August 2, 2016, https://www.arktimes.com/arkansas/thousands-of-arkansas-voters-flagged-for-removal/Content?oid=4518444 [https://perma.cc/XD3D-H3K6].

8. Ibid.

9. Ibid.

10. Leslie Newell Peacock, "County Responses to Flawed Felon Data Suggests Eligible Voters Have Been Removed from Rolls," *Arkansas Times*, August 4, 2016, http://www.arktimes.com/ArkansasBlog/archives/2016/08/04/county-responses-to-flawed

-felon-data-suggests-eligible-voters-have-been-removed-from-rolls [https://perma.cc/R3H5-UKT4].

11. Max Brantley and Benjamin Hardy, "Secretary of State Sends Stronger Guidance to County Clerks on Voter Data—Finally," *Arkansas Times*, August 11, 2016, https://www.arktimes.com/ArkansasBlog/archives/2016/08/11/secretary-of-state-sends-more-guidance-to-county-clerks-on-voter-data [https://perma.cc/P5VH-TTAZ].

12. Benjamin Hardy, email message to author, March 15, 2017.

13. Joseph Lichterman, "More Than a Thousand Reporters and Students Are Collectively Covering Voting Problems on Election Day," NiemanLab, November 7, 2016, http://www.niemanlab.org/2016/11/more-than-a-thousand-reporters-and-students-are-collectively-covering-voting-problems-on-election-day [https://perma.cc/SAP6-2FNB].

14. Ibid.

15. Blake Paterson and Andrew Kragie, "Voters Getting Incomplete ID Instructions at Polls," *Houston Chronicle*, November 2, 2016, https://www.chron.com/news/politics/article/Voters-getting-incomplete-ID-instructions-at-polls-10461851.php [https://perma.cc/X2W5-J4T6].

16. Allison Graves, "Fact-Check: Did 3 Million Undocumented Immigrants Vote in This Year's Election?" PunditFact, November 18, 2016, http://www.politifact.com/punditfact/statements/2016/nov/18/blog-posting/no-3-million-undocumented-immigrants-did-not-vote- [https://perma.cc/MR9U-X3N2].

17. Joshua A. Douglas, "Trump's Voter Fraud Lies: The Damage They Do," CNN, January 25, 2017, https://www.cnn.com/2017/01/25/opinions/trump-spicer-voter-fraud-lies-douglas-opinion/index.html [https://perma.cc/66XN-PL4X].

18. "Wednesday Editorial: Voter Fraud Claims Are Often Based on Flawed Analysis," *Florida Times-Union*, March 14, 2017, http://jacksonville.com/opinion/editorials/2017-03-14/wednesday-editorial-voter-fraud-claims-are-often-based-flawed-analysis [https://perma.cc/ZM8S-DQ5H].

19. Patrick Marley, "Absentee Ballots at Risk of Being Tossed," *Milwaukee Journal Sentinel*, October 7, 2016, https://www.jsonline.com/story/news/politics/elections/2016/10/07/absentee-ballots-risk-being-tossed/91728826 [https://perma.cc/6BBJ-V4EZ].

20. Patrick Marley, "State Makes It Easier to Fix Ballots," *Milwaukee Journal Sentinel*, October 14, 2016, https://www.jsonline.com/story/news/politics/elections/2016/10/14/state-makes-easier-fix-ballots/92052894 [https://perma.cc/ZWQ7-TXPT].

21. Patrick Marley, "DMV Gives Wrong Information on Voter ID," *Milwaukee Journal Sentinel*, September 29, 2016, https://www.jsonline.com/story/news/politics/elections/2016/09/29/dmv-gives-wrong-information-voter-id/91283462 [https://perma.cc/DN5F-3KKU].

22. One Wisconsin Institute, Inc. v. Thomsen, No. 15-cv-324 (W.D. Wisc. Oct. 13, 2016), available at http://moritzlaw.osu.edu/electionlaw/litigation/documents/OneWisconsin-OpinionandOrder.pdf [https://perma.cc/G3ZY-Y75K].

23. Anastasiya Bolton, "My First Vote as an American," 9 News, November 4, 2016, https://www.9news.com/article/entertainment/television/programs/next-with-kyle-clark/my-first-vote-as-an-american/73-348391138 [https://perma.cc/77XK-NEZ5].

24. Ibid.

25. Anastasiya Bolton, email message to author, March 16, 2017.

26. Ibid.

27. Brian Corley, in discussion with the author, March 15, 2017; "Is It Finally Time to Allow Online Voter Registration in Florida?" *Palm Beach Post*, April 23, 2015, http://opinionzone.blog.palmbeachpost.com/2015/04/23/is-it-finally-time-to-allow-online-voter-registration-in-florida [https://perma.cc/HL8Z-NZNL]; Steve Bousquet, "Online Voter Registration Gains Momentum in Florida," *Miami Herald*, March 8, 2015, http://www.miamiherald.com/news/politics-government/state-politics/article13027655.html [https://perma.cc/88UM-PQD4].

28. Carlos Duarte, in discussion with the author, March 27, 2017.

29. Ibid.

30. Ibid.

31. "August 22, 2018," *Ithaca Times*, August 22, 2018, https://issuu.com/ithacatimes/docs/august_22__2018 [https://perma.cc/4QC4-3SQB?type=image].

32. Email from Marshall Hopkins to Adam Eichen, August 25, 2018.

33. Molly E. Neck, Twitter, October 24, 2016, https://twitter.com/MollyENeck/status/790630554257330176 [https://perma.cc/AC4A-37ZQ].

34. Jim Malewitz, "In Some Counties, Early Voting Means Long Lines," *Texas Tribune*, October 24, 2016, https://www.texastribune.org/2016/10/24/some-texas-counties-long-lines-complicate-early-vo [https://perma.cc/W46F-LDYV]; Michael Wines, "As ID Laws Fall, Voters See New Barriers Rise," *New York Times*, October 25, 2016, https://www.nytimes.com/2016/10/26/us/elections/voter-id-laws.html.

35. Texas Secretary of State, Twitter, October 24, 2016, https://twitter.com/TXsecofstate/status/790655666314620928 [https://perma.cc/H22Y-HKM7].

36. "MALDEF Wins Court Order Requiring Bexar County Election Officials to Remove Illegal Voter ID Signs," MALDEF, October 28, 2016, http://www.maldef.org/news/releases/2016_10_28_MALDEF_Wins_Court_Order_Requiring_Bexar_County_Election_Officials_Remoe_Illegal_VoterID_Signs [https://perma.cc/DX4S-SPER].

37. Maria Taggart, Facebook, November 3, 2016, https://www.facebook.com/maria.taggart.9/posts/10154050500158225 [https://perma.cc/K3Y7-EBFK?type=image].

38. Ibid.

39. Ibid.

40. "State of the News Media 2016," Pew Research Center, June 15, 2016, http://www.journalism.org/2016/06/15/state-of-the-news-media-2016 [https://perma.cc/N4CN-4V76].

41. Ibid.

42. Jeffrey Gottfried, Michael Barthel, Elisa Shearer, and Amy Mitchell, "The 2016 Presidential Campaign—A News Event That's Hard to Miss," Pew Research Center, February 4, 2016, http://www.journalism.org/2016/02/04/the-2016-presidential-campaign-a-news-event-thats-hard-to-miss [https://perma.cc/PJX9-QE3F].

43. Joyce Dehli, "Rebuilding Local Journalism as an Essential Democratic Force," Pulitzer Prizes, http://www.pulitzer.org/article/rebuilding-local-journalism-essential-democratic-force [https://perma.cc/C5X7-4NUN].

44. Tim Carney, "A New Role for Public Media: Local Government Watchdogs," Knight Foundation, https://www.knightfoundation.org/public-media-white-paper-2017-carney [https://perma.cc/33BP-4DWM].

45. Michael Barthel, Jesse Holcomb, Jessica Mahome, and Amy Mitchell, "Civic Engagement Strongly Tied to Local News Habits," Pew Research Center, November 3, 2016, http://www.journalism.org/2016/11/03/civic-engagement-strongly-tied-to-local-news-habits [https://perma.cc/NRP7-GUVL].

46. Ibid.

47. Amber McReynolds, in discussion with the author, March 13, 2017.

48. "Ballot Selfies: A Look At Where They Are Allowed or Not," Associated Press, October 24, 2016, https://apnews.com/04c313da0672422ba28bb57c4e4a7ca0/ballot-selfies-look-where-they-are-allowed-or-not [https://perma.cc/EL3A-44HH].

49. Parker Smith, "No Good Reason to Deny Teens the Right to Vote," *Lexington Herald-Leader*, June 6, 2018, http://www.kentucky.com/opinion/op-ed/article212708569.html [https://perma.cc/AA4U-HRQS].

50. Shaan Merchant and Luke Kirkpatrick, "First-Time Voters Deserve to Have Say at the Polls," *Tennessean*, October 25, 2016, http://www.tennessean.com/story/opinion/contributors/2016/10/25/first-time-voters-deserve-have-say-polls/92731654 [https://perma.cc/RF2C-SN7N].

51. Chase Thomas and Judi Hilman, "Op-Ed: Automatic Voter Registration Would Boost Utah Democracy," *Salt Lake Tribune*, September 25, 2016, http://archive.sltrib.com/article.php?id=4358076&itype=CMSID [https://perma.cc/7QM8-K4SQ].

52. Taylor W. Anderson, "Do You Want to Register to Vote? Utah Enacts Widespread Election Law Changes, Including Election-Day Registration. Here Are All the Changes," *Salt Lake Tribune*, March 9, 2018, https://www.sltrib.com/news/politics/2018/03/08/do-you-want-to-register-to-vote-utah-enacts-widespread-election-law-changes-including-election-day-registration-here-are-all-the-changes [https://perma.cc/Q9NM-VV9B].

53. "Voting Rights Toolkit," Democracy Initiative, http://www.democracyinitiative.org/sample-op-ed [https://perma.cc/5Q58-P2P4].

54. "Stand Up for Voting Rights: Write a Letter to the Editor," Let America Vote, https://www.letamericavote.org/landing/action-write-letter-editor [https://perma.cc/G2BN-4TTM].

55. Phil Thompson, "People In, Money Out," *Spokesman-Review*, May 22, 2018, http://www.spokesman.com/stories/2018/may/22/people-money-out [https://perma.cc/5528-49LC].

56. Mike Clifford, "Readers Write: Redistricting in an Omnibus Bill, the Mideast, Polls, Out of the Mouths of Politicians, Twins Games on AM," *Minnesota Star Tribune*, May 15, 2018, http://www.startribune.com/readers-write-redistricting-in-an-omnibus-bill-the-mideast-polls-out-of-the-mouths-of-politicians-twins-games-on-am/482731021 [https://perma.cc/3WEW-4PEL].

57. Tonya Lundahl, "Letter: It Is Clear That Our Campaign System Is a Big Mess," *Salt Lake Tribune*, March 22, 2018, https://www.sltrib.com/opinion/letters/2018/03/22/letter-it-is-clear-that-our-campaign-system-is-a-big-mess [https://perma.cc/L8GQ-6VT8].

CHAPTER 12: THE PERILS OF ONLY PLAYING DEFENSE

1. Kristen Hubby, "How Many Americans Actually Vote?" *Daily Dot*, December 19, 2016, https://www.dailydot.com/layer8/voter-turnout-2016 [https://perma.cc/TKY6-9BJR]. *See also* Michael P. McDonald, "2016 November General Election Turnout Rates," United States Elections Project, http://www.electproject.org/2016g [https://perma.cc/79J7-T72P].

2. Edna Ralston, "The Right to Vote Is Under Attack," *Daily Camera*, February 11, 2017, http://www.dailycamera.com/guest-opinions/ci_30787592/edna-ralston-right-vote-is-under-attack [https://perma.cc/BSG7-BZEP]; Jeffery Adler, "Stories to Watch: Ballot Access and Voting Rights at Risk," Yahoo News, February 3, 2017, https://www.yahoo.com/news/ballot-access-and-voting-rights-at-risk-230230577.html [https://perma.cc/S3RP-YX4L]; Vanessa Williams and Katie Zezima, "Voting Rights Advocates Brace for 'Biggest Fight of our Lifetime' During Trump Administration." *Washington Post*, November 30, 2016, https://www.washingtonpost.com/politics/voting-rights-advocates-brace-for-the-biggest-fight-of-our-lifetime-against-trump-administration/2016/11/29/88bcaee8-b657-11e6-959c-172c82123976_story.html [https://perma.cc/UJ98-9ABC].

3. New State Ice Co. v. Liebmann, 285 U.S. 262, 311 (1932) (Brandeis, J., dissenting).

4. Joshua A. Douglas, "The Right to Vote Under Local Law," *George Washington Law Review* 85 (2017): 1073.

5. "H. R. 1, The For the People Act," Democracy Reform Task Force, Rep. John Sarbanes, Chair, https://democracyreform-sarbanes.house.gov/sites/democracyreformtaskforce.house.gov/files/H.R.%201%20SectiSe-by-Section_FINAL.pdf [https://perma.cc/3E4P-JK3G].

6. Ibid.

7. "Declaration of Independence: A Transcription," National Archives, https://www.archives.gov/founding-docs/declaration-transcript [https://perma.cc/78ER-B2JH].

8. "Voter Turnout: 2016 House of Representatives and Senate Elections," Australian Electoral Commission, http://www.aec.gov.au/About_AEC/research/files/voter-turnout-2016.pdf [https://perma.cc/DF6L-5QV5].

9. "Scotland Decides," BBC, http://www.bbc.com/news/events/scotland-decides/results [https://perma.cc/A2U4-QCBE].

10. Drew DeSilver, "U.S. Trails Most Developed Countries in Voter Turnout," Pew Research Center, May 15, 2017, http://www.pewresearch.org/fact-tank/2017/05/15/u-s-voter-turnout-trails-most-developed-countries [https://perma.cc/D2QZ-F7J2].

11. Frances Moore Lappé and Adam Eichen, *Daring Democracy: Igniting Power, Meaning, and Connection for the America We Want* (Boston: Beacon Press, 2017), p. 4.

EPILOGUE

1. Husted v. A. Philip Randolph Institute, 138 S. Ct. 1833 (2018); Gill v. Whitford, 138 S. Ct. 1916 (2018); Abbott v. Perez, 138 S. Ct. 2305 (2018).

2. To see the number of Electoral College votes in each state, visit https://www

.archives.gov/federal-register/electoral-college/allocation.html [https://perma.cc/JB2Q-RK6E].

3. Drew DeSilver, "Trump's Victory Another Example of How Electoral College Wins Are Bigger Than Popular Vote Ones," Pew Research Center, December 20, 2016, http://www.pewresearch.org/fact-tank/2016/12/20/why-electoral-college-landslides-are-easier-to-win-than-popular-vote-ones [https://perma.cc/6WFH-RWN9]. In 1824, Andrew Jackson won a plurality of both the Electoral College and the popular vote, but because he did not receive a majority in the Electoral College, the election was thrown to the House of Representatives—which chose his competitor, John Quincy Adams, for the presidency. Ibid.

4. Mario Trujillo, "After Bush v. Gore, Obama, Clinton Wanted Electoral College Scrapped," *Hill*, October 27, 2012, http://thehill.com/homenews/campaign/264347-obama-clinton-backed-reforms-to-electoral-college-after-bush-v-gore [https://perma.cc/KQ8D-DXR9].

5. Igor Bobic, "Democrats Push for Electoral College Reform After Hillary Clinton's Popular Vote Victory," *Huffington Post*, December 6, 2016, https://www.huffingtonpost.com/entry/electoral-college-popular-vote-reform_us_58471c4be4b0ebac58070c85 [https://perma.cc/9KAS-8GFG].

6. Bill Chappell, "Connecticut OKs Bill Pledging Electoral Votes to National Popular-Vote Winner," NPR, May 7, 2018, https://www.npr.org/sections/thetwo-way/2018/05/07/609060190/connecticut-oks-bill-pledging-electoral-votes-to-national-popular-vote-winner.

7. "National Popular Vote," *National Popular Vote*, https://www.nationalpopularvote.com [https://perma.cc/XTV6-CQD9].

8. Norman R. Williams, "Why the National Popular Vote Compact Is Unconstitutional," *Brigham Young University Law Review* 2012 (2012), p. 1523, https://digitalcommons.law.byu.edu/lawreview/vol2012/iss5/3 [https://perma.cc/26TR-GHF5]. Proponents have offered various counterarguments, stating that there are no constitutional issues with the National Popular Vote Interstate Compact. *See, e.g.*, Jessica Heller, "Dispelling the Major Legal Arguments Against the National Popular Vote Compact," FairVote, June 11, 2012, http://www.fairvote.org/dispelling-the-major-legal-arguments-against-the-national-popular-vote-compact [https://perma.cc/9FGU-AA6Y].

9. David Savage, "For the Fourth Time in American History, the President-Elect Lost the Popular Vote. Credit the Electoral College," *Los Angeles Times*, November 11, 2016, http://www.latimes.com/nation/la-na-pol-electoral-college-20161110-story.html [https://perma.cc/659P-QPFA].

10. Katy Collin, "The Electoral College Badly Distorts the Vote. And It's Going to Get Worse.," *Washington Post*, November 17, 2016, https://www.washingtonpost.com/news/monkey-cage/wp/2016/11/17/the-electoral-college-badly-distorts-the-vote-and-its-going-to-get-worse [https://perma.cc/V94T-VHSR].

11. Adam Liptak, "Smaller States Find Outsize Clout Growing in Senate," *New York Times*, March 11, 2013, http://archive.nytimes.com/www.nytimes.com/interactive/2013/03/11/us/politics/democracy-tested.html; "Impact of Increasing House Size," FairVote, http://archive.fairvote.org/?page=1765 [https://perma.cc/86XZ-3MUJ].

12. "Effort to Allocate House Seats to D.C., Utah Clears Major Hurdle in Senate,"

PBS NewsHour, February 24, 2009, https://www.pbs.org/newshour/politics/politics-jan
-june09-dcvote_02-24 [https://perma.cc/PX6N-YYD7].

13. Carl Hulse, "Advocates of Puerto Rico Statehood Plan to Demand Representation," *New York Times*, January 9, 2018, https://www.nytimes.com/2018/01/09/
us/politics/advocates-of-puerto-rico-statehood-plan-to-demand-representation.html.

14. Ted Barrett, "Here's What Senators Don't Want to Change Senate Filibuster
Rules," CNN, May 2, 2017, https://www.cnn.com/2017/05/02/politics/senate
-filibuster-rule-change-donald-trump/index.html [https://perma.cc/92W4-QZ3K]; Alex
Seitz-Wald, "The Nuclear Option: What It Is and Why It Matters," NBC News, April 3,
2017, https://www.nbcnews.com/politics/congress/nuclear-option-what-it-why-it
-matters-n742076 [https://perma.cc/F3WT-BV8L].

15. U.S. CONST. art. II, § 2.

16. Seitz-Wald, "The Nuclear Option."

17. "Fix the Court," Fix the Court, https://fixthecourt.com [https://perma.cc/
XG9U-NHP6].

18. Norm Ornstein, "Why the Supreme Court Needs Term Limits," *Atlantic*, May
22, 2014, https://www.theatlantic.com/politics/archive/2014/05/its-time-for-term
-limits-for-the-supreme-court/371415 [https://perma.cc/NWM5-XF85].

19. Erwin Chemerinsky, "It's Time to Reform the Supreme Court—Here Are Five Ways
to Do It," *Bill Moyers* (blog), July 15, 2014, https://billmoyers.com/2014/07/15/its-time-to
-reform-the-supreme-court-here-are-five-ways-to-do-it [https://perma.cc/5E9X-6N3S].

20. Kate Linthicum, "Bernie Sanders Slams New York's Closed Primary," *Los Angeles
Times*, April 19, 2016, http://www.latimes.com/politics/la-na-live-updates-new
-yo-bernie-sanders-slams-new-yorks-closed-primary-1461110907-htmlstory.html [https://
perma.cc/G8RM-GJ4T].

21. Tom LoBianco, "Trump Children Unable to Vote for Dad in NY Primary,"
CNN, April 12, 2016, https://www.cnn.com/2016/04/11/politics/donald-trump-ivanka
-vice-president/index.html [https://perma.cc/JFY4-LSPT].

22. Linthicum, "Bernie Sanders Slams New York's Closed Primary."

23. "State Primary Election Types," National Conference of State Legislatures, June
26, 2018, http://www.ncsl.org/research/elections-and-campaigns/primary-types.aspx
[https://perma.cc/WM4F-P8RF].

24. "Our Mission," Open Primaries, https://www.openprimaries.org/mission
[https://perma.cc/Z5S5-VAEC].

25. Cynthia McFadden, William M. Arkin, and Kevin Monahan, "Russians
Penetrated U.S. Voter Systems, Top U.S. Official Says," NBC News, February 7, 2018,
https://www.nbcnews.com/politics/elections/russians-penetrated-u-s-voter-systems-says
-top-u-s-n845721 [https://perma.cc/SMD7-K7EB]; Nicholas Fandos and Michael
Wines, "Russia Tried to Undermine Confidence in Voting Systems, Senators Say," *New
York Times*, May 8, 2018, https://www.nytimes.com/2018/05/08/us/politics/russia-2016
-election-hackers.html.

26. "2018 HAVA Election Security Funds," Election Assistance Commission, https://
www.eac.gov/2018-hava-election-security-funds [https://perma.cc/9UD4-C4TE].

27. Scott Shane and Mark Mazzetti, "Inside a 3-Year Russian Campaign to
Influence U.S. Voters," *New York Times*, February 16, 2018, https://www.nytimes
.com/2018/02/16/us/politics/russia-mueller-election.html.

28. Ibid.

29. Charles M. Blow, "Attacking the 'Woke' Black Vote," *New York Times*, February 18, 2018, https://www.nytimes.com/2018/02/18/opinion/black-vote-russia.html.

30. Patricia Zengerle and Donia Chiacu, "U.S. 2018 Elections 'Under Attack' by Russia: U.S. Intelligence Chief," Reuters, February 13, 2018, https://www.reuters.com/article/us-usa-security-russia-elections/u-s-2018-elections-under-attack-by-russia-u-s-intelligence-chief-idUSKCN1FX1Z8 [https://perma.cc/V3AN-BAWD].

31. Kenneth P. Vogel and Cecilia Kang, "Senators Demand Online Ad Disclosures as Tech Lobby Mobilizes," *New York Times*, October 19, 2017, https://www.nytimes.com/2017/10/19/us/politics/facebook-google-russia-meddling-disclosure.html; "The Honest Ads Act," Mark R. Warner—US Senator from the Commonwealth of Virginia, https://www.warner.senate.gov/public/index.cfm/the-honest-ads-act [https://perma.cc/77LY-MHE3].

32. Jack Nicas, "Facebook to Require Verified Identities for Future Political Ads," *New York Times*, April 6, 2018, https://www.nytimes.com/2018/04/06/business/facebook-verification-ads.html.

33. Sheera Frenkel, "Facebook and Twitter Expand Peek Into Who's Behind Their Ads," *New York Times*, June 28, 2018, https://www.nytimes.com/2018/06/28/technology/facebook-twitter-political-ads.html.

34. Andrew Ross Sorkin, "Demystifying the Blockchain," *New York Times*, June 27, 2018, https://www.nytimes.com/2018/06/27/business/dealbook/blockchain-technology.html.

35. Kevin C. Desouza and Kiran Kabtta Somvanshi, "How Blockchain Could Improve Election Transparency," Brookings, May 30, 2018, https://www.brookings.edu/blog/techtank/2018/05/30/how-blockchain-could-improve-election-transparency [https://perma.cc/573Z-K6FR].

36. Ben Miller, "West Virginia Becomes First State to Test Mobile Voting by Blockchain in a Federal Election," *Government Technology*, March 28, 2018, http://www.govtech.com/biz/West-Virginia-Becomes-First-State-to-Test-Mobile-Voting-by-Blockchain-in-a-Federal-Election.html [https://perma.cc/2VP7-8UR3].

37. Juliet Van Wagenen, "West Virginia Pilots First Blockchain-Powered Federal Voting App," *State Tech*, June 8, 2018, https://statetechmagazine.com/article/2018/06/west-virginia-pilots-first-blockchain-powered-federal-voting-app [https://perma.cc/NZH2-3SZ8].

38. "Voting Redefined," Voatz, https://voatz.com [https://perma.cc/7TY4-VT5X]; Mo Marshall, "Voatz Raises $2.2 Million to Make Elections Tamper-Proof," *Venture Beat*, January 8, 2018, https://venturebeat.com/2018/01/08/voatz-raises-2-2-million-to-make-elections-tamper-proof [https://perma.cc/Y76V-KYMG].

39. Dylan Love, "The United States Just Held Its First Blockchain-Enabled Election," Modern Consensus, May 14, 2018, https://modernconsensus.com/regulation/united-states/west-virginia-blockchain-federal-election [https://perma.cc/L3NN-EN6M].

40. "How to Report Bitcoin Contributions," Federal Election Commission, https://www.fec.gov/help-candidates-and-committees/filing-reports/bitcoin-contributions [https://perma.cc/5QKN-CUG6].

41. Lin-Manuel Miranda and Jeremy McCarter, *Hamilton: The Revolution* (New York: Grand Central Publishing, 2016).

42. Ibid.

43. Ibid.

44. Abraham Lincoln, "The Gettysburg Address," available at http://rmc.library
.cornell.edu/gettysburg/good_cause/transcript.htm [https://perma.cc/8SU3-3YCY].

INDEX